THE
FRENCH SECRETARIES
OF STATE IN THE AGE OF
CATHERINE DE MEDICI

by

N. M. SUTHERLAND

UNIVERSITY OF LONDON

THE ATHLONE PRESS

1962

Published by
THE ATHLONE PRESS
UNIVERSITY OF LONDON
at 2 *Gower Street, London* WC1

Distributed by Constable & Co. Ltd
12 *Orange Street, London* WC2

Canada
University of Toronto Press

U.S.A.
Oxford University Press Inc
New York

Printed in Great Britain by
WESTERN PRINTING SERVICES LTD
BRISTOL

DATE DUE

University of London Historical Studies

X

UNIVERSITY OF LONDON HISTORICAL STUDIES

THE FRENCH SECRETARIES OF STATE
IN THE AGE OF CATHERINE DE MEDICI

Nicolas de Neufville, seigneur de Villeroy, aged 65

TO GUY
WHO MADE IT ALL
POSSIBLE

PREFACE

As this book is largely based on French manuscript sources, the problem of what to translate and what to keep in the original has presented considerable difficulties. Opinions will always differ as to how the problem should be tackled, and there is no logical solution which does not, in practice, prove to be either absurd or impossible. It has therefore been necessary to compromise, and to treat each passage separately. Complete references have been given in every case. Abbreviated references to manuscripts and printed works used in the footnotes are explained in the bibliography. Where the French is quoted, the original spelling has been retained, but abbreviations have generally been extended. Where documents cited are dated in the old style, this has been shown in the usual way, thus: April 1546/7. Biographical notes on persons mentioned in the text may be found in appendix iii.

Formal acknowledgement will not convey the extent of my debt to Professor A. Cobban, for all that he has taught me, for his seemingly inexhaustible patience, and for many hours of work devoted to this study. I am also indebted to Miss F. A. Yates of the Warburg Institute, and Professor J. Hurstfield of University College, London, both of whom have generously given precious time to my work and advised me in revising it for publication. I would further like to thank Professor G. Dickinson of Westfield College, London, for help and advice during the early days of research in Paris, and for her constant encouragement and interest in my work. I am also indebted to Professor R. Mousnier of the University of Paris, and Professor M. François of the École des Chartes; also to the members of the Institut de France for the privilege of admission to their private library which contains an important collection of manuscripts. Finally I should like to thank Mr. P. W. Hasler for his patient help in correcting proofs.

For financial assistance, without which I should never have finished, I must record my gratitude to Newnham College, Cambridge, the trustees of the Central Research Fund of London University, and, particularly, to the council of Westfield College, London, for awarding me a two-year research studentship.

London   N.M.S.
May 1961

CONTENTS

PLATES

INTRODUCTION

This is a study of the twelve secretaries of state who held office in France between the years 1547 and 1588.

At the end of the chapter on the secretaries of state in his book *Les Institutions de la France au XVIe siècle* (vol. i, ch. v) Professor Doucet declared that any detailed work on the secretaries must be based on their correspondence preserved in the *Bibliothèque nationale* in Paris. That was the point of departure for this study which developed from a simple curiosity and a desire to find out as much as possible about the secretaries as individuals and the part which they played in the government of France. With the exception of Villeroy, it proved impossible to reconstruct more than the outline of their careers, and it is unavoidable that we know so much more about some than about others.

What remains of their once enormous correspondence is scattered among the many thousands of volumes of the *Fonds français*, and, to a lesser extent, among other French collections. A few historians, mostly of the late nineteenth century, have dipped into it here and there for specialized purposes, but no attempt has previously been made to locate and study it in its entirety. This was a lengthy but, in the end, rewarding task, because it opened a new window on to sixteenth-century France. Hitherto there have been only brief outlines of the history of the office written from a purely juridical point of view, together with a tantalizing page or two on each secretary, giving his coat of arms, his name, titles, parentage and the milestones, if any, in his public life.

In writing an account of French institutions of the sixteenth century, Professor Doucet has shown how France was governed in theory. But in drawing attention to neglected material, he rightly implied that there was a great deal more to know. Indeed, the theory can be very misleading. The government in sixteenth-century France was personal and flexible. Thus it is

B

only through attention to detail on the personal level that one can hope to learn anything new about what happened, and the way in which things were done. By combining analysis with a detailed, and sometimes even day-to-day, study of the activities of the secretaries, it is possible, not only to reveal their increasing importance, but also to throw some new light on the history of France in the second half of the sixteenth century, and on the working of the central government.

It will be seen that the secretaries of state developed out of the medieval *chancellerie* to become officers of the royal household. By the sixteenth century they were among the more important officers. Indeed, this was the great age of the secretary of state all over Europe because he was an ideal instrument for personal, despotic governments. Throughout the century in France, the credit of the individual secretaries determined the current conception of their office, which was slowly moulded by a combination of character and circumstance. It followed that the standing of a secretary, and his relations with the king and other officials, was constantly varying. This was also true in other countries, including England, where some of the 'principal secretaries' were modest administrative officers, while others were of outstanding importance.

The secretaries were chosen for their merits. They had to be men of some learning, with a certain knowledge of languages. They therefore came from the educated classes, which were not the old aristocracy but the upper bourgeoisie and the lesser nobility, many of whom had become ennobled through holding judicial or financial offices conferring this privilege, or through the purchase of land. The range of the secretaries' activity was vast. Their powers were neither defined nor limited and nothing was too great or too trivial to claim their attention. Owing to the fact that a secretary's signature was required to validate state papers and royal letters, they became the principal arm of the executive, and the main channel of communication between the king and the country. Each secretary normally underwent an arduous apprenticeship in the service of another—often a relation—and, on assuming office, inherited not an administrative routine, but a set of precepts and a fine tradition characterized by devotion to duty and a dedicated sense of service.

Little by little, from the last decade of the sixteenth century, the secretaries began to specialize, and what was originally the most personal of governments culminated in an impersonal, bureaucratic system in which the secretaries became ministers, each responsible for a separate department of state. For that reason, the dismissal of all three secretaries in 1588 provides the historian with a natural stopping-point.

PART ONE

The Origins and Work of the Secretaries

CHAPTER I

The Origins of the Secretaries and their Rise to Importance under Francis I

THE origins of the *secrétaires d'État* were already obscure by the seventeenth century. A memoir on this subject was drawn up on the instructions of Colbert, besides which there are three others. They all date from the seventeenth century and vary only in length and detail.[1] They were based on complex ordinances whose terminology was variable and imprecise, and the purposes and effects of which were no longer known. None of them, therefore, gives us a clear picture of the origins of the secretaries. Probably there had always been secretaries, in one form or another, so long as there had been kings, and there were a number of Latin names for them before the early French ones of *clerc* and *notaire*.[2] The name *notaire* appears as early as the tenth century, when the *notaires* were officers of the *chancellerie*.[3] In the eleventh century we note the existence of *clercs notaires du roi*. The *clercs* served the king, had their meals at court and enjoyed certain privileges and perquisites, while the *notaires* were still officers of the *chancellerie* and served the chancellor.[4]

In 1309, Philip IV reduced the number of his *clercs notaires* to thirty, of whom three were appointed *clercs du secret*, 'who were like the eye of the king, by which he saw with certainty everything that took place in his kingdom'.[5] In the next few years the

---

[1] B.N., Mss. Clairambault, 664, ff. 49–55, 65–95; Mss. fr. 18236, ff. 1–144; Mss. n.a.f. 9735, ff. 89–103, dated 1650.

[2] Miraulmont, 77–v.

[3] Robin, 4.

[4] B.N., Mss. fr. 18236, ff. 2v–3; Mss. n.a.f. 9735, f. 89v. The date is unknown.

[5] Du-Toc, 11; de Luçay, 4; Robin, 5–6.

name *secrétaire* emerged and, in 1317, using the names *clerc* and *notaire* interchangeably, Philip V decreed that three of the *notaires* who followed the king should be singled out for special duties. One, described as the *secrétaire*, was to work on the confidential affairs of the king, a second, *notaire du sang*, on criminal matters, and a third was to keep the registers of the council and *parlement*.[1] The name *secrétaire* was added to those of *clerc* and *notaire*, that of *clerc* carrying the right to eat at court and other privileges, that of *notaire* the right to draft and despatch letters concerning the *chancellerie*, and that of *secrétaire* to sign documents on the authority of the king.[2] Historians have seen in these two ordinances of 1309 and 1317 the only certain origins of the future *secrétaire d'État*.

We do not know what happened to the *secrétaire* and the two special *notaires* mentioned in the ordinance of 1317. *Secrétaires, clercs du secret* and *secrétaires des finances* are all spoken of in the fourteenth century without precision. But we may safely infer that their numbers increased and that as the title *secrétaire* replaced that of *clerc* for those who were employed close to the king and in his councils, so they all came to be called *secrétaires*. By about 1381, the name *secrétaire* was also being applied to any *notaire* indiscriminately. Not later than the last quarter of the fourteenth century, some of these *secrétaires*, probably the *clercs du secret*, acquired the right to sign documents concerning the finances, and came to be called *secrétaires des finances*.[3] By 1400, there were six *secrétaires des finances* and four other *secrétaires* in some way distinct from their colleagues. They were all forbidden to sign any letter except by virtue of an express command from the king, or possibly from the council, and this was the origin of yet another name for the chosen few, that of *secrétaires des commandements*, which was generally used in the later fifteenth century and until the latter half of the sixteenth.

The number of the secretaries always tended to increase and there were frequent ordinances reducing it. A lengthy ordinance of 1413 limited them to eight, and stated that they were to serve

[1] B.N., Mss. fr. 18236, f. 11; Mss. Clairambault, 664, f. 81v; Mss. n.a.f. 9735, f. 90; Miraulmont, 90; Du-Toc, 11, 12; de Luçay, 5.

[2] B.N., Mss. Clairambault, 664, ff. 49–v; Du-Toc, 12.

[3] De Luçay, 6, n. 1; Robin, 6.

in council, four at a time, in alternate months. It was also stipulated that the king was not to receive as a *secrétaire* anyone who was not already a *notaire*, and who had not been examined and sworn in by the chancellor.[1] The *notaires*, the ordinance specified, were all to be worthy, diligent and competent in Latin and French, 'of good morals, good life, loyal and well-spoken men'.[2]

The offices of *clerc*, *notaire*, and *secrétaire* were always enviable, and became increasingly so because of the opportunities they offered of advancement at court and of the privileges they carried which added greatly to the nominal value of their wages. The question of wages is confused and it is not known when they were fixed. In the early fourteenth century the *clercs* and *notaires* received six *sols parisis* a day, plus a clothes allowance, while those who followed the king also had their meals at court.[3] In addition, they received certain emoluments on the seals, known as *collation*. Mention is made, in one source, of *notaires* sometimes receiving payments in kind, in perishable foodstuffs, stockings, gloves and other trifles.[4] Each *notaire* made out a monthly wage claim, in a specified form, together with a report on his work and place of service, and presented it to the king's *audiencier*, who, under the chancellor, was the chief officer of the *chancellerie*. Each claim was considered individually and payment awarded according to the difficulty and merit of the work, the *notaire*'s past record and the expenses he had incurred in the king's service. The amount paid in each case was kept private. Towards the end of the fourteenth century, the *secrétaires* are generally said to have received twelve *sols parisis* a day, six more for the office of *notaire*, plus other emoluments and allowances in kind.[5] Louis XI raised their salary to 1,200 *livres* a year on condition that they renounced all other emoluments,[6] and a further rise took place, probably upon the accession of Charles VIII. In 1547 Henry II raised the salary of the *secrétaires d'État* from

[1] Isambert, vii, Ordinance of May 1413; de Luçay, 7.
[2] Isambert, vii, Ordinance of May 1413.
[3] *Sol* or *sou*; a *sol tournois* consisted of twelve *deniers* and a *sol parisis* of fifteen. Twenty *sols* made one *livre tournois* or *parisis*.
[4] B.N., Mss. fr. 18239, ff. 5v–6.
[5] Miraulmont, 90–v; de Luçay, 9.
[6] De Luçay, 9; the date is unknown.

1,623 *livres* 2 *sous* 6 *deniers*, which they received as *secrétaires des finances*, to 3,000 *livres*. They received a further rise in salary of 1,300 *livres* in October 1582.[1]

These officials, whether *clercs*, *notaires* or *secrétaires*, enjoyed many valuable privileges which were extended from time to time. One of the first of these was the exemption from all tolls levied on roads, rivers and bridges.[2] Their persons, property, incomes, goods and households were totally immune from any form of taxation, whether royal, seigneurial or urban.[3] They were also exempt from any form of military service and from the billeting of troops in their houses. They did not pay the usual fees on any legal documents which concerned them and they had certain other privileges in connection with litigation. In 1485 they were granted the most coveted privilege of all, which doubtless reflected the prestige they had already acquired; they were automatically ennobled on receipt of the office of *secrétaire* and, after four generations, their descendants were eligible for membership of any order of chivalry.

At least from the early fourteenth century, if not before, the *clercs* and *notaires* had begun to discharge a wide variety of administrative duties, at court, in council, in the *chancellerie*, the *chambres des comptes*, the *parlements*, and other provincial courts. Many of them had begun to sign charters and other state papers by the fourteenth century, noting at the end the names of those who had ordered them to be drawn up, and to whom they had to be re-read before being sealed. This practice continued well into the sixteenth century, by which time the customary signature of a *secrétaire* had acquired the force of law and become essential to validate a document. His signature was regarded as proof of the king's will, and gradually superseded the importance of the seal, which came to be a formality, although the chancellor could, and sometimes still did, delay business by refusing the seals.

From about the early fourteenth century there are examples of *secrétaires* being sent on diplomatic missions.[4] These were often difficult, fatiguing, costly and even dangerous, but they provided unparalleled opportunities for displaying address, tact, and

---

[1] De Luçay, 9.   [2] Robin, 10.
[3] Miraulmont, 97v; Isambert, x, 855 ff.
[4] B.N., Mss. fr. 18236, f. 6; Miraulmont, 97.

skill in argument. Envoys acquired specialized knowledge, and successful missions called for reward and recognition. Although it was a long time before prestige and distinction were attached to such missions, work of this kind undoubtedly helped to increase the influence of the secretaries.

Attached to the king, they were carefully selected as being able and cultured men, whom he chose to have about him to carry out his orders, to supervise the members of his household and to be ready at any moment to undertake important tasks in connection with affairs of state. The ordinance of 1399 described them as 'those whom [the kings of France] wished and intended to be present and perpetually available . . . to write and register their most important, most special and most secret business'.[1] There could be no clearer statement that the more important of the secretaries were very close to the king and that there were no public affairs calling for loyalty and efficiency upon which they might not be employed.[2] It is therefore not surprising that some of the most able, and perhaps agreeable, of the secretaries, who knew how to attract the king's attention and win his favour, should have risen above their colleagues.

By far the most important, distinguished and successful of the early secretaries was Florimond Robertet, ancestor of the two *secrétaires d'État* who bore his name. Quick, and able to make the most of his position, Robertet acquired great experience. We know more of the impression that he made upon contemporaries, who sang his praises, than of what he actually did and how he achieved his considerable renown. He is said to have been given wide powers under Charles VIII, and under Louis XII and Francis I he assumed the general direction of the government.[3] When he died in 1522, he had strongly influenced the government of France for a quarter of a century. It was even said that 'he governed the entire kingdom; for since the death of the legate d'Amboise he was the man who was closest to his master . . . and without any doubt I think he was more heeded than any man I have ever seen and of greater capacity than any who

[1] 'ceux qu'ils vouloient et entendoient etre presens et perpetuellement appelés ou aucun d'eux pour ecrire et enregistrer leurs plus grands plus speciaux et plus secrettes affaires.' B.N., Mss. Clairambault, 664, f. 85v.

[2] B.N., Mss. fr. 18236, ff. 6v–7.

[3] Chénon, ii, 404.

handled the affairs of France and who had complete charge of them'.[1] Robertet, by providing a great example and founding a great tradition, contributed more than anyone else to the creation of the *secrétaires d'État*. Philippe de Comines went so far as to honour him with the title of Monseigneur, and Du-Toc declared him the father of the *secrétaires d'État* who began to give to these officials the degree of importance and authority which they ultimately acquired.[2]

If the career and influence of Florimond Robertet were exceptional, there were, nevertheless, several other *secrétaires des finances* who achieved considerable distinction during the second half of the reign of Francis I, such as Nicolas de Neufville, grandfather of the famous secretary Villeroy, Jean Breton, seigneur de Villandry and Gilbert Bayard who served with Bochetel. Guillaume Bochetel and Claude de Laubespine deserve special mention because they were two of the four *secrétaires des finances* whom Henry II established as *secrétaires d'État* by his letters patent of 1547.

Bochetel was Robertet's chief clerk and therefore received his early training from Robertet himself. He witnessed his example, absorbed his precepts, inherited his tradition and, in turn, transmitted this inheritance to two of his sons-in-law, whom he trained for the office of *secrétaire d'État*. He must have begun his career of public service as a very young man, for he was granted permission to exercise his office of *greffier des aides, tailles et gabelles* of Berry while he was still under age.[3] However, his career began in earnest on 27 July 1518 when he became a *clerc, notaire et secrétaire du roi*.[4] It was not until 1530 that he received a commission to sign financial documents, and two years later he became a *secrétaire des finances*.[5] By this time Bochetel was also one of several secretaries to the queen, and a *secrétaire de la chambre du roi*.[6] By 1537 at the latest, Bochetel had become a councillor and,

[1] Fleuranges, quoted by de Luçay, 10–11.

[2] Du-Toc, 21. The register of Florimond Robertet was published by G. Robertet, *Les Robertet au XVIe siècle* (1888) but the intended study of his career was interrupted by the author's death.

[3] *Catalogue*, vii, no. 25615, undated.

[4] *Ibid.*, v, no. 16768, 27 July 1518.

[5] *Ibid.*, i, no. 3762, 22 August 1530; *ibid.*, ii, no. 4791, 28 August 1532.

[6] B.N., Mss. fr. 2952, ff. 28, 36, 50, 64v; *Catalogue*, x, 638, index, *secrétaires du roi*; Mss. fr. 3132, f. 55v.

in 1543, he was a member of the *conseil des affaires*, the king's most secret council, which included only four other members.[1] He continued to grow in favour: 'His ability and fidelity were so highly esteemed that the conduct of business devolved upon him and secrets of state were entrusted to his discretion.'[2] In 1542 he was rewarded for his services with the office of *greffier de l'Ordre de Saint-Michel*, upon the death of his colleague Jean Breton.[3] By the end of the reign, and after having served for at least twenty-nine years, Bochetel was undoubtedly the foremost of the secretaries.

It was just at the time when Bochetel was becoming really influential that Claude de Laubespine became a *notaire, secrétaire du roi*, on 10 March 1538.[4] He was fortunate enough to receive his training at the hands of Bochetel, becoming first his chief clerk and then his son-in-law. He was granted a special commission to sign financial documents on 23 August 1542 and became a permanent *secrétaire des finances* a few weeks later, upon the death of Jean Breton, seigneur de Villandry, who built the magnificent château which still bears his name.[5] When de Laubespine married Jeanne Bochetel on 14 January 1543, he received the *survivance*, or right of succession to Bochetel's office.[6] This was a favour to Bochetel, in recognition of his long services to the crown, 'in the despatch of our principal and most important business'.[7] Thus de Laubespine had made an excellent start on what was to be a brilliant career, with a powerful father-in-law to protect him at court.

During their years of apprenticeship, both Bochetel's and de Laubespine's work had been relatively humble, like that of any other young *secrétaire du roi*, and some of the acts of Francis I reveal interesting details about it. In 1521, when he was still very junior, Bochetel received the sum of 400 *livres tournois* for having, for more than a year, supplied the parchment and been responsible for the despatch of letters patent and royal letters,

[1] *Catalogue*, iii, no. 9431, 22 November 1537; Decrue, 12.

[2] B.N., Mss. fr. 18242, f. 1.

[3] *Catalogue*, iv, no. 12756, 29 September 1542.

[4] *Ibid.*, viii, no. 32789. This is sometimes given as 1537 which is the old style.

[5] *Ibid.*, viii, no. 33021; *C.S.P.D./F.*, 1542, p. 417. 7 September 1542, Paget to Henry VIII; *Catalogue*, iv, no. 12756, September 1542.

[6] B.N., Mss. fr. 6616, f. 37, 14 January 1542/3, de Laubespine's marriage contract.

[7] B.N., Mss. fr. 18243, f. 17, 23 October 1542 (copy).

especially those relating to the King of Navarre. He received the same sum the following year for despatching letters patent ordering bands of soldiers to disperse and return home without pillaging.[1] There are similar items for de Laubespine and others who served as clerks to more senior secretaries, for supplying parchment, drafting, writing and sending out technical documents. This was part of their routine duties.[2] It was normal for the secretaries to bear expenses initially and to claim for them later. One item records the repayment to Bochetel of eighteen *livres* which he had advanced for an express messenger to go from Chantilly to Paris to purchase some books and bring them back to the king.[3]

From a number of acts embodying gifts to Bochetel and to others of small or even considerable sums of money, the proceeds of fines and other amounts accruing to the king, we can see that he was in the habit of rewarding and encouraging his secretaries from time to time.[4] He was also mindful of the abnormally heavy expenses which they sometimes incurred in his service, and once he gave Bochetel 2,250 *livres* towards the wedding expenses of one of his daughters.[5]

Bochetel and de Laubespine were both employed by Francis I on more than one diplomatic mission, work which might result in their making a handsome profit or equally well in their sustaining a disconcerting loss. So far as we know, Bochetel's first mission was in 1530 when he went to Spain with the vicomte de Turenne to arrange for the king's marriage to Eleanor, Queen of Portugal, elder sister of the Emperor Charles V, and to see the captive dauphin (later Henry II) and his brother. Bochetel went to draft and write all the despatches, by means of which he kept the *grand maître*, Anne de Montmorency, informed of what was happening in Spain.[6] These are among the very few of

---

[1] *Catalogue*, v, no. 17441, 7 January–7 February 1521; *ibid.*, viii, no. 32372, 25 February 1522.

[2] *Ibid.*, vii, no. 28706, 1539; *ibid.*, viii, no. 29896, undated.

[3] *Ibid.*, vii, no. 28718, undated.

[4] *Ibid.*, iii, no. 8612, 17 August 1536, no. 9231, 21 August 1537, no. 9238, 25 August 1537, no. 10041, 21 May 1538.

[5] *Ibid.*, viii, no. 31709, undated.

[6] B.N., Mss. fr. 20639, ff. 231v, 235; Mss. fr. 20505, ff. 107, 121, 24 March, 13 February [1530], Bochetel to Montmorency; Mss. fr. 3005, f. 134, 23 February [1530], Bochetel to Montmorency.

Bochetel's still extant letters, and they show him performing what was always one of the most important functions of a secretary—that of liaison. Bochetel was further appointed one of the deputies to negotiate peace with England in 1535.[1] On this occasion he served as an ambassador rather than as a secretary, and his name appears in the commission at least theoretically on an equality with that of the admiral of France. For this mission he received the large extraordinary payment of 300 *livres*.[2]

Bochetel himself signed de Laubespine's instructions, on 8 July 1542, for his first diplomatic mission, which was to England. He was not yet even a *secrétaire des finances* when he left for London to join the French ambassador, Marillac, in seeking an audience with Henry VIII. He was to inform Henry that Francis had made a treaty with Sweden, Denmark and Prussia, that the King of Scotland would join it and that 'honourable place is left for the King of England to enter if he will'.[3] On 31 July, Paget, the English ambassador in France, wrote home that the French were longing to have de Laubespine's answer, 'for they have Henry in great jealousy for practising with the Emperor, and sent Laubeespine only to decipher him'.[4] The French envoys received a 'very short and meagre' audience but, if de Laubespine did not retain any very pleasant memories of his first diplomatic mission, he received the rather large payment of 787 *livres* 10 *sous* and £50 from the King of England. He also enjoyed a warm welcome on his return to court, his negotiation having 'given satisfaction to the Master'. If, indeed, he had gone to 'decipher' Henry, then he seems to have been entirely successful.[5]

De Laubespine took part in a further negotiation with England in 1544.[6] The king was evidently satisfied again since, shortly before his death in 1547, he entrusted de Laubespine, young though he was, with the sole charge of an important

[1] *Catalogue*, vi, no. 20912.
[2] *Ibid.*, iii, no. 7832, 12 May 1535.
[3] *C.S.P.D./F.*, 1542, p. 277.
[4] *Ibid.*, p. 318, 31 July 1542, Paget to Henry VIII.
[5] *Catalogue*, iv, no. 12626, 9 July 1542; *C.S.P.D./F.*, 1542, p. 742, app. B. no. 34, 2 August 1542, Chapuys to the Queen of Hungary; *ibid.*, p. 481 (28b); *ibid.*, p. 370, 23 August 1542, Marillac to de Laubespine.
[6] *Catalogue*, ix, 32; Du-Toc, 78.

mission to Strasbourg, where the deputies of the protestant towns and princes of Germany agreed to meet him. He tempted them with money which made them so wish for a French alliance that they handed him guarantees on behalf of their princes. De Laubespine reported to the king in a remarkably informal letter which suggests that he was on easy and friendly terms with his dying master, whom he was never to see again. It contains strong evidence of his outstanding ability.[1]

From being mere clerks of the *chancellerie* in the middle ages, the secretaries had by the sixteenth century become an essential part of the government of France. In trying to assess their position at the end of the reign of Francis I it is necessary to distinguish between the importance of the office and that of individual secretaries. The office had acquired a certain degree of permanent importance, if only because the signature of a secretary was normally considered necessary on royal letters and state papers. This alone meant that at least one of the secretaries was always in attendance on the king, a privileged and coveted position. Upon the accession of Henry II, the importance of the office was emphasized by the appointment of four specially chosen secretaries to the new distinction of *secrétaire d'État*. The regulation implicitly recognized that a few of the *secrétaires des finances* had been doing work at court which was more important than that of the majority of their colleagues. It was in these circumstances that some of them, especially Robertet and, to a lesser extent, Bochetel and de Laubespine, were able to exert a personal influence which was at times considerable. In the absence of any outstanding noble or officer of state, or possibly in time of war when the court might be temporarily deserted, opportunity could arise for an able secretary to increase his own influence. It was certainly no accident that Bochetel was most influential under Francis I during the years after 1541 when the autocratic constable Montmorency was in disgrace and absent from court. After the admiral, Claude d'Annebaut, the prevailing favourite, it was Bochetel and his colleague Gilbert Bayard who had most credit with the king, even in affairs of state.[2] But personal importance did not follow from the mere fact of hold-

---

[1] Ribier, i, 634, 26 March 1547, de Laubespine to the king.
[2] *Ibid.*, i, 557.

ing office; it was something fluctuating and variable, and dependent upon personalities and changing circumstances. This was dramatically illustrated by the palace revolution which followed the death of Francis I. Though not without their moment of anxiety, Bochetel and de Laubespine weathered this sudden storm to become two of the first four *secrétaires d'État.*

C

CHAPTER II

The First Four *Secrétaires d'État*

BOCHETEL and Bayard were with the king when he died in the round tower at Rambouillet early in the afternoon on the last day of March 1547. His illness had for some time interfered with business and, unable to obtain any instructions, the secretaries had letters which remained unanswered.[1] They trembled for their offices and that of de Laubespine, who was still away, knowing that there would be many changes at court on account of the bitter enmity between the households of Francis and Henry and between their rival mistresses, madame d'Estampes and Diane de Poitiers. Perhaps they used the letters as a pretext, for they managed to see the new king, Henry, before his hurried departure for Hautes-Bruyières the same afternoon, whence he summoned Montmorency back from disgrace, to meet him at Saint-Germain. Henry gave the two secretaries cause for hope and commanded them to follow him, which they did. Bochetel wasted no time in hurrying to Saint-Germain to present himself to Montmorency who had immediately assumed control over everything. He wrote to inform de Laubespine that Montmorency had received him well—they had already worked in close co-operation in the past—and had taken his son Jacques into his service. Bochetel did everything he could to ascertain his position and that of de Laubespine. Montmorency confirmed that the king would retain them, 'and I assure you', Bochetel wrote to de Laubespine, revealing the extent of his relief, 'that I have found more friends than I expected amidst such great and sudden changes'.[2] Bochetel

---

[1] B.N., Mss. fr. 18243, f. 23, 4 April 1546/7, Bochetel to de Laubespine; printed by Du-Toc, 25–7. This letter is far the most interesting document extant on the palace revolution of 1547.
[2] *Id.*

went on to recount the unjust treatment of Bayard, which only
served to emphasize their own good fortune, for he had been
dismissed on the trumped-up charge of having made some
indiscreet jest about the age and the charms of Diane de Poitiers. He died in prison two years later.[1]

The future careers of Bochetel and de Laubespine were
settled by the letters patent of 1 April 1547 by which they were
appointed two of four *secrétaires des commandements*, or, as they are
generally called from this date onwards, *secrétaires d'État*. When
he wrote to de Laubespine on 4 April 1547, Bochetel knew
nothing of this. Clearly the document was back-dated, as from
the king's accession, perhaps by as much as a week or two. He
did know, however, that Cosme Clausse was popular with the
king, and that Jean du Thier was an old servant of Montmorency, and he is therefore unlikely to have been surprised
when he learnt that they were all four to serve together as
secrétaires d'État to Henry II. They all came from a similar social
milieu, were known to each other, and had already had considerable experience during the previous reign.

Guillaume Bochetel, whose career we have already briefly
followed under Francis I, was the seigneur de Sacy and de la
Forest Taumier. He was often described as the seigneur de Sacy
and sometimes as the *greffier* Bochetel, by reason of his office of
greffier des aides, tailles et gabelles of Berry. Son of Bernadin
Bochetel, *secrétaire du roi*, *procureur du roi* in Berry and mayor
of Bourges, and of Catherine Babouin, he was probably born
about the turn of the century. His great-grandfather François
was also a *secrétaire du roi* and the mayor of Bourges in 1495. His
grandfather Jean was a *receveur général des finances*[2] and a *secrétaire
du roi* to Charles VII. Thus Bochetel inherited an already long
family tradition of public service. His wife, Marie de Morvillier,
was a sister of Jean de Morvillier, ambassador to Venice, bishop
of Orléans and later chancellor of France. They had four sons
and five daughters. Bernadin, the eldest son, became successively
abbé de Saint-Laurent and bishop of Rennes, *conseiller d'État*
and ambassador to the Empire, Venice and Switzerland.

[1] Du-Toc, 24; Cimber et Danjou, *Histoire particulière*, 286; B.N., Mss. Pièces
Originales, 770, f. 5, 1 June 1549.
[2] B.N., Mss. Cabinet d'Hozier, 49, f. 4.

Jacques, the second son, known as La Forest Bochetel, was ambassador to the Netherlands. A third son, Jean, became a *secrétaire du roi*. Of the daughters (Catherine, Jeanne, Marie and Anne) Jeanne married Claude de Laubespine, and Marie married Jacques Bourdin, who succeeded to his father-in-law's office in 1558. Bochetel's home was in Bourges though he probably had houses in other places such as Paris, Fontaine-bleau or Blois. We know little about his character, but he was much admired by his disciples and sons-in-law, de Laubespine and Bourdin.

The first of these sons-in-law, Claude II de Laubespine, chevalier, baron de Châteauneuf-sur-Cher, vicomte de la Forest Taumier, seigneur de Beauvoir-sur-Arnon, Hautrive, Rousson, Montgaugier and Coussières, was the son of Claude I de Laube-spine and Marguerite Berruyier. They were a family of lawyers from Orléans and the Beauce. Claude's father was the seigneur de la Corbillière and d'Erouville, and had been *bailly* of Saint-Enverte, *conseiller* and *échevin* of Orléans and, according to one source, a *secrétaire du roi*.[1] His grandfather, Gilles, was a merchant, bourgeois and *échevin* of Orléans, and his great-grand-father is said to have been *bailly* of Chartres and an *échevin* of Orléans in the middle of the fifteenth century.

By his first wife, Jeanne Bochetel, de Laubespine had three notable children, Claude, Guillaume and Magdalene. Claude became, in his turn, a *secrétaire d'État* and as such has a place in this study. Guillaume, *conseiller d'État*, *chancelier des Ordres du roi* and ambassador to England, married Marie de la Chastre—daughter of Anne Robertet—and their son Charles was marquis de Châteauneuf-sur-Cher, *garde des sceaux* and *gouverneur* of Touraine. Magdalene was one of the most celebrated women of her time, for her beauty, virtue and learning. She married the secretary Villeroy. De Laubespine also had three brothers of whom Sébastien, abbé de Bassefontaine, better known as the bishop of Limoges, was the most important. He played an outstanding part in public life until his death in 1582. He was one of France's principal ambassadors and a leading member of the council.

These remarkable family records have been given in detail

[1] B.N., Mss. Dossiers Bleus, 385, ff. 21, 77.

because the Bochetels and de Laubespines were two of the most celebrated families of the mid-sixteenth century and played a prominent part in public life. Their members were distinguished by their ability, integrity and popularity, their outstanding services to the state at court, in council and in diplomacy, their connections with other important families and by their position in the cultured, literary world.

We know little about de Laubespine's property or his family life. He owned a famous house in Bourges, which had belonged to Jacques Cœur, goldsmith to Charles VII, and he had lodgings in the Louvre, where he died. There is no evidence of his having bought land or built houses like some of the other secretaries, and it appears that he was not well off. Writing to the bishop of Rennes—Bernadin Bochetel, his brother-in-law—on 3 November 1560, he said that he was in debt as a result of having married his daughter eight or ten days before.[1] However, he possessed at least one fine château, at Châteauneuf-sur-Cher, which is still standing and inhabited today, surrounded on three sides by tall trees and commanding a fine view over the river and surrounding country. De Laubespine was buried in the chapel there in a marble tomb with an effigy and an epitaph. The chapel was rebuilt in the nineteenth century and his body was later transferred to a family tomb in the cathedral at Bourges.[2]

We have no contemporary description of de Laubespine, but there is an engraving of him as a young man, dated 1542, in which he appears to be tall and well-proportioned with a strikingly handsome oval face, dark hair, regular features, kind, lively eyes and a small pointed beard.[3] All that we know about his character must be deduced from the rectitude and integrity of his career, the insight and compassion of his letters and the great reputation he acquired. He became something of a legend in his lifetime, raising the *secrétaires d'État*, in the words of Saint-Simon, 'hors de page'. But, at the beginning of Henry's reign he was still young, and not yet the grave and eminent

[1] B.N., Mss. Cinq Cents Colbert, 394, f. 23, 3 November 1560, de Laubespine to Rennes.
[2] The cathedral was damaged during the Revolution but three of the de Laubespine family effigies may still be seen in the north aisle.
[3] See plate facing p. 97.

councillor that he became, saddened and matured by conflict and distress.

Cosme Clausse—Bochetel's and de Laubespine's colleague—seigneur de Marchaumont in Picardy, was the second son of Jean Clausse, *correcteur des comptes*, and younger brother of Engilbert, seigneur de Mouchy, a *conseiller procureur du roi en cour d'église au châtelet* and a *conseiller du parlement*. He married Marie Bourgensis, daughter of Louis Bourgensis, *secrétaire des finances* under Francis I and Henry II. Their eldest son, Henri, was a godson of the king whose name he bore. He became *grand maître des eaux et forêts* and married Denyse, sister of the secretary Villeroy. The second son, Pierre, *chambellan et surintendant de la maison et affaires* of François, duc d'Alençon, was often mentioned in the correspondence of the reign of Henry III, as he was employed on a number of missions. Another son, Cosme, became bishop of Châlons in succession to his brother Nicolas, who died. One of Clausse's daughters, Marie, married Florimond Robertet, seigneur de Fresne, who became *secrétaire d'État* in 1558 in succession to his father-in-law.

Clausse had been secretary to both the dauphins, Francis and Henry, and he supervised the affairs of Brittany.[1] At the time of the release of these princes from captivity in Spain, Clausse went with their governor René de Cossé, seigneur de Brissac, to meet them and take them letters from the king. He was later driven from court by the disfavour of madame d'Estampes[2] but the evidence of his surviving correspondence suggests that he did not, for that reason, cease to serve the dauphin Henry. He was therefore well known at Henry's court when he was appointed *secrétaire d'État* in 1547, upon the insistence of the king and madame—for, though the others were proposed by Montmorency, he was chosen by the king with whom he was popular. Henry also made Clausse *secrétaire controlleur général de ses guerres* on the death of the ill-fated Bayard, who had held the office for life.[3] The letters patent stated that as the office was important, it must be held by someone who was both 'highly agreeable to

---

[1] Du-Toc, 87.

[2] Romier, *Les Origines politiques*, i, 41, n. 4, the nuncio to cardinal Farnese, 31 March 1546/7.

[3] B.N., Mss. Pièces Originales, 770, f. 5, 1 June 1549.

the king', and also close to his person to answer for the *gendar-merie* as occasion arose.

In spite of his eleven children, Clausse was evidently pros-perous. In 1550 he acquired the seigneurie of Fleury-en-Bière. The château was then moated and consisted of a court and base-court, together with a dovecot, garden and adjoining farm buildings, all surrounded by high walls.[1] Clausse probably undertook fairly extensive alterations, and the château is still, for the most part, a fine example of the late French Renaissance style. He rebuilt the enclosing walls, weaving at regular intervals into the now mellowed brickwork two interlacing Cs, which were his initials. These may also be seen on the farm buildings, and even the metalwork of the great doors bears the same trace of his ownership. As a decorative motif, it is simple and effective. This same year, 1550, Clausse also employed no less an architect than Gilles le Breton to build or rebuild for him the neighbour-ing château of Courances, which is still one of the loveliest properties in the Ile-de-France. Both these châteaux were with-in easy reach of the much frequented royal palace of Fontaine-bleau, and were certainly honoured by Henry II when his hunting took him that way. The only faint hint we have as to Clausse's personality comes from Du-Toc who says that he was of an assiduous and intriguing disposition, involved in every-thing of importance which took place at court and in the king's secret council.[2]

The fourth secretary, du Thier, had like Clausse also served more in the court of the dauphin than he had in that of the king. Jean du Thier, seigneur de Beauregard, *receveur* of Sens, was the son of Olivier, *procureur* of Sens and *receveur des aides du domaine royal*, and of Marguerite de Voves. This was a fairly wealthy family on the fringe of the lesser nobility. By his wife, Marie Pelletan, du Thier had only one daughter, Jeanne, who was one of Catherine de Medici's famous troop of *dames d'honneur*, im-mortalized by Brantôme as the *escadron volant*.[3] He also had a

---

[1] *Acte de vente* 1550, lent by courtesy of the Marquis de Ganay, and kindly tran-scribed by Mademoiselle H. Michaud.

[2] Du-Toc, 87.

[3] Roy, 92. The *escadron volant* was a large group of young and beautiful ladies of good family who embellished the court and added to its gaiety by their ability to sing and dance, and perform masques and other entertainments. They were nor-

natural daughter, Catherine, legitimized by Henry in September 1554.[1]

Du Thier was the only one among the early secretaries who was not related to one or more of the others. He grew up at Sens in a busy and cultivated milieu and, in 1526, he became a *clerc à la recette des finances* attached to Jean Breton, the *secrétaire des finances*. He began, like Bochetel and de Laubespine, by doing the humble work of a clerk, copying and preparing documents. On 21 August 1528 he received only 200 *livres* for two years' salary.[2] At court du Thier came into contact with the powerful constable Montmorency. It was possibly through his favour that, in 1536, he became a *secrétaire du roi*,[3] and in 1538 received the title of *secrétaire du connétable*.[4] This was at the beginning of Montmorency's period of maximum influence under Francis I, when he, more than anyone else, was governing France, and du Thier must have received a thorough training at this time. According to Du-Toc, du Thier followed Montmorency when he was disgraced by Francis I, but his appointment as *secrétaire d'État* in 1547 was due to his own merit as well as to the constable's favour.

It appears that du Thier was reasonably rich and between 1547 and 1555 he gradually acquired a large domain of lands and seigneuries in the region of Blois.[5] The chief of these, and the one on which he lavished most care and attention was that from which he took his title, Beauregard, five miles to the south-east of Blois. According to a local tradition, the house, which is linked by a long, straight avenue to the château of Chambord, was originally built by Francis I as a hunting lodge. However that may be, du Thier acquired the property in 1545[6] and in 1550 he began to rebuild, making of it a sumptuous dwelling in which he assembled a fine library and valuable possessions. Beauregard, which Ronsard called 'ton œuvre', testified to du Thier's wide knowledge and good taste in architecture, litera-

---

mally in attendance upon Catherine, and were so named by Brantôme because they often followed her even when she travelled long distances at high speed. Contrary to popular belief, she governed them sternly.

[1] B.N., Mss. n.a.f. 7976, f. 45, signed by Bourdin.
[2] Roy, 73.
[3] B.N., Mss. Clairambault, 664, f. 105, 18 May 1536.
[4] Roy, 74.   [5] *Ibid.*, 77.   [6] *Ibid.*, 77–8.

ture and art. The king himself took an interest in the new château and made du Thier a gift of 1,500 trees—oaks, elms, hazels, hollies and beeches—to be taken from where they would cause least damage in the surrounding forests.[1] Some of these were probably for building and others for planting in the property. The celebrated architect du Cerceau, said of the house: 'L'édifice n'est pas grand, mais il est mignard, et autant bien accommodé qu'il est possible. . . . Tout, ainsi que le bastiment est plaisant et jolly, aussi est pareillement le jardin.'[2] The most remarkable of the alterations made by du Thier was the *cabinet des grelots*, a magnificent little study in exquisite taste, entirely constructed in light carved oak. Doubtless it was partly with du Thier's scheme in mind that the king made him a further gift of twelve oak trees together with their branches, to come from the neighbouring forests of Blois, Boulogne and Roussy, to help him complete his new dwelling at Beauregard, where he himself sometimes went to hunt.[3] The study is panelled from floor to ceiling and richly decorated in the finest sixteenth-century style. In the centre of the ceiling is a large octagonal caisson containing du Thier's coat of arms, azure three bezants (*azure à trois grelots d'or*). The three bezants form the chief decorative motif, both of the ceiling and of the lower panels of the walls.[4] Eight of the large upper panels bear paintings representing du Thier's catholic interests, showing him to be almost an *homme universel*. These interests were music, precious manuscripts, sculpture, painting and jewellery, also the art of war, hunting, games and agriculture. This latter must have included horticulture, for du Thier grew a collection of rare plants and trees in the gardens of Beauregard.

Still hanging in the entrance hall of the château is a sombre portrait traditionally said to be of du Thier. It is of an elderly man with a thick moustache and a big white beard entirely framing the rather square features. These have a composed and gentle expression, which certainly accords with the grave and fearless manner which Ronsard said he used in addressing

[1] B.N., Mss. Pièces Originales, 1045, 28 November 1551.
[2] Du Cerceau, ii, Beauregard.
[3] B.N., Mss. Pièces Originales, 1045, 13 January 1551/2.
[4] This was executed by Philibert de Lorme who designed the magnificent ceiling of Henry II's ballroom at Fontainebleau.

princes. The impression is of a heavy, thick-set man of medium height. He is simply dressed, wearing a little white ruff of the period 1540–60, and a dark velvet cap.

We know more about du Thier as a person than we do about his three colleagues. According to Ronsard, he was loved and esteemed by the king, and was no less highly regarded by both Montmorency and the cardinal of Lorraine, rivals whom he appears to have served with impartial loyalty. Du Thier's social position and his inclinations brought him into contact with the writers of the period, particularly the group of court poets to which Ronsard and du Bellay belonged, and of which he was a generous and much-loved patron. We do not know whether Bochetel and Clausse also mingled with this group, but de Laubespine certainly did and his children even more. Our knowledge of du Thier's personality is chiefly derived from Ronsard who sang his praises in extravagant pastoral verses in tune with the convention of elaborate *fêtes champêtres*. A poet in praise of his patron is not the most accurate of historical sources, and we must allow for poetic licence when he writes in a sonnet to du Thier, 'Depescher presque seul les affaires de France',[1] or when he proclaims him the companion of Apollo. But, making due allowance for gratitude, affection and the requirements of his art, what Ronsard said of du Thier was undoubtedly true in essence. He gives us a pleasing picture of a devoted servant of the king and a gentle, civilized man, revered for his virtue and wisdom. Du Bellay also wrote of du Thier's diligence, knowledge, wisdom and experience in public affairs, and Ronsard described his working day. In the morning he attended the *conseil des affaires* where, said Ronsard, crowds would throng round and importune him (this is unlikely), and in the afternoon there was the *conseil privé*. There were papers to be signed and countersigned and many royal orders in the course of the day. After attending the king's *coucher* in the evening he would sit up working far into the night. This routine will have been the same for all the secretaries. But in spite of the weight of responsibility he bore, Ronsard continued, he thrived on his work as a salamander thrives on fire; his green old age 'se nourrist du travail qui jamais ne te laisse'.[2] Ronsard said that du Thier was an excel-

---

[1] Ronsard, ii. 17–18, iii, 427 ff, v, 138 ff; Roy, 82 ff.
[2] Roy, 83 ff; Ronsard, v, 140.

lent poet. He was able to write in Italian, and in French he was known as a fine stylist. His compositions were a model of their kind.[1]

Not only Ronsard but others, including the naturalist Belon, also paid tribute to du Thier in speaking of his *bienveillance aimable* towards everyone, great and small, and his extensive knowledge. Ronsard himself loved his 'esprit vif, prompt, gaillard'.[2] He was no courtier but open and sincere, free of envy, pride and avarice; a man who remained simple in success and 'le protecteur de tout gentil esprit'.[3]

Of these four secretaries, Clausse is the only one who is known to have received a special commission in 1547. Probably the other commissions are lost. He was appointed as *secrétaire de nos finances en chef et titre d'office*, which rather suggests some kind of seniority, and he seems to have enjoyed considerable favour with the king and Diane de Poitiers.[4] The ambassador Alvarotti wrote to the duke of Ferrara on 31 March 1547 announcing the future importance of Clausse. Later in that year the papal nuncio, Dandino, sent to Rome, for the benefit of his successor, a list of persons in France whose goodwill it was important to secure; the only secretary mentioned was Clausse.[5] Bochetel himself tells us the same thing: 'Marchaumont [Clausse] is going ahead as fast as he can,' he wrote to de Laubespine, 'and I am withdrawing. Nevertheless,' he went on, 'I continue to despatch all the business I am accustomed to handling and consider that I am well treated.'[6] Bochetel behaved with discretion, gracefully ceding place. He realized that the best of his career was over, although he had once penetrated the secret council of Francis I, and no one comparable to him in knowledge, influence and importance had survived the changes upon the accession of Henry II. He was never again to be so influential, and to some extent de Laubespine shared this eclipse for he was less important than he had already been, and was later to become. But if Bochetel had lost his former position, he had not lost his credit, for, on 23 April 1547, the new king made him a handsome gift of

[1] Roy, 83 ff.   [2] Ronsard, v, 142.   [3] Roy, 83 ff.
[4] B.N., Mss. fr. 18243, f. 25, 1 April 1547, 'provisions de Cosme Clausse, extrait des registres de la chambre des comptes'. See app. ii.
[5] Romier, *Les Origines politiques*, i, 56, n. 6, August 1547.
[6] B.N., Mss. fr. 18243, f. 23, 4 April 1546/7, Bochetel to de Laubespine.

10,000 *livres tournois* for his services both past and future. Further-more his influence was still sufficient for him to acquire the *survivance* of his office for his chief clerk and future son-in-law, Jacques Bourdin, and the bishopric of Orléans for his brother-in-law, the wise and gentle Jean de Morvillier.

Were it not for the contemporary statements which have sur-vived to suggest that Clausse was more influential than his col-leagues, one would have accorded this distinction to du Thier or perhaps, increasingly, to de Laubespine. Clausse remains a shadowy figure and most of his letters are lost. Henry was evidently well served by him, but he does not seem to have been a person of the same calibre as the other three. His prominence may only have been temporary, or perhaps based more on per-sonal than on professional grounds. Certainly his *département*—the work which was allotted to him at the time of the appoint-ment of the four secretaries—was far less important than those of de Laubespine and du Thier who, between them, shared most of the work connected with foreign affairs. Du Thier, in par-ticular, had little else, and a certain prestige seems to have attached to this novelty.

CHAPTER III

The Secretaries and their *Départements*

THE permanent establishment of the *secrétaires d'État*—whose office was to develop and endure until the Revolution—was one of the first and most constructive acts of Henry II's reign. It was based on two regulations, the letters patent of 1 April and 14 September 1547.[1] The title *secrétaire d'État* which, for the sake of clarity, is usually employed from 1547 onwards, was not contained in either document. The secretaries had various designations, but as their special function was in connection with affairs of state, *secrétaire d'État* was an almost inevitable abbreviation. It is usually said that they received this title after the treaty of Cateau-Cambrésis because it was found by de Laubespine, at that time, to be applied to the Spanish secretaries. Though it was only generally used from about that time, it was by no means unheard of earlier.[2] Contrary to the opinion of de Luçay, who awarded this distinction to Claude de Laubespine the younger, Florimond Robertet, seigneur d'Alluye, was the first who actually received the title in his commission, dated 14 March 1559.[3]

What little remains to us of the letters patent, nominally issued from Hautes-Bruyières on the first day of the reign, is brief and to the point. It expresses the king's wish and intention that Guillaume Bochetel, Cosme Clausse, Claude de Laubespine and Jean du Thier, all described as *conseillers et secrétaires des commandemens et finances*, should have charge of the correspondence concerning affairs of state, and prepare the despatches and

---

[1] B.N., Mss. fr. 18243, f. 27; Du-Toc, 37–41, 44; de Luçay, 14–15.

[2] B.N., Mss. Pièces Originales, 1659, ff. 23, 27, 28; Mss. fr. 18152, f. 5; Du-Toc, 41 (registres du parlement, 27 July 1527); Doucet, i, 160, n. 4; Chénon, ii, 505.

[3] B.N., Mss. fr. 3942, f. 339, 14 March 1559; de Luçay, 579; Bondois, 48.

replies, each secretary for the places and districts thereafter specified:[1]

(1)	(2)
BOCHETEL	DE LAUBESPINE
(*Jacques Bourdin*, 1558;	Champagne
Claude de Laubespine, son, 1567)	Burgundy
Normandy	Bresse
Picardy	Savoy
Flanders	Germany
Scotland	Switzerland
England	

(3)	(4)
CLAUSSE	DU THIER
(*Florimond Robertet*	(*Florimond Robertet*
seigneur de Fresne, 1558)	*seigneur d'Alluye*, 1560)
Provence	Piedmont
Languedoc	Rome
Guienne	Lyons
Brittany	Dauphiné
Spain	Venice
Portugal	Levant

This document did not depart from the ancient custom of making a choice from among the *secrétaires du roi* of certain persons to perform special duties which, in 1547, were defined as 'la charge des expeditions . . . des affaires d'Etat', but it was the first time that their sphere of action had been specified in this way.

The purpose of the letters patent of 14 September 1547, which brought about the real change in the status of the four secretaries, was to raise their salaries from the sum of 1,623 *livres* 2 *sous* 6 *deniers*[2] which they received in common with other *secrétaires des finances* to 3,000 *livres* a year. Their office was described as being

---

[1] 'Le Roy veut et entend que maitres Guillaume Bochetel, Cosme Clausse, Claude de Laubespine et Jean du Thier, ses conseillers et secretaires de ses commandemens et finances ayent la charge des expeditions en ses affaires d'estat, et fassent les depeches et reponses en lieux et endroits cy-apres declarez selon le departement qui ensuit.' Du-Toc, 44.

[2] B.N., Mss. fr. 3132, f. 41; *Catalogue*, ii, no. 6576, 9 December 1535; *ibid.*, viii, no. 29893, 31 December 1537. Du-Toc and de Luçay give this sum as 1,623 *livres* 10 *sous*.

extremely laborious and calling for the greatest care and diligence. In order to perform their exacting duties, the secretaries
were attached to the king and required to remain continually
about his person, that is to say, within his immediate entourage.
Because of this their rise in salary was declared to be 'more than
reasonable', considering the excessive and unendurably high
cost of living, as well as the great and continual expenses which
they would necessarily incur in following the king.[1] The increase
in salary took effect retrospectively from the date of their
appointments, and they were paid at the beginning of every
third month. As it was exceptional for Henry II to stay for as
long as two weeks together in any one place, their office must
indeed have been expensive and demanding.

Thus, for the first time, the letters patent clearly raised the
secrétaires d'État above their colleagues. They were allowed a
much higher salary, they were commanded to remain at court
about the king, and the exacting nature of their work was
emphasized. But neither regulation specified the powers of the
secretaries, which were never defined. Their new *départements*
were stated to have been given them in order that each secretary
might know what he had to do, and be responsible for his
allotted areas, and also that from thenceforth confusion in the
handling of the despatches and state papers might be avoided
and the work done in an orderly fashion. The letters patent further stressed the supreme importance of these affairs of state,
and thus, by inference, the importance of the office of secretary.[2]

Though the *départements* of 1547 were purely topographical

---

[1] '. . . ayent egard a ce que nosdits . . . secretaires . . . pour satisfaire . . . a ce
qu'ils doivent pour nostredit service et entiere satisfaction de leurs charges qui sont
de grand et extreme labeur, soin, vigilance et diligence, sont abstraints de con-
tinuellement resider pres et allentour de nostre personne a grands frais et despens,
nous avons avise, comme il est plus que raisonnable de leur croistre et augmenter
jusques a trois mil livres tournois a chascun par an leurs gages . . . eu egard a la
cherte des vivres qui est excessive . . . qu'aussi a la grande et continuelle despense
que a cette occasion il faut qu'ils fassent a nostre suite.' Du-Toc, 38–9.

[2] '. . . nous eussions . . . fait election de quatre de nos amez et feaux conseillers et
secretaires . . . pour faire les expeditions et les depesches d'estat . . . pour distincte-
ment et respectivement en repondre afin que chacun d'eux sceut ce qu'il a à faire, et
que doresnavant telles expeditions et depesches d'estat, qui sont les choses plus
dignes et plus importantes qui soient à manier aupres de nostre personne, fussent
sans aucune confusion, mais avec l'ordre et dignite qu'il appartient, conduites et
maniees.' Du-Toc, 38.

and as such have been said to be inconvenient, there is no evidence of this except, perhaps, in military affairs. A similar division into *départements* continued until the end of the reign of Henry III, when the first signs of specialization appeared. The topographical division had the essential advantage of flexibility. It would have been much more difficult for heads of specialized departments to take over each other's work without warning. As it was, the same internal questions concerned all the secretaries to a large extent, and they were all informed of each other's business, both because they heard it discussed in council and because of their close personal relationships.

To what extent the secretaries kept to the work of their own *départements* is a pertinent and an interesting question. It is easy to multiply examples of their doing each other's work, as P. M. Bondois has done.[1] There was nearly always one of them doing another's work, and their ability to change about in this way was essential—if the system were to succeed—because the court was often divided, the secretaries were continually being sent out on missions of one kind or another, they were not infrequently ill and were occasionally away on holiday. They tended to work in pairs and to avoid, whenever possible, being absent together. Thus, de Laubespine and Bochetel, and later de Laubespine and Bourdin, would, if necessary, do each other's work. Du Thier and Clausse would also help each other in this way and the Robertet cousins, Fresne and Alluye, did the same. The fact that situations constantly arose in which the secretaries took over each other's work does not prove that the division into *départements* was never effective, as Bondois has claimed. It is easier still to multiply examples of their attending to their own countries and provinces, and they frequently referred, chiefly in letters to the duc de Guise, to the 'affairs of the places and areas under my control', or 'the places which are in my *département*', and other such phrases. By the reign of Henry III, which is much better documented than that of Henry II, the secretaries rarely took over each other's work, except in cases of absence. Few regulations were rigidly applied in the sixteenth century, and this one,

[1] Bondois, 49. He says: 'Cette division géographique fut méconnue dès les premières années où elle aurait dû être appliquée . . .' This opinion is not acceptable.

which was not worked out in detail, was clearly only intended as a general directive. Had it been an absolute rule, it would have made the work of administration impossible.

The eleven areas allotted to the secretaries in France—Normandy, Picardy, Champagne, Burgundy, Bresse, Provence, Languedoc, Guienne, Brittany, Lyons and Dauphiné—did not cover the whole country. They corresponded to ten of the eleven *gouvernements* which existed at the end of the fifteenth century, with the curious exception of the Ile-de-France, which may simply have been a copyist's error. Bresse, the eleventh area in the *départements*, was a newly conquered province which was lost again in 1559. These *gouvernements* were all frontier areas because the *gouverneur* was, in origin, essentially a military appointment. From the reign of Henry II onwards the powers of the *gouverneurs* rapidly increased, though the name was loosely and generally applied to persons holding dissimilar commissions and exercising differing degrees of authority.[1] From about 1560 the whole country had come to be divided into *gouvernements*, or at least lieutenancies, which might be areas broken off from a *gouvernement* for local, military or personal reasons. The numbers and areas of the *gouvernements* and lieutenancies varied from time to time and even at the end of the eighteenth century their limits were ill-defined. One of the most important duties of the secretaries was that of providing liaison between the king and the *gouverneurs*, keeping them informed of developments and opinion at court and transmitting to them the king's instructions. There was a period, from about the end of the reign of Henry II until it was revised in 1567, during which the original allocation of countries and provinces within the *départements* had become obsolete. The emphasis on the frontiers shows how public affairs had been thought of primarily in military terms, and particularly in terms of defence. The second group of *départements* reflected the shift of emphasis from external to internal affairs.

[1] On the *gouvernements* see Gaston Zeller, 'Gouverneurs de provinces au XVIe siècle', *Revue historique*, clxxxv (1939), and 'L'Administration monarchique avant les intendants', *Revue historique*, cxcviii (1947); Doucet, i, ch. ix. Both authors emphasize how little is at present known about this important subject and how imprecisely the terms *gouverneur*, *lieutenant général* and *lieutenant du roi* were applied. See also Chénon, ii, section 442, p. 449. The terms *gouverneur* and *gouvernement* cannot be correctly translated by the English words governor and government.

D

It was when Florimond Robertet, seigneur de Fresne, died on 22 October 1567 that the long-overdue revision of the secretaries' *départements* was made.[1] Comparison of the two lists, item by item, shows them to be very different from each other. But, apart from the removal of countries or provinces from one *département* to another, the actual additions were neither sudden nor arbitrary, but simply an official recognition of already existing facts. The system was flexible and it had developed—as it continued to do—as need arose. The new division was no less topographical than the first, but it nevertheless reflected the altered political and military conditions of the 1560s. It also reflected the pre-eminence of Claude de Laubespine over his colleagues, because he held in his new *département* the most important countries and provinces. The new allocation was as follows:

(1)	(2)
DE LAUBESPINE	ALLUYE
The Emperor	Piedmont
Spain	Levant
Portugal	Dauphiné
Flanders	Italy
England	Lyonnais
Scotland	Provence
Metz	Languedoc
Champagne	
Burgundy	
Ile-de-France	

(3)	(4)
DE LAUBESPINE, son	FIZES
Switzerland	Denmark
Normandy	Guienne
Picardy	Orléans
Germany	Touraine
Brittany	Maine
	Anjou
	Chartres
	Berry
	Poitou and La Rochelle

[1] B.N., Mss. fr. 18243, f. 44v, 24 October 1567, 'extrait d'un ancien registre parmi les papiers de Gassot'. Also Mss. fr. 21432, f. 124.

Of the provinces in his original *département* de Laubespine retained only Champagne and Burgundy. Switzerland he had already exchanged for the much more important England, at the time when Bourdin assumed the bulk of Bochetel's work, and Bresse and Savoy had ceased to be French since the treaty of Cateau-Cambrésis. Metz had been added at the time of its conquest in 1552, and for some years past he had already been dealing with the affairs of the Ile-de-France, which included Paris. Spain was the most important of the foreign countries, and, as we shall see later, for years de Laubespine had dealt with any special or secret negotiations with Spain, so that it was simpler and more logical to place that country in his *département*.[1] Spain and Portugal went together as did England and Scotland, and Flanders was inseparable from Spain.

Germany and Brittany were added to the young de Laubespine's *département* and the rest he received from Bourdin. In Alluye's *département* Italy replaced Rome and Venice, and Lyons became the Lyonnais, probably with the addition of some surrounding territory. He also received the large provinces of Provence and Languedoc, which were formerly in the *département* of his cousin Fresne.

It was Fizes' *département* which showed the most additions, only Guienne having been retained from the original list. Denmark had been added and a number of new *gouvernements*, for some of which Fresne had, in fact, already been responsible.[2] These additions were: Orléans, Touraine, Maine, Anjou (districts which had been separated from Guienne), Chartres (strategically and economically very important in civil war), Berry (the heart of France and important for holding the Loire against foreign mercenaries invading from the east) and, finally, Poitou and La Rochelle, also separated from Guienne.

Not knowing the exact boundaries of these areas (there may never have been exact boundaries) it is difficult to ascertain how much of France was still omitted, but probably it was only a relatively small area in the centre, comprising parts of Auvergne and Bourbonnais.

These *départements* of October 1567 were very short-lived for less than a month later the elder de Laubespine was dead, and

[1] See ch. ix.   [2] See ch. x.

they were immediately changed again. Those of 12 November 1567 were as follows:[1]

(1)	(2)
ALLUYE	FIZES
Italy	England
Levant	Scotland
Dauphiné	Denmark
Provence	Normandy
Languedoc	Brittany
Lyonnais	Paris, Ile-de-France
Auvergne and the rest of the	Orléans
gouvernement of the duc	Maine
de Nemours	Touraine and the rest of the
	gouvernement of the
	prince Dauphin

(3)	(4)
DE LAUBESPINE, son	VILLEROY
The Empire	Spain
Germany	Portugal
Metz	Flanders
Champagne and Brie	Picardy
Burgundy	Guienne
	Poitou and La Rochelle
	Anjou and Berry

Alluye, who became the senior secretary, moved to the head of this list with the same *département* as before, plus the addition of Auvergne and the rest of the *gouvernement* of the duc de Nemours. De Laubespine's highly concentrated *département* was split up again, causing alterations in the other three. It should be noted how important a *département* was given to de Laubespine's young successor, Villeroy, for even in his early youth he aroused great expectations.

This arrangement lasted for three years, until the young de Laubespine died on 13 September 1570. He was succeeded by Claude Pinart. Alluye, who died in the previous year, had been succeeded by Pierre Brulart.

[1] B.N., Mss. fr. 18243, f. 48, 12 November 1567; Mss. fr. 21432, f. 124v; de Luçay, 582. The heading quoted by de Luçay, 'après la mort de MM. de Laubespine père et fils', is an error. It refers to the fourth, not the third *département*.

The next *départements* of September 1570 were:[1]

(1)	(2)
FIZES	VILLEROY
Levant	Spain
Italy	Portugal
Dauphiné	Flanders
Provence	Picardy
Languedoc	Guienne
Auvergne	Poitou and La Rochelle
The rest of the *gouvernement* of	Anjou and Berry
the duc de Nemours	
The *gendarmerie*	
The king's household	

(3)	(4)
BRULART	PINART
The Empire	England
Germany	Scotland
Switzerland	Denmark
Metz	Brittany
Champagne	Paris, Ile-de-France
Brie	Orléans
Burgundy	Touraine
	Maine
	Normandy

Fizes, now the senior secretary, took over Alluye's former *département*. The Lyonnais, no longer mentioned, was certainly included under the *gouvernement* of Nemours. In addition, Fizes had two new items, the first heralds of specialization, the *gendarmerie* and the king's household. Villeroy, now second on the list, retained his original *département* of November 1567. Pinart took over that of Fizes unchanged, and Brulart received the young de Laubespine's.

This fourth allocation of *départements* lasted for nine years until Fizes died on 27 November 1579. His office was then abolished and, for the remainder of the period under consideration, there were only three secretaries. No lists have survived—if indeed there ever were any—of the changes made in 1579. It is usually

[1] B.N., Mss. fr. 18243, f. 48, September 1570; Mss. fr. 21432, f. 125; Mss. Clairambault, 664, f. 109.

said that Fizes' *département* and emoluments were divided among his three colleagues,[1] but this is an error. Villeroy, from then on the senior secretary, took over Fizes' *département*, at the same time keeping Spain, Portugal, Guienne, Poitou and La Rochelle from his own. The rest, namely Flanders, Picardy, Anjou and Berry, were added to Brulart's *département*. This arrangement remained unchanged until Henry III abruptly dismissed all three secretaries on 8 September 1588.

---

[1] De Luçay, 21–2. Others have copied him.

CHAPTER IV

The Work of the Secretaries and their Role in the Council

THE chief organ of government, and the chief centre of activity at court, both for the secretaries and for the king's ministers, was the council, which Henry II reorganized at the beginning of his reign.[1] The names, composition and sessions of the councils were constantly changing in the sixteenth century and one must beware of accepting too literally the contents of the ordinances or the theories of the jurists. No one sat in council as of right without being summoned by the king, and it often happened that nominal councillors were not summoned and that others were. At the beginning of the reign there were two councils, the *conseil des affaires*, also known as the *conseil du matin* because its sessions were held immediately after the king's levee, from about six to nine in the morning, and the *conseil privé* or *des parties*. This was the council proper. The *conseil des affaires* was the smaller, inner council, sometimes also known as *étroit* or *secret*. It was only held in the presence of the king and it discussed affairs of state and finance, questions of policy and all that was most urgent, secret and important. To it Henry summoned Montmorency, Guise, Lorraine, the Saint-Andrés (father and son), the King of Navarre, his son Antoine de Bourbon, Robert de la Mark, Villeroy,[2] as well as the president of the *parlement* of Paris, the chancellor, and Diane de Poitiers' nominee the treasurer

[1] Ordinance of 30 April 1547; Guillard, 38; de Boislisle, *Les Mémoires de Saint-Simon*, v, app. i, p. 464. See also vol. iv, app. i; Valois, *Arrêts du conseil d'état (règne Henri IV)* introduction; J. Caillet, *De l'administration en France sous le ministère du Cardinal Richelieu*; Léon Aucoc, *Le Conseil d'état avant et depuis 1789*.

[2] Nicolas de Neufville, seigneur de Villeroy, grandfather of the secretary Villeroy.

André Blondet. The four secretaries were also to be present (*assisteront*) but, in theory at least, without taking part in the deliberations of the council.

The *conseil privé*, the council *par excellence*,[1] sat in the afternoons and was seldom attended by the king who used, at that time of day, to visit Diane, to play the guitar, dally and recount to her the events of the morning. It was composed of the members of the *conseil des affaires*, together with the cardinals, bishops, dukes and one or two other persons. It dealt with all remaining business—affairs of state, administration, finance and justice. At this time the division of business between the councils was rudimentary and variable. The more important items discussed by the *conseil privé* were referred to the king for approval, but matters of general administration and justice were decided without him. An ordinance of 30 October 1557,[2] signed by de Laubespine, decreed that only the cardinals and the princes were to be of the *conseil privé*, as well as the four secretaries and Jacques Bourdin. He was to succeed Bochetel as *secrétaire d'État* and was probably already doing much of his work. Several others were mentioned by name including Villeroy, and the two Florimond Robertets, Fresne and Alluye, who were all three future secretaries. There is also a draft of 4 January 1559, in de Laubespine's writing, reaffirming this ordinance, which possibly had not been strictly observed.[3] From 1557 the council began to sit in different capacities—for instance it sat as the *conseil des parties* for judicial affairs from twelve to four o'clock on Tuesdays and Thursdays— and this period of changes and development lasted for at least a century.

Whereas under Henry II the *conseil des affaires* was the chief organ of government, under Francis II it was somewhat eclipsed while the Guises were in control. For a while, however, it was restored to its former prestige by the queen-mother, Catherine de Medici, at the beginning of the reign of Charles IX.

By a regulation of May 1561[4] the secretaries became full and equal members of the *conseil des affaires*, which they had probably

[1] Any reference to *the* council, was to the *conseil privé*.
[2] B.N., Mss. fr. 18152, f. 5, 30 October 1557.
[3] B.N., Mss. fr. 6617, f. 23, 4 January 1558/9.
[4] Valois, *Introduction*, xli.

already been in practice for many years past. After the declaration of his majority in 1563, Charles IX issued another ordinance reducing the membership of this council and reforming its procedure. The struggle for control of the council was a vital part of the struggle for control of the state, and the secretaries, who were constantly gaining in prestige and influence, were becoming an important element in this struggle. Catherine realized how useful they could be to her. She recognized and confirmed their position and also did what she could to attach them to herself and to the crown. In this ordinance of October 1563, the four secretaries were again expressly included in the *conseil des affaires* and its procedure was specified. All the packets and despatches were to be delivered to the secretaries, according to their *départements*, and to no one else. They were to hand them unopened to the queen-mother, who would afterwards show them to the king. When despatches or packets were presented to the queen in council, no one might approach her without being summoned, except the princes of the blood, the cardinal of Lorraine, the constable, the chancellor and the secretary presenting the packet.[1]

The *conseil des affaires* was nevertheless in decline. It was insufficiently secret, and was ill-adapted to a period of revolution during which intense personal suspicion among the leaders of France poisoned public affairs. The king came to treat his council with reserve; he would confer in a quiet corner of the room with a few chosen members or with the secretaries, or even sidestep the council altogether. About 1568 Charles IX actually formed a small, new, exclusive council in its place, known as the *conseil du cabinet*, of which his friend and favourite secretary Villeroy was one of the members.[2] The decline of the council necessarily had the effect of increasing the importance of the secretaries for, whereas other members could be ignored, they had to be summoned as it was they who had to take action.

---

[1] 'Quand il viendra des paquets et des lettres nul nen approche sans y etre appele si ce n'est Messieurs les Princes du Sang, le Cardinal de Lorraine, Connetable, Chancellier ou le secretaire qui apportera la depesche et que tous les autres paquets et lettres soient portes entre les mains des secretaires selon leurs departements sans les porter ailleurs lesquels les apporteront tous fermez a la Reine qui par apres les fera voir au Roy.' B.N., Mss. fr. 6627, f. 26, 23 October 1563, signed by Alluye.

[2] Cabié, 86, 15 April 1568, Charles to Alençon.

While the role of the *conseil des affaires* gradually diminished, that of the *conseil privé* continued to alter. Already since 1557 it had sat twice a week in a judicial capacity. In 1563 there were three new developments. Mondays were reserved for the *conseil des finances* attended by the secretaries in their capacity as members of the morning *conseil des affaires*. On Tuesdays there was a *conseil de la guerre* attended by the king and the secretaries, provincial *gouverneurs*, and other persons specially concerned. At the same time, and on Saturdays as well, the chancellor held the *conseil des parties* for judicial cases which, probably, the secretaries seldom attended, though if anything important arose the papers still had to be signed by one of them.[1] On Wednesdays and Sundays, immediately after dinner (dinner was, of course, in the morning), the king held a public audience for an hour for anyone who wished to see him, attended by one of the secretaries, each of them performing this duty in turn.

Jules Gassot, *secrétaire du roi*, who served under Alluye and Villeroy and who wrote a valuable memoir, informs us that during the years 1563–7, between the first and second civil wars, it was decreed that all cases arising out of the execution of the edict of pacification[2] should be reserved to the *conseil des parties*. As a result, the council spent so much of its time hearing private cases—and not only in those sessions expressly reserved for them —that the secretaries gave up attending altogether and contented themselves with being 'close to their Majesties in order to receive their commands'.[3] Thus the *conseil des parties* and probably also the *conseil des finances* were abandoned by the *secrétaires d'État*.

The once powerful *conseil des affaires* had been a stepping-stone for the secretaries. Then, as it declined in importance, they emerged above the council because they were closer to the king and the queen-regent than the council itself, from which the crown had largely withdrawn its confidence. The further history and development of the council barely concerns the story of the secretaries because they had already won their place among its members and could attend all its sessions. Whether in fact they attended or not depended upon the circumstances.

The Venetian ambassador, Giovanni Soranzo, reporting in

---

[1] Gassot, 58.   [2] See ch. ix.   [3] Valois, *Introduction*, l; Gassot, 58.

1558, gave a precise description of the procedure which was then followed in the *conseil des affaires*. We cannot be certain that it was the same at the beginning of Henry's reign as at the end but it is unlikely to have been substantially different, and it is said that the original membership remained constant throughout the reign.[1] The secretaries were summoned to the council separately, each for the business of his own *département*. The secretaries then made a draft from the instructions contained in the decisions of the council and—in 1558—if they related to military matters they took them to the duc de Guise, and if they referred to government or finance, to Lorraine. If Guise and Lorraine were satisfied they then showed them to the king.[2] In 1558 the constable, Montmorency, was a prisoner (he had been captured at the battle of Saint-Laurent, 29 August 1557) but, at the beginning of Henry's reign, all correspondence was undoubtedly taken to him, and it is unlikely that he showed more than a part of it to the king.

The secretaries, therefore, were then admitted to the council in a slightly subordinate position, but the fact of admission at all was a triumph. This was an important stage in the development of their office, as well as significant in a wider sense because they were the most stable element in the government. Unlike the nobility, who came and went, they were constantly present and were not distracted by other concerns. They were fully informed on every topic, indeed they were better informed than almost anyone else. A large part of the executive power of the state resided in them; it was in their power to delay or to expedite business, to give or to withhold information, to instruct, to warn, to explain, or to modify orders. It is impossible to believe that they consistently adhered to the letter of the ordinance of 1547 which admitted them to the council, not as full members, but only to deal with the affairs of their *départements* and receive instructions. We may safely assume that they also offered advice. Their greater freedom in the *conseil privé*—which was basically composed of the same personnel and dealt with business of a similar, if less confidential nature—doubtless helped to enhance their position in the more secret *conseil des affaires*.

[1] Cimber et Danjou, *Histoire particulière*, 282.
[2] Albèri, *Relazioni*, ser. i, vol. ii, 444.

A volume of registers of the *conseil privé* between the years 1547–53[1] gives some indication of the part which the secretaries played in the work of this council. Examples show the council dealing with foreign affairs, private litigation, orders for payment, petitions, financial, military and economic affairs. Either a *secrétaire d'État*, or a *secrétaire des finances* or *du roi* made minutes to be read back to the council at the end of the sitting or the beginning of the next and, in some cases, to the king. A *procès verbal* was then drawn up of the items as finally passed, and usually signed by a secretary. Only then would the decisions be acted upon. The *expéditions*[2]—in this case the letters sent out according to the decisions of the council—were sometimes in the same form as the *procès verbal*, over a secretary's signature and frequently prefaced by the phrase, 'collationé sur la minute originelle'.[3] Frequently the old custom was followed of indicating who had been present at the council. This was dying out, but only gradually. A volume entitled *Rolles d'aucunes expeditions commandees par le Roy*[4] for the year 1551 shows that they were prepared by a clerk and signed by the king. In some cases de Laubespine and du Thier have made additions in the margin in their own hands and either signed them or appended their sign-manual.[5] These additions were probably corrections made when the rolls were taken to the king for signature. Occasional signs-manual appear in the margin, sometimes of one of the secretaries, sometimes of a *secrétaire des finances*, and similarly the word *scelle*.

The secretaries also kept separate registers of the various documents (*expéditions*) which they had personally signed and despatched. These were copied by a clerk from the original rolls. One of Clausse's registers between the years December 1550 and July 1555, and one of Bochetel's containing entries between 1545 and 1559 are still extant.[6] The manner of keeping these registers was varied. Clausse's register is signed on the first and last pages. The items consist of gifts, grants and appointments.

---

[1] B.N., Mss. fr. 18153.
[2] *Expédition* was used as a generic term meaning, literally, that which was sent out. It included every type of document, state paper and official letter.
[3] De Bouard, i, 95.
[4] B.N., Mss. fr. 3154.
[5] *Ibid.*, de Laubespine, ff. 60v, 105v; du Thier, ff. 23, 27.
[6] B.N., Mss. fr. 5128, 5127.

At the beginning of each roll it is stated where and when the king had signed it and often who, among the more important councillors, had been present. For example: 'a Chambord le 29 decembre 1550. Monsieur le mareschal de Saint-Andre present.' Each item also bears the date on which it was despatched. In this register all the rolls from December 1550 to September 1552 were checked (*collationé*) and signed by the same *secrétaire du roi*, Dupoy, though they were copied in several different hands. A roll dated 19 September 1552 was signed by Clausse himself, the next two by a de Lomenie, and the next fifteen were not signed at all. One for 19 April 1553 was not only signed but also entered by Clausse personally, and the following roll was written by du Thier and signed by himself and the king. Many other rolls were not signed at all, but lines of Clausse's writing here and there show that he nevertheless kept an eye on his register.

Bochetel's register is similar. His name but not his signature appears on the title-page, together with the irrelevant and cryptic little message, 'a vous ma maitresse po^r avoyr'. There are no entries in Bochetel's own hand, neither has he signed any of the pages, but there are several marginal notes written and signed by Bourdin, Bochetel's chief clerk, who succeeded to his office, indicating that he had despatched things in Bochetel's absence. One such note says that the matter in question had been dealt with by the *receveur* of Sens—du Thier.

Besides these registers of outgoing business, the secretaries seem also to have kept other registers or letter-books. Those that have survived are only for the later period. There are nine for the secretary Pinart. Unfortunately we do not know what form these so-called registers were in before they were bound up into volumes. Their existence suggests that the secretaries kept copies of outgoing letters, and some of the volumes suggest that these copies were arranged according to their subject-matter. Others, however, do not point to such simple conclusions: they rather suggest that the registers were not kept regularly but were written up spasmodically and in arrears, and it is not unusual to find on the same sheet of paper documents bearing dates as much as two years apart. Several of the volumes belonging to Pinart are quite methodically kept. It is possible

that these were proper letter-books and the others merely collections of documents bound up at random.[1] One of the volumes of
Pinart's registers is a formulary.[2] Doubtless all the secretaries
possessed them, for they and their clerks were expected to have
certain technical knowledge and to be masters of protocol. It
begins with a section on forms of address, for they had to know
how to prepare correctly all letters, state papers, treaties, marriage contracts, commissions, etc. This could be complicated,
and varied according to the circumstances. If, for instance, the
king wrote in his own hand to the Queen of England, he must
begin, 'Madame ma Sœur'. But if the letter merely bore his
signature, then it must begin with the impressive flourish: 'A
tres haulte tres excellente et tres puissante princesse notre tres
chere et tres aimee bonne soeur et cousine la Reine d'Angleterre.' The same volume contains lists of benefices and their
values, of duchies, *bailliages*, *sénéchaussées*, the oath of a marshal of
France, forms of commissions for offices, gifts and *jussion*, en-
noblements and other factual and technical information.

The evidence of the registers appears inconclusive, and it is
difficult to escape the impression that the sixteenth-century
attitude to records and archives was casual. However, after
detailed study, Mademoiselle Michaud finds in these registers
evidence of a proper system of classification. The secretaries
inherited the papers of their predecessors, but we do not know
what happened to their records when the *départements* were
altered. Neither is it clear how treaties, contracts and other state
papers not falling within a particular *département* were kept. Du
Thier reveals in a letter to Brissac that, nearly four months after
it was signed, the treaty of Cateau-Cambrésis was in the possession of de Laubespine.[3] The perpetual peregrinations of the
court, followed by the vicissitudes of civil war, can have done
nothing to promote systematic habits. Most probably the archives
were placed in a chest and carted from château to château, exposed to the same risks as all other baggage. Only Villeroy ever

[1] B.N., Mss. fr. 3301–2, catalogued under Brulart's name, and 3305–11. Since
this was written Mademoiselle H. Michaud of the Bibliothèque nationale, Paris,
has made a detailed study of these registers for eventual publication in the *Bibliothèque de l'École des Chartes*.

[2] B.N., Mss. fr. 3311.

[3] B.N., Mss. fr. 20451, f. 219, 31 July 1559, du Thier to Brissac.

refers to what was probably some kind of filing system. In a series of extracts that he made for the year 1569, he says that he had placed a copy of a memoir 'dans la boitte'.[1] In another he refers to putting a copy of a memoir in the 'coffre'[2] and in a third he refers to the 'boitte' and the 'coffre' indifferently.[3] Documents put in the 'boitte' or 'coffre' sometimes bore a title and sometimes only the heading 'memoir of such and such a date'. The 'boitte' and the 'coffre' were certainly the same receptacle, but it is not clear what purpose it served.

We know very little about the staff the secretaries employed though it was certainly small, both for reasons of secrecy and because their constant wanderings precluded any fixed office organization. Du Thier wrote about his clerks to marshal Brissac on 11 August 1553 from Offemont, replying to the imputation that one of them had disclosed certain information.[4] After making inquiries, he said that he thought this unlikely. He watched them closely and, although they were often in very cramped and crowded lodgings, he made certain that the two who worked on affairs of state did so as privately as possible, and he had always found them loyal and faithful. He does not say who they were, but they were probably familiar figures or even future secretaries, for these had mostly served a long apprenticeship under another secretary before being appointed themselves. In this letter du Thier stated that he had two confidential clerks, but did not say how many others there were. In 1567 Bourdin, who became a secretary on the death of Bochetel in 1558, employed five clerks. Saint-Laurent, ambassador to the emperor, had written to ask Bourdin, his brother-in-law, to employ a young protégé of his. Bourdin replied on 6 April 1557 from Fontainebleau that he dared not employ a foreigner but only 'the most trustworthy young men from our own country whom I know', and that four out of the five were actually *secrétaires du roi* because, as he explained, 'our position is so ticklish and so many figures and important documents pass through our hands about which our clerks know almost as much as we do'. With a

[1] B.N., Mss. fr. 17528, f. 92, 10 May 1569.
[2] *Ibid.*, f. 104v, June 1569.
[3] *Ibid.*, f. 106, 27 June 1569.
[4] B.N., Mss. fr. 20524, f. 49, 11 August 1553, du Thier to Brissac.

foreigner, he said, he would be perpetually anxious about 'that which I fear as much as death'—he refers, presumably, to a leakage of information for which he would be held responsible.[1]

The secretaries and their staff were in charge of the preparation of official correspondence. The kings of France sometimes wrote letters in their own hands to certain people or in certain circumstances, and occasionally to create an impression. But the great bulk of their correspondence was necessarily written for them. Exactly how this was done varied at different times and cannot always be ascertained. Sometimes a letter was dictated, sometimes drafted upon a general instruction, sometimes drafted on the secretary's own initiative and, under Henry III, often directly prepared for signature. The king's letters were usually written by a clerk in a secretary hand (*écriture appliquée*) which was always small, neat and legible. Sometimes they were written by the secretary himself, in a secretary hand, and occasionally by a secretary in his own, normal writing. This was probably when they were harassed, overworked, seriously pressed for time, working in abnormal circumstances, or perched somewhere uncomfortably, which sometimes happened.

Regardless of who had written a letter, the secretary took it to the king for signature. He then added the date and the place and put his counter-signature and sign-manual at the end of a continuation line at or near the foot of the page. The continuation line served to ensure that nothing was illegally added to the text of the letter after it had been signed. Some of the secretaries' signatures varied with their different handwritings, while others always signed in the same way. Almost without exception the secretaries signed their family names, even when they were always known by another. Thus the two cousins Florimond Robertet, always known as Fresne and Alluye respectively, both signed themselves Robertet, and Villeroy invariably signed de Neufville.[2] Postscripts were often added by the secretary when a letter was signed by the king, to repeat or to emphasize a point, or to include a more recent item of news. These messages were usually from the king, but sometimes the secretaries made small

[1] B.N., Mss. Cinq Cents Colbert, 396, f. 267, 6 April 1557, Bourdin to Saint-Laurent.

[2] B.N., Mss. fr. 3213, f. 21, provides an exception, this letter being signed Alluye.

additions of their own. No letter, however, which was written in the king's own hand was ever countersigned, added to or altered in any way, which is why they are so frequently undated. Letters which the secretaries sent out under their own signatures were sealed with their own personal seal, bearing their coat of arms.

Officers of state and leading councillors often employed the secretaries in the preparation of their official or semi-official correspondence. This is proved by the frequent appearance on the letters of Montmorency—and to a lesser extent Lorraine and Guise—either of a postscript, the date and place, or sometimes the whole termination of the letter in the handwriting of one of the secretaries. Sometimes, no doubt, the secretaries supervised the preparation of such correspondence and sometimes they merely received it to date, seal and despatch. At other times, and not infrequently, they wrote the letters themselves in their ordinary writing. But they did not sign them. Only letters (as distinct from other forms of state paper) prepared for the king, and later for Catherine de Medici, were ever countersigned by a secretary.

It is difficult to determine, for the reign of Henry II, to what extent the secretaries dealt with the incoming despatches. We know from a letter to Marillac in England[1] that cardinal de Tournon, as Francis I's chief minister, received the despatches addressed to the king, had them deciphered, if necessary, read them and showed them to the king. We know from the same letter that Marillac also wrote to Bochetel direct; this correspondence will have contained the same information, plus other more detailed, frivolous or personal things. In the same way the minister replied himself as well as sending the official letter from the king—a task which was later performed by the secretaries. This system was undoubtedly continued at the beginning of the new reign, for Montmorency was too assiduous a worker, and too jealous of his position, to leave such important work to anyone else. But sometimes it was departed from as a result of physical circumstances, and increasingly as Montmorency and Guise were absent at war.

Ronsard, in a sonnet in which he attributes to du Thier the maximum credit for everything possible, indicated that as a

[1] *C.S.P.D./F.*, 1542, p. 373, 24 August 1542, de Tournon to Marillac.

E

secretary he had to sit down and study to compose the replies—
'soit en style commun, soit en style élevé avec la pureté de la
langue française'—to despatches which others had received and
opened. Outgoing despatches were usually drafted upon general
instructions discussed in council, as we can see from a letter from
Clausse to Lorraine. He said that the despatch was as he,
Clausse, had been commanded to prepare it, and that it had
been thoroughly disputed before any decision was reached.[1] A
suggestion might also be seen in this that they were not always
written on command. Du Thier wrote to Saint-Laurent,
ambassador in Switzerland in 1558, saying that the king had
left him with the queen 'and members of his council to receive
all the packets sent by himself, his ambassadors and others in
order to attend promptly to all urgent matters during his visit to
Calais'.[2] Du Thier must therefore have been both opening and
replying to despatches and there is nothing in the tone of the
letter to suggest that this was new or extraordinary, even though
it may have been exceptional. There are other examples of the
secretaries opening despatches but it is not certain when this
practice ceased to be in exceptional circumstances only, nor to
what extent the constant wanderings of the court made the
exception almost the rule. When Clausse wrote to Guise on
5 April 1552 from Fontainebleau[3] sending him an extract from a
despatch from Rome which had arrived that morning after the
king's departure, he must have been acting upon his own
initiative in promptly informing the duke of the latest news.
From the reign of Francis II there are an increasing number of
examples of this, which might be a matter of chance, or might be
due to the changed situation at court. It is certain that the
secretaries exercised more initiative towards the end than at the
beginning of Henry's reign, because Montmorency was then a
prisoner of war, Guise was away campaigning and Lorraine was
overworked.

In theory the secretaries followed the king but, if the court
divided, their services were also distributed. It was normal for a

---

[1] B.N., Mss. fr. 15881, f. 236, 5 December 1555, Clausse to Lorraine.
[2] B.N., Mss. Cinq Cents Colbert, 393, f. 187, 22 January 1557/8, du Thier to
Saint-Laurent.
[3] B.N., Mss. fr. 20514, f. 98, 5 April 1552, Clausse to Guise.

secretary to accompany a military expedition in or close to France, whether or not the king took the field. It was usual for a secretary to be appointed to a delegation to negotiate a treaty and to a temporary regency council, when there was one. If the king departed for a short while with a small company he almost always took one or sometimes two secretaries with him, leaving the others to attend to business at court. Although most of the secretaries' instructions came from the king, or the king in council, they also received instructions from the officers of state in connection with their particular functions, from leading councillors such as Lorraine, who held no specific office outside the church, and from the *gouverneurs* of the provinces in the respective *départements*, who, in the reign of Henry II, were still leading members of the nobility and as such social superiors and important persons in their own right.

These several considerations are all that is known about the work of the secretaries and how it was organized. If it seems remarkably little, this is not so much because of a lack of documentation, still less because the secretaries were idle, but rather because their work was never highly organized and never defined or limited. Their movements and their work were not predictable; what they were doing at any given moment and where they were doing it, depended upon the circumstances, and often upon where the hazards of the chase had taken the king. It would certainly be interesting to know more about their clerical habits and their staff. Probably this never exceeded more than five or six clerks to each secretary, both for reasons of secrecy—a problem which weighed on their minds—and because they were attached to an itinerant court and had no permanent offices.

The principal point to consider about the secretaries is always that of their relations with the king. At the beginning of the reign of Henry II, the king was closely surrounded by ministers and favourites, and the secretaries entered his inner council in a subordinate position only. How long this lasted we do not know; probably only for a few years. The council served them as a ladder by which they ascended, and fifteen years later they no longer had need of it. After the death of Henry II, they became more and more closely attached to the crown, first to Catherine de Medici as regent, and then, as Charles IX grew up, to the king himself. There was no longer anyone between the secretaries and the king. They were, so to speak, above the council, whose importance continued to fluctuate, and they gradually came to replace the great ministers and officers of state whom at first they had served. By the reign of Henry III, they had ceased to receive instructions except from the king and Catherine, and were rather in a position to command than to be commanded. Not infrequently they were addressed as Monseigneur. However, there was nothing inevitable about this development. It was not brought about either intentionally or as a result of ambition on the part of the secretaries, but arose naturally out of the circumstances.

CHAPTER V

The Secretaries and the Court
of Henry II

HENRY II, when he came to the throne, commanded the four newly-appointed secretaries to follow the court. It was very different from the one which they had known under Francis I, for Henry, who was discreet and seemly, disapproved of frivolity and licentiousness.[1] He changed the servants, dismissed many of the ladies and curtailed the habitual singing and dancing. Outwardly correct and well-regulated, his court was the most elegant in Europe, the centre of refinement and good taste, of courtesy and knightly chivalry. But the elegance, ceremony and elaborate forms were little more than a veneer glossing over a restless turbulence which frequently burst out in fits of anger and acts of violence and cruelty. Life at court was both public and dangerous.[2] It was still a large court, almost constantly on the move, in which the rooms—even the king's—were always crowded, where the activity and confusion were very great, and where the struggle for success was long and arduous.[3] Wherever it went, moving laboriously from château to château, there the secretaries were normally to be found, and there they did the greater part of their work. In order to understand them, therefore, and the circumstances in which they lived, it is necessary to have some idea, not only of what the court was like, but also of those who controlled it.

At the beginning of the reign, Montmorency and Diane de Poitiers, or the duchesse de Valentinois as she became in 1548,

---

[1] Albèri, *Relazioni*, ser. i, vol. iv, 61.
[2] See Bourciez, livre iii, ch. iii.
[3] Desjardins, *Negs. Tosc.*, iii, 193, 3–4 June 1547.

were supreme at court, the former over the crown and the latter over the king.[1] The Venetian ambassador, Contarini, even went so far as to report that for some time the court was doubtful which of them Henry loved the more.[2] When Montmorency emerged from his long conference with the king at Saint-Germain on 1 April 1547, he was in the highest possible favour.[3] He had become the king's principal councillor and minister. In the magnificent new château of Francis I he occupied the former apartments of madame d'Estampes. With the king, he and Diane made those changes in the court of Francis I that the dauphin and his company had for some years impatiently desired, and we have already seen in what way these changes affected the secretaries.

Montmorency was not popular, except with the king. His arrogance was said to be insupportable. He listened to no one, claimed to know everything, and did not even deal with the king's business promptly.[4] He was as much disliked for his overbearing ways and his monopoly of power[5] as he had been under Francis I, and this unpopularity was freely spoken of at court, even in the ante-rooms. Perhaps it coloured some of the reports of him, for Corregrani, the Mantuan ambassador, wrote home to his master in a more kindly strain, saying that Montmorency was indeed supreme, but that France was well governed and supplied and that he was worthy of his position.[6] The Venetian, Contarini, gives us this description of him: 'He is physically strong, of good understanding and has great experience. He is ... a good diplomat, a courageous soldier, and a wise councillor, but proud and ambitious both for himself and for his family.'[7] However, he was said to be less ambitious than the Guises, and more concerned for the public interest.[8]

Besides the constable, other favourites of the new king were Jacques d'Albon, known as Saint-André, and the young comte

[1] Cimber et Danjou, *Histoire particulière*, 281.
[2] Albèri, *Relazioni*, ser. i, vol. iv, 78.
[3] B.N., Mss. it. 1716, f. 99, 3 April 1547.
[4] Romier, *Les Origines politiques*, i, 36, n. 1, 8 July 1547, Alvarotti to the duke of Ferrara, State Archives of Modena, Cancelleria Ducale, Estero, Francia.
[5] Albèri, *Relazioni*, ser. i, vol. iv, 76.
[6] Romier, *Les Origines politiques*, i, 36, n. 3.
[7] Albèri, *Relazioni*, ser. i, vol. iv, 74–5.
[8] Romier, *Les Origines politiques*, i, 36, n. 3.

d'Aumale, better known as François, duc de Guise, as he became in 1550. Saint-André was handsome, lively and agreeable,
an excellent soldier and a subtle and accomplished courtier.
Though ruthless and undependable, he possessed to a high
degree the art of winning people's confidence by force of personality. Henry's he won absolutely and for life. He had been in
Henry's household since 1530 and they had shared the same
upbringing. They and their other young companions passed
their time in riding, hunting, games and violent exercises. The
melancholy Henry, unlike his elder brother Francis, then the
dauphin, was not drawn to letters and learning; he was all bone
and muscle. He and Saint-André developed fine physiques but
not penetrating minds. They received good advice but they
were not compelled to follow it. Their youthful energies and
high spirits were neither disciplined nor directed, and they and
their company freely indulged in brutal forms of horse-play
and hooliganism, seeking danger for amusement and constantly
quarrelling and fighting. These activities were only slightly
tempered by dancing and religious studies.

When Henry became the dauphin in 1536, he and Saint-
André went to serve under Montmorency in the king's army in
Provence. Their reliance on Montmorency was increased by the
growing antagonism between Henry and the king. By tempera-
ment and training the constable was congenial to them. They,
and indeed the prince's whole entourage, had always held him
in profound respect and admiration. Thus, as a very young man,
Saint-André became one of Henry's closest friends and, in
friendship as in love, Henry was constant. For this Saint-André
suffered disgrace at the hands of Francis I but in time he was
as richly rewarded as he expected to be. From being a simple
gentleman of the dauphin's bedchamber, and of humble origin
too, he became, all at once, the king's favourite and the
first gentleman of the royal bedchamber, a position which
gave him access to the king at times when even Montmorency
himself was excluded. Besides this, he became a marshal
of France in May 1547, an office of which he was undeniably
worthy, for he was considered to be one of the finest soldiers of
his time. Rewarded for his constancy and foresight, Saint-André
plunged into the luxury, ostentation and pleasure afforded by his

new position, making enemies but always able to attract new friends.

In spite of Francis I's dying warning against them, the Guise brothers, Aumale and Charles, archbishop of Reims, better known as the cardinal of Lorraine, immediately came to court upon Henry's accession. They too occupied apartments in the château of Saint-Germain, and their uncle, the then cardinal of Lorraine, was also welcome. Aumale, a little younger than Saint-André, was the king's own age, and Henry cherished him like a brother. Handsome, gifted, excelling in the same physical exercises and sharing the same passion for war, he had been, and continued to be, the king's natural and constant companion. His brother Charles was also important from this time until his death in 1574, for the Guises clung closely together, pursuing a single family interest. The grave and sinister cardinal of Lorraine—as Charles was shortly to become—remains an elusive and enigmatic figure. Cultured and austere—he knew Latin, Greek, Spanish and Italian and had a deep love of art—he made an excellent impression as a young man; he was pleasing and ingratiating, and a skilled and tactful courtier. He possessed outstanding ability as a theologian, financier and diplomat. He spoke with great eloquence, and authority came naturally to him. The Florentine ambassador, Ricasoli, was among those who were captivated by his charm. He said that he was 'not only most noble but also possessed of the highest virtue together with extraordinary gentleness and humanity'.[1] He lived a regular, ascetic life but his great gifts of brain and intellect were not equalled by qualities of character. In time he was to show himself cowardly, avaricious and mean, and quite unscrupulous in the pursuit of his restless ambition. Lorraine was the politician, and Guise the hero, a man of action, an excellent soldier, clear-minded, resolute, and generous in victory. He succeeded in inspiring widespread admiration and devotion, whereas Lorraine, if respected, came to be both feared and hated. He was the evil genius of the house of Guise.

Notwithstanding the sudden and drastic changes in the court, the new reign began auspiciously and great hopes were placed in the king, who, in France, was traditionally idolized. He

[1] Desjardins, *Negs. Tosc.*, iii, 215.

possessed those virile and chivalrous qualities expected of a prince; his appearance was pleasing and majestic and all accounts agree as to the beauty of his person. He was tall and well proportioned, strong, energetic and virtually tireless; he went hunting two or three times a week and took part in all court games and jousts, acquitting himself as well as any of the young nobles. Henry was by nature kind, gentle, virtuous and an excellent father, and never seen to be in anger, except occasionally out hunting. He was so friendly and affable in his ways and so courteous to everyone that he inspired universal devotion.[1] He spoke well in French, Spanish and Italian, had an excellent memory and was thought to be capable.[2]

But if Henry created a better impression than the turbulence of his youth or the paucity of his education might have suggested, he nevertheless came to the throne without knowledge or experience of affairs of state. His hopeless estrangement from his father had resulted in his exclusion from the council. It was natural, in these circumstances, that he should have turned to Montmorency, whom he had known and trusted for years and whose experience of war and politics was unrivalled. For the rest of his life Henry retained for him a strong, strange and emotional regard. Twenty-six years his junior, Henry possibly looked to him for the affection and guidance his father had denied him. There may also have been the attraction of a strong, intransigent nature for one that was yielding and pliable. Henry had no fixed purpose, no will or stable policy of his own. Seeing only immediate issues and with no independent judgement, he was an opportunist who could be worked upon by stronger characters. Accounts vary as to Henry's application to work. He was meticulous, honourable and painstaking and, on the whole, he was serious-minded, spending several hours in council every morning. It is said that he worked increasingly, more from a sense of duty than from inclination, but he never had the strength or confidence to dominate his council, nor was he a match for his rival ministers who were only too anxious to do everything for him. With his restless, almost neurotic desire for excessive

---

[1] Cimber et Danjou, *Histoire particulière*, 279. On Henry II see also Gaston Dodu, *Les Valois*, pt. iii, ch. ii.
[2] Albèri, *Relazioni*, ser. i, vol. iv, 60–1, 64.

physical exercise, he was not averse from leaving things to others and affairs of state were seldom allowed to interfere with the pleasures of the chase. Montmorency encouraged the king to take a great deal of exercise which, he pointed out, would prevent him from becoming fat, a possibility that Henry envisaged with disgust.[1] He was accused of keeping things from the king and of trying to exclude him from the government as much as possible. To some extent he held him in subjection and used a certain authority over him which was more that of a severe father than of a sagacious minister.[2] All sources are unanimous in saying that the constable controlled and did everything, at the beginning of the reign, and that the king seemed unable to speak or act without him. But Montmorency was not the only influence on Henry, who was said to have made no judgements except through the eyes, ears and opinions of those who controlled him.[3] He delivered himself so completely into the hands of his favourites as to allow them to pursue conflicting policies. His confusing affection for such bitter rivals as Montmorency and the Guises rapidly became, seems only to have been a naïve and childlike loyalty to those he had known in his youth.

Diane de Poitiers, Montmorency and the Guises had all known Henry for a long time, were aware of these defects in his character, and meant to profit from them. For this purpose they all remained as close to him as possible—indeed they followed him so closely that it was difficult for anyone else to approach, for Henry was most attentive to those about him, but an absent minister was temporarily disregarded and quickly lost ground.[4] The Guise brothers tried never to be away from court at the same time—while Montmorency, on the other hand, often tried to organize their absence. The Guises identified themselves with Diane de Poitiers, and it was through her favour that the cardinal was able to secure most of the benefices of his dead uncle, the former cardinal of Lorraine, which made him the richest and most powerful churchman in France. More attractive and apparently more promising than the brusque and ageing Mont-

[1] Albèri, *Relazioni*, ser. i, vol. iv, 65.
[2] Desjardins, *Negs. Tosc.*, iii, 228, 23 February 1548.
[3] Théodore de Bèze, i, 85.
[4] Paillard, 'La Mort de François Ier', *Revue historique*, v, 111–12, Saint-Mauris, despatch of June 1547.

morency, who was isolated in his unpopularity, the Guises inspired a much greater following at court, a clientele which they were at pains to foster and preserve. On the other hand, Montmorency was supported by the majority of the nobility and the *parlement*, while Saint-André, if he inclined to the side of the duchess and the Guises, retained the king's favour and confidence while adroitly managing not to be seriously involved in either faction.

The hostility between the Guises and Montmorency was carried to astounding lengths, although in 1547 the cardinal of Guise was only twenty-three and still lacked experience. Even in public Montmorency called him a great calf ('grant veau'), and Aumale habitually referred to Montmorency as 'that footpad' ('quel ladrone').[1] He and his brother appeared to contemporaries to be gaining in favour all the time. Montmorency's position was constantly threatened, and it was not expected that he would be able to maintain it. He used every means at his disposal to do so: his wealth, favour, authority and family connections. The struggle occupied him all the time and he found himself constantly in opposition. So long as he remained at court his influence was more or less equal to that of the Guises but, between 1547 and 1550, he gradually lost his initial supremacy.

Apart from their tireless vigilance at court and in council, watching for Montmorency's slightest weakness and awaiting his briefest absence to fill his place at the king's side, the Guises were singularly fortunate. Charles became a cardinal and succeeded to a vast inheritance, and François made a brilliant marriage to Anne d'Este, daughter of the duke of Ferrara and Renée de France, grand-daughter of Louis XII. This match greatly strengthened the Italian orientation of the Guise ambitions, and opened up the way for secret intrigue. Their goal was the kingdom of Naples, and Montmorency was naturally violently opposed to their policy of war in Italy. In the same year, 1547, their niece, Mary Stuart, better known as Mary, Queen of Scots, was brought to France and betrothed to the dauphin. In 1550, François succeeded his father as head of the family, thereby acquiring both wealth and prestige, and this

[1] Paillard, 'La Mort de François Ier', *Revue historique*, v, 117; Desjardins, *Négs. Tosc.*, iii, 229, 23 February 1548.

same year the Lady Fleming scandal helped to undermine Montmorency's position at court. Lady Fleming—the governess of the young Queen of Scots—was the temporary object of the king's affections and the constable had been taking him to her room every night. This resulted in a breach between Montmorency and Diane de Poitiers, and the Guises also blamed him for an affair which, they angrily declared, reflected dishonour upon their niece. So Montmorency received all the opprobrium of the king's liaison. Henry, as usual, bowed to the storm and for a while even refused to speak to Montmorency, whose grip seemed to be loosening. His real strength, however, lay in the king's affection for, when he was away, Henry lamented his absence. Nevertheless, he was unable to prevent the king from adopting the Guise policy and they took advantage of his discomfiture to get their supporters appointed to key posts in Italy. Italy slipped from Montmorency's control and events there moved rapidly towards the war which the Guises desired.

It is only in the light of this war of influence and these deep-seated family hatreds, which swelled to monstrous proportions, that the reign of Henry II can be understood. The king's fluctuating policy reflected, at any given moment, the state of credit or discredit of his principal councillors.

As Montmorency, Lorraine and Guise stood, politically, between the secretaries and the king, it is worth considering how their bitter rivalry and violent quarrels affected the secretaries who were obliged to serve them all in their conduct of affairs of state. The extent and degree of this antipathy, so clear to the ambassadors, must have been apparent to the whole court. How far it affected subordinates we shall never know. In a sense the quarrels of the great did not concern the secretaries, but they must, all the same, have had to exercise great discretion not to incur the displeasure of either faction. The Guises certainly fostered and maintained a loyal clientele, but there is no evidence that they ever tried to corrupt any of the secretaries who, fortunately, were well placed to serve these jealous councillors impartially. Three of them were nominees of Montmorency and the fourth, Clausse, had worked with him in the past. They had all known him for many years and, if he had manners that were not endearing, at least they were used to him. They had also known Aumale for some years, as a brilliant young noble of the dauphin's household. Aumale, who did not neglect to cultivate those who could be useful or who might be dangerous, may have made it his business to maintain friendly relations with the secretaries, and they were certainly aware that he and his brother might supplant the constable at any moment. Besides, it was part of their duty to serve so important a person—a peer, a favourite and a leading councillor—with courtesy and prompt attention.

In writing of the swarm of agents who supported the ambitions of the house of Guise, Romier has claimed, in a highly misleading passage based on the termination of one of his letters, that du Thier was a follower of Aumale.[1] All four secretaries, however, were liable to end their letters to Aumale, and to others, with elaborate expressions, sometimes of gratitude, and usually of desire to render services and to remain in their good favour. Such terminations might be as empty of meaning as any other polite formality; it was customary to write something of the kind.[2] To their lasting credit, there is no evidence to suggest that any of the secretaries supported either Montmorency or the Guises more than became their office, or to the disservice of the other. Nor are there grounds for supposing that their relations with either of them were anything but satisfactory, perhaps because their position was still too subordinate to compel or to enable them to take sides in that bitter rivalry. We may be sure that they privately preferred the policy—if not the person—of Montmorency, who strove for peace, for the secretaries consistently deplored the ravages and miseries of war.

[1] Romier, *Les Origines politiques*, i, 87; Michaud and Poujoulat, vi, *Mémoires-journaux du duc de Guise*, 25, 18 December 1549.

[2] B.N., Mss. fr. 15881, f. 236, 5 December 1555, Clausse to Guise; Mss. fr. 20555, f. 126, 5 October [1548], de Laubespine to Aumale; Mss. fr. 20457, f. 155, 2 February [1548], de Laubespine to Aumale; Mss. fr. 20552, f. 62, 27 July [1551], de Laubespine to Guise.

PART TWO

The Secretaries under Henry II

CHAPTER VI

The Secretaries Follow the Court, 1547–52

T HE secretaries were thus placed at the heart of a highly
personal system of government, depending on the sole
authority of the king, whose immense prestige still held in
check the latent forces of disorder. Their real position, like that
of anyone who took part in affairs of state, depended upon their
personal relationships and upon the circumstances of the
moment. Had this been a reign of peace and prosperity, the
work of the secretaries might have been confined to routine
administration. But as it formed the epilogue to a series of
foreign wars—still the normal occupation of a turbulent nobility
—its main events were concerned with foreign affairs and its
main preoccupation with defence. This, in turn, determined the
general trend of the secretaries' work. It was also a pre-revolu-
tionary period in which the unrelenting struggle for power
between Montmorency, the Guises, and their rival factions, continually influenced royal policy and consequently the careers of
the secretaries. They can therefore only be studied in relation to
those who controlled the king.

Little record remains of the activities of the secretaries during
the first year of their new appointments. They were undoubtedly
busy with such domestic matters as the establishment of the
royal households and preparations for the elaborate and
sumptuous coronation. The disputes over Boulogne, which was
held by the English, the expeditions to Scotland, whose queen,
Mary of Lorraine, was a sister of the Guises, and the fortifications on the northern frontier, must have made much work in
Bochetel's *département*. It may also be assumed that, besides the
negotiations with the emperor to decide the issue of peace or
war, de Laubespine was involved in others with the Swiss for the

traditional supply of mercenary troops, and with the fortifications of the long eastern frontier. Du Thier was concerned with
an embassy of the cardinal of Guise to Rome, a mission to the
Turk, the fortifications of Piedmont, and an attempt to draw the
Venetians into a defensive alliance in Italy. Clausse's *département*, not being important in the field of foreign affairs, was
relatively quiet. The only sign we have of him occurs in a number of letters written on behalf of the king to Jean d'Humières,
governor of the rather delicate children, over whose well-being
Henry watched with solicitous care. It seems that Bochetel was
away, perhaps ill, at this time. There is no trace of him between
October 1547 and July 1548, and de Laubespine countersigned
all the correspondence concerning his important province of
Picardy.

In January 1548 de Laubespine, Clausse and du Thier accompanied the king and Montmorency on a two weeks' hunting
tour between Fontainebleau and the Loire, during which time
they were constantly on the move from place to place.[1] This
tour is the first occasion upon which we find the secretaries
corresponding with Aumale, who remained behind, as the constable had no doubt intended, for their quarrels about that
time were particularly violent.[2] Most of the surviving personal
letters of the secretaries for the first half of this reign are
addressed to Aumale, doubtless because he was the most important person who was often absent from court. The letters make
it clear that they kept in close and personal touch with him,
sending him the latest news of their own *départements* and anything else they knew of.[3] If the king were sending a despatch,
they would often make haste to write by the same messenger.
Thus, at Ferriers on 30 January 1548, du Thier suddenly discovered that the messenger, Sansac, was about to leave with a
despatch for Aumale, and was already in a hurry to mount his
horse and ride away, 'comme un homme qui s'en va marrier a
une bien belle damoiselle sur la fin du nopce'. So du Thier,
perched on the edge of the constable's bed, hurriedly scribbled a

---

[1] B.N., Mss. it. 1716, f. 389, 4 February 1547/8.
[2] Desjardins, *Negs. Tosc.*, iii, 225, 7 February 1548.
[3] B.N., Mss. fr. 20542, f. 123, 23 January [1548], du Thier to Aumale; *ibid.*, f. 133,
30 January [1548], Clausse to Aumale; Mss. Clairambault, 341, f. 162, 24 January
1548, Clausse to Aumale.

brief line to Aumale, while Clausse was sealing down the king's despatch. What he said throws a little light on their manner of handling the despatches.[1] The cardinal of Guise, who was in Rome, and Jean de Morvillier, ambassador to Venice, had sent despatches by the same messenger. Du Thier, whose *département* included Italy, read them to the king, whereupon Henry commanded Clausse to prepare a letter to Aumale explaining their contents, and this is what he was closing while du Thier sat writing on the edge of the bed. In his letter, du Thier informed Aumale that the constable would send on the originals of the two despatches from Italy by their next messenger. This shows that it was the constable, not the secretaries, who kept possession of the incoming despatches at that time, and that while each secretary read to the king those despatches which concerned his *département*, the same secretary was not necessarily responsible for the resulting correspondence, which might be confided to one of his colleagues. In theory the despatches were read to the king in the *conseil des affaires*, early in the morning, to which the secretaries were summoned separately. But it is clear from du Thier's letter either that the secretaries were sometimes present in the council together, or else that the despatches might be read to the king at some other time.

As the secretaries' chief duty was to the king, it was normal for them, or for one or more of them, to follow the king practically wherever he travelled and even when the bulk of the court remained behind. When, in the spring of 1548, Henry II travelled through Burgundy to Piedmont, to see what work had been done on his frontier defences and to demonstrate to the emperor that there was no question of France ceding Piedmont, as he wished, the entire court accompanied him as far as Lyons. At such times the secretaries' routine work continued normally, as it would have done in Paris or at Fontainebleau. During this journey the French expedition to Scotland and the precautions and preparations against the English in Picardy—where Montmorency's brother, the *gouverneur* de la Rochepot, was building fortifications—were the most important affairs of the moment. Thus the king continued to write to de la Rochepot from many places on the way (Vauluisant, Aix-en-Othe, Troyes, Doulevant,

[1] B.N., Mss. fr. 20542, f. 142, 30 January [1548], du Thier to Aumale.

Vassy and Eclaron), his letters still signed, in Bochetel's absence, by de Laubespine. Montmorency's correspondence also continued, his letters often entirely written, and almost always added to, by de Laubespine. Bochetel, who, as far as we know, had been absent for ten months, resumed this work from Dijon, in July.

The secretaries also continued their normal liaison work which was necessitated by the court's not always travelling all together or by the same route. When Aumale went on ahead to make preparations for the reception of the king at Lyons, the capital of his *gouvernement*, both Clausse and Bochetel, in accordance with their instructions, wrote to keep him informed and sometimes, on Montmorency's orders, made him a digest of the despatches.[1]

De Laubespine, du Thier and Clausse all accompanied the king when he left Lyons, during the first week in August, with a rather small suite on account of the serious problem of lodgings, and crossed over the mountains into Italy.[2] From there also they continued to attend to the work of their *départements*. It is not very clear whether Bochetel went too but, from the spasmodic entries in his register[3] during these weeks, it seems most likely that he remained with the queen, the council and the majority of the court, who all went to Mâcon to await the king's return.[4]

Another of the duties undertaken by the secretaries, and certainly one of the least congenial and most exhausting, was that of accompanying military expeditions which took place within or close to the frontiers of France, again as liaison officers and to attend to all the civil and administrative matters which had to be arranged for the commander-in-chief. In such circumstances their normal routine work was usually done by a colleague who remained at court. But when the king himself was in the field, the secretaries accompanying him might have to carry on their normal work, or part of it, in camp.

[1] B.N., Mss. fr. 20640, f. 59, 8 July [1548], Bochetel to Aumale; Mss. fr. 20457, f. 103, 19 July [1548], Clausse to Aumale; *ibid.*, f. 107, 20 July [1548], Bochetel to Aumale; B.M., Add. Mss. 38031, f. 1 *verso*, 17 July [1548], du Thier to Aumale.
[2] B.N., Mss. it. 1716, f. 520, 29 July 1548.
[3] B.N., Mss. fr. 5127.
[4] B.N., Mss. fr. 3120, f. 63, 27 July 1548, Henry to d'Humières.

It was de Laubespine who was chosen to accompany Mont-morency when he and Aumale were sent by the king, in September 1548, to put down a rebellion at Bordeaux. News of this rebellion had disturbed the king's programme in Italy and brought him hurrying back to France. But the preliminary arrangements for suppressing it were made from Piedmont, by the king, Montmorency and de Laubespine.[1] It was decided to conduct a pincer movement upon the rebels, Aumale approaching Bordeaux via Poitou and Montmorency via Languedoc.

While the other three secretaries remained with the court, which slowly travelled back to Saint-Germain, de Laubespine left La-Côte-Saint-André with Montmorency on 14 September 1548.[2] It was his task on the way to Bordeaux to keep in touch with Aumale and to co-ordinate their movements. On 20 September, according to his instructions, he wrote to Aumale from Nîmes. The letter is badly damaged, but in it de Laubespine informs the duke of the constable's military preparations and of the news they had received that Bordeaux was already growing calmer every day.[3] From Toulouse, where it was dry and dusty and the plague was raging, de Laubespine assured Aumale that the constable's army was taking shape, but he did not think it would have much to do, for every day people were coming from Bordeaux 'a genoux s'excuser et promettre plus que l'on ne veut croire'. After having heard from Aumale, who was suffering from the heavy rains in Poitou, de Laubespine continued his letter, saying that the rebels were very much frightened by the approach of their two armies.[4] The affairs of Bordeaux were improving all the time, and the following day he again wrote that numbers of representatives kept arriving from Bordeaux to make their excuses, all of them claiming to be innocent. He said that Montmorency was leaving Toulouse the next day and advised Aumale that if things continued to quieten

---

[1] B.N., Mss. fr. 3134, f. 14, 3 September 1548, Henry to de la Rochepot; Mss. fr. 3316, f. 51, 3 September 1548, Montmorency to de la Rochepot; ibid., f. 55, 8 September 1548, Montmorency to de la Rochepot; Mss. fr. 20510, f. 18, 6 September 1548, Henry to d'Estampes.

[2] B.N., Mss. fr. 3316, f. 59, 12 September [1548], Montmorency to de la Rochepot.

[3] B.N., Mss. fr. 20555, f. 61, 20 September 1548, de Laubespine to Aumale.

[4] Ibid., f. 125, 5 October [1548], de Laubespine to Aumale.

down, there would be no need for his German mercenaries or many of his *gendarmerie* to cross the Garonne, a difficult and time-consuming operation. 'Toutteffoys,' he added playfully, 'jen parle comme ung clerc darmes.'[1]

De Laubespine proved to be right; there was no fighting in the south-west and, by 20 October, Bordeaux had already submitted to the constable's vindictive anger. Montmorency and Aumale lingered for some weeks to impose harsh penalties on the citizens and to restore such good order that the emperor would not be able to count upon any internal dissensions to assist him. Then, at the end of November, they were all recalled to court where Aumale's marriage to Anne d'Este in December was the occasion of more than a week of merrymaking, entertainments, games, tournaments and banquets.

De Laubespine was ill in April of the following year, 1549, and, on his return to work, he wrote a letter to Ménage de Cogny, ambassador in the Empire, which reveals something of a secretary's relations at that time with a French ambassador abroad. It is clear that they were in constant personal touch. Cogny, like most ambassadors, was in difficulties through lack of money and had appealed for de Laubespine's influence on his behalf. De Laubespine replied that he needed no prompting, for none was more willing to help than he, and that he had explained the case to the admiral, de Tournon, and the chancellor, who would raise it with the king when a suitable opportunity occurred. There were also other unspecified points upon which the ambassador appealed to de Laubespine, who answered that even while he was ill he had done what he could to attend to them, as Cogny could see from the king's despatches.[2] The implication is that the secretaries were able to produce results by working through important members of the council, but that they did not, at this time, personally consult and make decisions with the king or in the council.

While Montmorency and Aumale were occupied in the south-west there had been some alarm at court because the Emperor was said to be raising troops and planning an attack on the borders of Champagne. Both Bochetel and du Thier, however,

---

[1] B.N., Mss. fr. 20511, f. 10, 6 October [1548], de Laubespine to Aumale.
[2] B.N., Mss. fr. 17889, f. 30, 24 April [1549], de Laubespine to Cogny.

hastened to reassure Aumale that they did not take the rumour seriously.[1] By the summer of 1549 the emperor appeared to be a little less menacing and 'ne parle que de sucre et myel en notre endroit', de Laubespine wrote to Aumale. 'Touttelffoys,' he added ironically, 'vous scavez la bonne volunte quil nous porte de long temps. Et tout le bon que je y veoys cest que lon ne se fye gueres.'[2]

De Laubespine, Clausse and du Thier all accompanied the king when he left the court at Compiègne and joined the constable in camp at Montreuil on 17 August. Montmorency had gone on ahead to open the long-prepared campaign against England, in the hope of recapturing Boulogne. Later they advanced as far as Hardinghem near Guines and Wimille. Immediately after their departure de Laubespine wrote to Aumale on 8 August from Mouchy, to say that the king had delayed his despatch until he could announce his taking the field, which had not been without a great many tears from the ladies who were very distressed by the king's departure. Nevertheless he had managed to get away early in the morning.[3] On this occasion the secretaries were not in camp for more than a month, if as long, for they all three returned with the king early in September. Henry was discouraged by the wet weather and deeply anxious about the dauphin, who was seriously ill. Still following the king, the secretaries were back in Compiègne before 19 September, where upon arrival they sent off several letters to Aumale, so that de Laubespine was sure that there could be nothing left to tell him.[4] Du Thier informed the duke of the king's final decision to pay the high price demanded by the pope and to enter into a league with him. He did not say what the price was, but intimated that he thought the money ill spent. Nevertheless, he approved of the current policy of caution and said that they were being careful to avoid provocation while the question of Boulogne remained unsettled and preparations were in hand for the next season's campaigns. In conclusion, du

[1] B.N., Mss. fr. 20555, f. 133, 9 October 1548, du Thier to Aumale; *ibid.*, f. 137, 9 October 1548, Bochetel to Aumale; *ibid.*, f. 135, 9 October 1548, Clausse to Aumale.

[2] B.N., Mss. fr. 20534, f. 74, 8 August [1549], de Laubespine to Aumale.

[3] *Id.*

[4] *Ibid.*, f. 89, 20 September [1549], de Laubespine to Aumale.

Thier promised, if necessary, to send daily news of his *départe-ment*.[1] In his next letter, of 25 September, de Laubespine, who seems to have been doing Bochetel's work again, said that the English had shown signs of wanting to treat.[2] Clausse added that the English had been 'bien frottez', and the king had decided to build twenty ships in order to be stronger at sea than his enemies.[3] Late in October or early in November, Aumale returned to court and this correspondence ceased.

De Laubespine was evidently well-informed for, early in February 1550, while the court was in or around Fontainebleau, peace negotiations were opened with England at Outreau, near Boulogne, in an atmosphere of mutual distrust. It had become usual to send a secretary with a peace delegation and it was Bochetel—for England was in his *département*—who went with Montmorency, de la Rochepot, Gaspard de Coligny and du Mortier. In Bochetel's absence de Laubespine took charge of the king's correspondence with the deputies, who were author-ized to offer, if necessary, up to 400,000 *écus* for Boulogne.[4]

There is no record of the part played by Bochetel in the negotiation of this treaty, but in view of the presence of the brothers Montmorency and their nephew Coligny, it is unlikely to have been great. In theory, the commission applied to all the deputies equally, and Bochetel was there in the same position as he had already obtained in 1535 which technically, at least, was not inferior. He almost certainly drafted the French version of the treaty and, with the other deputies, he signed it on 24 March.[5] As de Laubespine informed Aumale—or Guise as he became upon the death of his father that very day, 12 April—Bochetel, with Coligny and du Mortier, had been chosen to go to England to receive the ratification of the treaty.[6] They left about 18 or 19 April while the king was at Boulogne.

The embassy was well received in England where it was met by a deputation of three boats at the mouth of the Thames, wel-comed at Greenwich by a gathering of sixty lords and gentle-

[1] B.N., Mss. fr. 20534, f. 91, 20 September 1549, du Thier to Aumale.
[2] *Ibid.*, f. 95, 25 September [1549], de Laubespine to Aumale.
[3] *Ibid.*, f. 113, 9 October 1549, Clausse to Aumale.
[4] B.N., Mss. fr. 3134, f. 8, 14 February 1549/50.
[5] The Latin text is in Rymer, *Foedera*, xv, 211.
[6] B.N., Mss. fr. 20511, f. 56, 12 April [1550], de Laubespine to Guise.

men, and escorted to lodgings. The next day they saw the king, and the day after received his oath amid an impressive assembly of the council and the court, and afterwards they dined at the king's table. They hunted with the king and supped in his private apartments. They also hunted with the marquess of Northampton and dined at Hampton Court.

In the summer of 1550, there was a ceremonial exchange of extraordinary ambassadors between England and France, and this time Jacques Bourdin, Bochetel's chief clerk, son-in-law and designated successor, went to England with de Morvillier. This further *entente* resulted in the treaty of Angers, signed on 19 July 1551 and negotiated, on the French side, somewhat on the run, the unfortunate, fatigued ambassadors and secretaries never being certain where the day's hunting might take the king.

When the deputies went to England in March 1550, the king wasted little time in going to see his newly recovered fortress of Boulogne. De Laubespine for once remained with the court at Saint-Germain to attend to business there, but Clausse and du Thier followed the king. While waiting for the army to arrive, du Thier found time enough to write to Guise on behalf of the constable, telling him that the king found the defences built by the English to be admirable and curious.[1]

During the following year, 1551, the secretaries remained at court, which stayed in or near the Loire valley and along the borders of Brittany. It was a period of intensive preparations for war—though it was uncertain who the enemy was to be—and of no less intensive quarrels at court.[2] The fighting which had broken out in Italy in May 1551[3] was reflected in a violent battle of influence which raged at court between the Guises, who wanted to intervene in Italy, and the constable who wanted at all costs to keep the peace. When Guise was absent, de Laubespine and du Thier, whose *départements* were involved, kept him informed of the complicated details of events in Italy and the Empire.

On 20 July 1551 du Thier wrote to Guise that his despatch about the affairs of Parma had been shown to the king in the *conseil des affaires* by the cardinal of Lorraine. 'Et me semble

[1] B.N., Mss. Moreau, 774, f. 169, 16 May 1550, du Thier to Guise.

[2] *C.S.P.F.*, 1547–53, pp. 75–6, 23 February 1550/1, Mason to the council; *ibid.*, p. 150, 20 July 1551, Northampton and others to the council; Desjardins, *Negs. Tosc.*, iii, 287, 31 August 1551.   [3] Romier, *Les Origines politiques*, i, livre ii, ch. ii.

monseigneur', du Thier went on, 'encores quil n'appartienne a personne si bas que moy de vous dyre ce mot, quil se peult touteffois excuser sur lentiere affection devotion et servitu que je vous porte. Que en telles rencontres selon les occasions . . . qui se presentent vous ne devez obliez a dire et faire entendre votre oppinion. Car combien que vous soyez absent de cest compaignye ou lon en peult disputter avec le Maistre et ses aultres ministres vous estes en lieu ou . . . vous pouvez plus aisement et facillement sans aucune passion ne confusyon faire en vous mesme ung petit recueil des raisons . . . que lon doibt avoir sur tels affaires. Et la dessus prandre et fournir une resolution qui ne scaurait estre trouve que tres bonne venant de vous.'[1] This letter could be taken to imply that du Thier had embraced the Guise faction at court and that he was himself in favour of war in Italy. On the other hand, it was his duty to keep in close touch with the duke over the affairs of Italy which were in his *département* and such a letter could have been written with the honest intention of furthering what was, undoubtedly, the king's policy of the moment. Events were moving fast in Italy and, at court, the battle was both lost and won. If, on 27 July, de Laubespine had nothing special to report,[2] on 1 August he wrote at midnight from the immense château of Chambord to say, 'when you come to court you will find the situation different from that obtaining at the time of your departure. And the king stays for nothing but your presence to come to a swift resolution which it would appear is very needful.'[3] Nothing could have been more diplomatic, and this letter, a little masterpiece of scrupulous impartiality, contrasts oddly with du Thier's of 20 July. But, if Italy had been in de Laubespine's *département*, might he not also have adopted du Thier's attitude?

The king, Lorraine, and Montmorency—who had been over-ruled—all wrote to Guise on 1 August to summon him back to court. Probably nothing much would happen that year, wrote Lorraine to his brother triumphantly, 'mais il est malaisé que du commencement de l'autre on ne joue le gros jeu'.[4]

[1] B.N., Mss. fr. 20552, f. 17, 20 July 1551, du Thier to Guise.
[2] *Ibid.*, f. 62, 27 July 1551, de Laubespine to Guise.
[3] *Ibid.*, f. 80, 1 August 1551, de Laubespine to Guise.
[4] Michaud et Poujoulat, vi, *Mémoires-journaux du duc de Guise*, 67, 1 August 1551, Lorraine to Guise.

CHAPTER VII

From Metz to Cateau-Cambrésis, 1552-9

BESIDES accompanying the king or his commanders in the field, the secretaries also played an important, if unspectacular, part in the work of preparing a campaign. Lorraine was correct in his hopeful forecast that war with the emperor could no longer be delayed and, in January 1552, there began a long series of letters from the king and Montmorency to the duc de Nevers, *gouverneur* of Champagne and a distinguished soldier, all written, signed or added to by de Laubespine, about the preparations for the forthcoming campaign and, in particular, the provision of adequate supplies of food and fodder, upon which so much depended.[1]

Not only the secretaries but the entire court went with the king in March to Reims, where he proposed to hold a council of war before taking the field in person, to attack the three bishoprics of Metz, Toul and Verdun which, in 1551, he had been invited to do by the German protestant princes. Catherine was appointed regent in the king's absence and du Thier and probably Bochetel, of whom there is no record for the whole year, remained with Catherine and the council at Châlons.

De Laubespine was with the king from beginning to end of the exhausting campaign, for three months from April to July, and Clausse, who was also there, seems to have been attached to Guise, for the whole army seldom moved together.[2] It is un-

---

[1] B.N., Mss. fr. 3130, and Clairambault, 345, *passim.*

[2] Montmorency occupied Metz on 5 April and the king arrived on 17 April. He moved east across the Vosges and reached Wissembourg on 12 May. There, fear of invasion from the Netherlands caused the king to split his army into three divisions, under Guise, the constable, and himself and Antoine de Bourbon-Vendôme. They moved rapidly west to the siege of Damvillers, from where the king went to Sedan, and disbanded his forces at Etréaupont in July. See G. Zeller, *La Réunion de Metz à la France, 1552–1648*, i.

fortunate that none of the personal letters of de Laubespine and Clausse remain for this strenuous and critical period. Only three letters prepared by de Laubespine during the campaign—two from the king and one from Montmorency to the queen, plus one set of instructions—have survived. Doubtless they are representative of the kind of work he was doing all the time and for which he and Clausse had very little clerical help, for three of the four documents are entirely written in his own hand. The queen had confirmed the news that there was a danger of invasion from the Netherlands and Henry praised the measures she had promptly taken and informed her of his decision to march quickly west and surprise the enemy. He asked Catherine to arrange with all speed for supplies of corn, flour and wine for the army.[1] This letter is a draft which was written by de Laubespine for the king and is exceptional in that instead of beginning with the usual 'Madame', it opens with the more intimate 'Mamye', which the king no doubt dictated.

Du Thier's correspondence from Châlons has fared equally badly: only four of his letters have survived, one to the constable —sending despatches and urging him to send instructions because the council was doing little or nothing about obtaining the necessary supplies[2]—and three to Guise. Two of the letters to Guise are purely personal. He must have kept in close and constant touch with the duke for he wrote on 6 May that his wife had arrived at Châlons and was well, and that he would send him news of her and forward her letters to him daily.[3] Du Thier excused himself for confiding to Guise something of his wife's gnawing anxiety for his personal safety, perhaps because he seemed to share her opinion that the duke should be more prudent. He also revealed his kindness of heart in protesting against those who were thoughtless enough to send the court ill-considered reports from camp, without stopping to think what effect they would have on the ladies.[4]

The administrative position during the Metz campaign is not very clear for, although the queen was formally constituted

[1] B.N., Mss. fr. 6616, f. 166, 12 May 1552, Henry to Catherine.
[2] *Ibid.*, f. 174, 7 June 1552, du Thier to Montmorency.
[3] B.N., Mss. fr. 20514, f. 117, 6 May 1552, du Thier to Guise.
[4] B.M., Add. Mss. 38031, f. 180v, 6 June 1552, du Thier to Guise.

regent[1] and disposed of the services of at least one secretary, as well as the council, the ambassadors actually followed the king in the field for nearly five weeks as far as the camp called Vaudrevange,[2] which meant that any business involving them would have to be done by the king or Montmorency, and de Laubespine and Clausse who were with them. But, in the middle of May, when the campaign was speeded up, the ambassadors were 'uncourteously commanded and licensed amongst other impedimenta to depart the camp' and address themselves to the queen at Châlons. The Englishman, Pickering, complained bitterly of his sufferings during what he indignantly called 'this camping time'.[3]

Clausse and de Laubespine, if more accustomed and long-suffering than the overstrained and underpaid ambassadors, cannot have suffered much less in fatigue, discomfort and inconvenience, in the midst of which they had to deal not only with the administration of the army—which must have involved a vast correspondence, though unfortunately it has not survived —but also, to a certain extent, with their normal, routine work, as the evidence of Clausse's register makes clear.[4] It contains rolls of *expéditions* from Joinville, the camp at Nomeny, and from four other camps before the siege of Damvillers, as well as from the camp at Etréaupont, where the army was disbanded. It also contains ecclesiastical business which was entered separately, and on different dates from the rolls. On 23 May at the camp of Vaudrevange, the king was mindful of a promise made to the seigneur de Clany of the abbey of Clermont, and commanded the secretaries to despatch the appropriate letter. This was signed by both Clausse and de Laubespine. Similarly a gift was made of the abbey at Saint-Benoît to Jacques Debilly actually during the siege of Damvillers, and another gift to cardinal Châtillon during the siege of Ivoy.[5] There are many gaps in the register, but nevertheless it illustrates the essential simplicity

[1] B.N., Mss. fr. 3900, f. 71, 1552.
[2] This is the usual French spelling. The English ambassador, Pickering, called the same place Walderfang. In fact there were no fewer than eight alternative spellings.
[3] *C.S.P.F.*, 1547-53, pp. 214-15, 19 and 26 May 1552, Pickering to Cecil.
[4] B.N., Mss. fr. 5128.
[5] Ivoy now called Carignan.

and mobility of the government. In spite of the existence of a regency and the council, where the king and a secretary were—· even on a battlefield—there was the government.

Jacques Bourdin, Bochetel's son-in-law, who had been away from court, returned about August 1552, possibly to relieve de Laubespine, who had certainly earned a holiday after his arduous three months with the army. He was away until 15 September. Bourdin was still only a *secrétaire des finances*, until he succeeded Bochetel some time in 1558, but he had possessed his *survivance* since January 1550. He had countersigned royal letters at least from 1549 and he appears to have done an increasing amount of work at court from the early 1550s onwards. We do not know how Bochetel spent the last years of his life but there is no sign of his having been at court after 25 September 1551, when he countersigned a royal letter to Nevers.[1] It therefore seems reasonably safe to conclude that Bourdin assumed sole charge of his office of *secrétaire d'État* from about 1552 or 1553, when there is a noticeable increase in the amount of his correspondence which has survived. In two news-letters to Guise of the year 1553, Bourdin refers to the affairs 'de mon coste'[2] and to 'ce qui est de ma charge',[3] which suggests that he was not merely deputizing.

Jacques Bourdin, seigneur de Vilaine, Chars and Villette, was the son of Jacques Bourdin, *conseiller*, *notaire* and *secrétaire du roi* and *controlleur général des finances* in Touraine, and of Catherine Brinon.[4] Like the Bochetels, who were almost certainly old friends, the family came from Bourges, where Bourdin's grandfather had been *receveur des aides* in Berry and *trésorier des guerres*. After a thorough training under Bochetel, as his chief clerk, Bourdin married Marie Bochetel in 1549 or 1550,[5] and the *survivance* of Bochetel's office of *secrétaire d'État*, said to be worth 10,000 *livres*, formed part of the marriage contract. They had three sons, Jacques, Nicolas and Jean, of whom Nicolas became a *secrétaire du roi*. Bourdin, like de Laubespine, certainly came

---

[1] B.N., Mss. fr. 3130, f. 44, 25 September 1551, Henry to Nevers.
[2] B.N., Mss. fr. 20517, f. 9, 11 December [1553], Bourdin to Guise.
[3] B.N., Mss. Clairambault, 347, f. 145, 18 December 1553, Bourdin to Guise.
[4] B.N., Mss. Dossiers Bleus, 123, dossier Bourdin, 1–14, ff. 7v, 9v.
[5] B.N., Mss. Cabinet d'Hozier, f. 59, gives this date as 12 January 1550. Du-Toc, 103, gives 14 June 1549. He is the more likely to be correct.

under the benign influence of Jean de Morvillier, and Du-Toc says that he followed the ideas and the example of Bochetel.[1] His brother, Gilles, *procureur général du roi au parlement de Paris*, was a man of culture, and his own education was probably no less good.[2] He acquired a great reputation for probity and simplicity. He was so much an enemy of display and ostentation that it was whispered he had some leaning towards the new religion. He nevertheless died a catholic, desiring in his will that he should be buried with the poor in the cemetery of La Trinité. Michel de l'Hôpital testified to his virtues, and the letters appointing his nephew de Laubespine the younger to his office, described him as 'jadis serviteur tres-digne . . . et dont la memoire demeure celebre par l'integrité de sa vie'.[3]

Bourdin was almost immediately involved in a clash of influence between Guise and Montmorency when he returned to court in August 1552. This interfered with his work and must have inconvenienced and annoyed him. Although both Guise and Montmorency were concerned in what was, so far, the biggest campaign of the reign,[4] they did not for one moment forget their private war. On 6 August, Bourdin wrote to the duke that he had been happy, on his return to court, to receive the constable's orders to prepare his despatch and to send copies of the news of the movements of the emperor's army. He also informed Guise of the French reverses on the northern frontier; du Thier, he said, was sending news from the Levant, Italy and Germany.[5] The sending of such information was apparently not the simple matter of routine that one might have supposed. The next day Claude, duc d'Aumale, wrote to his brother, Guise: 'Having learned this morning that the king had received news from Hungary, Germany and Italy, I chose an appropriate time when the constable was not with him to implore him to communicate and make the said news known to you, to which he gladly agreed and immediately commanded his grace of Sens and Bourdin to write to you and to send you the extracts. But I have learnt that after they had prepared the letters the constable

---

[1] Du-Toc, 103.   [2] Moreri, ii, 164.   [3] Quoted by Du-Toc, 107.
[4] Though the king had broken camp in July 1552, the war continued. Guise went to fortify Metz, which the emperor planned to retake, and remained there until January 1553.
[5] B.N., Mss. fr. 20515, f. 91, 6 August [1552], Bourdin to Guise.

desired to see them and commanded them to write to you more soberly. . . . Nevertheless they are sending you the said extracts.'[1] It is clear from this incident that the secretaries did not then, as later, prepare despatches, which were to be official, without orders to that effect. To what extent they may have supplied information not officially imparted, it is no longer possible to judge; neither can we tell how much information was officially suppressed, though the Guise brothers evidently did not think the constable above trying to do this, even in time of war, if there were any personal advantage to be gained.

When he returned from holiday on 15 September 1552, de Laubespine prepared frequent letters for the king to Guise and to Nevers—and for the constable, until he departed with Clausse to take reinforcements to Metz. The personal and official relations between a secretary and the *gouverneurs* of the provinces of his *département* could be particularly valuable in time of war. This proved to be the case when, in the autumn of 1552, while the emperor's forces were fully occupied with the siege of Metz, the king resolved to retake Hesdin (Pas-de-Calais), a project of which Nevers strongly disapproved. De Laubespine was able to assure him that the king had taken his protests in good part, but that arrangements for the siege were so far advanced that he was determined to carry on with the enterprise. There were many people, he said, who shared Nevers' opinion, but, at least, he added consolingly, Nevers need not worry that he would be blamed for anything that might come of it. He advised him to take precautions in the towns which were most suspect and had greatest need of them.[2] Nevers kept in close touch with de Laubespine, who thanked him for 'tant d'honnestres lettres', and assured him the following January, when the campaigns were over, that his presence was greatly desired at court and that the king had only refrained from recalling him so that he might have time to arrange for the safety of the eastern frontier in his *gouvernement* of Champagne.[3] Such a correspondence reveals how even the nobility felt able to write to the secretaries more con-

---

[1] Michaud et Poujoulat, vi, *Mémoires-journaux du duc de Guise*, 71–2, 7 August 1552, Aumale to Guise.

[2] B.N., Mss. fr. 3130, f. 88, 21 November 1552, de Laubespine to Nevers.

[3] *Ibid.*, f. 52, 15 January [1553], de Laubespine to Nevers.

fidentially than to the king or to their equals, and that they obtained from them assurance, encouragement and advice. In this way the secretaries often did much to explain and interpret formal and official correspondence, and to ease the doubts and fears which it produced in the minds of people serving far from court. We can also find examples of the secretaries doing their best to maintain good relations between the king and his officers in the provinces by toning down instructions where they could. Thus, in a letter of a later date to Charles de Cossé, comte de Brissac, *gouverneur* of Piedmont, who sometimes disagreed with the court, du Thier explained that he had done his best to make things easier for him, 'having on occasion endeavoured to modify things which, in the presence of the late king [Henry] and sometimes by the king himself, I was very harshly ordered to perform'.[1]

The years 1553 and 1554, during which the war continued on a smaller scale, are remarkably poor in material relating to the secretaries. On 16 May 1553, de Laubespine left on what was ostensibly a goodwill mission to England, but we know nothing of the real reasons for his going.[2]

Campaigning that year did not begin until after the harvest when Montmorency, accompanied as usual by Clausse, marched into the Netherlands. He was followed by the king, who took de Laubespine with him. The constable became seriously ill in September and the campaign proved brief and inglorious. The secretaries kept him as well informed of all that was happening during his long absence as they usually did the duc de Guise, and du Thier even sent him the gladdening assurance, 'quil tarde bien au Roy quil ne vous veoyt en ceste compaignye', and that the king had been sadly counting the days of his minister's absence.[3]

It was de Laubespine again, and this time du Thier, who went to camp with the king and Montmorency in June 1554. It was an angry campaign which proved a complete fiasco, after much wanton destruction, burning and pillaging which was abhorrent to the secretaries. From Dinan, du Thier wrote to

[1] B.N., Mss. fr. 20541, f. 219, 31 July 1559, du Thier to Brissac.
[2] *C.S.P.F.*, 1547-53, p. 280, 16 May 1553, Wooton and others to the council.
[3] B.N., Mss. fr. 15881, f. 232, 2 December 1553, du Thier to Montmorency.

G

Brissac in Piedmont that it was impossible for the constable to
write himself, because he was so burdened with work, having
the whole direction of the army on his shoulders, that he was at
a loss to know which way to turn. 'Il est vray', he continued
wearily, 'que entre nous autres scribendiers qui sommes icy
avons aussi une bonne part de la peyne avec les—incommodities
de la suicte dune armee.'[1] Du Thier was no longer young. He
had been lucky to escape the heat and distances, the rain and
hunger of the Metz campaign for, when his turn came, he did
not appreciate his 'camping time'. For two seasons the secretaries
had a rest from campaigning, for 1555–6 were years rather of
diplomatic activity.

It was at this time, in the service of Lorraine, that the future
secretary Fresne first began to play a part in public affairs.
Florimond Robertet, seigneur de Fresne, was the son of Jean
Robertet, *secrétaire des finances* and *président au parlement de Paris*.
His grandfather François was a brother of the famous Florimond,
and secretary to the duc de Bourbon. Fresne, as he will be called
to distinguish him from his cousin Florimond Robertet, seigneur
d'Alluye, became a *secrétaire des finances* in 1554, and in 1558 he
succeeded his father-in-law Clausse as *secrétaire d'État*. The
Robertet family, which died out with these two cousins, was, at
that time, as distinguished for its services to the crown as the
Bochetels, de Laubespines and de Neufvilles. Fresne was in-
directly related to them all through his brother-in-law, Henri
Clausse, who married Denyse de Neufville, sister of the future
secretary, Villeroy. We know little about Fresne, who died after
only nine years of service as a secretary. Du-Toc recorded that
he displayed great understanding and address.[2] He was a strong
catholic and—most probably on personal grounds—he sympathized with the Guises.

In the same way as du Thier, in his youth, had been attached
to the service of the constable, and Clausse to that of the
dauphin, so Fresne at the beginning of his career was befriended
and protected by Lorraine. Thus it was that in October 1555,
when Lorraine left for Rome with the cardinal de Tournon to

---

[1] Blank in the original to indicate du Thier's unprintable sentiments. B.N., Mss.
fr. 20524, f. 93, 13 July 1554, du Thier to Brissac.
[2] Du-Toc, 112.

conclude an offensive-defensive league with the pope, Fresne
had gone with him as his secretary. Since 1552 Pope Julius III
had been striving to make peace. Shortly before he died, he
achieved a conference at Ardres, attended by Montmorency,
Lorraine and de Laubespine. Lorraine ensured that nothing was
concluded because the new pope, Paul IV, was pro-French and
extremely bellicose. Thus Lorraine's mission to Rome, which
initiated Fresne into the mysteries of diplomacy, was a triumph
for the Guise policy, for they wished to continue the war in Italy.
During the embassy to Rome Fresne prepared all Lorraine's
despatches to Montmorency and the king, and the drafts of these
letters—the originals were sent in code—provide a detailed
account of the negotiation.[1] Lorraine, who was sick and
frightened by the rough sea, abandoned de Tournon at Toulon,
leaving him to brave the elements and to call in at Corsica, and
took Fresne with him by the overland route.[2] From Rome
Fresne wrote to Montmorency both about the political situation
and also about a personal assignment that he had undertaken
for the constable for, as well as negotiating a treaty, they found
time to search for works of art. He was arranging to send Montmorency some marbles and a statue by Christmas, and promised
to do everything in his power to see that they arrived intact.[3]

Lorraine was informed by both Clausse and de Laubespine
that there were struggles at court—which was only to be expected—over the official attitude to his embassy, or at least that
his despatches gave rise to heated disputes. On 5 December
Clausse explained, perhaps a shade apologetically, that the
despatch he was sending was 'telle quelle ma este commandee'.
De Laubespine also confirmed that it had been 'tant disputee'.[4]

While Fresne was serving Lorraine in Rome, de Laubespine

[1] B.N., Mss. fr. 15881, ff. 202, 203, 207, 209, 215, 220, 222, 223, 227, 229, 230,
235, 239, 245, 253, 266. On this negotiation see M. François, *Le Cardinal François de
Tournon*, also *Le Rôle du Cardinal François de Tournon dans la politique française en Italie,
janvier-juillet 1556*; G. Duruy, *Le Cardinal Carlo Carafa, 1519-61*; Baguenault de
Puchesse, 'Les Négociations de Henri II avec le duc de Ferrare', *Revue des questions
historiques*, v (1868).

[2] B.N., Mss. fr. 15881, f. 202, 22 October 1555, Lorraine to Montmorency.

[3] B.N., Mss. fr. 20442, f. 271, 27 November 1555, Fresne to Montmorency.

[4] B.N., Mss. fr. 15881, f. 236, 5 December 1555, Clausse to Lorraine; Mss. fr.
20624, f. 40, 5 December 1555, de Laubespine to Lorraine.

was helping Montmorency in spasmodic negotiations—proposed by the emperor—which resulted, on 3 February 1556, in the truce of Vaucelles.[1] However, during 1556, amid much talk of peace, events moved steadily towards war. Bourdin clearly saw that it was going to be a serious one and confided to his brother-in-law, Saint-Laurent, his fear that little by little they would become involved in war on all sides.[2] But he wrote more energetically, after the enemy had made attacks on Metz, Marienbourg, Montreuil, Corbie and Péronne, that God and reason were on their side.[3] 'We have not yet moved on the home fronts,' he wrote to Saint-Laurent in April, 'and I think it will not be possible before the next harvest for the lack of food which is general. God give us a good peace for I cannot love or wish for war, for the infinite suffering that it causes, which I fear in the end will bring down upon us the wrath of God.'[4] Not only was there famine in the provinces already ravaged by war, but in all France, so that one district could not relieve another; prices were soaring and many people actually dying of hunger, a thing unheard of within living memory.[5] Bourdin's fear of provoking the anger of God was no idle image or manner of speaking, but a terrible reality in the sixteenth century. His point of view, which was both professional and humanitarian, was shared by the other secretaries, who did not belong to the class which still regarded war as a normal occupation and the obvious means of winning an honourable reputation. Besides, a good crusade or a campaign in Italy was not at all the same thing as the constant devastation of French provinces.

The secretaries took advantage of the relative calm before the storm to take some leave, aware of the hard time they would

1 Thus the unrestrained rivalry of the king's ministers, simultaneously pursuing contradictory policies, had brought France to the ludicrous paradox of being committed—by Lorraine—to the protection of the pope against the emperor in Italy, at the same time as having signed a five years' truce with the emperor at Vaucelles. The deep, irreconcilable enmity between the Guises and Montmorency had never been more publicly nor more discreditably demonstrated. The Guises set to work to redeem the diplomatic situation and Montmorency's truce was doomed.

2 B.N., Mss. Cinq Cents Colbert, 396, f. 259, 13 January 1557, Bourdin to Saint-Laurent.

3 B.N., Mss. Cinq Cents Colbert, 396, f. 223, 13 February 1557, Bourdin to Saint-Laurent.

4 *Ibid.*, f. 263, 15 April 1557, Bourdin to Saint-Laurent.

5 B.N., Mss. it. 1719, f. 8, 23 March 1557.

have later in the year. Bourdin warned Saint-Laurent (who, as ambassador in Switzerland, came under his *département*) that he was handing over his work to de Laubespine, 'pendant que je iray faire ung tour en ma pauvre maison'. He said that he had heard from his wife that Bochetel was better than usual and growing stronger, and de Laubespine, who was already on leave, also confirmed this news.[1] Doubtless they were at home at Bourges, and it sounds as though Bochetel were both old and unwell.

While de Laubespine was on holiday, Bourdin became seriously ill and du Thier had to do his work. There is no record of Clausse at this time, though he may have been at court. Montmorency, himself barely recovered from a severe illness, hastily recalled de Laubespine.[2] On receiving the message he travelled as fast as he could, in long stages, and reached the court at Villers-Cotterêts on 1 May, where he found Bourdin, 'God be praised over his fever', he informed Saint-Laurent, but so tired and ravaged by the sickness that his only wish was to quit that inferno (the court), which he did that same day, leaving work behind him for de Laubespine to disentangle. Bochetel, de Laubespine added in the same letter, was still in Berry, and in very good heart. At court everyone was talking of marriage, for it was the wedding day of the young François de Montmorency to the king's natural daughter Diane, duchesse de Castres. 'Apres ces nopces', de Laubespine concluded, 'on parlera de guerre car le feu commance fort a sallumer et en aura on plus de passetemps que lon ne vouldroit.'[3]

Only Bourdin, who had evidently recovered from his illness, went to camp with the constable and Saint-André when the campaign began on 22 July 1557. De Laubespine, Clausse and du Thier remained with the king. At court, tension was rising; there was a growing sense of impending disaster; something was about to happen. Suddenly the king was struck by the danger to Saint-Quentin, and despatched de Laubespine with a sharp message for the constable. He was to say that the king was angry

[1] B.N., Mss. Cinq Cents Colbert, 396, f. 267, 6 April 1557, Bourdin to Saint-Laurent.

[2] B.N., Mss. it. 1719, f. 11 *verso*, 2 April 1557.

[3] B.N., Mss. Cinq Cents Colbert, 303, f. 71, 4 May 1557, de Laubespine to Saint-Laurent.

that so important a place had not been better provided for, and Montmorency was to attend to the matter forthwith.[1]

The loss of the battle of Saint-Laurent outside Saint-Quentin —at which the constable and Saint-André were both captured— precipitated the greatest crisis of the reign.[2] In the words of an eyewitness, Fresne, who wrote an historical memoir at this time, the king found himself suddenly without an army, his frontier undefended, 'lacking generals, men and supplies. . . . This was the state of the king's affairs on Wednesday, 11 August 1557.'[3] In this grave and sudden crisis, the secretaries must have come into more frequent and closer contact with the king than ever before, for of his habitual councillors, only Lorraine was at court, and it was the king himself who tackled the emergency. The secretaries must have worked both day and night, for Fresne says that within two days they had sent off more than two hundred different despatches. He himself was sent to Paris with a message for Catherine, who was striving to raise money. On 12 August the king, de Laubespine and Clausse also left Compiègne for the relative safety of Paris.[4]

The overworked secretaries were soon joined in Paris by their colleague Bourdin, who had gone to camp with Montmorency and shared in the disaster. Not until 21 August—perhaps while the king was hunting—did he find time to write to his brother-in-law Saint-Laurent about this 'punishment of God' and to tell him how he had escaped from camp during the battle, not without the loss of part of his baggage, and other troubles which he did not reveal. 'We are trying to reassemble our forces with all speed and hope that money will not be lacking. Above all send us some of your men [Swiss troops] . . . in order, if it be God's will, to redeem our shame and loss and to prevent the enemy from doing any worse harm in this kingdom, where he

---

[1] B.N., Mss. it. 1719, ff. 75v, 251 (decoded), 2 August 1557.

[2] On the battle of Saint-Laurent and the loss of Saint-Quentin, see Michaud et Poujoulat, xl, *Mémoires de Gaspard de Coligny; Registres du bureau de la ville de Paris*, iv, 493 ff.; *La Guerre de 1557 en Picardie*, Société académique de Saint-Quentin.

[3] B.N., Mss. fr. 4742, *Histoire des choses advenues en France depuis la prinse de Monseigneur le Connetable . . . jusques a la prinse de Thionville . . .*, 1557–9. See also Henri Furgeot, 'L'Attitude de Henri II le lendemain de la journée de Saint-Quentin', *Revue des questions historiques*, xxxii (1882). This is largely based on Fresne, though without acknowledgement.

[4] B.N., Mss. it. 1719, f. 251 *verso* (decoded), 11 August 1557.

hopes to reduce us to extremity.'[1] Fresne tells us that Nevers and the prince de Condé went to Laon to reassemble an army. They were trying hard to starve the enemy out of France by a scorched-earth policy, and the systematic destruction of wind- and water-mills and anything the enemy might use.[2] 'We must often stop our eyes,' Fresne lamented in his history, 'and commit acts of cruelty which make our hearts bleed.' He, like Bourdin, was deeply distressed by the horrors of war.

Guise, who was in Italy, had been summoned home immediately after the loss of Saint-Quentin, and when the welcome news arrived that he had landed at Marseilles, de Laubespine hastened to write to him by the first despatch to congratulate him upon his return, 'it being the thing of which the king and the kingdom had and still have the most need'. He said that he had little news to report of his *département* because he had been ill for nearly two weeks, 'de ceste malhereuse cocqueluche'. Practically no one had escaped it and de Laubespine had had such severe pains in the head that he could not so much as look at paper.[3] This was not whooping-cough but something like cholera, and the epidemic was serious.[4] About the war, de Laubespine said that it was not believed that the enemy would do much more that year as it was late in the season and the rains were coming. But for these same reasons and also because the country had been so terribly devastated, de Laubespine feared for the new French army, which had been so rapidly assembled: 'I am very much afraid that our own will have a great deal to endure', but he added with his usual humility, 'I do not speak as one who knows much or indeed anything of such matters.'[5] Du Thier added his greetings to those of de Laubespine. He too did not have much news of his *département*, but he was worried about Guise's deputy, Brissac, who, with loud protestations, was demanding his arrears of pay which amounted to such a huge sum that it was quite impossible to satisfy him. Du Thier's letter

---

[1] B.N., Mss. Cinq Cents Colbert, 396, f. 235, 21 August 1557, Bourdin to Saint-Laurent.

[2] Michaud et Poujoulat, vi, *Mémoires-journaux du duc de Guise*, 381-2, 29 August 1557, Henry to d'Humières.

[3] B.N., Mss. fr. 20529, f. 13, 1 October 1557, de Laubespine to Guise.

[4] B.N., Mss. it. 1719, ff. 128v, 130v, 21 September 1557.

[5] B.N., Mss. fr. 20529, f. 13, 1 October 1557, de Laubespine to Guise.

also revealed that the king had appealed to the Turk for help by land and sea.[1]

It appears from one of de Laubespine's letters to Saint-Laurent that the enemy was already beginning to withdraw and the first murmurings of peace were heard. 'There is nothing new,' he wrote on 19 October, 'except that we are beginning to grease our boots to go to camp, unless there should be some composition. At any rate my lord of Guise is to leave the day after All Saints.'[2] Bourdin was again chosen to accompany him to Calais, his supposedly secret destination, though de Laubespine said that all the pages were talking about it openly.[3] Bourdin's departure put an end to de Laubespine's hopes of going on holiday. He grumbled to Saint-Laurent that he expected to have to endure a long spell at court without any further hope of getting away, as he had planned, after the feast of St. Martin. 'Ce sera quant il plaira a dieu', he added with typical resignation.[4]

Well briefed, and with news and letters for the duc de Guise, Fresne left the court on New Year's eve, which was also the eve of the siege of Calais. At Calais he joined Bourdin, who was fully occupied with the innumerable arrangements and despatches of a commander-in-chief, and obliged to suffer the full rigours of a mid-winter campaign in atrocious weather conditions. De Laubespine was certainly better off in Paris, although he was having to work abnormally hard for Lorraine, whose chief concern was 'de me tourmenter pour avancer nos deniers'.[5] They were also preparing for a meeting of the States General, which opened in Paris on 5 January.

Fresne, who was used by Guise as a messenger, arrived back from camp on 9 January—while the court was celebrating a wedding and the king was dancing—with the news of the capture of the castle of Calais, which the English had held for two centuries. Not content with announcing the happy news to the court, Fresne wrote an account of this siege in his history, in

---

[1] B.N., Mss. fr. 20982, f. 84, 2 October 1557, du Thier to Guise.

[2] B.N., Mss. fr. 20472, f. 17, 19 October 1557, de Laubespine to Saint-Laurent.

[3] B.N., Mss. Cinq Cents Colbert, 393, f. 165, 28 December 1557, de Laubespine to Saint-Laurent.

[4] Ibid., f. 139, 25 October 1557, de Laubespine to Saint-Laurent.

[5] B.N., Mss. fr. 23191, f. 1, 1 January 1557/8, Lorraine to Guise.

which he revealed his great admiration for Guise because he did everything he could to protect the inhabitants, and especially the women, from his troops. The king, said Fresne, was as relieved and delighted as one might imagine and at once determined to see Calais for himself.[1] Bourdin, who remained in camp, was therefore soon joined by de Laubespine who arrived with the king and Lorraine.

Meanwhile du Thier remained in Paris with the queen and the council to receive despatches from the king, his ambassadors and others, and to attend promptly to all urgent matters. During this time, he was doing the work of at least three *départements*, his own, de Laubespine's and Bourdin's. Du Thier clearly implies that he was left alone. There is no record of Clausse at this time, and although he seems to have been at court at least within a month of his death, some time in November 1558, the increasing activity of his son-in-law and successor, Fresne, may mean that he was doing less and less work towards the end of his life. Bochetel also died some time that year. He slips quietly out of the picture and we know nothing about his death. It is likely that he was in retirement in his native Berry. De Laubespine was gradually coming to the fore. For some time he had been at the centre of government, not going to camp unless with the king, and employed on all that was most important whether by Montmorency or Lorraine. He worked in close co-operation with his more junior brother-in-law, Bourdin, and so far as we know they were never absent from court together.

The campaign over, first de Laubespine and then Bourdin went home on holiday. This time it was du Thier who became seriously ill. De Laubespine returned before Easter 1558 to a situation precariously balanced between war and peace. Everything was being prepared for war, which the victorious Guise intended to continue, but there had also been vague, spasmodic rumours of peace since October 1557. The origins of the negotiations which culminated in the treaty of Cateau-Cambrésis have never been clarified. They were promoted by the dowager duchess of Lorraine, a cousin of Philip II and reputed to be a great enemy of France, and by Montmorency and Saint-André who were prisoners. The king also wished for peace, both

[1] Fresne's history. B.N., Mss. fr. 4742, f. 36v.

in order to obtain their release, and because he was anxious to turn his attention to the problem of heresy.[1] From the beginning de Laubespine was connected with the official negotiations. The first public move for peace was a conference at Péronne, to which Lorraine was accompanied by de Laubespine, Fresne, and a large and splendid following.[2] They left the court on 5 May 1558. The usually reliable de Thou has claimed that, on this occasion, Lorraine entered into a treacherous agreement with Spain. If this is true—and it is probable—it explains why the duchess of Lorraine should have laboured to achieve the meeting. Clearly it had to take place before Montmorency could be ransomed, or he would have been present at every interview. It is impossible to believe that Lorraine was seriously trying to make peace, but he may have thought that to undertake the negotiation himself was the safest way of ensuring its failure.

We know nothing of de Laubespine's work at the conference but we may be certain that it was concerned with the outward efforts to find some basis for negotiation. At least a week was wasted initially in a dispute about their place of meeting; in this connection Fresne made several journeys. He tells us that the same points were raised as had been discussed at a previous conference in 1556, but they were ill-received by the Spanish.[3] He evidently believed in the sincerity of Lorraine's negotiation, but de Laubespine, as usual, does not disclose his opinion.[4] We cannot tell how much he knew, or how much, in fact, there was to know.

Bourdin accompanied Guise on the campaign which followed the rupture of this conference, and it seems certain that Fresne went too, since he wrote an account of the siege of Thionville.[5] De Laubespine, du Thier and Clausse remained with the king. Peace negotiations continued, this time through the agency of Saint-André who had been released for two months, allowed to see Montmorency, and sent to obtain definite proposals from the king.

[1] Some of the early and secret stages of the negotiations are described by the Venetian ambassador: B.N., Mss. it. 1719, f. 201, 18 October 1557, f. 146, 15 November 1557, f. 274v (decoded), 3 December 1557.
[2] B.N., Mss. Cinq Cents Colbert, 393, f. 358, 18 April 1558, de Laubespine to Saint-Laurent; Mss. it. 1720, f. 29, 6 May 1558.
[3] Fresne, B.N., Mss. fr. 4742.   [4] Id.   [5] Id.

Some time in September the services of a secretary were requested by Montmorency who, while still a prisoner, was working for peace, and it was de Laubespine who was sent.[1] When commissioners were finally appointed, it was de Laubespine, his uncle de Morvillier, Montmorency, Saint-André and Lorraine who represented France. Work began on 13 October 1558. At the outset de Laubespine did not consider the negotiations very promising: 'Things . . . are still so troubled', he wrote to d'Humières at Péronne on 25 October, 'that one cannot be sure of anything, added to which the English are spoiling everything on account of Calais.'[2] On 2 November, de Laubespine and de Morvillier were left alone while Montmorency, Saint-André and Lorraine went to see the king at Beauvais. Henry was overjoyed to see Montmorency again. It was even believed by the Guises that they entered into some private agreement about the terms of the treaty. Working for such a discordant commission must have taxed de Laubespine's diplomatic skill to the utmost. There is an example of his tactfulness in a letter written to Guise when Lorraine—ahead of Montmorency and Saint-André—returned to the conference alone. 'The cardinal's return', he wrote, 'has consoled us all, and gives us hope that we will not labour in vain', though he must have been perfectly well aware that Montmorency was far more willing than Lorraine to make the concessions upon which the peace depended.[3]

The diplomatic situation was altered by the death of the Queen of England on 17 November, and the conference was adjourned until 8 February 1559. We learn from the Venetian ambassador that before the deputies actually dispersed, Fresne, whom he calls 'Roberteteo', went to consult Lorraine, Montmorency and Saint-André upon a proposed mission to England. This, it appears, was prompted by the Guises, to urge the claims to the English throne of their niece, Mary Stuart, newly married to the dauphin, or perhaps to threaten Elizabeth that France would only recognize her accession if she agreed to renounce Calais. But we hear no more of the matter and, luckily for

[1] B.N., Mss. it. 1720, f. 93, 23 September 1558.
[2] B.N., Mss. fr. 3128, f. 157, 25 October 1558, de Laubespine to d'Humières. The general history of the conference has been told in detail by A. de Ruble, *Le Traité de Cateau-Cambrésis*.
[3] B.N., Mss. fr. 23192, f. 34, 7 November 1558, de Laubespine to Guise.

Fresne, he was spared what would certainly have been a highly disagreeable embassy.[1]

De Laubespine, this time with his brother Limoges and de Morvillier, returned to the conference at Cateau-Cambrésis on 20 January 1559. Montmorency, Saint-André and Lorraine followed later, and peace was finally signed on 2 April. De Laubespine had been present, at Montmorency's request, from start to finish of the negotiations, and it is likely that his contribution was not negligible. Had he merely been doing clerical work, he would not have been accompanied by his brother Limoges, and his uncle de Morvillier. It is usual to point out that de Laubespine, whom the Venetian Michiel described as one of the four secretaries, and possibly the principal one, took the title of *secrétaire d'État* in signing the treaty.[2] If this title had often been used before, the fact of its appearing in a treaty of the first importance was nevertheless something like public recognition of the prestige that the secretaries' patient and efficient work had won for them.

During these months of negotiation the other secretaries were at court, busily helping the king and Guise to disband the large French army. In November and December 1558, du Thier was absent, either on holiday or, at such a time, more likely ill, and Bourdin and Fresne shared his work between them. Bourdin, the senior of the two, worked closely with the king at this time when, of the important councillors, all but Guise were away.[3] Du Thier was no sooner back than Bourdin fell seriously ill. During this illness, in February 1559, he sent Guise a long letter written by a clerk. After thanking the duke for kind inquiries about his health, he wrote of the desirability of detaching the negotiation with Spain from that with England, which was bedevilled by the problem of Calais. This letter strongly suggests that Bourdin was in a position to influence the duke, and through him, the king, or he would not have troubled to write while he was so ill.[4]

During the months which followed the signing of the treaty of Cateau-Cambrésis, the secretaries were at court employed on the

[1] B.N., Mss. it. 1720, f. 121, 28 November 1558.
[2] Flassan, i, 424 (ed. 1809).
[3] Petitot, xxx, *Mémoires de du Villars*, 263, 269.
[4] B.N., Mss. fr. 15872, f. 27, 16 February 1558/9, Bourdin to Guise.

ratification, and on drafting the marriage contracts of Elizabeth of France and the king's sister Marguerite, to Philip II and the duke of Savoy, respectively. As a change from affairs of state, the secretaries were also employed on the organization of elaborate and costly festivities. 'The king will receive the deputies of the catholic king in the upper hall of the Louvre,' begins a draft in Fresne's worst handwriting, 'the ball will take place in the lower hall. Three lodgings will be prepared, for the deputies, for his grace of Savoy... and other principal nobles ... namely at the Louvre, the palace and the Tournelles.' Such an influx of important people created a serious problem over lodgings, which were already insufficient for the court. There follows a detailed list, made by Fresne, of celebrations, banquets and balls with the king scheduled to move his lodging from one place to another. The *prévôt des marchands* was to be ordered to clean the streets and clear out the ditches of Paris for the occasion.[1]

The story is well known how these magnificent celebrations ended abruptly in the death of the king—long foreseen by the astrologers. Judged, as he was, by feudal, chivalrous and romantic standards, Henry was loved and admired. His death was a grievous shock, swiftly followed by sorrow and then by fear.[2] Michiel, the Venetian ambassador, tells us why. From the moment that Montmorency was ransomed and returned to court, he displaced Lorraine from the position of chief minister. He resumed control over affairs of state from the very evening of his arrival, shortly before Christmas 1558. The wheel had turned full circle, and the position was once again that of 1547. As a result, such violent quarrels broke out between Montmorency and the Guises, even within the château of Saint-Germain itself, that unless effective disciplinary action were taken, Michiel, for one, thought the situation critically dangerous.[3] Nothing had occurred to alter it during the six months since that unquiet Christmas, and there were no more foreign campaigns to divert and occupy the nobility. France was bankrupt, ravaged, exhausted and divided, suffering from famine and waves of epidemic sickness. The heir to the throne was a delicate boy

[1] B.N., Mss. fr. 15872, f. 86 [? June 1559].
[2] Desjardins, *Negs. Tosc.*, iii, 400, 9 July 1559.
[3] B.N., Mss. it. 1720, ff. 128v-9, 131, 23 December 1558.

of sixteen whose early death was generally expected. In dying, Henry diverted the course of French history and left his country a prey to terrible disasters which only his continued presence might have averted. His life was like the sluice gates damming up a flood. By his death the waters were released.

For the secretaries, this twelve-year reign had been a time of stabilization and experience. The simple establishment of 1547 had worked extremely well, and the individual secretaries had shown themselves to be valuable servants of the monarchy, loyal, efficient and adaptable. They were already the most stable factor in the administration and their presence and position was neither queried nor resented by any of their superiors. The year 1559 was one of crisis and a turning-point in their careers.

PART THREE

The Secretaries under Francis II and Charles IX

Claude de Laubespine the elder, 1542

CHAPTER VIII

The Changing Position of the Secretaries under Francis II, 1559–60

THE reign of Francis II was brief, sinister and full of foreboding. It witnessed the downfall of Montmorency and the beginning of the struggle for power between the houses of Guise and Bourbon which was to fill France with bloodshed and desolation. Deprived of the king's support and denied that of the princes of the blood—Antoine de Bourbon, King of Navarre, and his abler, more ambitious brother, Louis, prince de Condé—Montmorency was helpless. The Guises, on the other hand, were able to dominate the king, who was too young and too unwell to rule, through his queen Mary Stuart, who was their niece. But their supremacy was gravely threatened by the Bourbon princes who, dissatisfied with their treatment, had remained away from court during most of Henry's reign, and by Montmorency's nephews, the Châtillon brothers, Coligny, admiral of France, François d'Andelot and Odet, cardinal of Châtillon, all of whom showed marked signs of favouring the protestants.

In their struggle for supremacy, both factions had to reckon with the queen-mother, Catherine de Medici. As a woman who had only occasionally played any part in public affairs, the grief-stricken Catherine was at an initial disadvantage upon the death of Henry II. She had lived a quiet, domestic life, and no one yet suspected the latent ability and tremendous force of character which made her such a redoubtable defender of the throne for her sons, its rightful occupants. In 1559 Catherine justly feared both the Guises and the Bourbons. Together they forced her into a life-long struggle to keep the peace in France; for contrary to

H

what is often said, Catherine never wavered in her policy of keeping the peace and protecting the throne, though circumstances frequently obliged her to alter her tactics. It was not because she believed in the sincerity of the Guises, but because with their hold over the king they were simply too strong for her, that they assumed control over the kingdom immediately Henry died.

The first major sign of this struggle was the conspiracy of Amboise, in March 1560, reputedly organized by Condé with protestant support, and directed against the Guises though naturally they insisted that it was aimed at the king himself. The plot was betrayed, and many of those who were captured were hanged from the terrace and battlements of the château of Amboise. But the trouble and unrest which broke out about that time in almost all the provinces of France was never suppressed, and during the summer there was much fear and danger of a general rising. Contemporaries alleged that Condé's complicity in a vast conspiracy for rebellion was proven by intercepted letters. He was arrested in Orléans at the end of October and condemned to die on 10 December, the opening day of the States General. But his life was saved by the sudden death of the king, which put an end to the Guise supremacy.

It required no great prescience on the part of the secretaries to imagine, during the ten days in which Henry II lay dying, what changes would be made at court upon the accession of Francis II. But it was not so clear that his reign would see the beginning of a new stage in the development of their office, and in the personal careers of those secretaries concerned, more especially de Laubespine. For some years past de Laubespine had slowly but surely been emerging as the principal secretary. He had worked extensively both with Montmorency and, latterly, in his absence, with Lorraine as well. It was not by accident that he was sent to the peace conference when the captured Montmorency requested the services of a secretary, nor that his brother Limoges and his uncle de Morvillier joined him there. Nor was it without significance that de Laubespine was the first to sign a treaty as *secrétaire d'État*, a designation that was currently used from then onwards. Indeed, not only de Laubespine himself, but his whole family was coming to be of the utmost importance to France as secretaries, ambassadors and councillors. Besides his uncle de Morvillier (a future *garde des sceaux*), and his brother Limoges, there were his brothers-in-law Jacques Bourdin, La Forest Bochetel, and Saint-Laurent (now bishop of Rennes). There were also his brilliant son Claude and, most outstanding of them all, his son-in-law Villeroy, both of whom were future secretaries. Together with others in that moderate, hard-working milieu of *gens de robe longue* they formed a nucleus in the council. They unswervingly supported the crown which they served with selfless devotion at all times and in all places for negligible financial rewards. Indeed they were the only remaining bulwarks of good order and administration during the years of revolution which followed the death of Henry II.

De Laubespine's first delicate and disagreeable duty as secretary to Francis II was to go to the disconsolate constable, left to grieve and mount guard over the body of the much-lamented Henry, take from him the king's personal seal (*cachet*) and deliver it to Lorraine.[1] This, finally, was the end of Montmorency's career as a minister. The distressing incident was almost symbolic for in a sense de Laubespine himself was to be the old constable's real successor.

In the past Montmorency had been the effective head of the administration, but he was the last of the great officers of state to serve as a minister. Their role from then onwards was to become increasingly ceremonial and honorary. Lorraine, who held no lay office beyond that of councillor, was content to direct general policy and leave the details to others, so that much of the work of government devolved upon the secretaries. Here, writes Decrue, the constable's biographer, are the new leaders of the administration.[2] There was no longer any barrier between the secretaries and the crown and, theoretically at least, there was nothing to prevent them from rising to high place. It was natural that the secretaries should grow closer to the crown, upon which they depended, and that they should give loyal support when its dignity and authority were menaced by the nobility who enlisted the explosive forces of revolution and the assistance of foreign princes in the service of their own overweening ambitions.

[1] B.N., Mss. it. 1720, f. 202, 12 July 1559.   [2] Decrue, 255–6.

When, upon the death of Henry II, the secretaries presented themselves to the young king Francis, he referred them straight to the queen-mother, telling them to take all their business to her, as she was to be in charge of the kingdom. Thus they heard from the king himself that authority was to be vested in his mother. In practice, however, they were obliged to serve the king through his uncles, the Guises, as they had, at times, already done during his father's reign. What then was the secretaries' real position in the three-sided struggle between Catherine, Guise and Bourbon?

The elderly du Thier probably did not live long enough to adopt any definite attitude to the new division of power. The countries and provinces of his *département* were such that he had worked more closely than his colleagues with the agreeable duc de Guise, which must have given him a certain understanding of the Guise point of view and may have caused him to see the worst in Montmorency's character. We do not know whether this resulted in a friendship with the duke, extending to Lorraine, or in any deterioration in his relations with Montmorency, his first master and protector. But there is nothing which authorizes us to think so. Probably, like de Laubespine, whose esteem he retained to the end, du Thier behaved with tact and equanimity and remained on good terms with everyone.

Fresne, it will be remembered, had from the beginning of his career been attached to Lorraine, who had trained and promoted him. So had his cousin, the young Florimond Robertet, seigneur d'Alluye, who succeeded to du Thier's office of *secrétaire d'État* on the recommendation of Guise.[1] Both the cousins were strongly catholic and known to be sympathetic to the Guise faction. What does this imply? The political and the personal situation at court was neither simple, clear nor static, and it must not be concluded from this affiliation that the Robertets were not on good terms with their colleagues, whose sympathies differed from their own, or that they failed to render the loyal service required of their office. Besides, Fresne and Alluye also were, and remained, on easy and friendly terms with Navarre. Their attachment to the Guises was, in the first place, personal and even coincidental. Their religious convictions may

[1] B.N., Mss. fr. 20976, f. 129.

also have drawn them to the self-proclaimed champions of the catholic church. But there is no evidence—rather to the contrary—that either these convictions or their attachment to the Guises led them to share the catholic opinion—whether merely professed or sincerely held—that a civil war for the faith was a lesser evil than any form of toleration. For the Robertets at least, their connection with the Guises was something which had existed before the problems and conflicting loyalties of the 1560s had arisen. In 1559, this did not require the explanation, or even justification that it does to us, who cannot easily exclude from our judgements the knowledge of events which were still in the future. Unable to forget a not entirely proven, but nevertheless inescapable belief that Lorraine was sold to Spain and corroded by ambition, it is difficult not to be suspicious of the Robertets who were devoted to him. But, in their defence, it must be remembered that they may neither have known nor suspected what we know and suspect or, if they did, they may, in all sincerity, have placed a different interpretation upon it. However this may be, it seems unlikely that the circumstances of their early careers or their private affiliations greatly influenced their conduct as secretaries, for in practice it was perfectly clear what they had to do.

De Laubespine's sympathies were definitely not with the Guises. This may have been because, like many people, he disliked Lorraine's treacherous character, while admiring his abilities; it was perhaps that having been present at all the conferences which resulted in the treaty of Cateau-Cambrésis, he may have been deeply suspicious of the cardinal's relations with Philip of Spain; it may have been because the ambition and cupidity of the Guise family far exceeded the limits of what was reasonable and legitimate; most likely there were a number of reasons. If de Laubespine became the first of a series of secretaries to be Catherine's close confidants and advisers—and from this time on she always had at least one of them especially devoted to her service—it was because the association was so natural as to be inevitable; they shared the same political outlook, which was simply that the government must remain in the hands of the rightful king. It is unlikely that Catherine and de Laubespine had had much to do with each other before the death of Henry

II, or that their close association arose instantaneously. But it grew rapidly. Bourdin may safely be assumed to have shared de Laubespine's point of view because, in the affairs of their *départements*, they always worked in close co-operation. They were also bound together by family ties and by their experience and early training under Bochetel, whose principles and example they are both said to have followed.

From the beginning de Laubespine stood by Catherine, but with his habitual tact and diplomacy which rendered him *persona grata* to everyone. Their similarity of outlook may first be seen in their attitude to the rejected constable, who still found in de Laubespine a friend and sympathizer at court, though whether this was on Catherine's advice, as a matter of policy or simply of courtesy, we cannot tell. When, in obedience to his uncles, the young king received the constable coldly, not to say cruelly, Catherine tried to soften the blow and used all her influence to keep him at court. But her efforts were unavailing. He departed to Chantilly and Catherine became, to some extent, a victim of the Guises.

De Laubespine showed his friendship for the constable in the tone and content of his letters, in which he not only told Montmorency of things which he might not have learnt from other sources, but also confided some of his own feelings, as to a friend. Thanking the constable for a letter, he said that it was a great honour and pleasure that the constable was pleased to remember him, who all his life would offer him humble and devoted service and, referring to something that Montmorency owed him, de Laubespine said, 'I could not think of ever importuning you and trust in your good pleasure to conclude the matter.'[1] When Lorraine informed Montmorency of warnings of the protestant plot that he had received early in 1560, de Laubespine referred only to the 'petites follyes dont en sent le vent parmy ce Royaume', thereby avoiding any disagreement he may have felt with the Guise version of the impending conspiracy. Thus while he can have left Montmorency in no doubt as to his friendly attitude, de Laubespine's letter contained nothing to which Lorraine, had he seen it, could have objected.[2]

[1] B.N., Mss. fr. 3158, f. 51, 25 February 1559/60, de Laubespine to Montmorency.   [2] *Id.*

After the conspiracy of Amboise, de Laubespine sent the constable what is probably one of the first, and certainly one of the most graphic and authentic accounts of it ever written. As one might expect, his reactions were of the utmost horror. He hoped that the capture of the leaders would put an end to their designs 'which are so wicked and disastrous that the thought of them horrifies me. It is something unheard of in this kingdom.' The prisoners, he said, were men of all kinds, and it was his belief that they had all been misled by 'je ne scay quels predicans'. He says nothing of the terror which, according to the Venetian Michiel, prevailed in the closely guarded château of Amboise, perhaps because he was so much more frightened by the general state of France. 'God grant', he prayed, 'that this fire may not spread for it is highly dangerous and of great consequence in this kingdom, which begins to be strongly tainted by the [new] religion and more than one would have imagined.'[1] To de Laubespine, this uprising had been a shock and a revelation which disturbed him profoundly. Of the political aspects he said nothing, presumably out of discretion only, for he had himself decoded intercepted letters, allegedly from the authors of the plot. They wrote of their intentions to 'chastise those two villains'—namely Lorraine and Guise—which made it clear enough that if the rank and file were fighting for religion, their leaders' motives were rather different.[2] In a postscript, de Laubespine excused himself to Montmorency for a letter which, he confessed, was badly composed and badly written, 'mais elle est faite a la haste par un homme accable d'affaires y ayant tantost deux mois que je trayne seul cette charrue'. This was because du Thier, who had gone to help him, died within eight or ten days. De Laubespine said that he was greatly distressed, and the king had thereby lost an old and very devoted servant.[3] So de Laubespine confided his regrets and his exhaustion to the constable, who thereby learnt, if he had not already heard, of the death of his former secretary. According to one historian, du Thier died in his house at Blois and was buried on 22 March.[4]

[1] B.N., Mss. fr. 3158, f. 54, 19 March 1559/60, de Laubespine to Montmorency.
[2] B.N., Mss. it. 1721, f. 12v, 16 March 1560.
[3] B.N., Mss. fr. 3158, f. 54, 19 March 1559/60, de Laubespine to Montmorency.
[4] Roy, 91. He quotes from Jacques Taveau.

His death coincided with that of the chancellor, François Olivier, and Jules Gassot wrote of them both: '[ils] ont esté deux personnaiges bien entenduz et excellens en leurs charge et profession'. Alluye, he noted, was placed in du Thier's office.[1]

Florimond Robertet, seigneur d'Alluye, had become a *secrétaire des finances* in January 1556 upon the resignation of his father. The letters patent appointing him referred to the training (*nourriture*) that he had already received 'under certain of our special secretaries', and said he had acquitted himself very well both at court and in Italy where he had been employed in the king's service by some of his principal ministers.[2] In France he worked for du Thier, to whose office he succeeded on 14 March 1560.[3] In 1564 he further received that of *général président de la chambre des comptes de Blois*, formerly held by du Thier with a salary of 1,200 *livres* a year and other perquisites such as a fuel allowance.

Alluye must have been wealthy. After his death, however, his brother François dissipated the Robertet fortune, and the family, that had for so long served the king of France, was ruined by debts and bad management.[4]

Already possessing a house in the rue des Poullies in Paris (now the rue du Louvre), on the death of his father in 1567 Alluye inherited the family property in and near Blois. The hôtel Alluye (rue Saint-Honoré), a splendid town house in Blois, was built by the first Florimond Robertet in brick and stone. The Robertet arms can still be seen over the doorway and the initials F.R. on the gables. It originally consisted of four wings surrounding a rectangular courtyard with galleries on the ground floor. Only one of the galleries now remains, decorated with medallions of the Caesars. The interior has been considerably altered but there is still the *grande salle* containing a superbly delicate, carved Renaissance fireplace, a painted wooden ceiling and the original wooden shutters carved with the motif of the Robertet arms and the tame parrots of the first madame Robertet. The room is as fine as anything that sur-

---

[1] Gassot, 21.

[2] B.N., Mss. fr. 3942, f. 335 *verso*, January 1556.

[3] *Ibid.*, f. 339. Du-Toc is mistaken in giving the date of du Thier's succession to office as September 1559.

[4] Gassot, 84.

vives in the neighbouring château of Blois and testifies to the wealth and good taste of the secretaries, who rivalled even the king himself in the magnificence and luxury of their houses. Alluye also inherited the almost legendary château of Bury on a rising above the Loire, on the edge of the forest of Blois, where Henry II sometimes sent his children. It was begun by Robertet in 1515 and built in the finest contemporary style. There are two engravings of it in du Cerceau[1] showing it to have consisted of four wings—including a ground-floor gallery—round a central courtyard, incorporating at the corners the round towers of the medieval castle. There was also a second court and service wings. The whole structure was moated, each court having its own drawbridge. It was spacious and said to contain many precious objects in a magnificent gallery—souvenirs, no doubt, of journeys to Italy. In the centre of the courtyard stood a valuable bronze statue of David by Michelangelo, brought from Rome in 1508. It is clearly visible in du Cerceau's engravings. Later in the century the property was acquired by Villeroy but again disposed of by his son Charles, who removed the statue to his house at Villeroy, and put a fountain in its place. What became of the statue is a matter for conjecture, and the château, one of the finest of its style, fell into disrepair and was eventually used as a quarry.[2]

Besides these two fine properties, Alluye also acquired from du Thier's widow the reconstructed château of Beauregard and the Robertet arms can still be seen in various parts of it. It seems unlikely that Alluye was able to enjoy these properties to any great extent because his brief public career kept him almost constantly at court. But he had one other house which he particularly liked and probably used much more. It was called La Rocquette and stood at the Porte Saint-Antoine, on the eastern extremity of Paris.

Alluye made a brilliant marriage to Jeanne d'Hallewin de Piennes, reputedly one of the most lovely and most courted of Catherine's *filles d'honneur*, who was socially far superior to him.[3]

[1] Du Cerceau, ii, Bury.   [2] La Saussaye, 252.

[3] Léon Marlet in his frivolous article on Alluye, 'Florimond Robertet, son rôle à la cour et ses missions diplomatiques', *Revue des questions historiques*, xlvii, has made a glossy romance of this marriage. He quotes from a letter to the duc de Nemours of 22 April 1557 (Mss. fr. 3199, f. 13) in which he claims that Alluye betrays his love

She had once been engaged to François de Montmorency but the engagement was forcibly broken off by the constable, who intended that his son should marry the king's daughter, Diane. We do not know the date of Alluye's wedding—a marriage by which he had no children—but it was not before the summer of 1564 when, from Roussillon, during the journey round France, he wrote amusingly to the duc de Nemours of his impatience to be married: '. . . si une foys je vous monstre le chemyn a tous vous aultres amoureux . . . a la fin vous serez marries come on dict que je le doys estre. Je ne sais quant ce sera mays ce ne sauroyt estre trop tost a mon gre. Aussi ay je rayson de le desyrer ainsi car il y a de quoi.'[1]

During an important embassy to Piedmont in 1562, Alluye showed himself to be proud and sensitive to any offence, but warm and simple over family matters and the personal difficulties of others. Accustomed to the gay and active French court he felt bored and exiled elsewhere, and in Piedmont he longed for letters. He replied to them with serious decorum to the queen, and friendly intimacy or even cheerful frivolity to his cousin Fresne. Thus, when he was unable to get on with his work, he informed his cousin that he had nothing to write about, 'sinest du marriage de deux dames veufves qui toutes deux espousent deux bons partenaires'.[2] If Brantôme is to be believed, Alluye was not very popular at court, and when he returned from his mission to Piedmont with a fine gold chain worth 2,000 écus, a present from the duke of Savoy, he was taunted about his Italian gold. It was, of course, the custom for ambassadors to receive presents, but Brantôme implies that Alluye received rather more than was usual. In an interesting little sidelight on Alluye's character, Brantôme says that he lost his chain to René de Villequier at cards, for they were both great gamblers.[3] To judge from his letters, Alluye appears both gay and compassionate. Jules Gassot, a better witness than the entertaining Bran-

for mademoiselle de Piennes. Not only does it not refer to her, but it was written by his cousin Fresne; so was another letter to Nemours (Mss. fr. 3200, f. 139, 5 July [1557]), which he also attributes to Alluye. In fact we know nothing about the circumstances of Alluye's courtship and marriage.

[1] B.N., Mss. fr. 3211, f. 8, 10 August 1564, Alluye to Nemours.
[2] B.N. Mss. fr. 15877, f. 88, 18 September 1562, Alluye to Fresne.
[3] Brantôme, v, 81.

tôme, and who worked for Alluye and knew him well, said that he was a 'gentil et vertueux seigneur et vrayment noble'.[1]

Not much evidence has survived of the secretaries' work during this short reign of Francis II. For Fresne there is little but drafts of letters from Lorraine to Limoges, ambassador in Spain —Spain being in Fresne's *département*—and for his young cousin Alluye there is nothing of any interest. Bourdin has not fared much better. De Laubespine went away towards the end of August 1559, not having had a break for a long time owing to his incessant labours at the peace conference of Cateau-Cambrésis. He appears to have been absent for about three months while Bourdin did his work. Bourdin, in turn, must have been away during the troubled months at the beginning of 1560, since de Laubespine was alone at Amboise, and complained of being overworked. During the first week in May, de Laubespine again went home to Bourges, whence he wrote to his brother-in-law, the bishop of Rennes, that he found all his friends in good health. He was busy with family affairs and referred to certain 'partaiges' which could have been legacies left by Bochetel.[2] Whatever they were, they caused trouble which distressed both de Laubespine and Bourdin, and gave rise to litigation which they mentioned, on and off, for several years. In another letter from Bourges, de Laubespine told Rennes— newly appointed ambassador to the Empire—that he would be at home until 20 or 25 July. This meant an absence of nearly three months, but still he thought the time too short, both because he found the court was no place 'pour avoir l'esprit en repos', and because it was not long enough in which to settle his private affairs. They would have to remain in their present confusion until better times, and he could see no certainty of that for a long time to come.[3] It seems that even on holiday de Laubespine did not enjoy the blessing of a quiet mind, for he was deeply perturbed by the situation in France. He knew that it could not be quickly rectified by assemblies and edicts. 'People talk a little', he wrote to Rennes, 'of these new disagreements.

---

[1] Gassot, 84.
[2] B.N., Mss. Cinq Cents Colbert, 394, f. 1, 8 May 1560, de Laubespine to Rennes.
[3] B.N., Mss. Cinq Cents Colbert, 394, f. 4, 22 June 1560, de Laubespine to Rennes.

But it is a general disturbance throughout the kingdom which threatens some much greater trouble than we can yet envisage.' These growing troubles in the country were focused at the court, where de Laubespine was forced to tread so carefully, and this was another reason for his wishing to remain at home, if only it were possible to excuse himself from returning 'y estans les troubles tels quils sont'—a cautious, cryptic little phrase, burdened with significance.[1]

All four secretaries were present at the assembly of notables held at Fontainebleau in August 1560, to discuss the problems of religion and the stupendous national debt. Their role was undoubtedly a subordinate one and probably confined to taking notes and possibly orders. But when Coligny openly presented two petitions on behalf of the protestants, one to the king and one to Catherine, the king ordered de Laubespine to read them aloud.[2]

In November the secretaries went with the court to Orléans to prepare for the forthcoming assembly of the States General. The Guises had surrounded the city with troops and virtually held it in the grip of martial law. When Condé was suddenly arrested there, de Laubespine wrote to inform the bishop of Rennes at his post in the Empire. He said that many people were astounded, but he did not know what result it would have. He seems to have approved of the arrest, for he added, 'cependant toutes choses se pourront plus doulcement accorder pour le repos que nous desirons en ce Royaume'.[3] Bourdin, who had been ill with dysentery, referred without comment to Condé's arrest, but remarked that things were notably quieter since the king had arrived with an army. He prayed that God would give them the peace that they needed, and a holy union in religion—a prayer that was not to be answered.[4]

For the secretaries, as for everyone else, the reign of Francis II was like a moment of hesitation. It was at once an interlude and,

[1] B.N., Mss. Cinq Cents Colbert, 394, f. 4, 22 June 1560, de Laubespine to Rennes.

[2] Delaborde, i, 463. The text of the petitions is printed in the *Mémoires de Condé*, ii, 645–8.

[3] B.N., Mss. Cinq Cents Colbert, 394, f. 23, 3 November 1560, de Laubespine to Rennes, quoted by de Ruble, *Antoine de Bourbon*, ii, 410.

[4] B.N., Mss. Cinq Cents Colbert, 396, f. 207, 1 November 1560, Bourdin to Rennes.

all too clearly, a prelude to troubles which were growing more serious every day. While there was nothing the secretaries could do, de Laubespine and Bourdin, if not also the Robertet cousins, clearly saw the extent of the danger to France. In 1560 this understanding was rare, because there were so few people who stood detached, and afraid for France, anxious above all to protect the throne and to ensure peace and good order. Almost everyone was committed in advance, whether through fealty and patronage, religion, ambition, greed, passion or, more likely, a confusion of motives and an inability to resist the force of circumstances.

CHAPTER IX

The Secretaries and
Catherine de Medici, 1560–3

WHEN Catherine realized that Francis was dying she seized the opportunity of dislodging the Guises and of assuming control of the government herself, with Navarre, the first prince of the blood.[1] In effect he became lieutenant-general of the kingdom—though he did not receive this title until March 1561—and keeper of the royal seal, surrendering to Catherine his claim to the regency. This arrangement was sanctioned by the States General in January 1561. Montmorency was recalled to court and at first the Guises acquiesced in what appeared to be inevitable. When the king died, the court remained unusually calm.[2]

Catherine wrote to tell the king's sister Elizabeth, Queen of Spain: 'Dieu . . . m'a haulté vostre frère . . . et m'a laysée aveque troys enfans petys, et en heun reaume tout dyvysé, n'y ayent heun seul à qui je me puise du tout fyer, qui n'aye quelque pasion partycoulyère.'[3] This was her dreadful predicament, the crux of the situation and the explanation of her conduct. It was also the secretaries' great opportunity for it was natural, in the circumstances, that Catherine should turn to them and, in struggling to free and preserve the crown, she released them from the control of any intermediary. De Laubespine recorded

---

[1] *Mémoires de Condé*, ii, 211.

[2] B.N., Mss. n.a.f. 3102, f. 17, 7 December 1560, Charles to Limoges; La Ferrière, *Lettres*, i, Introduction, lxxxviii.

[3] *Ibid.*, i, 158, December 1560, Catherine to the Queen of Spain. 'God . . . has deprived me of your brother . . . and left me with three small children, and in a kingdom utterly divided, in which there is not a soul in whom I can trust at all, who has not got some private purpose of his own.'

in his register that, upon Charles' accession, he and his three colleagues were summoned and commanded by the child king to follow the queen, and no one else. They were to receive their orders from her, and to despatch no letters or state papers unless at her command.[1]

From then onwards any ambassador desiring an audience applied to the appropriate secretary and saw the queen directly, without previously explaining his business to any minister. The Florentine Ricasoli recorded that all the secretaries had recourse to Catherine and all the despatches were referred to her and passed through her hands.[2] Instead of showing everything to Lorraine, she referred, if necessary, to the council, of which the secretaries were members. This new arrangement proved very satisfactory. The Venetian ambassador said that it was well organized. Each secretary attended to his own *département* and everything was done quickly without the slightest confusion.[3] This was the more remarkable since, previously, the ambassadors had constantly complained of the confusion at court and in the negotiations. For the first time, their business was in professional, disinterested hands. It was further decided, at the same time, that Catherine should open the despatches. The secretaries were to present them to her sealed, and she would look at them on her own (*à part*).[4] This should not be taken too literally, for the purpose of the regulation was certainly to give Catherine the opportunity of concealing things from Navarre. It is impossible to believe that de Laubespine or, in certain circumstances, his colleagues, never opened the despatches.

Nothing is more difficult to gauge than degrees of influence, but it appears that from this time onwards no one was more in Catherine's confidence than de Laubespine, and no one more constantly at her side. The surviving evidence indicates that she entrusted to him all that was most confidential or actually secret, regardless of whether or not it fell within his *département*.

[1] 'Ledit seigneur commanda que doresnavant ils se tinssent pres de ladite dame et la suivissent et non autre pour recevoir d'elle ses bons commandements et ne faire aucunes expeditions des affaires de cedit Royaume que celles que leurs seraient par elle ordonne.' B.N., Mss. Dupuy, 128, f. 9v, 7 December 1560.

[2] Desjardins, *Negs. Tosc.*, iii, 430, 10 December 1560.

[3] B.N., Mss. it. 1721, f. 208, 8 December 1560.

[4] De Ruble, *Antoine de Bourbon*, iii, 13.

There can be no doubt that from 1561 until his death in 1567, de Laubespine's personal influence with the queen was paramount, and that he enjoyed her absolute confidence. He sympathized with her problems, which were insoluble; he shared her fatigues, which were great; he expressed the same fears and, if he were less optimistic, he also entertained the same hopes. We know that he was popular, successful and respected, and that he bore a great burden of work with admirable devotion and integrity. We know too that he was most discreet and diplomatic, never giving himself away, and never writing anything that could be charged against him, and his patience must almost have equalled that of Catherine herself. He was not swayed by faction and—though we know nothing of his own possible heart-searchings—he appears to have seen things simply and clearly. With acute penetration, he grasped at a very early stage the essential tragedy of the following forty years, namely that it was already too late to do anything effective about religion and that a conflict, which would bring about the ruin of France, was as inevitable as it was useless.[1] It is clear that he understood the complex and unedifying nature of the struggle, and knew that it could only work itself out painfully and in time.

De Laubespine probably approached the zenith of his career towards the end of 1563. The English ranked him at that time among the principal persons about the queen, on whom he was in constant attendance.[2] He was a power in the land, and Sir Nicholas Throckmorton declared that de Laubespine 'principally governs the Queen Mother'[3] and Sir Thomas Smith that he 'has most credit with the Queen'.[4] Nothing, they believed, was treated without his knowledge.

De Laubespine's close association with Catherine is most clearly illustrated by their letters to his brother Limoges, ambassador in Spain. Spain was in Fresne's *département* and it was Fresne who prepared and countersigned the official despatches from the court. These dealt with certain aspects of policy and

[1] B.M., Add. Mss. 35125, f. 6, 30 September 1561, de Laubespine to the Queen of Scots.
[2] *C.S.P.F.*, 1563, p. 4, 2 January, Smith to Cecil.
[3] *Ibid.*, p. 542, 5 October, Throckmorton to the queen.
[4] *Ibid.*, p. 626, 19 December, Smith to the queen.

the usual diplomatic exchanges, and were semi-public documents. But, besides Fresne's routine correspondence, Catherine
also carried on a secret correspondence with Limoges. It was
written by de Laubespine who personally received the replies
wherever he happened to be. They were brought to him by
special messenger. Sometimes de Laubespine drafted these
secret letters himself and sometimes Catherine dictated them.
At other times, probably when she was very busy, she simply
asked him to write at length to his brother and explain everything himself. These letters were concerned with aspects of
policy which Catherine wished to keep secret because they explained with great frankness her real position in France.
Probably we now have only a fraction of this secret correspondence but what remains is sufficient to illustrate de Laubespine's
special position, as well as the extent to which he identified himself with Catherine's point of view and her struggle against the
Guises.

In the official despatch from Charles IX, which Fresne prepared upon the king's accession, Limoges was informed of the
ostensible situation at court—of the death of Francis II and the
assumption of the government by Catherine.[1] But, in their very
different, secret letter written twelve days later, Catherine and
de Laubespine informed Limoges of the *real* situation at court,
and of the reason why Catherine had linked Navarre with the
throne, when he was *persona non grata* to Philip II. She took care
to make it plain that he was 'soubz moy et mon auctorité'. The
reason given was that she was doing everything she could to
'contenir ung chacun avecques contentement'. She and de
Laubespine went on to express her secret fears: 'il est malaisé
que ceste farce se joue à tant de personnages sans ce qu'il y en
ayt quelqu'un qui ne face mauvaise myne, et que la diversité des
esprits meuz de beaucoup de passions dont ce monde est si
plain, est grandement a craindre, mesmement que ung si sou-
dain et inopiné changement ne se peult, comme je doubs
craindre, gouster si tost par tout le monde, principalement par
ceulz qui ont dernièrement tenu les premiers lieulx.'[2] This was a
graphic, if complex picture of the explosive situation at court.

[1] B.N., Mss. n.a.f. 3102, f. 17, 7 December 1560, Charles to Limoges.
[2] La Ferrière, *Lettres*, i, 570, 19 December 1560, Catherine to Limoges.

I

The heads of the rival factions were there, and so many people were involved in what Catherine, with bitter humour, called 'this farce', that sooner or later someone was likely to give trouble. She feared the ambitions that seethed around her, and she feared that the Guises and their supporters would not quietly stomach their recent overthrow.

One of the topics Catherine reserved for her secret correspondence was the proposed marriage of Mary, Queen of Scots with Don Carlos, prince of Spain. This was sponsored by Mary's uncles, the Guises. De Laubespine had already approached his brother on the matter and Catherine ordered Limoges to confine any mention of the subject to his letters to de Laubespine.[1] She was anxious to prevent the match because, at the time, she hoped to strengthen her relations with Spain by marrying her daughter Marguerite to the prince. Catherine, de Laubespine and Limoges were all well aware that the secret relations between the Guises and Spain were a constant threat to her security, which was another reason for wishing to thwart this plan devised by Lorraine. Catherine warned Limoges to watch for signs of Guise activity in Spain, and to keep herself and de Laubespine fully informed, 'afin que nous ne chemynions point en ténèbres en cest endroict'.[2] Later in March 1561, there is another letter in this series written by de Laubespine for Catherine, explaining French affairs to Limoges. It is an untidy draft in his own hand and unmistakably in his own style.[3] He said that trouble had arisen at court because, as men's minds are easily disturbed for very little reason, so Navarre had decided that Guise was enjoying too much favour and authority, and was therefore stubbornly determined that Guise must leave the court.[4] Catherine temporarily placated Navarre by allowing his brother, Condé, to return to court. On the accession of Charles IX Condé had been released from prison and had withdrawn to La Ferté in his *gouvernement* of Picardy. This quarrel between

---

[1] B.N., Mss. fr. 6617, f. 131, draft by de Laubespine; Mss. fr. 6605, f. 18, original; La Ferrière, *Lettres*, i, 572, 16 January 1561, Catherine to Limoges.

[2] La Ferrière, *Lettres*, i, 585, 3 March 1561, Catherine to Limoges.

[3] B.N., Mss. fr. 6614, f. 230 [March 1561], draft by de Laubespine. This interesting document, which has no opening, termination, date or place, has unfortunately been overlooked by the editor of Catherine's letters.

[4] La Ferrière, *Lettres*, i, 586, 3 March 1561, Catherine to Limoges.

Navarre and Guise caused great alarm because it could so easily have resulted in civil war. Catherine was anxious that Limoges should be accurately informed about it so that, in Madrid, he could carefully minimize the gravity of the crisis.[1] In his letter de Laubespine pointed out that Catherine's urgent wish was for a reconciliation, in the first place between Navarre and Guise, and secondly between Condé and Guise. The former had been outwardly achieved, but Condé rejected any reconciliation with the duke, 'dequoy je ne suys pas en peu de peine', de Laubespine wrote for Catherine, because they were afraid that it would result in even worse trouble.[2] This they were struggling to prevent. But in the official despatch, which was prepared by Fresne, Catherine contented herself with saying, 'le Prince . . . s'est rendu ung peu plus difficille touteffoys jespere qu'il se layrra [se laissera] conduyre a la raison'.[3]

In another official despatch of 27 March about the dispute between Navarre and Guise, only the outward events are mentioned—the fact of a conspiracy to oust Catherine from power, Navarre's demand that Guise should leave court, and the settlement reached by which he became lieutenant-general of the kingdom and commander of the army. In return he renounced his claim to the regency, thus leaving Catherine absolute and supreme in the state. With this arrangement, the letter said, Catherine was well content.[4] It therefore fell to de Laubespine to explain to his brother the complexity of the situation left by this crisis, and how nervous Catherine was of the religious concessions she had felt obliged to make to conciliate Navarre and his followers, while awaiting a council to settle the whole religious question. Limoges was asked to explain to the Spanish queen how hard-pressed Catherine was, in order that she might 'preparer le Roy son mary a ma juste justificacion pour les choses qui peuvent survenir'—this because 'il n'est pas expedient de tenter tous remeddes et fault dissimuler beaucoup de choses pour ny pouvoir donner ordre . . . *et toute*

---

[1] La Ferrière, *Lettres*, i, 586, 3 March 1561, Catherine to Limoges.

[2] B.N., Mss. fr. 6614, f. 230 [March 1561].

[3] B.N., Mss. fr. 15874, f. 153, March 1560/1, draft by Fresne, Catherine to Limoges; La Ferrière, *Lettres*, i, 171.

[4] B.N., Mss. fr. 6617, f. 139, 27 March 1560/1, Fresne to Limoges; La Ferrière, *Lettres*, i, 176, 27 March 1561, Catherine to Limoges.

la matiere de cette depesche est affin que je soys excusee envers luy et tout le monde de ce qui succedera de ceste affaire de la religion'. Thus Catherine hoped to make it clear in Spain that if she did not appear over-zealous in the cause of catholicism, it was because there was no practicable way of enforcing religious unity. She declared that she was the first to regret this predicament, but to eradicate protestantism, as Philip II wanted, it would be necessary to reduce half the kingdom to ashes. Besides, de Laubespine added, for his brother's eyes alone, even if they were prepared to ruin the kingdom in an attempt to exterminate the protestants, who was there who could be trusted to do this, and how could it be done? 'Car en cela et beaucoup d'autres choses', de Laubespine concluded on behalf of Catherine, 'a vous dire verite *ne scay je vraiment a qui me fyer.*' These were admissions that Catherine could never have made openly.[1]

In April there was still 'no small amount to do', wrote de Laubespine in another draft, owing to the divergent passions and partialities of those at court. Only by the grace of God and the most skilful direction could they hope to prevent there being evil results.[2] In this letter, de Laubespine mentioned Catherine's fear that Navarre and his followers might go on trying to increase his authority at her expense. She was anxious that, on the pretext of trying to recover the part of his little kingdom which was held by Spain, he might 'souffler quelque feu qui allumeroyt une guerre', and at the same time favour the protestants. This was a further, secret topic which could not be discussed in the official despatches. Catherine proposed in absolute secrecy that if Limoges could arrange for a meeting between herself and Philip II, she could then raise Navarre's hopes of recovering his lands or of receiving some compensation. This would be a means by which she could restrain the King of Navarre and consequently, she said, the whole kingdom. Until she knew what hope there was of achieving such a meeting with Philip, Catherine did not wish a living soul—apart from de Laubespine

[1] B.N., Mss. fr. 6614, f. 230 [March 1561], draft by de Laubespine for Catherine to Limoges. My italics.

[2] La Ferrière, *Lettres*, i, 188. Under 21 April 1561, the editor prints parts of this letter of which the beginning and, unknown to him, the end are missing. B.N., Mss. fr. 6618, f. 98, 22 April 1561, is a draft of this document. The two versions are not quite identical.

and Limoges—to hear of her plan. Limoges was to send back the express messenger to de Laubespine at his own house and from there he would secretly inform Catherine of his brother's opinion. She intended to bide her time until she received the reply.[1]

It is difficult for us to tell what was obvious at the time and what was obscure, but there is nothing to suggest that any secretary other than de Laubespine, who occupied a special position, was really well informed as to what was happening. It is possible, if unlikely, that Fresne knew more about Franco-Spanish relations than meets the eye, but there is nothing to show that he did. A memoir which he drafted on this subject in November 1561 refers only to matters of common knowledge.[2] What he did know was that things were being concealed from Navarre, for whom he often worked. In March 1561 he wrote to Limoges: 'You will find three letters in this packet, a first and two other later ones. The first and the second are sent to you privately and you must answer them in a separate letter. As for the other, which concerns the King of Navarre, this one has been shown to him. You should answer it in your letter to the king, which he will also see. It is necessary to do things this way in such times as these.'[3]

So far as we can tell, de Laubespine alone realized the truth about Catherine's position—that she was isolated, afraid of Spain and quite unable to trust her ostensible allies, the catholics. Bourdin may possibly have known too, since he worked in close co-operation with de Laubespine. But that Alluye, for one, did not realize this is shown by a letter he wrote to Nevers on 29 November 1561, in which he identified the crown with the catholic cause, apparently unaware that Catherine, in great perplexity, was actually dallying with the protestants.[4] De Laubespine himself was very guarded to everyone but Limoges, the only person to whom he dared express his anger, or reveal his sympathy for Catherine as a human being. Referring to the

[1] B.N., Mss. fr. 6618, f. 98, 22 April 1561, draft by de Laubespine for Catherine to Limoges.
[2] B.N., Mss. fr. 15875, f. 279 [November 1561].
[3] B.N., Mss. fr. 6617, f. 139, 27 March 1561, Fresne to Limoges, quoted by de Ruble, *Antoine de Bourbon*, iii, 13.
[4] B.N., Mss. fr. 3221, f. 29, 20 September 1561, Alluye to Nevers.

outward reconciliation between Condé and Guise which Catherine finally achieved in August 1561, de Laubespine wrote to Rennes the non-committal observation that it was 'a beginning towards greater peace in this kingdom'.[1] But, knowing how little it really meant, he wrote more graphically to Limoges, 'pour cela je ne sais si leurs estomacs sont bien . . .' Clearly he thought otherwise, because of the continual news of fresh alarms and disputes, which all recoiled upon Catherine and worsened her predicament. Thus, he said, 'ceste pauvre reine porte la paste au four et est grandement a plaindre n'osant deplaire a pas ung et etant peu obeie si non en les gratifiant de ce qu'ils veulent'.[2]

Writing at length to Limoges, at Catherine's own request, he explained just how badly the catholics were treating her. In March 1561 Guise, Montmorency and Saint-André banded together in a close catholic alliance known as the *triumvirat*, in which Chantonnay, the Spanish ambassador, was also involved. The *triumvirat* managed to seduce Navarre, and constituted a serious threat to Catherine, against whom, it is sometimes alleged, they harboured violent intentions. De Laubespine wrote to Limoges that the *triumvirat* was threatening Catherine with the power of Spain. Indeed there were many rumours and even disquieting signs that Philip was planning an invasion of France. Philip's ambassador, 'ce beau Chantonnay', as de Laubespine acidly called him, kept appearing at court at all hours to complain about the state of religion in France. Even more outrageously, the ambassador sent his secretary to tell the queen that he, Chantonnay, could no longer refrain from informing his master of what he saw and heard in France. De Laubespine was glad that Catherine had dealt firmly with him. He was angry that she should be so rudely treated, 'sans consulter la peine ou elle est de se comporter et vivre parmi une telle tourmante que celle qui est presentement icy'. He told his brother that the members of the *triumvirat* exploited Chantonnay's machinations. Only the night before (28 August 1561),

[1] B.N., Mss. Cinq Cents Colbert, 394, f. 183, 24 August 1561, de Laubespine to Rennes.
[2] B.N., Mss. fr. 6618, f. 8, 29 August 1561, de Laubespine to Limoges. Quoted by de Ruble, *Antoine de Bourbon*, iii, 203–4. His reference is to the coded version of the letter.

Guise and the constable had alarmed the queen by appearing at
midnight to say that they observed that the catholics were arming and the kingdom was in danger of being split into two.
These, de Laubespine said, were vexatious things for his brother
to learn, and the presence of the *triumvirat* was making everything much worse. De Laubespine was afraid. He had no illusions, and fully realized that the other side was also making
preparations because they would never be content until they had
hounded the Guise faction from court. 'God grant', he concluded despairingly, 'that all may be well, but we are living in
terrible times.' This revealing letter was sent in code, and it is
interesting to note that where there was no need for pretence,
there was no talk of religion.[1]

To settle the country and deprive the leaders of both parties
of the pretext for their actions, it was essential to reach some
settlement of the religious problem. Catherine was therefore
very anxious that there should be a general council and, failing
that, she determined to hold a national one. But all she finally
obtained, after much delay, was a new session of the council of
Trent. It was Bourdin who largely assisted her in the work which
this entailed. Du-Toc tells us that Bourdin prepared almost
single-handed all the memoirs and instructions that were sent to
the council, and undertook the French negotiations 'avec une
vigueur et une majesté dignes de la grandeur de cette couronne'.[2]
If Du-Toc is a little flamboyant, Bourdin certainly did the work
with quiet efficiency and won for himself an excellent reputation.

Neither Bourdin nor de Laubespine had any real faith in the
success of Catherine's daring plan to hold what was called the
'colloque de Poissy', in which both catholics and protestants
were to be heard. Bourdin wrote to the bishop of Rennes that he
expected no good results from it. On the other hand, he admitted
that things had to be decided either one way or the other: 'fault
il que les choses preignent resolution en une part ou une autre
car de demeurer longuement en la diversite et contension ou
nous en sommes il ne se peut aucunement'.[3] De Laubespine
expected no more: 'a en parler franchement', he wrote to the

[1] B.N., Mss. fr. 6618, f. 8, 29 August 1561, de Laubespine to Limoges.
[2] Du-Toc, 103.
[3] B.N., Mss. Cinq Cents Colbert, 396, f. 191, 30 June 1561, Bourdin to Rennes.

bishop of Rennes, 'sans grande grace de dieu je y veoy peu d'esperance et le mal empire tous les jours'.[1] To Limoges, as usual, he expressed his real opinion more freely. He said that the prelates had begun to consider reforms, which was neither the matter nor the root of the divisions, instead of discussing doctrine, as it was intended. Now, as you know, he went on to his brother, 'quelques esprits et cervaulx sont divises et composes d'estranges passions', and this was as true of the prelates as it was of the nobles. There was not one among them, in de Laubespine's opinion, who was not afraid lest he be obliged to mend his way of life, and go to attend to his flock.[2]

At the same time as the colloque de Poissy, the States General were in session at Pontoise, in theory to bring the replies from their constituents as to what they were prepared to do about the national debt, which had risen to well over forty million francs. There is no detailed information as to what part the secretaries played in the meetings of the States—most probably they were concerned with their preparation and with formal and technical matters. An engraving of the States of Orléans which met in December 1560 and January 1561 shows all four secretaries seated together at a table placed in a central position. The only certain thing is that they were present, and that the results of the States of Pontoise troubled de Laubespine very much. The nobles and the people, he wrote to Limoges, claimed that the church should pay the king's debts, while the clergy, enraged, offered little help. 'Et la conclusion de tous les deux etats est d'avoir temples pour y faire librement prescher . . . et changer peu a peu la vieille religion ce qui trouble beaucoup car la plus parts des grands y poussent.'[3]

During this first year of Charles' reign, the other two secretaries, the cousins Robertet, were mainly occupied with their routine duties. Fresne had an expanding *département*, for the troubles of the early 1560s brought about certain changes and additions to the *gouvernements* of which the secretaries' *départements* were partially composed, and a considerable in-

---

[1] B.N., Mss Cinq Cents Colbert, 394, f. 183, 24 August 1561, de Laubespine to Rennes.

[2] B.N., Mss. fr. 6618, f. 8, 29 August 1561, de Laubespine to Limoges. See de Ruble, *Le Colloque de Poissy (septembre–octobre 1561)*.

[3] B.N., Mss. fr. 6618, f. 8, 29 August 1561, de Laubespine to Limoges.

crease in activity between the provinces and the crown, which created additional work for the secretary concerned. It was Fresne who was responsible for the vast areas of the south and west of France—Provence, Languedoc and Guienne—chiefly affected by the religious disturbances, and in which most of the changes took place. The chief innovation in these years was the appointment for towns, as opposed to provinces, of *gouverneurs* or lieutenants-general—neither of these terms was precisely defined or consistently used—and of temporary, roving commissioners, either for military or administrative purposes.

Guienne, extending from the Spanish frontier to the Loire, was clearly too large an area for one person to control in time of trouble. Thus Bayonne and Bordeaux each received a lieutenant-general and a series of additional officers were sent as need arose, either as lieutenants-general or as special commissioners. All these were controlled through Fresne's *département*. In the north of the province there were similar changes. At least before 6 December 1560, Guy de Daillon, comte du Lude, had been appointed *gouverneur* (not lieutenant-general) of Poitou. La Rochelle received Guy Chabot, seigneur de Jarnac, as lieutenant-general at some date before October 1562. Later on, Poitou and La Rochelle, effectively detached from Guienne, came under one and the same *gouverneur*.

In May 1562, as civil war was breaking over France, Fresne must have been nearly overwhelmed with work, drafting and preparing instructions for so many different officials. Thus he warned Joyeuse in Languedoc to provide for the frontier town of Narbonne,[1] instructed the seigneur de Bury at Bordeaux to call out the local nobility, to attend to the safety of Bordeaux and to break up assemblies of protestant troops forming to go to the help of Orléans.[2] He sent a warning to the vicomte d'Orthe, *gouverneur* of Bayonne, to expect the arrival of 3,000 Spanish troops,[3] to Jarnac at La Rochelle to watch for signs of English help for the protestants,[4] and to Estampes in Brittany to attend to the defence of his fortresses.[5]

[1] B.N., Mss. fr. 15876, f. 10, 6 May 1562, Charles to Joyeuse, draft by Fresne.
[2] *Ibid.*, f. 12, 8 May 1562, Charles to Bury, draft by Fresne.
[3] *Ibid.*, f. 7, May 1562, Charles to d'Orthe, draft by Fresne.
[4] *Ibid.*, f. 13, May 1562, Charles to Jarnac, draft by Fresne.
[5] *Ibid.*, f. 40, 10 May 1562, Charles to d'Estampes, draft by Fresne.

The other secretaries had comparable work, but none was so heavily burdened as Fresne. He kept up an almost constant stream of correspondence relating to the requirements of war or the enforcing of peace, because his *département* contained a much larger area of France than any of the others. It is not possible to determine to what extent he himself decided the content of the instructions sent to the lieutenants and commissioners, but knowing more about this *département* than anyone else, it is reasonable to suppose that his opinions were consulted. The issuing of these instructions, besides his correspondence with the ambassador in Spain, his duties at court and in council, and the missions he accomplished for Catherine, were the chief elements in Fresne's work, and they explain why he became an authority on protestant affairs, then called R.P.R.—*les affaires de la religion prétendue réformée*. It was only a matter of chance, and in no sense attributable to any personal inferiority, that Fresne was not involved in more spectacular work like the embassies of his cousin Alluye.

For Alluye we have only a meagre record for the first eighteen months of Charles' reign. He was probably less busy than his colleagues, for his *département* contained only two provinces in France, Lyons and Dauphiné. It was natural that Alluye should have been on close terms with the duc de Nemours, who was *gouverneur* of Lyons, especially as Alluye and his cousin had been friendly with him for some years. He kept the duke informed of what was happening, and in touch with events at the court. Brantôme describes Nemours as 'la fleur de toute chevallerie'.[1] He was rich, handsome and accomplished, the dazzling idol of a brilliant court. But, in May 1561, he was absent from court, on account of a scandalous lawsuit with mademoiselle de Rohan whom he had seduced. Alluye, who watched over his interests and the progress of his case, which lasted many years, wrote to him on 22 May advising him that things were well disposed for his return to court, even though he might not think so from the letter the queen wrote him.[2] 'If I were wise enough to know how to advise you,' Alluye wrote with feigned modesty, 'I

[1] Brantôme, iv, 165.
[2] La Ferrière, *Lettres*, i, 197, 21 May 1561, Catherine to Nemours. On this affair see de Ruble, *Le Duc de Nemours et mademoiselle de Rohan, 1531–92*.

would willingly tell you that you should not squander more time in Savoy than you need to attend to your affairs', adding that he was certain that Nemour's presence at court would be as greatly welcome as his absence was regretted.[1]

The relations of Alluye and Nemours illustrate the potentially important role of the secretaries in forestalling or dissolving misunderstandings between important persons and the court, in preventing the proud and touchy nobles from feeling neglected, forgotten or insufficiently esteemed in their absence, in championing their personal and public interests and sometimes even in preserving their loyalty to the crown. De Laubespine, for instance, was in constant touch with Gaspard de Saulx de Tavannes, lieutenant-general in Burgundy, and, upon the death of marshal Bourdillon, informed Tavannes that he was not—as he had expected—to receive the vacant office of marshal. De Laubespine managed the matter so tactfully that the incident passed off without trouble. He persuaded Tavannes that he should rejoice in the 'certain assurance of their Majesties' goodwill', and that the honour, which he deserved, would not be long withheld.[2]

The secretaries had also to bear the brunt of a deluge of complaints from the *gouverneurs* about their lack of money—money which, as a rule, was both owing and urgently needed in the public interest. They had to explain, apologize and prevaricate, to reconcile conflicting claims, to battle for the money at court, and, above all, to stave off the anger or despair—which could be dangerous—of those who were kept waiting for it.

Towards the end of 1561 the situation in France was rapidly worsening. Every day, Bourdin told Rennes, there was news of fresh trouble, especially in the south, 'and we are threatened in so many other districts that the king is obliged to arm in order to quell such wicked and disloyal temerity'.[3] This brought new work for the secretaries. On 18 November, de Laubespine was sent to Tours following a tumult there, one of many incidents of the kind which were taking place all over France. The next day

[1] B.N., Mss. fr. 3200, f. 133, 22 May 1561, Alluye to Nemours.
[2] B.N., Mss. fr. 4641, f. 60, 11 April 1561, de Laubespine to Tavannes.
[3] B.N., Mss. Cinq Cents Colbert, 396, f. 203, 6 October 1561, Bourdin to Rennes.

he sent a report to Guise saying that the garrison had been distributed according to orders. De Laubespine, who hated violence and disorder, was very much moved by the state of Tours, and the people begged him to intercede for them with Guise and the king. He agreed to do so upon obtaining a promise of obedience. He pointed out to the duke that the commander, Richelieu, was not a gentle person, and that his troops were getting themselves fed at the expense of those on whom they were billeted, which was wrong. He further told the duke that all the wicked troublemakers who committed the recent follies had withdrawn, so that any severity would be visited upon the innocent. 'Il y a une merveilleuse pitye', he pleaded, because there was not a single house without three, four of five tenants, craftsmen who could only live by their hands and whom one was constrained to evict, thereby destroying their livelihoods. Five or six hundred of them had left the town in ten or twelve days.[1] We do not know what mercy, if any, de Laubespine obtained for Tours but this was only the beginning. From then on he was constantly to witness such suffering. He cannot have stayed in Tours for more than a day or two because by 23 November he was back at Saint-Germain, where Catherine needed him. That December, Sir Nicholas Throckmorton wrote to Sir Thomas Challoner that it was de Laubespine, together with Condé, Coligny and the chancellor who 'do all indeed'.[2]

The four secretaries were all at court during the first troubled months of 1562, during which Catherine was hesitating between the catholic and protestant factions. Guise, who had been away from court for some months, was recalled to attend the council and to control the disorders in his *gouvernement* of Dauphiné. He came, but—a fact which has often been obscured—he came as a rebel in arms and, disobeying Catherine's orders to join her at Monceaux, went straight to Paris, entering by the royal Porte Saint-Denis, when the city was already occupied by Condé. There was not room for both of them. Guise was the stronger and Condé and his followers departed and took possession of Orléans.

Except for Bourdin, all the secretaries were involved in the complex series of negotiations which then began with Condé's

---

[1] B.N., Mss. fr. 15875, f. 376, 19 November 1561, de Laubespine to Guise.
[2] *C.S.P.F.*, 1561–2, p. 450, 20 December 1561, Throckmorton to Challoner.

faction, and of which there are not two identical accounts. On 8 April the two Robertets were sent to Orléans with Artus de Cossé, seigneur de Gonnor, *surintendant des finances*, and they returned on 10 April.[1] Three days later Gonnor was sent a second time with Alluye and, on 24 April, de Laubespine went to Orléans with de Morvillier, the bishop, who witnessed the sack of his cathedral. While they were there Coligny feigned illness and refused to see them.[2] They returned from Orléans on 2 May and reported to the queen in the garden of the Louvre— Catherine loved to walk in a garden while discussing business— in the presence of Navarre, Montmorency, the chancellor and the other secretaries.[3] The substance of all their messages was the same: Condé refused to lay down arms and return to court unless the *triumvirs* disarmed and withdrew. Furthermore, he demanded the full application of the edict of January. This edict granted limited toleration to the protestants, but had been modified owing to strong catholic opposition.[4]

After their several journeys to Orléans, the three secretaries all wrote to Limoges. Fresne said that they had reached the 'crise de la malladie' and they would soon know what their fate was to be. He, personally, had made two journeys to Orléans, and he was troubled, he said, because he saw not the slightest sign of either side giving way, and the answers had always been the same. If, within a month, passions were not appeased, he foresaw the total ruin of the monarchy. 'I do not doubt', he said, 'that from over there you feel our trouble as we do ourselves, but if you saw with your own eyes what we are seeing, you would deplore our calamity even more'. He wrote, he said, in strict confidence, knowing that he could trust Limoges.[5] It seems perfectly clear from this letter that, for all his affiliations with the Guises, Fresne was not blinded by partisan opinion, greed or passion, and that he contemplated civil war and the

---

[1] Paschal, 20, 22.

[2] Baguenault de Puchesse, *Jean de Morvillier*, 147; *C.S.P.F.*, 1561–2, pp. 633–5, 27 April 1562, Throckmorton to the queen. He gives the date of de Laubespine's journey to Orléans as 26 April.

[3] Paschal, 30–1.

[4] The text of the edict of 17 January 1562 is printed by Delaborde, ii, app. i, 547–51.

[5] B.N., Mss. fr. 6618, f. 94, 17 April 1562, Fresne to Limoges.

ruin of the monarchy, not with the equanimity of his early protectors, but with the same horror, foreboding and distress as de Laubespine and Bourdin. The same may be said of Alluye, who also wrote to Limoges to say that in several journeys to Orléans he had been able to obtain little. 'We are so wretched that we are now up to our eyes in war and, save for the intervention of God, we shall be in it even deeper.' What was more, he could not see that there were any grounds for agreement. 'You are very fortunate', he concluded sadly, 'still to be far away and not to see before your eyes the mischief that we see every day.'[1]

The import of de Laubespine's letter was similar. He said that a great 'fureur du peuple' had swept the country, and not even Condé and Coligny could control it. 'Je prie dieu,' he wrote characteristically, 'quil pardonne a ceulx qui sont cause de ce mal qui est si grant quil pourroyt bien tirer la Reine de ce Royaume.' Meanwhile, he said, each side was preparing to take up arms and not forgetting to employ foreign mercenaries, the consequences of which Limoges could judge for himself.[2]

Once again de Laubespine seems to have been alone among the secretaries in understanding what was really happening. That he did understand is illustrated by another of his letters to Limoges. In mid-May 1562 three of the secretaries accompanied Catherine to Monceaux, where she went to demonstrate that she and the king were not being held prisoners by the catholics. Fresne remained in Paris to work for Navarre. De Laubespine makes it perfectly clear that if Catherine were not exactly a prisoner, neither was she free. Her cause was still different from that of either side, although she was constrained to work with the catholics who were *legally* in control of the king's forces. He told Limoges that Catherine had sent to Condé to entreat him to disarm and disband his troops, and that she would do the same to Guise and the constable. 'God grant that they will be prepared to believe and obey her', he said, but there was a great lack of confidence between the two sides and 'peu d'honneur . . . *Et est bien malaise a juger qui a la plus grand tort* . . . cependant le Royaume se ruine je vous asseure.'[3]

---

[1] B.N., Mss. fr. 6618, f. 172, 17 April 1562, Alluye to Limoges.
[2] B.N., Mss. fr. 6609, f. 61, 5 or 6 May 1562, de Laubespine to Limoges.
[3] B.N., Mss. fr. 6614, f. 129, 18 May 1562, de Laubespine to Limoges. My italics.

The secretaries were having to work desperately hard at this time. They were constantly on call if the queen should want them[1] and de Laubespine, who was anxious for his brother's company, counsel and support, warned him—and only half in jest—that when he returned from Spain 'vous . . . nen aurez pas meilleur marche'.[2] Besides all his other worries, de Laubespine was anxious about his wife who was in Touraine, which was not safe, and he could neither reach her himself, nor could she come to him, and for some reason unknown to us, he was afraid she might fall ill. If things became any worse, he told Limoges, she would go to Berry but, in fact, it was not really safe anywhere. There are very few references to his wife in de Laubespine's correspondence, but those there are all indicate affection and concern for her, suggesting a happy marriage. Later in the same month he sent his son to see her because she was in great distress, and he himself very anxious. Their home town of Bourges, which up till then had been spared, had finally shared the fate of other towns and the churches had been destroyed. For the first time there seems to be a note of near despair in de Laubespine's supplication, 'Notre seigneur nous regardera en pitye quand il luy plaira. Et nous donnera plus que nous ne meritons car je ne veoy nul conclusion dun coste ni dautre.'[3]

Catherine, whose only hope was to make peace before anything conclusive could happen in the field, was to receive loyal service from all four of the secretaries who were perpetually in attendance on her. Though unsuccessful, their negotiations with Condé continued—even after Navarre and Guise had taken the field on 1 June 1562. There are various accounts and interpretations of what happened and of the constant comings and goings, in which Alluye and Fresne were particularly active.[4] For a week after the end of June, it seemed that peace was secure and, from Talcy, Fresne drafted letters and instructions for persons to go out to the provinces to publish and enforce it.

[1] B.N., Mss. fr. 6609, f. 61, 5 or 6 May 1562, de Laubespine to Limoges.
[2] *Id.*
[3] B.N., Mss. fr. 6614, f. 129, 18 May 1562, de Laubespine to Limoges.
[4] De Ruble, *Antoine de Bourbon*, iv, pp. 244–52, 256; Delaborde, ii, ch. iv, gives a different account. De Ruble is supported by the evidence of the Venetian ambassador, B.N., Mss. it. 1722, f. 414, 5 July 1562. Even to contemporaries it was not clear what was happening.

Then, when Fresne returned to the protestant camp at Orléans for certain particulars concerning a promise of Condé's to leave the country, he found that there had been a change of mind and he went back to warn Catherine 'qu'il falloit autre chose que du papier pour le mettre dehor'.[1] Catherine departed and de Laubespine, Bourdin and Alluye accompanied her to Vincennes, while Fresne went to Blois to serve Navarre.

We do not know what part the secretaries played in the negotiations which continued not only during the summer of 1562, but also during the siege of Bourges which followed, for it was a peculiar feature of this whole period that there were acts of war during all the intervals of peace, and peace negotiations almost continually throughout the wars. Conditions were similar whether in time of war or of peace. When Catherine and the king entered Bourges on 1 September 1562, it was in de Laubespine's house that they stayed for nearly a week. Then, after some hesitation, it was decided to go to Normandy to attempt the recapture of Rouen and, on 12 October, Fresne wrote to Nemours to describe the siege, but 'in haste being the only one here among my companions and so burdened with work that I do not know which way to turn'.[2] However, it appears from one of Catherine's letters that Bourdin had been there three days before.[3] There was no sign of de Laubespine, who may have remained at Bourges, and Alluye had been sent on an important mission to Piedmont, during which Fresne did his normal work.

It was decided in council at Blois, on 13 August 1562, that four French towns in Piedmont should be restored to the duke of Savoy. His friendship was becoming increasingly important to Catherine, as the situation in France became more serious, and it was only by ceding the towns that troops stationed in Piedmont could be released for service in France. Besides, if Brantôme is to be believed, there was a secret agreement in the treaty of Cateau-Cambrésis by which the French towns were to be restored if the duke of Savoy and his wife, Marguerite, were

---

[1] De Ruble, *Antoine de Bourbon*, iv, 257–68.

[2] B.N., Mss. fr. 3200, f. 128, 12 October 1562, Fresne to Nemours, partially printed by La Ferrière, *Lettres*, i, 414, n.

[3] La Ferrière, *Lettres*, i, 416, 9 October 1562, Catherine to Rennes.

to have a son.[1] As she was already thirty-six at the time of her marriage this was considered extremely unlikely. But the unexpected happened, and a son was born. A commission to restore the towns was therefore issued in the names of Imbert de la Platière, seigneur de Bourdillon, lieutenant-general in Piedmont, de Morvillier, René de Birague and Alluye, or any two of them.[2]

It was not new for a secretary to go on a foreign mission. Bochetel had been to Spain, and he, de Laubespine and Bourdin had all been to England. But this was the first time that a secretary had undertaken so difficult, responsible and urgent a negotiation abroad. Their work had always been determined, at least in part, by circumstances, and their advance was hastened by the civil war; twenty, or even ten years earlier, such a mission would not have been entrusted to a *secrétaire des finances* but to a noble or perhaps a senior churchman. In 1562, when the *noblesse* was split between hostile factions, it seemed natural to send a secretary. Alluye was doubtless chosen because Piedmont was in his *département* and because his colleagues were otherwise engaged. It is true that Alluye was only one of an equal commission of four, but it was he who did most to keep the negotiation alive and to bring it to the desired conclusion. What happened in Piedmont reveals more than we had previously known of his character. He emerges as an able young diplomat, undaunted in the face of persistent problems and unflurried by a clamour of protest and complaint. Furthermore, his ability to extract money from close and wily Italian bankers justly elicited Catherine's praise.

Alluye departed, perhaps from de Laubespine's house, where the court was staying at Bourges, on 2 or 3 September 1562. He was charged with the despatch of troops to France—in the first place to Tavannes who was desperately trying to pacify his *gouvernement* of Burgundy[3]—with the restitution of four fortress towns to Savoy and, later, with the negotiation of loans from Florence, Genoa and Venice. He seems also to have had some personal commission from Navarre in connection with his perpetual efforts to recover the lost part of his kingdom, for Navarre

---

[1] Brantôme, v, 72.   [2] B.N., Mss. fr. 15534, f. 162, 13 August 1562.
[3] La Ferrière, *Lettres*, i, 392, 2 September 1562, Catherine to Maugiron.

K

hoped, apparently, that Savoy might intercede for him with the King of Spain. Brantôme also says that if Alluye were successful in this, Navarre promised to help him win the hand of mademoiselle de Piennes, whom he wanted to marry. This may or may not be true, but Navarre was dead before Alluye returned.[1]

Alluye immediately encountered difficulties when Bourdillon, as lieutenant-general in Piedmont, refused to obey the order to restore the four towns to the duke of Savoy, on the grounds that he could not do so in the name of a king who was a minor, or anyway not without a form of exoneration (*descharge*) which, he well knew, it was totally impossible to procure.[2] Thus began a long delay. Nearly a month later, on 10 October, Alluye and de Morvillier moved from Fossano to Turin where they were expecting a messenger to arrive with despatches and further orders from the court.[3] Meanwhile Alluye occupied himself with trying to raise money from Italian bankers. To Fresne he complained vigorously about the excessive delay which made it appear, there in Italy, that they had only been sent 'pour charmer le temps', as though they were not acquainted with the confidential details of the matter for which they were sent.[4] This was damaging to their prestige, and the problems in Piedmont were becoming ever more complicated. So many people all round him wanted so many things that an angel from heaven would be unable to satisfy everyone. The longer they waited, the more schemes and machinations there would be. He ended as crossly as he had begun, with a demand for clear instructions for everyone and, in the name of God, for his own recall.[5]

The courier finally arrived on 24 October[6] with letters and instructions from which Alluye, in turn, learnt something of the difficulties with which his cousin Fresne had had to contend in France, for he had been present at the siege of Rouen. Alluye was only partially satisfied. Besides writing to the queen himself,

---

[1] Brantôme, v, 75.

[2] B.N., Mss. fr. 3195, f. 35, 15 September 1562. See also Mss. fr. 6626, ff. 78, 80, 18 September 1562, Alluye to the queen.

[3] B.N., Mss. fr. 15877, f. 205, 10 October 1562, Alluye to the queen.

[4] *Ibid.*, f. 309, 16 October 1562, Alluye to Fresne.

[5] B.N., Mss. fr. 15877, f. 309, 16 October 1562, Alluye to Fresne.

[6] *Ibid.*, f. 304, 25 October 1562, Bourdillon to Catherine.

he asked Fresne to explain to her the uselessness of trying to hurry anything in Italy without sending money. He found it necessary to state the obvious, he explained a little acidly, because back at court, they seemed to think they need only whistle in order to restore the towns, whereas there were 'tant de cordes a toucher'. There in Italy, Alluye was exposed to all the winds which were blowing, namely the 'passions de tout le monde'. He swore that if he were not soon recalled, he would come without instructions. He also asked Fresne to beg the queen to do something for Bourdillon, who was now willing to obey.[1] Catherine, for her part, had written frankly to Alluye, who was bearing the brunt of the negotiation, and in whom she showed complete confidence, inviting him not to hesitate to inform her of any other difficulties and of the remedies he proposed for them. Catherine desperately needed the troops from Piedmont because, after the fall of Rouen, d'Andelot, with German troops, was threatening Orléans. She further said that she approved of Alluye's proposals for borrowing money in Genoa and that if he could find a way of extracting one or two hundred thousand *écus*, it would be no small achievement and no small success in their affairs. 'Si vous estes si bon harangueur,' she continued, 'que vous en pussiez tirer quelque chose, je diray que vous estes habille homme.'[2] It may be said that he was an able man, for he was successful, and the money was paid in two instalments the following year.

Alluye was anxious to return to France—a journey for which his instructions were already prepared, probably by himself—to explain to Catherine in person certain problems about Bourdillon, who was still making difficulties although he had said that he was prepared to obey.[3] But the duke of Savoy refused to allow Alluye to go, anxious, no doubt, lest his absence be used as an excuse to delay the negotiation still further.[4] However,

[1] B.N., Mss. fr. 15877, f. 300, 25 October 1562, Alluye to Fresne.
[2] La Ferrière, *Lettres*, i, 423, 20–26 October 1562, Catherine to Alluye.
[3] It appears likely that Bourdillon was making difficulties because he was in sympathy or in touch with the prince de Condé.
[4] Léon Marlet, in his article on Alluye, claims that he returned to court between 10 and 12 October, alleging that he was spurred on by love, evidently to superhuman speeds. The error arises from his attributing to Alluye, Fresne's letter to Nemours of 12 October, from Rouen (B.N., Mss. fr. 3200, f. 128). The editor of

things suddenly became easier for Alluye. He had done his best to obtain some adequate compensation for Bourdillon, and, besides money, he was promised the first vacant office of marshal.[1] He soon received that of Saint-André, who was killed at Dreux in the first pitched battle of the war, on 19 December 1562.[2] Lorraine, who was passing through north Italy on his way to the council of Trent, succeeded in facilitating the negotiation so that, on 2 November, Alluye was able to write that their difficulties were at an end and he did not see what fresh trouble could arise.[3] By 12 December operations were nearly complete and he was ready to mount his horse to return, first taking leave of the duke and duchess. Thus he hoped to kiss the queen's hand at Christmas.[4]

During the first three months of 1563 de Laubespine, Fresne and Alluye worked in the closest co-operation with Catherine. We may safely assume that Limoges, who had returned from Spain, and de Laubespine, who was involved in all the peace negotiations, were Catherine's constant advisers at this time. Lorraine was away at the council of Trent and Guise was with the army; Navarre had died at the siege of Rouen and Saint-André was also dead. Condé and the constable had both been captured; Coligny was in the enemy camp and Nevers and Nemours were in their *gouvernements*. Thus the court was virtually deserted, and there was no one to detract from the secretaries' importance.

Their efforts and those of Catherine herself were entirely directed towards raising adequate sums of money and restoring peace. Writing to Nemours in the previous December, Fresne had referred to Catherine's great desire and even greater hope

Catherine's letters also made this same mistake (i, 420, n., column 2). Marlet then wonders why Alluye, back in Piedmont, wrote to the queen as though he had not recently seen her, accounting for this by his annoyance at having to leave Rouen, where mademoiselle de Piennes was with the court, and where his rival in love had happily been killed. This romantic story is entirely fictitious.

[1] Brantôme, v, 76.

[2] Fresne described this battle in a letter to Nemours, B.N., Mss. fr. 3180, f. 74, 22 December 1562. It is quoted in full by Marlet, 507–8, but attributed to Alluye.

[3] B.N., Mss. fr. 15877, f. 336, 2 November 1562, Alluye to the queen. Mss. fr. 3195, f. 15, 2 November 1562, the treaty with the duke of Savoy.

[4] B.N., Mss. fr. 15877, f. 454, 12 December 1562. See also the *Acte de delivrance des villes*, Mss. fr. 3195, f. 39, 12 December 1562, and the *procès verbal de la restitution*, *ibid.*, f. 1, December 1562.

for peace, saying that 'tant y a quon faict la guerre dun coste obstinement et elle faict la paix du sien malgre le ciel et tous les elements'.[1] Since then neither the circumstances nor Catherine's attitude had altered.

De Laubespine was in constant communication with his friend the seigneur de Gonnor, to whom he wrote in January that he had been wearing down his pen writing about the peace and trying to arrange a meeting between the captives, Montmorency and Condé.[2] He was deeply concerned, and with good reason, about the truly desperate financial situation. He asked Gonnor—*surintendant des finances*—to try to make this quite clear to Guise, who was then preparing to lay siege to Orléans, because de Laubespine found it very curious that one should launch into such great expenditure without having considered it exhaustively and without understanding it more clearly. He wished he could make everyone realize that this lack of money was no mere manner of speaking 'car gueres ne le croyent'.[3] Meanwhile, he could detect nothing but bad faith, 'chacun fait du pis quil peult'.[4]

Indeed this problem of money became so acute as to threaten to disturb de Laubespine's relations with Gonnor after the conclusion of peace. The normally patient secretary showed signs of irritation, warning Gonnor that there would be further money troubles and that it was futile to get into a rage about it. But he soon relented, admitting, 'you have reason to be angry with me for I know well that I vex you, and myself even more by writing to you so often on the subject of money'.[5]

Alluye, for his part, was plagued by the same problem. Nemours' troops were badly needed at Orléans, but without money he could not send them. Applying to the queen and then to Gonnor, Alluye did everything he personally could to procure money for Nemours but, for lack of it, he said, they were almost dying of hunger. Even at court there was no money, he told Nemours, and every time there was a journey to make,

[1] B.N., Mss. fr. 3180, f. 114, 12 December 1562, Fresne to Nemours.
[2] B.N., Mss. fr. 3216, f. 37, 28 January 1562/3, de Laubespine to Gonnor.
[3] *Ibid.*, f. 47, 4 February 1562/3, de Laubespine to Gonnor.
[4] *Ibid.*, f. 51, 13 February 1562/3, de Laubespine to Gonnor.
[5] B.N., Mss. fr. 3219, f. 60, 25 March 1562/3, and f. 117, 2 April 1562/3, de Laubespine to Gonnor.

money had to be borrowed for it. 'We are in such a state of poverty', he wrote, 'that you could hardly believe it.'[1] Like de Laubespine, he realized how serious the situation was, and wholeheartedly supported Catherine in her efforts to make peace. 'The queen is doing everything in her power', he informed Nemours, 'to achieve a peace, of which there are so many rumours that with the help of God I hope she will be successful, and indeed, my lord, our need of it is inexpressibly great.'[2]

Alluye and Bourdin were also entrusted with tasks connected with the military situation. In January Alluye was sent from the court to see Guise in his camp, to obtain his opinion on the various problems of war and peace. He brought back the message that Catherine should make peace if she could do so quickly, but meanwhile his forces ought to be increased because the enemy was expecting further help and showed signs of moving towards Champagne, whence it would come.[3]

Bourdin left court some time after 18 January 1563 to carry out a military mission for Guise, to negotiate 'capitulations' with the comte de Rocandolf and colonel Grombach for German troops. On 17 February he wrote to explain the whole situation to Guise[4]—a letter which the duke probably never received, for on 18 February he was attacked by an assassin and six days later he died.

The death of Guise completely altered the situation since there was no longer any major catholic leader to oppose Catherine's will. De Laubespine's reactions are lost to us, but they are unlikely to have been substantially different from those of Catherine. She was angry and shocked at the murder, if somewhat relieved by the elimination of a dangerous and doubtful ally. The absence of Guise simplified her immediate position; on the other hand she was well aware that nothing could be more diabolically calculated to sustain the quarrels in France. The two Robertets were not only outraged but also suffered an acute sense of personal loss, which they at once expressed to

---

[1] B.N., Mss. fr. 3180, f. 59, 19 February 1562/3. Alluye to Nemours.
[2] *Ibid.*, f. 47, 14 January 1562/3, Alluye to Nemours.
[3] B.N., Mss. it. 1722, f. 671, 26 January 1562/3.
[4] B.N., Mss. fr. 3899, f. 387, 17 February 1563, Bourdin to Guise.

Nemours. 'It is, my lord, a loss that both the king and you have sustained,' wrote Fresne from Orléans, 'he of one of the greatest and worthiest servitors this monarchy has had in five hundred years, and you of the most assured and worthiest of friends.' He praised the manner of the duke's dying and expressed his earnest desire for peace, for the longer the war lasted the more 'gens de bien' would be killed.[1] Alluye, who was at Blois, had already written to tell Nemours that Guise had been wounded. He had been at the bedside and assured Nemours, on the authority of the surgeons, that the wound was not serious and Guise in no danger.[2] So, when he died, Alluye took the news grievously to heart. 'I do not know where to begin my letter to you,' he wrote to Nemours, 'for I am so afflicted that I can neither breathe nor speak.' In his first access of anger and sorrow, he urged Nemours to think of revenge. 'I shall never believe that there is a God if I do not see this wicked deed revenged. You my lord have lost a good friend among the surest you will ever have, and I a good lord and master. It is pitiful to see this poor lady [madame de Guise] for such grief has never been seen and she has great need of consolation.'[3] Alluye knew that this would touch the duke, for it was common knowledge that he loved her.

De Laubespine was the only secretary to take part in the highly secret negotiations which occurred soon after the death of Guise, as a result of which the constable and Condé were finally brought together. They met on an island in the Loire on 6 March, with de Laubespine and one or two others, who are not named, standing by.[4] According to de Laubespine, who said that he was imprisoned on the island for six days, there were three or four meetings at which every means was tried to find a *modus vivendi*. Finally, considering the state of desolation of the kingdom, they were induced to make peace through religious concessions. This at least could be a temporary measure until such time as God might work something better. De Laubespine said that everyone there was likely to agree, but he did not know

[1] B.N., Mss. fr. 3218, f. 87, 24 February [1563], Fresne to Nemours. The date 1568 has been added to this document, but in error.
[2] B.N., Mss. Cinq Cents Colbert, 24, f. 42, 20 February 1563, Alluye to Nemours, partially quoted by La Ferrière, *Lettres*, i, 512, n., column 1.
[3] B.N., Mss. fr. 3180, f. 62, 25 February 1562/3, Alluye to Nemours.
[4] *C.S.P.F.*, 1563, pp. 199–201, 12 March, Smith to the queen.

how the peace would be received elsewhere. He was clearly thinking of Spain and he wrote to his brother-in-law the bishop of Rennes, 's'ils avoyent le feu si avant chez eulx je croy quils seroient bien aupres d'en eschapper'.[1] This had been another period of extremely hard work for de Laubespine. On returning from the island he apologized to his friend Gonnor for having neglected him, offering by way of excuse that every day and for more than half the nights he had been in camp, he had been 'harrasse comme ung chien'. He promised in future to write more often because he was about to go home, where he expected to have an easier time serving his wife than he had had at court serving the queen. The invincible, indefatigable Catherine was not always an easy taskmaster.[2]

Whether or not they welcomed it, the secretaries, together with the rest of the court, were now to have a change of occupation, for Catherine on moving to her favourite residence, Chenonceaux, plunged into a series of costly and spectacular celebrations. So it was that instead of attending to affairs of state, Fresne found himself organizing complex and elaborate court festivities. One of his most illegible drafts tells us a little about them. Then, as now, the approach to Chenonceaux was by a long avenue, from which, on the arrival of the king, singing sirens were to emerge, answered by nymphs who stole from the woods. At the sound of their song, satyrs appeared and would have carried them off, were it not for the timely succour of gentle knights. The king was greeted by a salute of artillery and a blaze of fireworks. All the lords and ladies were dressed in the most costly and magnificent clothes; there was dancing, a masque, a river fête, a picnic and more fireworks.[3]

The court might amuse itself, but the secretaries were unable to forget that the aftermath of the war was hardly less terrible than the war itself. Alluye wrote feelingly to Nemours of the

---

[1] B.N., Mss. Cinq Cents Colbert, 394, f. 287, 11 March 1562/3, de Laubespine to Rennes. 'If their own house were burning as fiercely as ours, I think they would be in a hurry to escape from it.' Mss. fr. 3196, f. 26, 12 March 1562/3, printed in the *Mémoires de Condé*, iv, 305. The edict of Amboise, often referred to as the edict of pacification, was signed on 19 March 1563. The text is printed in the *Mémoires de Condé*, iv, 311.

[2] B.N., Mss. fr. 3219, f. 117, 2 April 1562/3, de Laubespine to Gonnor.

[3] B.N., Mss. fr. 15881, f. 329 [April 1563], draft by Fresne.

fearful sufferings they were witnessing. He said that they were so great that he could never have believed them, were it not that he had seen them.[1] From Chenonceaux where the court was delayed by the non-departure from France of the *reîtres*—the hired German cavalry—Bourdin wrote to Gonnor that they were such a terrible scourge that Catherine did not know which saint to invoke and, for his own part, he said, 'if we do not recognize that it is the anger and punishment of God we are blind indeed'.[2] De Laubespine went away to his property at Hauterive some time before 19 April 1563, with similar thoughts in mind, and no less preoccupied with the miseries of France. He dared not go to Bourges which was in the grip of plague and famine. 'These are express visitations of our God,' he wrote to Rennes, almost echoing Bourdin's very words, 'that we may clearly understand the extent of his anger against us, whose pity I implore, that he may give us peace.'[3] De Laubespine's respite and sad reflections were interrupted, as often seemed to happen, when Bourdin succumbed to an attack of gout, a malady to which he was prone. As Alluye was away in England, and Fresne could not manage at court alone, the unfortunate de Laubespine was obliged to leave home and return to school, as he put it, 'qui m'est grande peine et annuy'.[4]

In May 1563, Alluye was sent on a second, and by no means unimportant mission, this time to England.[5] One of the many problems left by the war was the occupation of Le Havre by the English, with whom Condé and Coligny had concluded the scandalous treaty of Hampton Court.[6] In return for 100,000 *écus* and 6,000 men they had guaranteed the restoration of Calais to England. Elizabeth declared that she would only cede Le Havre—which the English called Newhaven—in return for Calais, and Catherine determined that she would recover Le

---

[1] B.N., Mss. fr. 3180, f. 64, 21 March 1562/3, Alluye to Nemours.

[2] B.N., Mss. fr. 3219, f. 121, 19 April 1563, Bourdin to Gonnor, printed by La Ferrière, *Lettres*, ii, 15–16, n.

[3] B.N., Mss. Cinq Cents Colbert, 395, f. 99, 6 May 1563, de Laubespine to Rennes.

[4] *Ibid.*, f. 103, 3 June 1563, de Laubespine to Rennes.

[5] B.N., Mss. fr. 17832, f. 16, undated contemporary copy of the instructions for Alluye; Mss. Cinq Cents Colbert, 102, f. 7, 21 May 1563, another, later copy.

[6] See C. Marchand, 'Le Traité des huguenots avec les Anglais en 1562', *Revue des questions historiques*, lxxvii (1905).

Havre without ceding Calais. But first she would negotiate. By the treaty of Cateau-Cambrésis, France was to cede Calais to England in 1567. Catherine, if she drove Elizabeth to war, could then claim that England had broken the treaty and therefore forfeited her rights. She had first to render peaceful agreement impossible, for fear that the protestants might refuse to support her against their recent ally, Elizabeth.

Alluye departed on 23 May 1563, and went first to see the constable at Chantilly before going to England, where he arrived about 29 May. Catherine may possibly have thought that Alluye, being very young, would be unacceptable in England and so serve her purpose all the better. This was the first comment made by Henry Middlemore to William Cecil, 'He is very young for so great a charge.'[1] Thomas Randolph reported Catherine to have said that she never had a great opinion of Alluye, 'but as of a young man . . . without a beard', but this is gossip.[2] Being young, rich and successful, he was possibly a little self-opinionated.

Alluye was to demand the evacuation of Le Havre, and to offer to ratify the treaty of Cateau-Cambrésis and to give hostages. He was not intimidated by the cold reception he met with in England and even at his first meeting with Elizabeth 'there grew such altercation betwixt her and them as they [the French] required to have conference with certain of their Council [sic. the privy council] with whom they might, as they said, speak boldly and be plainly answered'.[3] The next day Alluye and the French ambassador met five members of Elizabeth's council, who insisted upon conducting the proceedings in Latin, 'saving that d'Allouy for lack of Latin used French'.[4] This was a calculated discourtesy considering that they were not ignorant of French and that the usual diplomatic language was Italian, which Alluye could speak. On 3 June Alluye had a further meeting with Elizabeth and roundly demanded her answer as to whether she would relinquish Le Havre and abide by the terms of the treaty concerning Calais—for to obtain such an answer was the principal item in his instructions. Elizabeth said

[1] *C.S.P.F.*, 1563, p. 365, 24 May, Middlemore to Cecil. Alluye was thirty.
[2] *Ibid.*, p. 399, 13 June, Randolph to Cecil.
[3] *Ibid.*, p. 387, 5 June, Cecil to Smith.
[4] *Ibid.*, p. 388, 5 June, Cecil to Smith.

that she would exchange Le Havre for Calais, whereupon the negotiation ceased.

Alluye had had a thankless task in England. He did not make a good impression there, for Cecil wrote to Smith that 'in his manner of negotiation here [Alluye] has showed nothing but pride and ignorance'.[1] Elizabeth also said that he appeared 'to be an instrument rather to increase discord than to make peace' —an uncomfortable mission one must suppose.[2] Elizabeth had evidently grown angry, for back at Vincennes on 15 June—he had tarried in England for nearly a week before returning— Alluye reported her to have said that she had taken Le Havre in revenge for Calais and that she intended to keep it. The French felt strongly about Calais, and this was possibly just the result that Catherine had wished to obtain. Certainly in Bourdin's opinion it was the best solution.[3] Whether she relied upon Alluye's personality to achieve it, or whether he had secret or verbal instructions to behave as he is alleged to have done, it is impossible to say. Smith, who knew that Elizabeth had not actually intended to push the matter to the point of war, declared that he was sorry that Alluye and La Haye—a protestant envoy who went with him—had not negotiated better 'but the fault is not altogether in them', because he could see no inclination 'to such commission as should bring peace or reason to be done with quietness, but all to the war'.[4]

By the summer of 1563, when some outward semblance of unity had been restored in France, the situation was already very different from that prevailing on the accession of Charles IX. In the first place Catherine was established as queen-regent and, from then until her death, she was a power in the land. The rapid alignment of parties, of which there were three—the crown, the house of Guise, in general but not exclusively supported by the catholics, and the houses of Bourbon and Châtillon, in general but not exclusively supported by the protestants —led to the first civil war. This, unhappily, was neither lost nor won.

[1] C.S.P.F., 1563, p. 388, 5 June, Cecil to Smith.
[2] Ibid., p. 442, 5 July, the queen to Smith.
[3] B.N., Mss. fr. 3219, f. 119, 17 April [1563], Bourdin to Gonnor, printed in La Ferrière, Lettres, ii, 26, n.
[4] C.S.P.F., 1563, p. 421, 19 June, Smith to the queen.

The quarrels of the *noblesse* were not those of the crown, yet, hopelessly impoverished and with his forces legally controlled by the catholics, the king was neither able to stand aside nor to dominate either faction. The crown was therefore left dangerously, if not always obviously, isolated. As a result, civil wars alternated with periods of armed truce for thirty years until, with the accession of Henry IV, the interests of the crown were finally identified with those of one of the factions. Only then could it impose peace.

In these circumstances the secretaries were among the most loyal supporters the crown possessed. When Navarre, Guise and Saint-André had all perished, when the old constable was no longer active, and when, for a time, Lorraine attended to the affairs of the church, the secretaries were virtually the only people left with any experience of affairs of state, and they proved unwavering in their support of Catherine, who was the monarch in all but name. They were her councillors, ambassadors and friends. De Laubespine was her close confidant. They followed her restless movements, dealt with her correspondence, undertook her negotiations, seconded her efforts to make peace and, when it was done, helped to organize her festivities. Their letters provided a distressing commentary on the terror and suffering of civil war, and are all the more impressive since, largely detached from the quarrels about them, the secretaries understood what was happening. De Laubespine, at least, had written to his brother, Limoges, stressing Catherine's predicament and the isolation of the crown. He was aware that the flames were being fanned by the King of Spain—who was to do so much to perpetuate the strife in France; he deplored the degeneracy of the higher clergy; he saw that by 1561 the religious controversy was too far developed to be settled by anything swifter or less painful than time, and he did what little he could to drive home the gravity of the financial crisis.

No revolution can be simply tabulated or reduced to an easy formula; nevertheless, these four points—the isolation and the bankruptcy of the crown, the danger from Spain, and the corruption of the church, together with the problem of toleration—are fundamental to any analysis of the state of France in the early 1560s—but it is doubtful if more than a handful of de

Laubespine's contemporaries would have seen or expressed the situation in quite that way.

If such clear-sighted objectivity was not shared equally by all the secretaries, one or more of them at least always possessed it. During his own lifetime, de Laubespine's opinions were largely shared by Bourdin and, when he died, his mantle fell on Villeroy, who saw as clearly and reasoned as honestly. The other secretaries, so far as we know, were all moderates, and all equally steadfast in their loyalty to the crown. Even the Robertet cousins threw themselves into the work of mediation, although they owed everything to the Guises and were stricken by the news of the duke's death. All the secretaries were horrified by the outbreak of civil war and sympathized with Catherine's strenuous efforts to make peace, as Fresne said, in spite of the very heavens themselves and all the elements.

CHAPTER X

Changes in Personnel, 1564–7

HAVING recaptured Le Havre from the English and declared the king of age at Rouen, Catherine turned her attention to pacifying the quarrelsome nobles, concluding a treaty with England, and to making the long progress round France during which she would have a meeting with her daughter Elizabeth, if not with Philip II himself. She had had this in mind for three years.

It would be a mistake to suppose that because civil war did not break out again for four years, this was a peaceful interlude in France. They were, on the contrary, most unquiet years, dominated by such a degree of fear, suspicion and tension that the renewal of war must almost have come as a relief.

Even before Catherine returned in October 1566 from her journey round France, there was imminent danger of fresh internal strife. Coligny stood accused of the murder of Guise which, on both sides, produced emotions of violent intensity, and these were aggravated by lesser quarrels among their supporters. At the beginning of 1564 the admiral was said to be in arms and the Guises were raising forces, while the Spanish ambassador, sowing his evil seed in fertile ground, was going round from house to house busily intriguing.[1] The slightest incident could have touched off a serious tumult in Paris.[2] The king reserved this quarrel to his own judgement, deferring the decision for three years. When the time came, Coligny was declared innocent, but this did not end the trouble. More serious than the quarrel itself was the state of mind it had engendered. No agreement was considered binding because neither

---

[1] B.N., Mss. it. 1725, f. 47, 23 November 1563.
[2] *Ibid.*, f. 46, 23 November 1563.

side believed that the other would respect it. Each side claimed to act in self-defence and each placed a threatening interpretation upon the other's actions. Their constant complaints of the danger to their lives and property were well founded, for it is hardly possible to exaggerate the extent to which everyone with an enemy lived in fear and danger of sudden death, and fear proved to be a fruitful source of trouble. This breakdown of confidence was like the endemic plague which erupted periodically with sudden force. It was the dominant characteristic of the remainder of the period of this study and, together with an evil blend of hatred and ambition, was one of the chief causes of disintegration in France.

Bourdin's name is associated with the treaty of Troyes, 12 April 1564, which Catherine wished to conclude with England before taking the king and the court on her journey to Guienne. It does not appear, however, that he played a large part in the rather acrimonious interviews which had been taking place at irregular intervals for nearly eight months. De Laubespine, his son-in-law Villeroy, *secrétaire des finances*, and Limoges were, at one time, also involved, and one or two meetings with the English ambassadors took place in Villeroy's house. When, in March 1564, the English requested commissioners with whom to treat formally, Bourdin and de Morvillier were appointed. De Laubespine would undoubtedly have been named rather than Bourdin, both because of the importance of the negotiation and because it concerned his *département*, but he seems to have been absent from the end of December 1563 until some time in May 1564, and Bourdin was doing his work. Presumably he was ill or else had some private trouble, for he never went on holiday in the winter or with such important business on hand.

Bourdin and de Morvillier finally succeeded in inducing the English to accept Catherine's first and only offer of a mere 120,000 crowns in settlement of the long dispute over Calais, a triumph of bluff and obstinacy.[1]

---

[1] On this negotiation see La Ferrière, *Lettres*, ii, Introduction, xlii–xliii, and 'La Paix de Troyes avec l'Angleterre', *Revue des questions historiques*, xxxiii (1883); *C.S.P.F.*, 1563, 1564–5, *passim*.

The treaty signed, the court, a vast army of 8,000 horse covering several leagues, departed on the first stages of a truly fantastic itinerary through Champagne, Lorraine, Burgundy, Languedoc, Guienne, Touraine and Auvergne, ending at Saint-Maur-des-Fossés in April 1566.[1] This involved a colossal removal from place to place of the government of France. Not all four of the secretaries were with Catherine throughout the journey but, so far as we know, there were at least two and often three of them with her all the time, and they undoubtedly had to endure the greater part of the strain, fatigue, danger, discomfort, heat, cold and lack of food. Bourdin and the two Robertets set out with Catherine in April and de Laubespine joined them at Dijon in May. Thereafter they seem to have taken it in turns to be absent.

De Laubespine, Bourdin and Fresne were all present at the climax of the journey, Catherine's meeting with her daughter, the Queen of Spain, and her ministers, which took place at Bayonne between 15 June and 2 July 1565.[2] The letters in which de Laubespine referred to these important meetings appear to be based on personal knowledge, and are more authoritative than those of Bourdin who relied upon what was reported. De Laubespine, in spite of his suspicion of the Spanish, was fairly optimistic that something good might come of it. 'Up till now one can detect nothing but good cheer and hope of good results', he wrote to marshal Montmorency, gouverneur of Paris, on 16 June. 'You have known the Spanish for a long time and provided that we lose nothing over this it seems to me that we will have gained a great deal.'[3] Bourdin's attitude was more one of boredom and distaste for the costly celebrations which he

---

[1] On this journey see Abel Jouan, *Recueil et discours du voyage du Roy Charles IX*; Jean Bonnerot, 'Esquisse de la vie des routes', *Revue des questions historiques*, cxiv (July 1931); Pierre Champion, *Catherine de Médicis présente à Charles IX son royaume, 1564–6*.

[2] On this meeting see La Ferrière, 'L'Entrevue de Bayonne', *Revue des questions historiques*, xxxiv (1883). This gives an account of the meetings, although the suggestion that there was any connection between the interview at Bayonne and the massacre of St. Bartholomew has long since been discredited. Alva's instructions for the conference are printed on pages 483–4. See also B.N., Mss. it. 1725, ff. 87–90, 22 July 1565.

[3] B.N., Mss. fr. 3249, f. 92, 16 June 1565, de Laubespine to marshal Montmorency.

evidently thought excessive, and which interrupted business. 'Nous aurons tous nos esprits tenduz a caresses festins combats et dix mille sorte de festoiemens et gentillesses', he wrote to Pomponne de Bellièvre, ambassador in Switzerland.[1] 'Farces festoyements et triomphes . . . se continuent encores tous les jours', he wrote again a week later, and there was no news either of Elizabeth's departure or that the meetings had produced any other result than that of domestic pleasure. Thus Bourdin dismissed the festivals of Bayonne, which were among the most splendid and most famous that the Valois court ever contrived, and which have been immortalized in the Valois tapestries.[2] When it was all over, de Laubespine informed the marshal Montmorency that Elizabeth was leaving, that the two queens were happy to have seen each other, and that he hoped Franco-Spanish relations would benefit, '*quen est tout ce que nous remportons de ceste assemblee*'.[3]

De Laubespine departed from court about 20 July and Fresne followed him as soon as Bourdin had recovered from an illness, so only Bourdin and Alluye accompanied Catherine on the return journey.

We know very little of the secretaries' work and careers during the two years after the court returned from Bayonne. It moved about a great deal and strove to enforce the edict of pacification, which Catherine rightly continued to believe was the only hope for France. The little of their work that has survived was of the routine, administrative kind. Of Alluye we know almost nothing at this time, and of the rather enigmatic Fresne we hear virtually nothing more at all before his death on 22 October 1567. As for Bourdin, who had always been subject to attacks of illness, his health was definitely failing. He was away between February and June 1566, either ill or on holiday; he was ill in August and September and again in March 1567. He went home to Vilaine about 20 April and it is doubtful if he ever returned to court, for de Laubespine was still doing his work until shortly after his death on 6 July. De Laubespine himself, who had all this extra

[1] B.N., Mss. fr. 16013, f. 156, 15 June 1565, Bourdin to Bellièvre.
[2] *Ibid.*, f. 162, 22 June 1565, Bourdin to Bellièvre; F. A. Yates, *The Valois Tapestries*, pt. ii, ch. i.
[3] B.N., Mss. fr. 3249, f. 73, 1 July 1565, de Laubespine to marshal Montmorency. My italics.

L

work, was also nearing the end of his term, but without the prelude of recurrent illness and with no political decline. In fact he had never been more powerful with the queen-mother. When he departed on holiday after the interview at Bayonne, Catherine at once wrote after him asking him to investigate an outrage which had occurred at Tours, to find out what had really happened, to see what he thought could be done, and to report his findings to her, because, she said, he could do that better than anyone else, thus openly declaring her confidence in him.[1] In 1567 Sir Henry Norris, the English ambassador, informed Cecil that it was Catherine, de Laubespine, Limoges and de Morvillier who 'do all'.[2] He meant, of course, that they, primarily, made political decisions, and it is significant that not one of Catherine's chief advisers was a great noble. De Laubespine also continued to write to the ambassador in Spain, now Fourquevaux, as he had already done under Francis II.[3] On 13 May 1566 Catherine, writing to Fourquevaux, ordered him, in a postscript, to prepare a separate packet whenever he had anything to say about her marriage plans for Charles IX and his sister, Marguerite, besides other secret matters, to address it to de Laubespine and to give orders that it should be delivered to him personally. Everything else should be sent in the ordinary way and handed to the *secrétaire de la charge*, who was Fresne.[4]

De Laubespine, Alluye and possibly Fresne and the young de Laubespine were with the court at Meaux when the long-awaited storm burst in September 1567. The atmosphere of fear and suspicion, which had been so menacing before the journey of the court round France, was unchanged upon its return in the spring of 1566, and the next eighteen months proved to be nothing but an anxious prelude to the second civil war. The Venetian ambassador wrote that the hatreds between the two houses of Guise and Châtillon were once again as strong as they had ever been and might easily result in a serious breach of the

[1] B.N., Mss. fr. 15881, f. 201, 21 July 1565, Catherine to de Laubespine, draft by Fresne.

[2] *C.S.P.F.*, 1566–8, p. 171, 2 February 1567, Norris to Cecil.

[3] On Fourquevaux see C. Douais, *Dépêches de M. de Fourquevaux*, and G. Dickinson (Ed.), *The Instructions sur le Faict de la Guerre of Raymond de Beccarie de Pavie, sieur de Fourquevaux*.

[4] La Ferrière, *Lettres*, ii, 363, 13 May 1566, Catherine to Fourquevaux.

peace.[1] Mutual complaints of murder plots and armed gatherings were serious and continual, and none the less dangerous for sometimes being ill-founded. The unrest was greatly increased by trouble in the Netherlands and fear of the possible repercussions in France. During the summer of 1566, when there was trouble in Languedoc and alarm over an alleged protestant plot to murder the king, all the huguenot chiefs were expelled from Paris. The following year it became increasingly obvious that the protestants were preparing for war. Charles, who was very much alarmed by the situation both at home and abroad, raised a levy of 6,000 Swiss troops. This levy, the disfavour of the protestant leaders at court, and the supposedly definite coming of Philip II to the Netherlands, finally rendered peace in France impossible. Protestants everywhere were said to be arming and the situation was rapidly getting out of control. When the crisis of confidence had reached a point at which it could no longer be contained it was to de Laubespine and de Morvillier that Catherine turned for advice. In August de Morvillier had gone to Brussels to compliment the duke of Alva and the duchess of Parma on being appointed to govern the Netherlands. On his way back he learnt of a protestant plot to capture the court at Meaux, which he at once revealed.[2] This was by no means the first rumour of its kind, and Catherine sent for Castelnau, seigneur de Mauvissière, who later became de Laubespine's nephew by marriage. In the king's study he found, not the council, as he might have expected, but only de Morvillier and de Laubespine. Together they decided that it was necessary to take action and, after reconnoitring, Castelnau confirmed the immediate danger. The king was obliged to flee by night. He reached Paris safely, if not uneventfully, thanks to the protection of his 6,000 Swiss troops. The Florentine ambassador commented at this time on the great confusion, especially of women and baggage, adding that the kingdom was upside down.[3]

With the protestants outside Paris at Saint-Denis, doing their

[1] B.N., Mss. it. 1726, f. 21, 23 May 1566.
[2] Baguenault de Puchesse, *Jean de Morvillier*, 197-8.
[3] Desjardins, *Negs. Tosc.*, iii, 528, 29 September 1567. On the 'incident de Meaux' as it is called, see Delaborde, ii, 480 ff., which gives the protestant point of view, and Petitot, xxxv, *Mémoires du duc de Bouillon*, 56 ff.

best to blockade the capital by controlling the rivers, the
secretaries began to write to their provinces to order a general
mobilization. Alluye, who was deeply shocked by what had happened, wrote to Nevers, lieutenant-general in Piedmont, that
they were so busy they did not know where to turn.[1] The shock
and fright in general had been very great, for it had come to an
act of open war against the king's sacred person, which no pious
talk could erase or excuse.

Hostilities and peace negotiations opened simultaneously. De
Laubespine, the constable—who was well armed—his son,
marshal Montmorency and the seigneur de Gonnor, met the
admiral Coligny, cardinal Châtillon, d'Andelot and La Roche-
foucauld at Saint-Denis on 10 October.[2] The interview was
brief because of a big storm, but they met again the next day and
talked until the constable and Châtillon quarrelled. Catherine,
and certainly de Laubespine, were distressed by this failure to
reach agreement, which meant that they must once again endure the scourge of foreign troops on French soil. The king,
however, as well as the city of Paris, was anxious for war.
Catherine, who never gave up easily, sent de Laubespine back
to Saint-Denis on 26 October, this time with de Morvillier and
marshal Montmorency.[3]

It was de Laubespine's last mission. What took place we do
not know, but something which to him was very terrible, for
contemporaries believed that the experience precipitated his
rather sudden death. Upon his return he fell seriously ill. 'The
miseries', said Du-Toc, 'affected him so deeply that he fell ill and
died in the apartment that he had in the Louvre.'[4] Norris, the
English ambassador, also wrote to Cecil: 'At his [de Laubespine's] being at St. Denis the Prince [of Condé] burdened him
that he should seek his blood and that of others of the nobility,
and showed him a letter signed with his hand to that effect,
which thing he took so to heart as upon his return he sickened
and died.'[5]

[1] B.N., Mss. fr. 3221, f. 12, 9 October 1567, Alluye to Nevers.
[2] B.N., Mss. it. 1726, f. 152v, 12 October 1567; Du-Toc, 80.
[3] B.N., Mss. it. 1726, f. 159v, 31 October 1567; Desjardins, *Negs. Tosc.*, iii, 549,
22–29 October 1567; Baguenault de Puchesse, *Jean de Morvillier*, 199.
[4] Du-Toc, 81.
[5] *C.S.P.F.*, 1566–8, p. 374, 29 November 1567, Norris to Cecil.

During this last illness it was Villeroy, his designated successor, who did de Laubespine's work. On 6 November, Villeroy wrote to Fourquevaux in Spain regretting that he was the secretary responsible for that despatch on account of the illness of one of Fourquevaux's best friends, 'which has been such that two days ago it did not appear that he could ever do you service again'.[1] He had rallied a little, and Villeroy added that he still hoped he would recover. The young de Laubespine also wrote to Fourquevaux by the same despatch, curiously enough making no reference to his father's illness. He only said that if it were not that 'les passions sont si estranges de coste et dautre' everything could be peacefully settled. As it was, he foresaw a terrible battle.[2] It took place at Saint-Denis four days later. The constable was mortally wounded and, by this strange coincidence, he and de Laubespine both died on the same day, 11 November, after almost thirty years of service together. De Laubespine died in his lodgings in the Louvre, where Catherine visited and consulted him on his deathbed, and he is said to have made important recommendations for the good of the state.[3] Norris, writing to Cecil of de Laubespine's death, says that he 'made a very goodly confession of his faith contrary to that the papists did look for, being very penitent that to please Princes he had so long dissimuled. . . . A like confession of his faith made M. De Bourdin.'[4] But there is no other indication that de Laubespine died a protestant. In the case of Bourdin, Du-Toc tells us that although he was thought to have some leanings towards the new religion, he died a catholic, assisted by Claude d'Espence, rector of the University of Paris.[5] Catholic or protestant, they were both first and foremost good secretaries and good Frenchmen.

It seems almost symbolic that first Bourdin, then Fresne and finally de Laubespine should have died in quick succession in 1567, at the time when idealism, or even the pretence of it,

[1] 6 November 1567, Villeroy to Fourquevaux, seen at Messrs. Sotheby & Co., April 1957, sale catalogue no. 2081.

[2] 6 November 1567, de Laubespine, the younger, to Fourquevaux, seen at Messrs. Sotheby & Co., April 1957, sale catalogue no. 2081.

[3] B.N., Mss. Dossiers Bleus, 385, f. 77v; Petitot, xliv, *Mémoires d'Estat de Villeroy*, 21; Du-Toc, 81; Moreri, i, 484.

[4] *C.S.P.F.*, 1566-8, p. 374, 29 November 1567, Norris to Cecil.

[5] Gassot, 68, n. 3.

vanished, when the war ceased to be an aristocratic pastime and became almost total, merciless and bitter. Death, as a natural phenomenon, was accepted almost casually in the sixteenth century. These deaths which came at a moment of dramatic crisis, Fresne's on 22 October amidst the negotiations at Saint-Denis, and de Laubespine's together with Montmorency's the day after the battle of Saint-Denis, seem to have passed almost without comment, or, if there were any, it has not survived. Whatever feelings Alluye had for his cousin were concealed in his bare statement to Nevers, 'M. de Fresnes est mort il y a huict jours.' He added that de Laubespine was dying and Villeroy had been appointed to succeed him.[1] On 11 November he wrote again, 'Nous perdrons cest nuyct monsr. le connetable et cest apres dysnee avons perdu le pauvre monsr. de Laubespine'.[2] Writing only a few hours later from the same place, and showing by the simple words 'le pauvre' at least some degree of affectionate interest, it seems unlikely that Alluye would not have known, and would not have commented on a dying confession of the protestant faith. But we cannot be sure.

Bourdin was succeeded by his nephew, the young Claude de Laubespine—he was known as 'le jeune'—Fresne by Simon Fizes, and de Laubespine by his son-in-law de Neufville, better known as Villeroy.

Nicolas III de Neufville, seigneur de Villeroy, d'Allincourt and Magny, *ministre d'État* and *trésorier des Ordres du roi*, was the most distinguished of all the sixteenth-century secretaries and the one about whom we know the most. By the middle of the century the de Neufville family was no less eminent than the de Laubespine, but their origins had been humble. One source records that a great-great-grandfather, also Nicolas de Neufville, *maître d'hôtel* to Philippe duc de Bourgogne, had risen from being a fishmonger.[3] His grandfather, known as Nicolas I de Neufville, was a *secrétaire du roi* in 1507, *trésorier de France*, *secrétaire des finances* and *secrétaire de la chambre* in 1515. Under Henry II he was a member of the *conseil des affaires* and died in 1549. Villeroy's father, Nicolas II, *chevalier*, seigneur de Villeroy,

[1] B.N., Mss. fr. 3221, f. 47, 2 November 1567, Alluye to Nevers.
[2] *Ibid.*, f. 55, 11 November 1567, Alluye to Nevers.
[3] Nouaillac, 2, and n. 1.

d'Allincourt, Magny Bouconvilliers and other places, had a most distinguished career, was well known in court circles and had a wide knowledge of affairs. He was a *secrétaire des finances* in 1539, *trésorier de France*, lieutenant-general of the Ile-de-France, *gouverneur* of Pontoise, Mantes and Meulan, *prévôt des marchands de Paris* 1568, and *trésorier de l'Ordre de Saint-Michel*. He died in 1594, as a very old man.[1] He married Jeanne Prudhomme, daughter of a *secrétaire des finances*.

Born in 1543, Villeroy probably grew up at court, and in the company of his future brother-in-law, Claude de Laubespine, who was one year his junior. At the age of sixteen, in June 1559, he became a *secrétaire des finances* and Catherine began to employ him at once. In 1559 he was sent to Spain to implement some point in the treaty of Cateau-Cambrésis and later to Rome to treat of a matter of precedence between France and Spain.[2] According to Matthieu, Villeroy claimed to have been employed on the edict of pacification in 1563[3]—doubtless he was working for de Laubespine—and it was Villeroy who went to Paris and announced the news of the peace to the *parlement* there.[4] On 12 July 1567, the Venetian ambassador reported Villeroy as having returned from Scotland, adding that there had been no mention of what hope he had received from the Queen of England of a marriage with the king's brother, the duc d'Anjou.[5] He is also reported by the historian, Matthieu, to have been at the conference at Saint-Denis in 1567, probably to assist de Laubespine.[6] Matthieu said of the youthful Villeroy that 'son entende-ment alloit desia d'un air tout autre que les communs'[7] and when, in November 1567, at the age of twenty-four, he became *secrétaire d'État* in succession to de Laubespine, he already had eight years' experience. However, Villeroy had not grown up in the safe expectation of this office, for de Laubespine's *survivance* had been held by his son Claude. It was doubtless when Claude received Bourdin's office, before his father's death, that Villeroy began to hope that he might receive de Laubespine's. No one

---

[1] Nouaillac, 8, gives this date as 1598; Moreri, vii, 990, gives 1594.
[2] Matthieu, 15; Du-Toc, 131; Moreri, vii, 993.
[3] Matthieu, 14.
[4] La Ferrière, *Lettres*, ii, 5, 1 April 1563, Catherine to Messieurs les gens; *Mémoires de Condé*, iv, 331.
[5] B.N., Mss. it. 1726, f. 132, 12 July 1567.   [6] Matthieu, 28.   [7] *Ibid.*, 15.

held Fresne's *survivance*, but when he died on 22 October 1567, Villeroy was passed over in favour of Fizes, who was probably older. This was very likely a disappointment, yet not more than a week later, when de Laubespine was desperately ill, Villeroy was promised his office. In the letter to Fourquevaux of 6 November, in which Villeroy informed him of de Laubespine's illness and his hopes of his recovery, he also revealed his pleasure at having been promised the office of secretary, confessing that he wanted it, but had not wished to ask for it.

Villeroy could hardly have had a better start to his long, exemplary career. He was equally fortunate in his birth, upbringing, inheritance and marriage. He was also fortunate in his political associates, his father-in-law, de Laubespine, and his uncles, Limoges and de Morvillier. 'Rien que le temps,' said Matthieu, 'ne s'opposeroit à sa fortune.'[1] He enjoyed to an unusual degree that 'puissante faveur' which Matthieu says was indispensable for laying the foundations of a career at court. He had not to carve his own way there, for he was already known and, with his brother-in-law Claude, the poet Amyot and the comte de Retz, he was a favourite with the young Charles IX, who called him 'son secrétaire' and confided to him his secret thoughts.[2] It was to Villeroy that Charles is said to have dictated his *Livre de chasse et de vénerie* and various poems—for the young king was a pupil of Ronsard—among them the lines which he addressed to Ronsard himself—perhaps apropos some minor incident long since forgotten:

'Ton esprit est Ronsard plus gaillard que le mien,
   Mais mon corps est plus jeune et plus fort que le tien . . .'

to which Ronsard good-humouredly replied:

'Charles tel que je suis vous serez quelque jour
   L'Aage vole toujours sans espoir de retour.'[3]

Not only Villeroy and de Laubespine, but also Rennes—Villeroy's uncle by marriage—who had a pleasing voice, was in favour with Charles, who sometimes employed him to read poetry and made him *maître de la musique de la chambre*.[4]

[1] Matthieu, 13.   [2] *Ibid.*, 18.   [3] *Id.*
[4] Pierre Champion, *Ronsard et son temps*, 233.

Villeroy, who attended the celebrated Collège de Navarre, has been said to have had only a slender education. As he began his public career at the age of sixteen, his formal studies cannot have been prolonged. Richelieu said of him in his memoirs that he had 'grand jugement non aidé d'aucunes lettres', and Sully that he was not eloquent and had a bad style. Both were jealous critics. No one has ever claimed that Villeroy was eloquent but the Venetian ambassador, Pietro Duodo, said that the many letters which Henry IV sent out were all in Villeroy's style, and that without doubt he wrote better than anyone else when he wanted to.[1] Sully doubtless meant that Villeroy's style was not elaborate, larded with classical quotations or abstruse allusions. Matthieu records that Henry IV was 'amazed that such a head knew so many things without having been filled in his youth by that which is learnt from studying or drawn from books'.[2] But books, school and college are not the only means of education and Villeroy managed very well without them. He came from a highly cultivated family and grew up in a highly cultivated court, among cultured people of good taste. He stayed in houses and palaces which were gems of Renaissance art; he witnessed the court masques and entertainments and he heard the king's musicians. He could hardly have failed to absorb a certain culture. Besides this, he married the beautiful and learned Magdalene de Laubespine, who was much admired in the literary world and at court, and was considered by Ronsard and Desportes, who sang her praises—indeed they admired her whole family—to be a worthy daughter of her distinguished father. Magdalene not only wrote a great deal of poetry but also translated the epistles of Ovid. Jean Bertaut, who wrote her epitaph, said of her, 'et peut-on jugement tesmoigner de sa vie, que pour mourir hereuse il falloit vivre ainsi'.[3]

Pierre Champion has drawn attention to a manuscript volume of verses which, he said, belonged to the de Neufville family and was compiled and partly written by Villeroy himself as a kind of *tombeau littéraire* in memory of the two de Laubespines,

[1] Albèri, *Relazioni*, ser. i, app. 190.
[2] Matthieu, 53.
[3] There is a portrait of Magdalene de Laubespine in the Musée Carnavalet, Paris.

who were the subject of many of the verses.[1] These are mostly sonnets and other short pieces by Ronsard, Desportes, Jamyn, Nicolas, Delbene, du Bellay and Passerat in French, Latin, Spanish and Italian and copied in the *chancellerie*. Villeroy's signature appears on a fly-leaf under two lines in Latin, and so does that of Jules Gassot, his clerk, besides a certain amount of scribbling. Champion claims that Villeroy wrote the Latin lines and that he copied in a number of the verses in Latin,[2] one in Spanish[3] and one in Italian[4] and that in all his writing appears on some thirty pages. From this he concludes not only that Villeroy was a friend of the poets—which is well known— but also that he was conversant with Latin, Spanish and Italian, and that he was by no means as ill-educated as some critics have pretended. While Champion is wrong in thinking that Villeroy copied any of the verses in this volume, his other claims are unquestionably correct, for Villeroy's name frequently appears, both in the poems and in the dedications, and he would certainly have been familiar with anything written about his brother and father-in-law. Ronsard himself, in verses addressed to 'très vertueux seigneur Nicolas de Neufville' in 1584, mentioned the Greek, Latin and French epitaphs that Villeroy commissioned for the two de Laubespines and Jean de Morvillier.[5] This, in itself, does not prove his knowledge of foreign languages, ancient or modern, but, as Spain was in Villeroy's *département* from 1567, and Italy from 1579, it is most unlikely that he was ignorant of those two languages at least. Some of the poems were composed and others copied by Desportes, *secrétaire de la chambre*, who served under Villeroy, and others were probably copied by Gassot, Villeroy's chief clerk.[6] There was, in fact, no clear distinction between the cultured world of the poets and that of the *chancellerie* to which the *secrétaires* and *notaires* belonged. They lived and worked together at court.

Villeroy was undeniably more practical than imaginative, and more businesslike than artistic, but he nevertheless moved in this *société lettrée* and, if he were not a *grand lettré* himself, he

---

[1] B.N., Mss. fr. 1663; Pierre Champion, *Ronsard et Villeroy*.

[2] B.N., Mss. fr. 1663, ff. 16, 26v, 27, 34, 95, 95v, 96v, 118, 118v, 119v, 122v, 124, 124v.

[3] *Ibid.*, f. 36.   [4] *Ibid.*, f. 64.   [5] Schweinitz, 39.   [6] Pierre Champion denies this.

was a sympathetic onlooker, the friend and patron of the poets and 'a perfect humanist'.[1] As a young man he must have spent much time among the court poets, both because of his friendship with the king, and because of the inclinations of his lovely wife whose 'beaux yeux bruns' were praised by Ronsard, Desportes and Bertaut. Not only did Ronsard admire Magdalene, he also loved Villeroy and delighted in visiting him at his country house, 'ta belle maison de Conflans . . . qui regarde Paris . . . sejour des rois', where Villeroy had a fine library, founded by his father. Ronsard wrote with evident pleasure of the gardens, the woods and surrounding fields, the good air, the river and the orange trees.[2] It was there in the late summer, in September 1570, that he wrote a sonnet for Villeroy ('pour aborder une ile planteureuse'), only a few days before the untimely death of the young Claude de Laubespine, which distressed them so much. Villeroy also possessed another fine house at Villeroy, on the way to Fontainebleau, completed in 1560. Whether for Conflans or Villeroy, we find him importing rare and beautiful things for the house and garden, such as melon seeds from Italy, Indian seeds, and a *tapisserie de cuire doré* from Spain.[3] He also sent for marbles from Italy, and for tapestries and pictures from Holland, as well as for an instrument for emptying water out of a canal. The property of Villeroy was described in the early seventeenth century as one of the loveliest places in all the Gâtinais, two leagues from Corbeil. 'Il y a deux grands corps de logis . . . le château est composé de belles salles, galeries et chambres richement garnies . . . s'y voit aussi une très belle chapelle; au dela du château sont les jardins de plaisance ou se voit de belles fontaines, puis un bois fait en allées, dans lesquelles se voient de beaux cabinets de verre et des peintures excellentes.'[4]

Ronsard was not alone in 'adoring' Villeroy,[5] whose only fault, he said, was that of working too late at night. He was

---

[1] Pierre Champion, *Ronsard et Villeroy*, 36.

[2] Pierre Champion, *Ronsard et son temps*, 242.

[3] B.N., Mss. fr. 16092, f. 44, 18 February 1583, Villeroy to Maisse; Mss. fr. 16109, ff. 27, 59, 23 January, 10 March 1584, ff. 325, 387, 7 October, 8 December 1585, Longlée to Villeroy.

[4] Nouaillac, 287-8, n. He quotes the *Histoire générale des pays de Gastinois, Senonois et Hurpois* (1630).

[5] Pierre Champion, *Ronsard et son temps*, 240.

reassured when Villeroy, 'le bon pilote', was 'assis sur le haut de la poupe', for he was 'prudent, mesuré, pacifique apaisant les querelles, si obligeant aussi'.[1] Villeroy had that calm quality which inspires confidence and the belief that if he were there all would be well. All accounts join in a chorus of praise and affection for him. 'Qui ne donne des honneurs à M. de Villeroy,' wrote Matthieu, 'les refuse à la vertu.'[2] The Venetian ambassador Duodo said that Villeroy was loved by Catherine de Medici, Charles IX and Henry III, and was no less esteemed by Henry IV for his unbelievable excellence (virtù), which indeed was very great.[3] Villeroy had limitations but no real faults. He was perhaps a little solemn, with a slight tendency to self-righteousness, but he was well aware that in politics it is not sufficient to be good; it is necessary also to appear good. Matthieu recorded that he never tarnished his reputation by any act of disloyalty, and that he possessed 'l'ordre en ses discours, le jugement en ses escrits, la sincerité en ses opinions, la constance et le secret . . . aux resolutions'.[4] He acquired a very thorough knowledge of affairs, but he never pretended to know everything. He was neither servile nor arrogant. He was incredibly industrious and efficient but not precipitate. He did not allow work to accumulate and he did not make rash decisions out of spite, vexation or anger. He never put private before public interests, but embraced the king's business as most men would their own. Even those who were not his friends admitted that he had outstanding qualities, 'une grande integrité espurée de toute avarice, une grande modestie, une exquise proprieté et une vigilance incroyable'.[5]

There is some doubt about the date of Villeroy's marriage to Magdalene de Laubespine but it was probably in 1561 when they were eighteen and seventeen respectively.[6] They had two sons and a daughter, but only one son lived. In January 1567 was christened Charles, by his godfather, Charles IX, thus departing from the family name of Nicolas. He became the seigneur d'Allincourt, chevalier des Ordres du roi, gouverneur of Lyonnais, Forez and Beaujolais and ambassador to Rome. By

[1] Pierre Champion, Ronsard et son temps, 238-9.   [2] Matthieu, 5.
[3] Albèri, Relazioni, ser. i, app. 190.   [4] Matthieu, 8-9.   [5] Ibid., 56.
[6] Ibid., 13; Petitot, xliv, p. l., Notice sur Villeroy et sur ses mémoires.

his second wife he was to have a son, Nicolas, who became the
duc de Villeroy, a peer and a marshal of France. It was a source
of disappointment to Villeroy that he did not have more children, as he admitted to his relative Mauvissière[1] when con-
gratulating him on the birth of a son, 'mais je diray quil ne tient
pas a moy', he added sadly, 'au moins je le pensse ainsy'.[2]
Magdalene died at Villeroy in May 1596. In his will Villeroy
made provision for the rest of his family.[3] It is an engaging
document typical of its author in showing kindness, charity and
thoughtfulness. Besides leaving money to two religious foundations and requesting the simplest of funerals for himself, Villeroy
provided for his grandson's tutor, for his own chaplain, his
maître d'hôtel, and his concièrges at Conflans and Villeroy. He left
pensions for his cook, his wine steward, his coachman and even
for his serving boy, and money for a little lackey to be appren-
ticed for three years. Like du Thier, he had remained simple in
success.

Villeroy was buried in 1617 in the church of Magny-en-
Vexin for which he left 2,000 livres for structural repairs. Classi-
fied as an historical monument, it survives today very much as
Villeroy must have known it, a rare and delicate example of
Renaissance architecture. On the south side there is a triple
marble effigy of himself in middle age, wearing the order of the
Saint-Esprit, of his father, to whom he was devoted, and between
them, the celebrated Magdalene.

Claude III de Laubespine, Villeroy's childhood companion
and friend and later his fellow secretary, had a brief but dazzling
career—dazzling more for what he was than for what he did, for
his mere three years of office provided no extraordinary opportunities. Born almost literally into affairs of state, he added his
own brilliance and popularity to the immense, inherited advantages of the prestige, respect and goodwill which his name alone
evoked. He enjoyed as much, if not more 'puissante faveur' than
Villeroy, and was destined, like his father, for a great career. He
and Villeroy together would undoubtedly have formed a strong,

[1] Mauvissière married a niece of Villeroy's wife.
[2] B.N., Mss. Cinq Cents Colbert, 472, f. 33, 30 January 1571, Villeroy to
Mauvissière.
[3] B.N., Mss. fr. 17864, f. 252v, 26 August 1609.

unique and remarkable partnership in the state, and his early death was an incalculable loss. On 26 March 1560, at the early age of sixteen, he was granted the *survivance* of his father's office, and very likely began to work under him. On 23 June 1564, he left the court, which had stopped at Lyons, to take letters to Jean d'Ebrard de Saint-Sulpice, ambassador in Spain, and to tell him that everything in that protestant stronghold was quiet and orderly.[1] It seems unlikely that this, and various items of news, were the sole reasons for his mission. He may also have had to find out what he could about the prospects of a meeting with Philip II and Elizabeth at Bayonne. He was not away very long for he set out on his return journey on 31 July. In May 1567, he was again sent to Spain, ostensibly to obtain news of the health of the queen, Elizabeth, to discover whether Philip II was really going to Italy and to conclude a league with the pope and the emperor. Catherine was also anxious to know whether Philip intended to visit the Netherlands in person, to quell the rebellion there, and whether there might be any chance of the meeting with him which she still desired, in order to conclude a close alliance with Spain.[2] When de Laubespine arrived in Spain the king departed. He had to wait for three weeks before receiving an audience, and Catherine was annoyed.[3] He was back at court by 12 July and confirmed that Philip intended to go to the Netherlands in August or September.[4] Nevertheless, he did not go.

De Laubespine returned from Spain either just before or, more probably, just after the death of Bourdin on 6 July. It is therefore to be supposed that he had acquitted himself well, for he was immediately made a *secrétaire d'État*, and thus for four months he served together with his father. De Laubespine appears to have been very brilliant, charming and popular and much was hoped of him. He was a particular favourite with the young king Charles IX whom he must have known from early childhood. Something of an *enfant terrible*, a great huntsman and

[1] B.N., Mss. fr. 3899, f. 82, undated, de Laubespine's instructions.
[2] B.N., Mss. fr. 10753, f. 131, undated, instructions for de Laubespine, printed by La Ferrière, *Lettres*, iii, 33, n. He gives the reference to Mss. fr. 10751 which is an error.
[3] B.N., Mss. it. 1726, f. 122v, 25 June 1567.
[4] *Ibid.*, f. 132, 12 July 1567.

great card player, more given to gaiety and amusement than to hard work in his extreme youth, de Laubespine drew a sharp reprimand from his uncle de Morvillier, the *garde des sceaux*, that in spite of the king's favour, he had a greater duty to attend to his work than to his pleasures.[1] Devotion to duty, first and foremost, was almost a religion among the few leading families of public servants. Du-Toc says in de Laubespine's defence that he only mingled in the pleasures of his master as much as was necessary to obtain his confidence.[2] Nevertheless de Morvillier thought highly of his young nephew and is alleged to have said to him, 'mon neveu voicy un penible mestier [that of chancellor]. Vous estes du bois de quoy on fait les chancelliers et les gardes des sceaux; qu'il ne vous en prenne jamais envie; ce n'est pas celuy d'un homme de bien.'[3]

De Laubespine's death on 13 September 1570 at the age of twenty-six was deeply mourned, and his friends the court poets, Ronsard, Desportes, Jamyn, Passerat and Dorat, lamented in unison his youth and his charm.[4] Villeroy felt his loss as keenly as that of a brother, and he placed a marble plaque, with a Latin inscription, in the wall of the Couvent des Jacobins where his heart was laid with that of his father. Villeroy expressed his grief in a letter to his lifelong friend Bellièvre: 'You can imagine what good reason I have to feel afflicted, having lost my best friend with whom I had grown up and made my fortune. My consolation is to have learnt, after this too great loss, by how many worthy people he was loved for his virtue and goodness, having been mourned and lamented as much as anyone of his kind who has died for a long time past.' Villeroy determined to emulate his example, and to console himself by serving those who had loved him.[5] De Laubespine had married Marie Clutin, but he left no children.

Simon Fizes, *chevalier*, baron de Sauve in Languedoc, was the only one of this group of secretaries to come from the south of France and, apart from du Thier, he was the only one not related by blood or marriage to any of the other secretaries or

[1] Du-Toc, 120.
[2] *Id.*
[3] Baguenault de Puchesse, *Jean de Morvillier*, 219.
[4] Schweinitz, 39.
[5] B.N., Mss. fr. 16023, f. 125, 20 September 1570, Villeroy to Bellièvre.

councillors. In April 1569, when the court was at Metz, Fizes married one of Catherine's ladies, the famous Charlotte de Beaune, mademoiselle de la Boissière, reputedly one of the most beautiful women of her time, who is said to have been the mistress of Henry of Navarre—not to mention Condé, Guise, Alençon and Montpensier. Fizes began his career, so far as we know, as secretary to the *garde des sceaux* Bertrandi, in 1553 and, in the same year, he became a *notaire secrétaire du roi*.[1] He accompanied Lorraine to the council of Trent, and by November 1559 he was both a *secrétaire des finances* and also Catherine's principal private secretary, for which he received 600 *livres* a year.[2] It was Catherine who fostered his career and had him appointed *secrétaire d'État* upon the death of Fresne. He is a shadowy figure and it is impossible to form any clear idea of what he was like. He seems to have been involved—perhaps involuntarily—in a good deal of court intrigue which, in the absence of explanation, appears a little sinister. There is no doubt that Fizes played a greater part in public affairs than can now be demonstrated, but he did so more behind the scenes than in the public eye. He was close in Catherine's councils and, more than any of the others, her particular secretary for some years.

Although it was Fizes who was attached to Catherine, it was Villeroy who came closest to being de Laubespine's successor. He inherited de Laubespine's office, much of his prestige and potentially his importance; but he did not occupy a similar position at court. Charles IX was growing up and, although Catherine continued to be powerful for many years and influential all her life, nevertheless the centre of gravity in the state was beginning to shift. Villeroy and Catherine were, and remained, on close and excellent terms—indeed they often worked smoothly and successfully together—but he was not, so far as we know, her confidant in quite the same sense as de Laubespine had been because the circumstances were no longer comparable. Whether under Charles IX or Henry III, Villeroy was principally the king's secretary and, living in the mainstream of public life, he rapidly became a national figure.

[1] Du-Toc, 125; Moreri, v, 173.   [2] B.N., Mss. fr. 21451, f. 361.

CHAPTER XI

The Secretaries in War and Peace: I, 1567–70

WHEN de Laubespine died in November 1567, with a protestant army once more at the gates of Paris, Alluye, at the age of thirty-four, became the senior secretary, senior that is in order of appointment. He was older than Villeroy and the young de Laubespine but probably younger than Fizes. He seems to have played a more prominent part than the others in the events of the following year. Alluye was equally involved both in the negotiations for peace and in the abortive preparations for war which, as usual, were conducted simultaneously.

The negotiations broken off by Montmorency and de Laubespine before the battle of Saint-Denis were resumed at the end of November and others were opened by Condé in December.[1] As a result, Alluye was exceptionally busy and he complained of being so overworked that he hardly had time to eat and drink.[2] Besides negotiating, Alluye took the precaution of showering on Nevers, who was then besieging Mâcon, exhortations to hasten the junction of his forces with those of the duc d'Anjou, recently appointed lieutenant-general of the kingdom, because he knew that the enemy was taking full advantage of the interlude.[3]

Fizes at this time was serving Anjou in the field. He informed the court that Anjou and his advisers were in favour of making peace and returning to the edict of Orléans of 1563. This was because they feared that to fight would only result in the destruction of the king's army without preventing the enemy

[1] Delaborde, ii, 503.
[2] B.N., Mss. fr. 3221, f. 120, 16 December 1567, Alluye to Nevers.
[3] Id.; B.N., Mss. Cinq Cents Colbert, 24, f. 262, 2 December 1567, Charles to Anjou.

M

from joining forces with their German mercenaries. In fact the army was paralysed by camp quarrels, which Catherine did her best to compose. Commanded by the marshals Cossé and Carnavalet, it was believed by the Florentine ambassador that they were in close touch with Coligny to ensure that the army could not or did not fight. Confusion reigned, and anyone anxious for battle was kept well to the rear, a league or two away from the main body of the army.[1]

Peace was therefore the only solution. A further effort failed in January 1568[2] but, late in February, Alluye, Limoges, de Morvillier and the marshal Montmorency were appointed as commissioners to treat formally.[3] It is significant of the importance of Alluye that he took an active part in the negotiation which followed at Longjumeau, on a basis of equality with the other commissioners. Some time before 6 March he returned to court, greatly discouraged because the demands from the protestants (who meanwhile continued to batter Chartres) were exorbitant.[4] By 10 March, Alluye had returned to court a second time with a further set of excessive demands from the huguenots —who were fully aware of the king's weakness—including the insolent demand that he should pay the German troops they had hired to dethrone him.[5] Finally, on 13 March, the deputies agreed upon a truce[6] and, on 23 March, the 'little peace' of Longjumeau was signed. But everyone, wrote the Tuscan ambassador, acted in bad faith, because nothing was certain.[7] This was the general opinion.

---

[1] Desjardins, *Negs. Tosc.*, iii, 563, 2 January 1568.

[2] B.N., Mss. fr. 15544, f. 75, 19 January 1568; Mss. it. 1726, f. 183, 1 January 1568; Du-Toc, 116.

[3] B.N., Mss. it. 1726, f. 207, 27 February 1567/8; Mss. fr. 3410, f. 54, 27 February 1568, commission signed by Villeroy and de Laubespine.

[4] B.N., Mss. it. 1726, f. 208v, 6 March 1568; Mss. fr. 3410, f. 63, 4 March 1568, *articles bailles par le cardinal de Châtillon.*

[5] B.N., Mss. it. 1726, f. 210, 10 March 1568; Mss. fr. 3410, f. 57, 7 March 1568, memoir of Condé's deputies.

[6] B.N., Mss. it. 1726, f. 213v, 13 March 1568.

[7] Desjardins, *Negs. Tosc.*, iii, 573, 9 April 1568. See also B.N., Mss. fr. 6611, f. 47, 21 March 1568, the commissioners to the queen; Mss. fr. 3410, f. 60, 28 March 1568, *Memoire de ce que le seigneur d'Alluye aura a faire entendre a leurs majestes*; La Ferrière, 'La Seconde guerre civile. La Paix de Longjumeau', *Revue des questions historiques*, xxxvii (1885). He does not mention that Alluye was one of the commissioners.

With the end of Anjou's abortive attempts at campaigning, Fizes, who had been in camp, returned to court, where business was soon brought to a standstill by the illness of the queen-mother. A resumption of arms was constantly expected and the Venetian ambassador said that no one knew for certain whether they were at peace or at war.[1]

That summer the secretaries were lodged at Neuilly, while the court was scattered, because the king was ill in the château of Madrid, in what is now the Bois de Boulogne. This meant that the secretaries had to do a great deal of riding about in the heat. On 20 August, the king went to convalesce in Alluye's favourite residence, La Rocquette, 'a delightful little house', on the way to Saint-Maur-des-Fossés. This was a source of pride for Alluye and Gassot, who was then his chief clerk, and they both hoped that they might have an opportunity of preparing some ordinance so that they could put at the bottom, 'donné à La Rocquette'.[2] The arrival, on 27 August, of three successive messengers with the news that Condé and Coligny had left Burgundy in arms and crossed the Loire, heading for La Rochelle—which had never submitted to the king—more than fulfilled their childlike wish, but not in the way they would have chosen. From La Rocquette, they were obliged to write immediately to all the *gouverneurs* and lieutenants-general, to send out commissioners for raising troops and to place the whole country in a state of alert.[3]

Fizes once again accompanied Anjou to deal with all the civil and administrative matters that might arise when, in the first week of October, he left Paris to join the army at Orléans and go to the support of the duc de Montpensier in Guienne.[4] The young de Laubespine was in Catherine's service and Villeroy and Alluye both remained with the king.

We possess a remarkable account of the campaigns and

---

[1] B.N., Mss. it. 1726, f. 227, 9 May 1568.

[2] Gassot, 79.

[3] *Id.*; B.N., Mss. it. 1726, ff. 261, 262v, 28, 30 August 1568; Desjardins, *Negs. Tosc.*, iii, 576, 27, 30 August 1568. On the flight of Condé and Coligny from Burgundy, see also Delaborde, iii, 40 ff.

[4] There are many drafts of letters written by Fizes for Anjou during this campaign, B.N., Mss. fr. 15543-4-5. There are also many drafts of letters written by his secretary Ruzé whom Anjou—as Henry III—made a *secrétaire d'État* in 1588.

events of the next nine months, compiled and almost entirely
written by Villeroy himself.[1] It begins on 25 October 1568,
when Anjou and his army were at Amboise on their way to
Guienne, and ends abruptly in July 1569 shortly before Villeroy
went to serve Anjou in camp. Sometimes writing from day to
day, and sometimes in arrears, Villeroy made a digest of all the
incoming despatches, often giving a detailed picture of the complicated manœuvres of several armies, as well as the movements
of the court, and other events. There is no indication why Villeroy kept this 'Estat des affaires', as he called it. Probably it was
for some confidential purpose, since he not only analysed the
troubles from which France was suffering but also expressed his
own critical opinion with unusual frankness. From his early
youth Villeroy had been perfectly clear about the nature of the
troubles in France, the extent of the danger and its probable
results. He revealed his great admiration for Catherine and his
abiding respect for the throne and the person of the king. In
spite of the prolonged civil wars and the weakness of the last
Valois kings, this sentiment was still very strong in France, and
it is only in the light of it that the history of the sixteenth
century can be understood. The wars were in no sense a repub-
lican movement, and neither side ever attempted or intended to
undermine the prestige of the throne; their leaders were much
too anxious for its possession. Villeroy also revealed his private
determination to do his duty and to place his faith in God. This
gave him sufficient strength of purpose never to despair and
never to stop working for the restoration of peace and prosperity
in France. It was because of this steadfast devotion that Villeroy
survived over thirty years of revolution almost without enemies,
enjoying a respect, trust and admiration that were practically
universal.

    Some time between 11 and 16 November 1568, Villeroy was
sent from court to Anjou (who was in camp in the modern
'département' of Vienne) possibly in connection with the king's
intention to approach his army, or even to take the field in per-

---

[1] B.N., Mss. fr. 17528. This has been fairly extensively quoted by S. C. Gigon, *La
Troisième guerre de religion*, and is undoubtedly the most important single source for
that subject. There is another account of the campaign written by Gassot: Mss. fr.
5783. It covers the period August 1568 to November 1569.

son. During this time Villeroy's 'Estat' was written up for him in a different hand, probably by one of his clerks. He returned to court at Orléans on 21 or 22 November[1] with news of a considerable skirmish, but not of a pitched battle as had been hoped, and he wrote in his 'Estat' in his own hand a 'discours du camp', giving the military details.[2] A few days later Alluye was sent to Anjou's camp, apparently on account of some obscure trouble over the cavalry.[3] He returned to court, which was then at Melun, on 10 December[4] with the message that Anjou was expecting the vicomte de Joyeuse with reinforcements, and that Anjou and his officers thought the king ought to go to Blois and assemble all his forces there, while Aumale held the eastern frontier against the invasion of protestant troops from Germany.

It was after a meeting of the council to discuss the situation which arose in December, that Villeroy first expressed his private opinion in his 'Estat'. The danger of invasion, on the one hand by the prince of Orange in the north, and on the other by the German duc de Deux-Ponts (Zweibrücken) in the east, had kept the king within reach of Paris. At the same time lack of money, food and supplies, together with the terrific cold—snow, and rain that froze as it fell—had forced Anjou to withdraw. It was difficult, so it was said, to remain standing, let alone to fight a battle.[5] Villeroy found for once that he had 'un peu de loisir', and may have clarified his own mind by recording what he described as 'the opinion of a young fool with little experience of affairs'. There was one primary cause of the troubles in France, as he saw them: this was the personal quarrels between the house of Guise on the one hand, and the houses of Montmorency and Châtillon on the other. In his opinion, the root of these quarrels was ambition, which also caused the disobedience and temerity of those who took up arms against the king. Because of this, Villeroy believed that they were moving as

[1] B.N., Mss. it. 1726, f. 299, 22 November 1568.

[2] B.N., Mss. fr. 17528, f. 21.

[3] *Ibid.*, f. 25.

[4] B.N., Mss. fr. 3222, f. 71, 13 December 1568, Alluye to Nemours; Gassot, 13, gives this date as 8 December. Gassot was reliable on facts but not always accurate over dates.

[5] B.N., Mss. it. 1726, f. 311v, 22 December 1568.

fast as they could towards ruin and perdition. 'The sinews of war', he wrote, 'is money, which we lack', or at least they had not sufficient to retain those who, having served with the army for the customary term of five months, were inclined to break camp and go home. Nor had they enough to attract to the standard those who had not volunteered to serve in the first place. Thus it was impossible to keep an army together. The king needed 8–9,000 *livres* a month for his extraordinary expenses, and Villeroy had once hoped that such necessity would open men's eyes, and that the king would 'take action against so many calamities. . . .' But, he said, 'in truth I fear it is too late and that he has waited too long. For all the above nothing will be done. Thus with tears in my eyes I leave it to my readers to draw their own conclusions.'[1]

Villeroy was provoked to an outburst of anger by the inability of the duc d'Aumale and the duc de Nemours to agree to co-operate in the face of two invading armies, those of the prince of Orange and the duc de Deux-Ponts. Orange withdrew, and Deux-Ponts joined forces with Coligny, and then died. Villeroy complained in his 'Estat' of this 'grand malheur', by which he meant the mutual jealousy of the nobles, 'pour l'autorite et commandement'. For this they wasted time and opportunities alike, without pity for the people or the slightest consideration for the king's service. As the military situation grew more dangerous in March 1569, Villeroy returned to a longer discussion of this consuming canker, the importance of which he could hardly exaggerate, for the hatred, jealousy and conflicting ambitions of the nobles effectively sabotaged every attempted settlement of the troubles in France. 'Je tiens,' he wrote, 'pour le moins nostre bon maistre sera en bien grand hazard de perdre sa couronne.'[2]

On 25 or 26 March 1569, Alluye who, like Villeroy, had accompanied the court to Metz—where it was detained by a long and serious illness of the queen-mother—was despatched to Anjou[3] a few days after the arrival of news of the victory of Jarnac and the death of Condé. He went to congratulate Anjou, and

---

[1] B.N., Mss. fr. 17528, ff. 38v–39.   [2] *Ibid.*, f. 69v.
[3] *Ibid.*, f. 77v, Villeroy gives the date as 26 March; Mss. fr. 5783, f. 42v, Gassot gives 27 March; Mss. it. 1727, f. 14v, 30 March 1569.

took with him an edict by which the king allowed all those who had served Condé to return home upon swearing never again to bear arms against the king.[1] Alluye was also authorized to confer Condé's *gouvernement* of Picardy on the duc de Longueville; Villars[2] was to be created admiral in place of Coligny, from whom the office was confiscated. Finally, Alluye was to extend to Condé's widow a warm invitation to go to court; this was in the hope of removing her son from Coligny's influence. It was Alluye's last mission, from which he never returned to court. He remained with Anjou for about two months, taking the place of Fizes who went to Metz, where he was married in April.[3] Alluye was still in camp at Montbron (Charente) on 13 May when he wrote a memoir for Anjou to the king.[4] He went to Paris at the end of May or the beginning of June, on his way to meet the king, and died in his house in the rue des Poullies, 'to the very great regret of his majesty, of the queen, of monseigneur [Anjou] and of one and all'.[5] Alluye was only thirty-six and it seems likely that he had contracted the pestilent fever that was raging in Anjou's camp.[6] It was Brulart—whose daughter, Magdalene, later married Alluye's brother and heir François Robertet—who received Alluye's office of secretary, though probably not his *département*. All Alluye's other offices, as well as his property, went to his wife by virtue of her marriage contract, but she nevertheless neglected to pay his debts.[7]

The young de Laubespine accompanied Catherine when she joined Anjou's camp near Limoges at this time, and took up her quarters among the Swiss troops.[8] As Anjou no longer had any of the secretaries in his service, de Laubespine's letters to the king assumed an additional importance.[9]

[1] B.N., Mss. it. 1727, f. 14v, 30 March 1569.
[2] See app. iii.   [3] Gassot, 85.
[4] B.N., Mss. Cinq Cents Colbert, 24, f. 389, 13 May 1569, Anjou to the king.
[5] B.N., Mss. fr. 5783, f. 42v. Gassot says that Alluye died on 6 June, but he must have been mistaken, for the queen, who was near Limoges, had already heard of Alluye's death by that date. See the letter of 6 June 1569 from de Laubespine to the king, printed by Baguenault de Puchesse, *Les Opérations de l'armée royale*, 10. This letter was in the author's own possession.
[6] B.N., Mss. it. 1727, f. 49, 9 July 1569.
[7] Gassot, 84-5.
[8] Desjardins, *Negs. Tosc.*, iii, 590, 13 June 1569.
[9] Baguenault de Puchesse, *Les Opérations de l'armée royale*, has printed three of these letters, 6 June, 10 June (B.M., Add. Mss. 21405, f. 68, the end of the letter is

In a lively letter of 6 June, from La Souterraine near Limoges, written shortly after their arrival, de Laubespine seems to have been infected with something of Catherine's energetic enthusiasm and high hopes of seeing a battle for, after she had inspected part of the army, he assured the king that it was the biggest and finest that had ever been seen in France, even in the days of his predecessors. The queen, he said, had been so anxious to witness the battle which everyone was expecting, that they had followed the army. This they did with a reckless disregard for safety, since their outriders had actually scared some of the enemy. On Catherine's instructions, de Laubespine wrote again on 10 June to tell the king how they had marched with the Swiss to Limoges. During the march de Laubespine himself served as messenger between Catherine and Anjou, work which the gay and active young secretary probably much preferred to his writing-table. But, since 6 June, de Laubespine reported, the opportunity of fighting the enemy had been lost as the *reistres* had refused to march, because they were without wine, bread and fodder. Seeing this, two regiments of cavalry had also deserted. Having hoped every day for a week to be able to give battle, Anjou had left the baggage well to the rear. The troops had lodged in the open, de Laubespine informed the king, the majority of them dying of hunger and thirst, and cursing those whom they believed to be the authors of their misery. This was the real picture, now dutifully described, and the army no longer appeared so great or so fine as it had before their hopes had been dashed. The next letter contained a detailed description of the military position and warned the king that more and more of his cavalry was deserting for lack of money, food and fodder.[1]

In August 1569 the secretaries—except for de Laubespine, who was ill in Paris[2]—accompanied the king and Catherine to

missing) and 14 June 1569 (B.N., Mss. fr. 15549, f. 206). He has mistaken the identity of the secretary de Laubespine. He calls him François de Laubespine, seigneur de Bois le Vicomte, *président au grand conseil*. François was Claude de Laubespine's uncle, who died that same year, 1569. Catherine also had in her service another Claude de Laubespine, son of Gilles, a first cousin of the young secretary. He was a *secrétaire des finances* and *greffier du conseil* and lived until 1627. It was he who received the *survivance* of Villeroy's office in 1588.

[1] Letter of 14 June 1569.
[2] B.N., Mss. fr. 3344, f. 83, 12 August 1569, Villeroy to Nevers.

Amboise and on to Tours. Anjou came to see them there, to discuss his plan of campaign.[1] It was probably when he left Tours, on 3 September according to Gassot, that Villeroy went with him to camp.[2] De Laubespine and Fizes were both ill at that time, so Brulart was left alone at court to do all their work. De Laubespine appears to have been ill for some time and may, perhaps, have contracted something from which he never recovered, since he died almost exactly a year later. Villeroy remained in camp at least until 17 October and probably longer, because in the autumn both the king and Catherine themselves went to camp, or else stayed very close to it.

Though only a few of the letters and memoirs of this period have survived, Villeroy wrote to the king and queen every day, both officially for Anjou and on his own behalf. He kept them fully informed of the duke's well-being and progress, though it seems that not all of their despatches arrived, as they were both scolded by Catherine for not having written sufficiently often.[3]

In camp, where he witnessed the victory of Montcontour on 3 December, Villeroy experienced to the full the bitter truth of what he had written in his 'Estat', that lack of money would make it impossible to keep an army in the field. Bad weather—it was after all mid-winter—and lack of munitions increased the problem of desertion. In memoir after memoir and letter after letter, Anjou and Villeroy pleaded the urgent need for money and supplies. Villeroy did not hesitate to express himself to Catherine in very clear language. Thus, on 7 October, from Parthenay, he wrote that he had already asked her majesty for the supplies which were essential for her service, and 'I am obliged to tell her again', he repeated, 'that if she is not pleased to provide us with what we need, I foresee that this army will gradually dis-

---

[1] Marguerite de Valois, who accompanied her mother, recalls this journey with amusement. 'Portée des aisles . . . de l'affection maternelle', she said, Catherine made the journey from Paris in the record time of three and a half days, 'qui ne fust sans incommodité et beaucoup d'accidents dignes de risée, pour y estre le pauvre M. le cardinal de Bourbon, qui ne l'abandonnait jamais, qui toutefois n'estoit de telle humeur ny de complexion pour telles courvées'. Petitot, xxxvii, *Mémoires de Marguerite de Valois*, 35–6.

[2] B.N., Mss. fr. 5783, f. 45.

[3] B.N., Mss. Cinq Cents Colbert, 24, f. 407, 17 October 1569, Anjou to the king; Mss. fr. 15550, f. 74, 17 October 1569, Villeroy to Catherine.

integrate, for one and all are departing, some with permission and others without a word. Madam,' he concluded almost peremptorily, 'your majesty will please take the necessary action.'[1]

Neither Villeroy nor, so far as we know, the other secretaries played any direct part in the peace negotiations which began in November 1569 and dragged fitfully on, like the war itself, until August 1570. Some time in the first half of January 1570, while the other three secretaries remained at court, Villeroy accompanied by Gassot—who, since the death of Alluye, had become his chief clerk—went on a mission to Germany to conclude a negotiation for the king's marriage to Elizabeth, second daughter of the emperor, Maximilian II.[2] At the time, the purpose of his mission was kept secret, for the well-informed Venetian ambassador said that since he was a person of great experience and well loved by the king, it was supposed that he was going for some important negotiation, though it was not then known what it might be.[3] Villeroy and Gassot went to Innsbruck via Lyons, Turin, Mantua and Trent, and thence on to Prague where they were met by the fat duke Albert of Bavaria.[4] Matthieu considered that Villeroy learnt a great deal from this successful mission and that it was an excellent thing for him to travel and to see for himself countries which might become hostile to France.[5] By 7 April Villeroy was back from Germany bringing with him a portrait of the king's future wife, as well as an agreeable message from the emperor who was willing to accompany his daughter wherever and whenever the king wished.[6] According to Gassot, Villeroy reported to the king at Argentan in Normandy: a part of the summer was spent moving about and then the court returned to Saint-Germain in July. There, on 5 August, it was Villeroy who read out in council the articles of the peace. It was also he who drafted the

[1] B.N., Mss. Cinq Cents Colbert, 24, f. 402, 7 October 1569, Villeroy to the queen.

[2] B.N., Mss. it. 1727, f. 113, 17 January 1570; Gassot, 88–9.

[3] B.N., Mss. it. 1727, f. 113, 17 January 1570.

[4] Gassot, 91. Villeroy wrote a letter to Tavannes from Prague, B.N., Mss. fr. 4641, f. 62, 2 March 1570.

[5] Matthieu, 29.

[6] B.N., Mss. it. 1727, f. 149, 7 April 1570; Desjardins, *Negs. Tosc.*, iii, 619, 8 April 1570.

edict of pacification and signed the treaty on 8 August.[1] This peace was sarcastically known as *boiteuse et malassise*, after the infirmity of Biron who negotiated it, and the name of his associate. It was this treaty of Saint-Germain which set the fatal precedent of granting the protestants *places de sûreté*.

[1] La Ferrière, *Lettres*, iii, 325 n., 326 n. The articles of the peace are printed in the *Memoires de l'Estat de France sous Charles IX*, i, 7 ff.

CHAPTER XII

The Secretaries in War and Peace:
II, 1570–4

AFTER the exhausting summer of 1570 in which Villeroy
had first been to Germany and then concluded the peace
of Saint-Germain, he went home to his house at Conflans
on the Seine outside Paris. It was while he was there in September, enjoying a visit from the poet Ronsard, that his colleague and childhood friend, the young de Laubespine, died at
the Cloître de Notre Dame in Paris.[1] Brantôme wrote of de
Laubespine that he was, 'l'un des vertueux et honnestes
seigneurs de son temps et qui aymoit la noblesse . . . tant que,
quand il mourut en fort jeun aage et en sa grande beauté,
comme il estoit très-beau, ell'y perdit beaucoup. Il me tenoit
pour [un] de ses grands amis, et se plaisoit quelques fois à me
conter des nouvelles.'[2] It was Claude Pinart—who married de
Laubespine's first cousin—who succeeded to his office.

Pinart, and Brulart who succeeded Alluye, are the last two of
the twelve secretaries with whom this study is concerned.

Pierre Brulart, seigneur de Crosnes and de Genlis—sometimes
known as the seigneur de Crosnes—came of a family which,
according to Moreri, was ancient and illustrious both in law and
in the field. Brulart's great-grandfather, also called Pierre, was a
conseiller et secrétaire du roi in 1466, his grandfather, Jean, a
conseiller au parlement, and his father, Noel, procureur général du
parlement. His mother was Isabelle Bourdin, sister of the secretary
Bourdin.

Born in 1535, Brulart became a secrétaire du roi in 1557 at the

[1] B.N., Mss. it. 1727, f. 199, 17 September 1570; Gassot, 91.
[2] Brantôme, ii, 156–7.

age of twenty-two, and it was probably then that he worked under his uncle Bourdin, who is said to have trained him and fostered his career.[1] In 1564 he became *secrétaire des commandements* to Catherine, which was an important position. As Catherine was then ruling France, there was little of interest or importance which did not pass through Brulart's hands before 'issuing forth to take effect in the world'.[2] He succeeded to Alluye's office of secretary in 1569 when he was thirty-four but, according to Du-Toc, he also retained that of *secrétaire des commandements de la reine mère*, and managed to satisfy both the king and the queen.[3] This dual role may not have lasted, for during the reign of Henry III it was Pinart who became her especial secretary, while Brulart served the king.

In September 1571 Brulart married Magdalene Chevallier, by whom he had five sons and at least one daughter. His eldest son Gilles was his designated successor, but retired in 1588 when the three secretaries were dismissed. His daughter, Magdalene, married François Robertet, seigneur d'Alluye, younger brother of the secretary. Of Brulart's character we know little. Du-Toc said that he did much to uphold the royal authority, and there is no doubt that he served the king honestly and loyally at a time when dishonesty was commonplace and disloyalty would have paid. Like his colleagues, he warmly admired Catherine and yearned for a permanent peace in France, even at the price of a disadvantageous settlement. There is some evidence that he was not always very diligent when entrusted with his colleagues' *départements*, and the English ambassador, Sir Edward Stafford, complained of his cold nature and of his taciturnity. Stafford, who preferred to do business with Pinart, wrote to Walsingham on one occasion: 'to speak to Brulart . . . Pinart not being here, it were as good speak to a stock'. But he nevertheless considered him honest, patriotic and anxious for the well-being of France.[4] He was a competent secretary, if not outstanding, but he has been eclipsed by his

[1] Du-Toc, 147.
[2] *Id.*
[3] *Ibid.*, 148; Gassot, 84; Moreri, ii, 322.
[4] *C.S.P.F.*, 1583-4, p. 621, 17 July 1584; *ibid.*, 1584-5, p. 525, 5 June 1585; *ibid.*, 1586-8, pp. 259, 352-3, 24 March 1587, 14 August 1588, Stafford to Walsingham.

colleagues both because their work was more interesting and also because we know more about them.[1]

Claude Pinart, *chevalier*, seigneur de Cramailles, first baron de Valois, was the son of François Pinart, seigneur de Malines, *maître d'hôtel* to Charles duc de Bourbon, and grandson of a Jean Pinart who came from the south of Brittany.[2] He began his career as secretary to Saint-André, the favourite of Henry II. Du-Toc said that his master was in the king's confidence, and Pinart in the confidence of his master. There was therefore little in the way of 'belles intrigues' or important negotiations with which he was not acquainted.[3] After Saint-André had been killed at the battle of Dreux in 1562, Pinart succeeded in attracting the attention of the queen-mother. She made use of his services, came to know him well, and commanded him to follow her. This he did for the rest of her life. The Venetian ambassador said that he was one of her personal secretaries before he succeeded the young de Laubespine as *secrétaire d'État*.[4]

In November 1568 Pinart was sent to Lyons, to hurry the collection of taxes, which were urgently needed at court.[5] In January the following year, while he was still only a *secrétaire du roi*, he was sent on a mission to the duke of Alva in the Netherlands to try to obtain permission for the sale of French property there, or to cede it against a loan. The mission failed, but Pinart was able to give the king a good account of conditions in the Netherlands.[6] That same year, Catherine made him a *secrétaire des finances*. He had little hope of further promotion at the time, as all four of the secretaries were very young, but when de Laubespine suddenly died in September 1570, Pinart succeeded

---

[1] The secretary Brulart has often been confused with the *président* Brulart, his first cousin. He has also been confused with Pierre Brulart, vicomte de Puisieux et de Sillery, son of Nicolas Brulart, chancellor of France, and grandson of Brulart's first cousin the *président* Brulart. It is under Sillery's name that the bulk of the secretary Brulart's correspondence is catalogued in the Fonds français at the Bibliothèque nationale in Paris.

[2] B.N., Mss. Dossiers Bleus, 524, Pinart, f. 4v. Moreri says that Pinart was a native of Blois. This seems unlikely since his property was in the Ile-de-France.

[3] Du-Toc, 157.

[4] B.N., Mss. it. 1727, f. 199, 17 September 1570.

[5] B.N., Mss. fr. 3222, ff. 27, 86, 22 November, 20 December 1568, Charles to Nemours.

[6] B.N., Mss. fr. 17528, ff. 49v–50, 3 February 1569; Mss. fr. 3187, f. 138, 11 February 1569, Villeroy to d'Humières.

to his office. His marriage to Marie de Laubespine, his pre-
decessor's first cousin, admitted him to an *élite*, and probably
helped to further his career. If, unlike other secretaries, he had
not been trained by an elder relation in the certain anticipation
of high office, he was at least befriended by the good and influential Jean de Morvillier, from whom he may well have
learnt a great deal, like Bourdin, Villeroy and the young de
Laubespine before him.[1]

As a personality Pinart, like Brulart, never quite emerges
from the surviving evidence. The English ambassador, Sir
Edward Stafford—not necessarily a reliable witness—declared
that he was 'covetous in all extremity', and that he was
'nought', and 'gross-headed', but possibly only because he
thought him an 'enemy to all protestant princes'.[2] Far from
being 'nought', Pinart was clearly able, efficient and long-
suffering. Furthermore, he had risen by his own merits, without
anyone to help him in the struggle for survival at court. We
receive the impression of a quiet, unassuming person, who was,
like the others, content to do his duty and trust in God, and who
reacted to adversity with philosophical resignation. He had a
profound respect and admiration for Catherine, whom he
served with the utmost devotion. After the death of Fizes in
1579, he worked with her very closely, especially during her
many illnesses, the most intimate details of which were known
to him. He owed everything to Catherine and she expected
him to work with the same tireless energy and invincible spirit
that she herself possessed. She called upon him to follow her on
journeys which lasted for months and even years. She summoned him to her service at any hour of the day or night, at all
places and in all weathers. To Pinart she entrusted the principal charge of her enormous correspondence. She wrote a great
deal herself, dictated a great deal more, and left Pinart to compose the rest.

From the point of view of a study of the secretaries, the two
years which followed the peace of Saint-Germain in August
1570 were uneventful, although they were critical years for
France. De Morvillier, the secretaries' guide and mentor, is said

---

[1] Baguenault de Puchesse, *Jean de Morvillier*, 231–4.
[2] *C.S.P.F.*, 1583–4, p. 621, 17 July 1584.

to have dominated the council at this time, and wielded a great influence over Catherine. He was strongly averse to the policy of war in the Netherlands, which the admiral, Coligny, was then urging on the king, and he carried with him the opinions of Villeroy, Pinart and Brulart, though we cannot be sure about that of Fizes. Pressed by Coligny, Charles was induced to agree to a plan of campaign in the Netherlands, which he tried to keep secret from Catherine who was always opposed to war.[1] Charles employed Fizes as his secretary in this matter, enjoining him to secrecy. But, if Fizes were high in the king's favour, he was equally so in Catherine's, and his name is associated with that of Albert de Gondi, duc de Retz, who tried to mediate between Catherine and the king.[2] Indeed, Fizes and de Retz informed Catherine, who was absent from court, of the king's decision to go to war in the Netherlands. She returned with all speed and, in the violent scene which followed, Fizes excused himself as best he could, and Charles forgave him.[3] The episode illustrates the embarrassing predicament in which disunity between Catherine and the king could place the secretaries. We are ignorant of Fizes' motives in informing Catherine of what had taken place in the king's councils, but he does not seem to have suffered as a result of the incident.

Fizes is the only one of the secretaries who may have been involved in the massacre of Saint Bartholomew, which took place soon after this crisis at court.[4] According to Du-Toc, he was the only secretary to have advance knowledge of the massacre, and all the secret despatches concerning it were entrusted to him.[5] This statement must be treated with the utmost reserve, since there is no kind of proof that the massacre was ever planned or ordered, or that any such despatches ever existed. But, if Fizes were commanded to prepare despatches concerning a massacre, it would have been virtually impossible for him to refuse. The

[1] See on this subject, H. Hauser, *François de la Noue.*

[2] Desjardins, *Negs. Tosc.*, iii, 769, 22 April 1572.

[3] Delaborde, iii, 409–11; *Memoires de l'estat de France sous Charles IX*, i, 251.

[4] Much has been printed about the massacre, a great deal of which is propaganda. See H. Butterfield, *Man on his Past*, ch. vi, and S. England, *The Massacre of Saint Bartholomew*. The most interesting comments are made by Gassot (97 ff.). This event must be considered in its context and as an act of war, not as a sudden, isolated outrage.

[5] Du-Toc, 125.

secretaries might argue, protest and advise, but there is no recorded instance of their declining to obey an order.

Villeroy and Pinart were also at court at this time, and we learn some interesting information about Villeroy from Gassot, his clerk. In the evening of the day on which the admiral was wounded, the king sent Villeroy to see him, presumably to learn how he was. Villeroy returned about seven o'clock and, during supper, he told the king that the admiral's wound was not serious ('qu'il n'en auroit que le mal') and that he was being attended by a good surgeon. 'We were seated at the end of the lower table', says Gassot, who was there, and with them was Charron, one of the king's valets, a gay fellow who was a good friend of Villeroy. Having heard what Villeroy said to the king, Charron informed the company that the almanac of the celebrated astrologer Nostradamus contained the entry, 'pris en dormant' for that night, 24 August 1572. Gassot never learnt how the massacre came about, and we may safely assume that Villeroy shared his ignorance, for if one of them had known, the other would have known too.[1]

The massacre of Saint Bartholomew precipitated a further resort to arms over much of the country, including the protestant stronghold of La Rochelle. A siege of this town was therefore decided upon. Fizes once again took the field with the duc d'Anjou when he left Paris as lieutenant-general, on 14 January 1573, and remained with him at camp for six months, until peace was concluded in July. His correspondence and that of Villeroy has unfortunately been lost. Pinart and Brulart wrote regularly to Anjou, sending him news from court and copies of the outgoing despatches. Sometimes Pinart prepared letters for Anjou, on Catherine's instructions, and sent them to La Rochelle for him to sign.

Early in May 1573, Pinart was sent to La Rochelle to 'travail for an end' to hostilities.[2] This was desirable for many reasons, but particularly on account of the candidature of Anjou for the throne of Poland, and because of the great and dangerous disorders in the royal camp. Anjou's younger brother Alençon was there with Henry of Navarre, the young Condé, and Bouillon.

[1] Gassot, 103.
[2] C.S.P.F., 1572-4, p. 330, 3 May 1573, Dale to Burghley.

N

The chief purpose of these turbulent young princes was not the overthrow of the king's enemies, but the overthrow of his brother and heir Anjou, and the organization of a revolution, but their own indiscretions betrayed them to Anjou.[1] Because of this, Pinart was authorized to tempt the rebels with great offers of privileges and full religious liberty if they would acknowledge the king and admit a royal garrison. But, owing to the incompetence of the king's forces and the divisions in his camp, the affairs of the rebels were going well. They therefore felt able to demand that all protestants everywhere be included in the agreement. For this reason, Pinart's mission was unsuccessful. On his way home through areas in his own *département*, he made arrangements to have ammunition for Anjou sent by water to Châtellerault, and to establish a depot at Saumur. He returned to Fontainebleau on 13 May and—in Dr. Dale's picturesque phrase—the court fell into 'a damp' about the failure of his mission.[2]

At the end of the month, Brulart went to La Rochelle bearing news of the election of Anjou to the throne of Poland, together with most generous articles of pacification, and instructions to try to compose the quarrels between Anjou and Alençon— something which no one ever succeeded in doing.[3] He found that the situation had deteriorated still further; he was no more successful than Pinart and he returned to court on 9 June. The king was out hunting too late to consider his message that night, but no time was too late for Catherine, who dragged Pinart from his bed to write to Anjou in the middle of the night.[4]

The others having failed, it remained for Villeroy to go to La Rochelle. Many times he ventured right into the rebel territory, not without danger since the siege continued with renewed force, and Anjou himself narrowly escaped death.[5] After nearly a month of negotiation, Villeroy brought about an agreement

[1] Petitot, xxxvi, *Mémoires de Cheverny*, 49–50; *ibid.*, xxxv, *Mémoires du duc de Bouillon*, 81 ff.; Hauser, *La Noue*, 61 ff.

[2] B.N., Mss. fr. 15557, f. 235, 12 May 1573, Pinart to Anjou; Desjardins, *Negs. Tosc.*, iii, 877–8, 18 May 1573; *C.S.P.F.*, 1572–4, pp. 330, 336–7, 3, 16 May 1573, Dale to Burghley.

[3] *C.S.P.F.*, 1572–4, p. 350, 31 May 1573, Dale to Burghley; Desjardins, *Negs. Tosc.*, iii, 879, 31 May 1573.

[4] B.N., Mss. fr. 15536, f. 54, 9 June 1573, Pinart to Anjou.

[5] B.N., Mss. it. 1728, f. 38, 20 June 1573.

which included the towns of La Rochelle, Nîmes and Montau-
ban, but which left protestants in other parts of the country still
in arms.[1]

The following months were spent in preparations for Anjou's
departure for Poland, and the secretaries with the entire court
accompanied him towards the frontier. On the way, the king
collapsed at Vitry with the illness from which he never recovered. This caused an alteration in his itinerary, which alone
delivered him from the treachery of Alençon. Having failed to
murder Anjou at La Rochelle, Alençon was now planning to
despatch the king and seize the throne in his brother's absence.
There was no lack of flatterers at court to urge him to declare
himself the leader of the rebels. The situation in France could
hardly have been more perilous: the king was dying, the heir
was absent, and half the provinces were in arms. In these circumstances Alençon prepared a *coup d'état* at court, which was intended to coincide with a general rising on 10 March 1574, but
the plan miscarried. The king left Saint-Germain precipitately
for the greater safety of Vincennes and, in the confusion which
followed, Alençon admitted his complicity. He and Navarre
were confined to the château where they spent their time planning to escape. Though the conspiracy had miscarried, it was
not abandoned, and the corollary to the events at Saint-Germain was the arrest, and imprisonment in the Bastille, of the
marshals Cossé and Montmorency. Though this was unquestionably essential for security, it had the effect of paralysing all
negotiation with the protestants who were in arms in most parts
of the country.[2]

To meet this alarming situation, Catherine hoped to be able
to negotiate separate agreements with the protestant leaders, La
Noue in the west and Damville[3] in the south. This would have
had the effect of pacifying part of the country and separating
the genuine protestants from the *politiques* and the *malcontents*,
thereby reducing Alençon's following. Catherine, who never

[1] B.N., Mss. it. 1728, f. 43, 2 July 1573.
[2] Petitot, xxxv, *Mémoires du duc de Bouillon*, 91 ff., and xxxvii, *Mémoires de Marguerite de Valois*, 57 ff.; Desjardins, *Négs. Tosc.*, iii, 903 ff., 1 March 1574; La
Ferrière, 'Les Dernières conspirations du règne de Charles IX', *Revue des questions
historiques*, xlviii (1890); Cimber et Danjou, viii, *Discours de l'entreprise de Saint-
Germain*, 107 ff.   [3] See app. iii.

shrank from the impossible, chose Pinart and Villeroy to undertake this insuperable task. Pinart left on 27 March 1574 for
talks with La Noue in Poitou or Guienne, and Villeroy, with
Saint-Sulpice, left on 2 April to try to see Damville, *gouverneur* of
Dauphiné and Languedoc.

Pinart travelled extremely fast, reaching Loudun (Vienne) by
31 March, where he showed his instructions to Montpensier
who was assembling a royal army. It was not easy to contact
La Noue who was constantly moving about from place to place
and who was in no mood for negotiating. Pinart therefore found
himself in the curious position of following an enemy army in an
attempt to negotiate with its commander, while Montpensier
was assembling forces with which to oppose it. One of the things
which Pinart was to offer was that the king should come in person, and hear and receive his people's grievances in an assembly
of the local States. But the king lay dying, and the future was all
uncertain. It is greatly to Pinart's credit that he managed to see
La Noue at all. That he should have been back in court by
20 May with 'minimal results' was only to be expected.[1]

For his part, Villeroy wrote to Damville on 23 February 1574
to announce his visit and request a safe-conduct or such escort as
might be necessary beyond Lyons. The purpose of his mission,
as described in his instructions, was to confer with the protestants and if possible to negotiate a good peace. He and Saint-
Sulpice were also provided with a second, secret instruction,
containing details of concessions which they might make if
necessary. The king also offered to visit this province in person.
Failing a peace, Villeroy was to conclude a truce, and arrange
for Damville to lead a protestant deputation to court, a proposi-
tion which was hardly realistic.[2]

Villeroy and Saint-Sulpice went no further than Avignon,
and Damville refused to meet them. They understood why when
they received a curious, autograph letter from the king, informing them of the arrest of the marshals Cossé and Montmorency,
an event which was already known to Damville. By the same

[1] B.N., Mss. fr. 15559, *passim*; Institut de France, Mss. Godefroy, 258, f. 143,
7 April 1574, Pinart to Alençon; B.N., Mss. it. 1728, ff. 221, 303, 28 February,
20 May 1574.
[2] B.N., Mss. fr. 20507, f. 149, 23 February 1574, Villeroy to Damville; Mss.
n.a.f. 7178, f. 83, 26 February 1574, f. 126, undated.

messenger, they received a commission under the great seal to arrest Damville in the king's name. They were astounded at this request, being unarmed, in Damville's *gouvernement*, surrounded by his forces, 'not having any reasonable grounds for hoping that this was something which we could effect . . . without any forces or other means with which to do it'. On the contrary, wrote Villeroy in his memoir, whereas they were supposed to be arresting Damville, it would have been very easy for Damville to arrest them.[1] They lingered, dangerously no doubt, for three weeks, warning the local authorities and the inhabitants of Dauphiné and Languedoc no longer to recognize or obey Damville as their *gouverneur*.

When they rejoined the court in June, they found that the king had died.[2] Villeroy's grief, which he expressed to his friend Bellièvre, was clearly genuine: 'if I was distressed not to have been able to make peace in Languedoc and Dauphiné, I was very much more distressed on my return to find my master dead, for I had special reason to be, more than the others'.[3] Brantôme testifies to Villeroy's particular intimacy with Charles, by whom he was 'tant ayme et chéry', and regretted that he never wrote a commemorative book on the young king. Charles had recommended Villeroy to Anjou, upon his departure for Poland, and dying, he recommended him again, this time to his mother.[4]

Pinart, Brulart and Fizes were all with the court at Vincennes when Charles died. Fizes was one of the witnesses when, in the presence of Alençon and Navarre—who were under detention—Charles declared Henry of Anjou his rightful successor, and his mother the regent until Anjou returned. According to Du-Toc, it was Fizes whom Charles commanded to prepare all the necessary papers for declaring and establishing the regency, which was ratified by the *parlement*.[5] All three secretaries took immediate steps to inform the provincial authorities.

[1] Petitot, xliv, *Mémoires d'Estat de Villeroy*, 24-5. Villeroy writes about this mission at some length because of the fatuous accusation, invented later, that he was sent to Languedoc to murder Damville.

[2] Charles IX died in the afternoon of 30 May 1574, of pulmonary tuberculosis. Gassot, 125-6, says that though not quite twenty-four he was lined and bent.

[3] B.N., Mss. fr. 15903, f. 75, 17 June 1574, Villeroy to Bellièvre, quoted by Nouaillac, 44, n. 1.

[4] Brantôme, v, 285; Matthieu, 31.

[5] Du-Toc, 127; Brantôme, v, 268-9.

By the death of Charles IX in 1574, the secretaries had already for some years been engaged in that struggle to make, execute and keep the peace which was to be their constant occupation until 1588. Time had passed, and the *dramatis personae* had changed, but the quarrels between the rival noble houses and the adherents of the two religions were still unresolved. Besides this, the activities of the king's youngest brother Alençon added a new, and if possible even graver cause for anxiety. Alençon was ambitious, vain, undisciplined and unscrupulous. He achieved nothing because his incompetence was equalled only by his infirmity of purpose. But already he had tried to murder his brother, the heir presumptive, and twice conspired against his other brother, the king. He was one of the principal sources of trouble and, throughout the next ten years until he died in 1584, he remained a living threat to the king's safety and the peace of France. The secretaries—and more particularly Villeroy—had repeatedly to grapple with the crises that he caused.

PART FOUR

The Secretaries under Henry III

CHAPTER XIII

The Rise of Villeroy, 1574–7

VILLEROY'S services had already become so necessary, wrote Matthieu, that after the death of his first master he was no less cherished by the second.[1] Villeroy went with Fizes and Cheverny, a future chancellor of France, to meet the king at Turin, on his return from Poland, and to explain the affairs of his new kingdom.[2] The king, said Villeroy, received them 'très-humainement'. Villeroy had already enjoyed Henry's support, favour and protection in the past. Now, bearing in mind how his brother, the late king Charles, had appreciated him and recommended his services, Henry reserved for Villeroy an especially warm and gratifying welcome, more than any of them had presumed to hope for.[3] It was a disappointment for Brulart that he was not sent to Turin, for he had hoped to share the honour of going to meet the king.[4] Instead, he left Paris a few days after Catherine, and the whole court assembled at Lyons where the king arrived on 6 September 1574.[5]

The secretaries are generally said to have suffered a setback at the beginning of Henry's reign, owing to the changes which he quickly made in the customary manner of granting gifts and concessions, which had formerly been left very much to the secretaries' own discretion.[6] The setback, however, was more apparent than real, and cannot be regarded as a calculated

[1] Matthieu, 32.
[2] Petitot, xxxvi, *Mémoires de Cheverny*, 64.
[3] Petitot, xliv, *Mémoires d'Estat de Villeroy*, 27.
[4] B.N., Mss. fr. 15903, f. 116, 13 July 1574, Brulart to Bellièvre.
[5] Catherine took Alençon and Navarre with her. They were still under detention since the conspiracy of Saint-Germain, but were released by Henry III.
[6] Petitot, xliv, *Mémoires d'Estat de Villeroy*, 27–8, 'le changement de la forme ancienne des expeditions des dons et bienfaicts'.

blow to the secretaries' well-earned prestige. Nor did it mean
that the king held any adverse opinion either of their office or of
their persons. He had worked with them before his accession and
knew them well—particularly Fizes and Villeroy—and he was
soon to make greater use of their services than any of his predecessors had done. He at once admitted them to his council
whereas, even of the princes of the blood, only the cardinal of
Bourbon and the duc de Montpensier were included.[1] Nevertheless, in September 1574 the king commanded that nothing
was to be granted or despatched until he had seen and signed
the petitions himself, and for this purpose they were presented to
him in the presence of the secretaries, who received his instructions.[2] Thus they were deprived of the discretionary power,
allowed them by Charles IX, to bestow or to withhold benefits in
the king's name.

According to Saint-Simon, it was on account of Villeroy's
favour and importance ('en sa considération') that, from the
time of his appointment under Charles IX, the secretaries had
begun to sign all kinds of documents for the king ('toutes sortes
d'expéditions'), but Henry III wished, at first, to exercise a
strict control over them himself.[3]

Villeroy claimed that these powers had been exercised with
discretion and integrity, and his comments on their cancellation
are extremely revealing. Indeed, it was one of the rare occasions
upon which, by implication, he criticized the king. He said that,
far from thereby eliminating abuses which the secretaries or
their clerks were alleged to have committed, the king abolished
the only controls which existed over the granting of petitions.
His explanation was that Charles IX, following the example of
his predecessors, had granted all petitions, but passed them on
to one of the secretaries, who refrained from implementing them
if they were contrary to the law. Otherwise he entered them on
a special roll, which was read to the king in the presence of his
mother and anyone else he chose to summon—which shows,
incidentally, that in spite of precise ordinances, the composition
of a council was still variable. The king would then declare his
will (which might be written in the margin) and sign the roll,

[1] Petitot, xxxvi, *Mémoires de Cheverny*, 66.
[2] *Ibid.*, 67; Gassot, 130.   [3] De Luçay, 19.

Nicolas de Neufville, seigneur de Villeroy, as a young man

and the secretary drew up and despatched the necessary papers to implement the gift or concession. In this way the law and the secretaries stood between the king and the possible discontent of his subjects and, being held entirely responsible for their decisions, the secretaries were scrupulously careful about what they signed. Villeroy recalled that one day the comte d'Escars brought him a petition signed by the king. It granted the count permission to tax the people of his estates to pay for a number of soldiers to guard his château. Villeroy, acting as he always had, refused to implement this petition because, as he said rather tartly, they had not yet taken to having private houses guarded at the expense of the people. But d'Escars complained to the king, and Villeroy received a sharp reprimand. He was accused of wanting to control the king, informed that he and his colleagues were to desist from interfering and that they were to act promptly upon any order signed by the king. This, Villeroy said, they did from then on. As a result, he disclaimed any responsibility for orders of this kind which he signed and despatched under Henry III, whereas for those of Charles IX, he accepted it in full.[1] No doubt the same was true of his colleagues.

Besides this loss of control over petitions, the secretaries were, for the moment, forbidden the king's room. Temporarily, they received their orders from Cheverny, who was high in favour, having kept a close watch on Henry's interests during his absence in Poland.[2] The humiliation which Villeroy felt at this time is reflected in a letter to Nevers, *gouverneur* of Piedmont, in which he wrote, 'considerez Monseigneur que je suis un pauvre serviteur qui suis tenu . . . dobeir au pied de la lettre a ce quil m'est commande'.[3] Nevers had been commanded, against his will, to evacuate three towns in Savoy, and Villeroy wished to excuse himself for sending what he knew Nevers would consider an unsatisfactory form of exoneration (*descharge*).[4] But it was not for long that Villeroy or his colleagues had any reason to feel like this.

[1] Petitot, xliv, *Mémoires d'Estat de Villeroy*, 27–30.
[2] La Ferrière, *Lettres*, v, 85 n.
[3] B.N., Mss. fr. 3315, f. 55, 11 October 1574, Villeroy to Nevers.
[4] Henry sent Fizes to Nevers with a commission to return three towns, but there are no details of his work in Italy. B.N., Mss. fr. 3315, f. 33, 10 October 1574, Henry to Nevers.

Historians have attached importance to this question of the petitions because of the relatively long passage which Villeroy devoted to it in his memoir, and possibly also because it is one aspect of procedure upon which we have an unequivocal statement. Villeroy himself attached importance to it because Henry's alteration of the old procedure was contrary to his own best interests, and destroyed a means whereby the secretaries could render him good service. He also deplored the new regulation because the king decreed that no one might make any request or present any petition except for himself alone. The result was that those about the king were in an unjustly advantageous position and became the objects of such violent envy as to have caused, in Villeroy's estimation, a large part of the troubles of Henry's reign. How long the new procedure lasted in practice, we cannot tell. Henry certainly continued to make gifts that were unreasonable and contrary to the law, but they were probably not made in this way.

If the secretaries were mortified at the time by the apparent implication that they could not be trusted, Villeroy was perfectly well aware when he wrote his memoir in 1589—though possibly not in September 1574—that the regulation had not reflected any positive distrust of the secretaries but had proceeded from the desire which the king experienced at that moment to control and direct his affairs himself. Henry III began his reign with an access of energy, rising early and working hard, treating with reserve, if not suspicion, those whose authority had increased in the immediate past, and unwisely preferring the immature councils of a few youthful intimates. In his defence, it should be remembered that not only was his throne menaced, but also his life, and it was necessary for him to proceed with caution. This mood was of brief duration, but it was characteristic. The episode foreshadowed a future discontent which was to spring from Henry's increasingly extravagant behaviour. In fact the secretaries had never been so close to the king as they were under Henry III and it was therefore natural that they should have been among the first to suffer from what they must soon have realized was one of the fundamental contradictions in his character: his spasms of energy, accompanied by an almost obsessive desire to do everything himself, alternating

with a longing—already apparent—for seclusion from the publicity of life at court. This often led him to the opposite extreme
of abandoning the government to his ministers, even in times of
crisis.

In his early youth Henry had promised well and much was
expected of him. The campaign of 1568-9 earned him a military
reputation which, however, was largely misplaced, for he was in
no sense a man of action, and his disinclination to action increased with time and ill-health to almost pathological proportions. Contemplative and thoughtful, Henry had excellent
qualities of mind and intellect, greatly superior to those of his
father or his brothers, but he lacked the qualities of character
and physique which are necessary for sustained effort. He had
no realistic grasp of cause and effect and little sense of propor-
tion; he was also a hopelessly poor judge of character. For long
periods he allowed others to do his work and yet, in moments of
stress, he had no certain conviction as to whom he could trust.
This, combined with a strain of morbid suspicion, was liable to
result in fiercely irrational decisions, and behaviour which was
not only unpredictable but also highly irresponsible. In his ill-
balanced nature there was a curious disjunction between his
thought and his actions, his motives and his achievements; a disjunction which prevented him from bridging the gap between
analysis, of which he was capable, and effective action, of which
he was incapable. This was a source of anguish to himself and
those about him, and of disaster to his people. It is impossible to
rationalize the character of this unfortunate prince, whose many
good qualities—save perhaps his eloquence and his commanding presence—were not those required of a king who mounted a
bankrupt throne during the anarchy of civil war, to rule over a
turbulent people whose leaders were consumed with ambition,
greed and vengeance. Yet is is only through some understanding
of this kaleidoscopic character that we can hope to explain
either the tragedy of his reign or the story of the secretaries who
became the bewildered victims of what, in the end, was surely a
disequilibrium not far removed from insanity.[1]

[1] The opinion that Henry III was a homosexual has long been uncritically
accepted. It is supported by Gaston Dodu in *Les Valois*, pt. iv, ch. ii, who gives an

The secretaries' correspondence is extremely sparse for the first six months of Henry III's reign, during which the troubles in the provinces increased and nothing constructive was achieved. In mid-November the court went to Avignon—the secretaries in a boat which nearly capsized. There the king attended the States of Languedoc, and Villeroy and Brulart were also present, at the foot of the dais, seated on a bench before a table.[1]

It was Pinart who was most active at this time. Dr. Dale, the English ambassador in France, writing to Burghley two days before Christmas, is alone in telling us that he was sent to Paris 'to deal with Montmorency by fair and by foul to persuade his brethren'—presumably to come to some kind of composition with the king. It was also rumoured that Pinart would go on to Germany to see Condé, the count Palatine and the Landgrave.[2] Pinart's activities must have been kept secret, for he was even reported to have gone to England to urge the queen not to help the rebels in France.[3] We cannot be sure what he really did except that, at the end of 1574, or the beginning of 1575, he went as ambassador extraordinary to the King of Sweden—an incredibly long and arduous journey to make in mid-winter— and it is quite possible that he performed some mission in Germany on the way.

The ostensible reason for his journey was to see the King of Sweden's sister who was said to be very beautiful and, if she really proved to be so lovely, to bring back her portrait with a view to opening marriage negotiations for the king. The Venetian ambassador discovered later what he believed to be the real reason for Pinart's embassy, namely to convey the

interesting account of Henry's character. It should be pointed out, however, that this opinion is usually based upon the presence at court of the so-called *mignons*. This represents a mis-interpretation of the word, which had not then acquired its present connotation, and merely signified a favourite. Moreover, given the frequent references to the king's private affairs in the remarkably uninhibited correspondence of the period, it is significant to find no indication of the belief that he was a homosexual. Proof is naturally difficult to obtain, but unless or until reliable evidence is produced, this opinion should be treated as a matter of speculation, and not as though it were a proven fact.

[1] C. Devic and J. Vaisseté, xi, 599.
[2] *C.S.P.F.*, 1572–4, p. 583, 23 December 1574, Dale to Burghley.
[3] B.N., Mss. it. 1728, f. 513, 29 December 1574.

king's thanks for their having sent a gentleman to France, offering to use Swedish influence to prevent the election of another
king to the throne of Poland.[1] But it does not appear that the
marriage negotiation was only a pretext, or it would not have
been necessary to send a secretary in response to a message
delivered by a mere gentleman. Dymock, the English ambassador in Stockholm, reported to Burghley on 25 March that
Pinart went to see the duke Charles and the princess Elizabeth
and spent five days 'where was great cheer, with presents and
the Lady Elizabeth's picture for the French king, so it is thought
there will be a marriage between them'. He also reported that
one night Pinart became drunk and made some gravely un-
diplomatic remarks about the Queen of England.[2] We learn
from de Thou that when Pinart received instructions to break
off the negotiations, the King of Sweden came very close to mal-
treating him.[3] Pinart must have been furious and grievously
embarrassed to learn that during his mission Henry had actually
married Louise de Vaudemont at Reims on 15 February
1575.

When Pinart returned from Sweden he found the court
steeped in an atmosphere of mounting tension. The dangerous
situation, already deplored by Villeroy in 1568, had returned.
The quarrels between the princes and nobles were such that
everything was in a state of confusion and there was imminent
danger of more serious trouble.[4] This closely concerned the
secretaries, and particularly Villeroy, for whom Alençon was
becoming a source of increasing work and worry. The importance of Alençon's position, as heir apparent to the throne, was
exalted by the universal belief that the king would remain
childless and die young. Alençon wanted the throne and he
feared his brother. He quarrelled with Navarre, both of them
being in love with madame de Sauve, wife of Fizes, and both
hating the able, ambitious catholic duc de Guise. The Venetian
ambassador, describing Alençon in 1574, when he was twenty,
said that he was deceitful, evilly disposed and inordinately

---

[1] B.N., Mss. it. 1728, f. 541, 12 February 1574/5.
[2] C.S.P.F., 1575-7, p. 34, 25 March 1575, Dymock to Burghley.
[3] Quoted by Petitot, xxxvi, Mémoires de Cheverny, 68, n. 2.
[4] Desjardins, Negs. Tosc., iv, 38, June-July 1575.

ambitious, and that in order to dominate he would hazard any great enterprise whatsoever.[1] Villeroy was involved in almost all the negotiations to which Alençon's mismanaged affairs gave rise, and his authority and persuasive manner were repeatedly employed to control and restrain the young duke's grandiose ambitions. Alençon was the pivot and focus of rebellion and disorder in France, constantly involving the king in peril at home and the danger of foreign war.

Villeroy was naturally fully aware of the gravity of the situation and, in September 1575, he wrote to Mauvissière, ambassador in England: 'we talk of nothing but war upon the rumours of the coming of the *reistres*', meaning the military help that the protestants were awaiting. 'It seems to me that the longer we delay the more difficult it will be to make peace.'[2] However, there was nothing which he, personally, could do but await the crisis which quickly followed when, after several abortive attempts, Alençon, aided by his sister Marguerite, fled from court on the evening of 15 September. So many people flocked to join him that the situation was very sinister. 'We cannot fail to have a great deal of trouble', Brulart wrote to Nevers who was in the field, and with whom he kept in close touch.[3]

It was not long before Villeroy was needed. Accompanied by Fizes, Catherine immediately followed Alençon, and Villeroy, who left Paris very suddenly, had joined them at Chambord before 30 September. There, for the first time, he was directly associated with Catherine in the negotiation of an agreement. They were to work together on many future occasions during the following fourteen years.

Villeroy then made several journeys in quick succession between Catherine and the king. He was back at court by 1 October,[4] probably to inform the king that there was no hope of making peace while the two marshals, Cossé and Montmorency, were still held prisoners, and he rejoined Catherine a second time on 4 October, with the news of the release of the marshals

---

[1] Albèri, *Relazioni*, ser. i, vol. iv, 320.

[2] B.N., Mss. Cinq Cents Colbert, 472, f. 19, 3 September 1575, Villeroy to Mauvissière.

[3] B.N., Mss. fr. 3323, f. 25, 18 September 1575, Brulart to Nevers.

[4] *Ibid.*, f. 69, 1 October 1575, Henry to Nevers.

and, it was thought, with orders from the king about ceding Blois to Alençon.[1] Catherine then sent Villeroy with Montpensier to see Alençon in person.[2] The 10th October found him once more at court, having brought good hopes of peace if the king would release the marshals unconditionally.[3] Villeroy then remained at court, watching the situation deteriorate. He wrote to Mauvissière on 23 October that they still had very little hope of peace, and added that he, personally, had made two journeys to see the queen and Alençon. But it was not, he said, only Alençon who was at fault. 'Il y a aussy de mauvaises volontes dun coste et d'autre qui traverssent les bonnes.' Meanwhile everyone was preparing for war.[4] Villeroy was growing depressed and anxious as Catherine remained at Blois. 'Voila,' he concluded, 'tout ce que je vous puis escrire de nostre miserable France laquelle je tiens pour ruinee et desolee a jamais si dieu ne nous donne la paix avant que les barbares d'un coste et dautre y mettent le pied.'[5] He referred, of course, to the coming of foreign troops. That the king's own brother and heir should prove so intransigent was, after all, a shocking and a terrible development.

On the same day, 23 October, Brulart wrote to Jacques Viart *gouverneur* of Metz—in his *département*—a letter which reveals that he also experienced a similar anguish and foreboding at this time, as well as the warmth of his appreciation of Catherine, whose gruelling tragedy dragged on before their eyes, and whose grief on this occasion had been more than she was able to conceal. 'We find ourselves prepared to suffer many misfortunes,' he wrote, 'and eventually to be completely overwhelmed by them if God does not take pity on us and reveal the grandeur of his power before our despair becomes any greater. As for the opinion that the negotiation at Blois is unlikely to come to any good end, I am not certain what the outcome will be, but I consider that no other measure could be more appropriate and if we are so unfortunate that nothing comes of it, it will nevertheless

---

[1] La Ferrière, *Lettres*, v, 147, 5 October 1575, Catherine to the king.
[2] *Ibid.*, 150, 7 October 1575, Catherine to the king.
[3] B.N., Mss. it. 1729, f. 311, 11 October 1575.
[4] B.N., Mss. Cinq Cents Colbert, 472, f. 21, 23 October 1575, Villeroy to Mauvissière.
[5] *Id.*

O

serve to show the world how much trouble the queen was willing to take.'[1]

In the middle of November Villeroy fell ill and was away for a month. He took no further part in the negotiation until about 8 January 1576 when he was sent to Bourges, which had been given to Alençon as part of the price of a truce to which he had agreed.[2] It was Villeroy's task to try to persuade the town to co-operate, but he met with a firm resistance from the people, who told him that they would sooner die than admit their enemies and the protestant cult.[3] They even refused to admit Villeroy who must, if only by virtue of his marriage to Magdalene de Laubespine, have been well known there. Disliking his mission they lodged him without the walls, and he achieved nothing.[4]

The situation was calamitous. Villeroy had every reason to feel distraught, since Catherine was ill and the king hid himself in a windowless room to read poetry by candlelight with a group of young people. Villeroy expressed his feelings to his friend Mauvissière, to whom he wrote that Navarre had left the court for Guienne, where he had a large following, that the armies of both sides were moving fast, and that the truce had never been observed. He prayed that they still might not come to war because, he said, that would result in the complete and final destruction and ruin of the nobility, and consequently of the crown.[5]

Villeroy did not approve of the peace, which he announced to Mauvissière three months later, because it involved the king in crushing expenses and because the other conditions were so advantageous to Alençon's party 'qu'il n'est possible de plus'. 'But', he added, 'since they have been concluded we must praise God for everything and strive to accomplish what remains to be done so that we may enjoy either the reality or the illusion of peace.'[6] Brulart did not approve of the peace either,

[1] B.N., Mss. fr. 3365, f. 49, 23 October 1575, Brulart to Viart.

[2] B.N., Mss. it. 1729, f. 442, 17 January 1575/6.

[3] B.N., Mss. Cinq Cents Colbert, 472, f. 47, 7 February 1576, Villeroy to Mauvissière.

[4] B.N., Mss. it. 1729, f. 461, 30 January 1575/6.

[5] B.N., Mss. Cinq Cents Colbert, 472, f. 47, 7 February 1576, Villeroy to Mauvissière.

[6] Ibid., f. 39, 5 May 1576, Villeroy to Mauvissière. The peace of Monsieur, 6 May 1576. It was from the time of this treaty that Alençon took the title duc d'Anjou, formerly held by his brother.

but he believed more firmly than Villeroy that any peace was better than none, because he thought the continuation of such wars as dangerous for the victors as for the vanquished.[1] The peace he considered costly and dishonourable but better even so than their former miserable condition 'et le pis qui nous menassoyt'.[2]

The secretaries were very busy throughout the summer, which was spent in trying to raise the enormous sum of two million *livres* accorded by the peace to the enemy's foreign troops. This proved as difficult as Villeroy expected when he said that they would need a miracle of God.[3] In June he and Brulart went with the king and Catherine to Rouen and Dieppe to try to raise money for Bellièvre, *surintendant des finances*, who had been sent to pay the mercenaries and by whom he was detained and mal-treated. 'Your letters are so pitiful', Villeroy wrote to him kindly, 'that they melt the hardest of hearts', but he had no more substantial consolation to offer him.[4]

Villeroy went home for a month's holiday on 5 September by which time the money had actually been raised. We learn from him that Pinart was ill at this time with a quartan fever.[5] We know nothing of Pinart's life from January to September 1576 and it is possible that he had been ill for some time. We do not know anything of Fizes either. It may have fallen to him to accompany Catherine on another journey which she made to Chenonceaux to see Anjou—who was anxious to intervene in the war in the Netherlands—and to Cognac to see Navarre who, it was feared, might not keep the newly-made peace.[6]

In November the four secretaries and the whole court assembled at Blois for the meeting of the States General which the king had promised to call. It is evident that the secretaries had a definite part to play in connection with the work of the assembly though we do not know about it in any detail. In

[1] B.N., Mss. fr. 15560, f. 43, 12 November 1575, Brulart to Hautefort, brother of Bellièvre and ambassador in Switzerland.
[2] B.N., Mss. fr. 3318, f. 42, 17 May 1576, Brulart to Vulcob, ambassador in the Empire.
[3] B.N., Mss. Cinq Cents Colbert, 472, f. 39, 5 May 1576, Villeroy to Mauvissière.
[4] B.N., Mss. fr. 15904, f. 166, 26 June 1576, Villeroy to Bellièvre.
[5] B.N., Mss. Cinq Cents Colbert, 472, f. 45, 4 September 1576, Villeroy to Mauvissière.
[6] B.N., Mss. it. 1729, f. 813, 8 August 1576.

February 1577, the king assigned the *cahier* of each of the three States to one of the secretaries, while the fourth was to write down the decisions taken. Work began on the *cahier* of the clergy, which was given to Villeroy. The clergy demanded that there should be only one religion, and the other *cahiers* were in agreement.[1] The king's announcement—in accordance with this request—that he wished there to be one religion only, precipitated a crisis, as it was interpreted as a declaration of renewed war upon the protestants. This crisis was typical of the king's undependable character and his moments of suspicion. He disgraced Villeroy's uncle Limoges, temporarily excluded Bellièvre from the council, and even de Morvillier found some excuse for withdrawing to Paris. These were excellent and honest councillors, but they had all been appointed by Catherine, with whom from time to time Henry quarrelled, exerting his authority in rash and ill-considered ways. On this occasion they all advised him against making war. This mood of sudden obstinacy in the king soon gave way to one of vacillation, but not before much damage had been done. A heavy share in its reparation was to fall on Villeroy.

For a time Villeroy was afraid that war would follow. In January 1577 he wrote to Saint-Sulpice that at court they were awaiting news from Montpensier and Biron, who had gone to see Navarre, 'pour savoir de quelle mort nous devons mourir. Il faut lever les yeux aux ciel', he said, and more laconically to Mauvissière on the same day, 'I can only say that as we are about to go to war again, we have no cause for rejoicing.'[2] It was a state of partial war that ensued.

In April 1577, Brulart, who had remained at court much more than his colleagues, went to camp in the service of Anjou who, temporarily reconciled to the king since the peace of Monsieur, was sent to retake the towns of La Charité, Ambert and Issoire. Brulart remained in the field until some time in July when he suffered from the heat, and fever at night.[3] Meanwhile Villeroy played host to the king in one of his houses, be-

---

[1] Gomberville, *Mémoires de Nevers*, i, 173.

[2] Cabié, 328, 30 January 1577, Villeroy to Saint-Sulpice; B.N., Mss. Cinq Cents Colbert, 472, f. 33, 30 January 1577, Villeroy to Mauvissière.

[3] B.N., Mss. fr. 3337, f. 96, 16 July 1577, Brulart to Nevers, from Thouran (Haute Vienne).

fore going with Pinart and Fizes to join Catherine at her favourite château, Chenonceaux.

It was from Chenonceaux—on 4 June—that Villeroy left for Bergerac on what proved to be his first really important negotiation. He had served on other missions and extraordinary embassies but it was the treaty of Bergerac that established his reputation. There had been negotiations for many months before Villeroy went to Bergerac, but it was he who directed the concluding stages, which lasted for three and a half months.[1] Montpensier, Monluc bishop of Valence, Paul de Foix, Biron, La Mothe-Fénelon and Saint-Sulpice were all associated with Villeroy in this negotiation, but Gassot said that in his devotion, diligence, understanding and conduct, Villeroy shone out as much as or, without wronging them, more than all the rest together, and the conclusion of peace redounded to his honour.[2] When the king decided to send Villeroy with La Mothe-Fénelon, who had come with a message from Navarre, he described them as 'personnages de qualite', an expression which twenty, or possibly even ten years previously, would never have been used in reference to a secretary.[3]

Villeroy did not want to undertake this negotiation. He did his best to excuse himself because he considered that his instructions—to induce Navarre and his associates to abandon their claims to be allowed to celebrate the protestant cult—were impossible to carry out. Villeroy explained this problem in his memoir. He said that during the meeting of the States at Blois, the king had declared that he would never make peace with the huguenots unless they agreed to renounce their cult, and that if, through necessity, bad advice, or for any other reason, a different peace were made, it was contrary to his will and he would not respect it. While Villeroy was positive that the huguenots would never agree to renounce the cult, the king was given to believe that they might do so, 'a quoy', said Villeroy, 'je les trouvay très-contraires'.[4]

The negotiation did not begin for some time, and then

[1] B.N., Mss. n.a.f. 7260, letter to Du Vair.
[2] Gassot, 146-7.
[3] Cabié, 352, 4 June 1577, Henry to Saint-Sulpice.
[4] Petitot, xliv, Mémoires d'Estat de Villeroy, 31-2.

immediately became involved in serious difficulties which, considering Villeroy's instructions, was only to be expected. The
proceedings were kept very secret and no one knew much about
what was taking place. For this reason it was Villeroy himself
who made journeys to the court at Poitiers to discuss problems
with the king. He arrived there about 4 July to explain the
exorbitant demands of the protestants, particularly for the
exercise of the cult in many places. He also bore the sombre
message from Navarre that if the king did not quickly make
peace he, Navarre, would be unable to do so. Fortunately for
Villeroy, he was authorized to make concessions, because the
king feared—and the protestants hoped—that his brother Anjou
would grow weary of commanding a royal army, and be
tempted and attracted by offers which were reaching him from
the Netherlands.

Villeroy was back in conference by 15 July, and he tried to
win over Navarre personally in the hope of isolating him from
the party. But, in August, the conference again reached a deadlock and Villeroy went to Poitiers a second time. Instead of
discussing the matter in council, as was usual, Villeroy and
Biron conferred with the king and Catherine alone. They
returned to Bergerac on 2 September, to try once more to bring
the negotiation to a successful conclusion.[1]

The most interesting document relating to this treaty is a
letter which Villeroy wrote to the king on 8 September 1577.[2] It
was written in code and sent in secret by a lackey who served
Montpensier's wife. No one but Montpensier and Villeroy
knew of its existence. It does not tell us much about the terms of
the negotiation, but it does tell us a great deal about Villeroy,
his relations with the king and the importance of the role he was
playing. It also proves that it was he who was leading the negotiation. Villeroy disapproved of the instructions with which he
had returned to Bergerac on 2 September. We do not know
what they contained, but he had now to tell the king that they
had brought the conference to the point of rupture, and he
actually asked to be recalled. Although the king had completely
departed from his original policy, Villeroy was still in funda-

[1] Cabié, 372, 31 August 1577, Henry to Saint-Sulpice.
[2] B.N., Mss. fr. 3395, f. 44, 8 September 1577, Villeroy to the king, decoded.

mental disagreement with him, so much so that, in spite of his deep-rooted hatred of war and violence, he wrote: 'Sire, I believe that God . . . has created these difficulties for the best to prevent the conclusion of peace, because I foresee that if it is made according to the conditions which you have authorized us to grant, it will not only be very difficult to implement but also so full of problems and contradictions that you will find it worse than war.' That was a very strong statement for Villeroy to make, not only because war was known to be abhorrent to him, but also because he was fully aware of the disastrous gravity of the financial situation, and that the king was then squandering money with criminal profligacy.[1] 'I know', Villeroy continued, 'that there are men already moving about from place to place in this province inciting the nobles and the towns to band together to oppose the peace, to which some pay attention out of fear of the King of Navarre, some for fear of losing their freedom to pillage and others on account of various private passions. . . . If this is brewing here [he meant in the vicinity of the court and the king's person] you can imagine, Sire, what is happening and will happen elsewhere.' Wishing to drive his point home, Villeroy concluded; 'Pardonnez moi si je vous le dict encores une autre fois qu'il vous sera bien difficile de remedier aux inconveniences qui en viendront.'[2]

These were the words of a minister from whom nothing was concealed, to whom the most arduous of all tasks were entrusted, and who was in a position privately to impress his considered opinion upon the king. The importance of this letter can hardly be exaggerated. It was nothing less than a serious and accurate warning of the developing tragedy of the next twelve years—into which the king seemed to move with a kind of mechanical fatality—for it was not to be Navarre and the protestants who finally ruined their country and hounded the king from his throne, but this nascent catholic league. The peace of Bergerac declared all leagues illegal; thus the development of the catholic league was temporarily arrested.[3] If Villeroy was not, at the time, aware of the full significance of his letter, his warning was

[1] B.N., Mss. it. 1730, f. 79, 14 June 1577.
[2] B.N., Mss. fr. 3395, f. 44, 8 September 1577, Villeroy to the king.
[3] See app. iv.

none the less prophetic. That Henry did not heed it or accept his advice was no reflection upon the position or the powers of a secretary. Had Villeroy been a peer of France he would not have been any closer to the king, who alone had the right to initiate policy and who did not consistently act upon anyone's advice but swung uncertainly from one course to another.

We do not know what the king replied but only that the negotiation continued painfully. Saint-Sulpice informed the king on 14 September that they were working without wasting a single moment but in the face of such difficulties that if for part of the day they hoped for peace, for the rest of it they feared the continuation of war, but that day he really expected a conclusion.[1]

Villeroy was back at Poitiers by 22 September, having dealt with further demands of the protestants, made after the conclusion of peace on the 14th.[2] He was overwhelmed with work because it was he who had to draft the edict—known as the edict of Poitiers—which was finally printed for distribution because it was too long to have sufficient copies made by hand.[3] Knowing almost nothing of the secret negotiation of this treaty, beyond the journeys between Poitiers and Bergerac, and the rise and fall in the hopes of those who strove for peace, we can only imagine the phenomenal amount of work which it must have entailed, consisting, as it did, of sixty-four articles which were published, and forty-eight secret articles concluded with Navarre. We do not know what these articles were, but it seems likely that the king remained secretly in touch with Navarre.

The king was well content with the treaty of Bergerac and it was Villeroy who received the credit for it. The part which he played in its negotiation illustrates the predicament of a secretary who found himself in disagreement with the king, and whose advice was not accepted. Villeroy began by trying to excuse himself from the mission because he knew that his instructions were impossible to carry out, and that any agreement reached would be contrary to the king's statement at Blois. It is likely that he also bore in mind the unjust fate of his uncle

[1] Cabié, 374, 14 September 1577, Saint-Sulpice to the king.
[2] B.N., Mss. it. 1730, f. 143, 20 September 1577; *ibid.*, f. 149, 25 September 1577.
[3] Cabié, 377, 26 September 1577, Villeroy to Saint-Sulpice.

Limoges, who was made a scapegoat for the peace of Monsieur when the king temporarily changed his mind about the advantages of having come to terms with his rebel subjects. However, having received a clear order, it was Villeroy's duty to obey. As a secretary he might guide or influence policy but, as he did not direct it, he was not responsible for it. He was responsible only for his actions under the crown, for the sincere execution of the king's will, to the best of his ability. His own disagreement with this will might often prove a source of anguish and discomfort, but not of a sense of guilt. Besides, Villeroy's conception of any problem was practical, not abstract or academic. He saw things in terms of the possible, preferring to work for a lesser good rather than to abdicate on a point of principle and achieve nothing at all. Confusing changes of policy such as Henry frequently indulged in, were alien to the scrupulous, clear-sighted Villeroy. But he was obliged to adapt himself to them, and he learnt to do so without any loss of personal integrity, and without embittering his relations with the king.

France was still a prey to the confusion which followed the massacre of Saint Bartholomew when Henry III ascended the throne in 1574. The early years of his reign marked a new stage in the civil wars, when Henry of Navarre fled from court to assume the leadership of the protestant party, vacant since the death of Coligny. Once again, as in 1562, two parties were emerging whose quarrels were not those of the crown. Navarre always behaved with moderation, and declared that it was not the king but the duc de Guise who was his enemy. Both cherished dynastic claims and therefore paid lip-service to the king, who was isolated. From about 1576, the real enemies of the devout and sincerely catholic Henry were not the protestants but the catholics themselves. This was one of the outstanding problems of the reign, and one which was never really faced and only spasmodically acknowledged. It was in fact a problem without solution, pointing the way to tragedy. Villeroy was aware of it, but he was powerless to do anything effective about it.

The situation was further complicated by the king's younger brother, Alençon. He had already shown himself to be dangerous. Now he came out in open opposition to the throne, except for brief periods of partial and insincere reconciliation. He attracted to his selfish cause some degree of support, and much of the military scum of Europe.

In these difficult circumstances, the work of the secretaries was further complicated by the character of the king and his unpredictable changes of policy. Villeroy was always his favourite among the secretaries, and this was a critical period in his career. From this time on, he became increasingly eminent, assumed an even greater burden of responsibility and was one of the few to have any real grasp of public affairs.

CHAPTER XIV

Villeroy and the Struggle for Peace, 1578–81

THE years 1578–81 were primarily devoted to the struggle to enforce the peace in France, to attempts to restrain Anjou from intervening in the revolt in the Netherlands and to trying to arrange a marriage for him—endeavours with which the secretaries were closely concerned and which gave them a restless period of travelling.

By this time Villeroy's credit and prestige had become very great and his pre-eminence was undisputed. From being the most favoured of the secretaries, he had become one of the most important public figures in France, esteemed and also courted by all parties. After witnessing his skill at the conference of Bergerac, the King of Navarre offered him an annual pension of 2,000 écus.[1] It was paradoxical that this situation should have resulted, to a considerable extent, from his conclusion of a treaty which he had strongly opposed and which he feared would prove disastrous.

Villeroy enjoyed the advice and support of his close friend and associate, Bellièvre, but he had lost that of de Morvillier, who died in October 1577 leaving to him and his cousin de Laubespine his houses and their contents at Paris, Fontainebleau and Saint-Germain.[2] He had also lost the active support of Limoges, who was living in retirement and died in August 1582. Though well able to stand alone, Villeroy missed their wise counsel. There was no one with more experience of public affairs than Limoges, and no one, according to Villeroy himself, whose

[1] Petitot, xliv, *Mémoires d'Estat de Villeroy*, 109.
[2] Baguenault de Puchesse, *Jean de Morvillier*, 353.

advice and judgement he esteemed more highly in affairs of state.[1] Until his death, Villeroy went to visit Limoges when he could.[2] The death of Fizes, which occurred on 27 November 1579, also tended to increase Villeroy's importance and gave him and Brulart considerably more to do, for Fizes had no successor. Villeroy took over his *département* and divided his own with Brulart.[3]

Villeroy's work in restraining Anjou began again without delay. After the treaty of Bergerac, Anjou went to see ambassadors from the Netherlands at La Fère in Picardy, where the king promptly sent Villeroy to dissuade him from concluding any agreement.[4] Villeroy was at least temporarily successful and the duke soon returned to court.

If it was difficult for him and his brother to live together peacefully, it was impossible for their respective households, and the following months were marked by frivolous, but violent quarrels, which threatened to destroy all that had been achieved since Anjou's flight from court in September 1575. Already in January, Villeroy thought there was a danger of renewed war but hoped that the king's determination to keep the peace would still prevail.[5] What he thought of the hatreds, jealousies and squabbles of the vain and idle young men who thronged the court, may be deduced from the laconic disgust with which he wrote to Mauvissière, 'Je ne vous escriray rien de nos folies qui sont trop grandes et extraordinaires.'[6]

It therefore came as no surprise to Villeroy that, when Anjou fled from court a second time in the night of 14–15 February 1578, he should be sent off the very next morning in pursuit of

---

[1] B.N., Mss. Cinq Cents Colbert, 472, f. 9, 23 July 1579, Villeroy to Mauvissière.
[2] He went for Easter 1581, B.N., Mss. fr. 15906, f. 298, 26 March 1581, Brulart to Bellièvre.
[3] See ch. iii.
[4] On Anjou and the Netherlands, see P. L. Muller and A. Diegerick, *Documents concernant les relations entre le duc d'Anjou et les Pays-Bas, 1576–83*; La Ferrière, *Les Projets de mariage de la reine Élizabeth*, contains a certain amount about the Netherlands and, as the title indicates, about the tortuous marriage negotiations with queen Elizabeth. The sources for this are given by F. J. Weaver, 'Anglo-French Diplomatic Relations, 1558–1630', *Bulletin of the Institute of Historical Research*, iv–vii.
[5] B.N., Mss. Cinq Cents Colbert, 472, f. 87, 15 January 1578, Villeroy to Mauvissière.
[6] *Ibid.*, 472, f. 89, 12 February 1578, Villeroy to Mauvissière.

him.[1] Villeroy was followed by Catherine, who left the same afternoon, but travelled much more slowly, with a large suite. This was the first of many journeys to see Anjou, and of many long arguments with him. There is some evidence that he liked Villeroy, or at least realized that it was worth while trying to win his sympathy.[2] Villeroy could do more with Anjou—who would sometimes request his help—than anyone but Catherine. Indeed, it was reported of him a few years later, that he allowed himself to be governed by Villeroy.[3] But, short of imprisonment, no one could restrain him for long. On this occasion Villeroy did not catch up with Anjou until he was half a day's journey from Angers, where the duke received him graciously and gave him letters and explanations for the king, claiming that he was threatened with imprisonment and that his flight was innocent.[4] Nevertheless, he had substantial demands to make. Villeroy must have met Catherine somewhere on his way back, for she heard what he had to say and went on to Angers. She there proceeded to lecture Anjou for no less than six hours, after which it was thought that he would not do anything rash for some time to come.[5]

Villeroy arrived back at court before noon on 22 February and spent the greater part of that day with the king in his study. The court learned of Anjou's honeyed words, but Villeroy's lengthy consultation with the king gave cause to think that his message 'contained higher matter'.[6] Villeroy was consoled at this time by the king's firm resolution to enforce the peace he had recently concluded; but he wrote to Saint-Sulpice, three days after his return, that events at court had lately been so strange and so diverse that he did not know what comment to make on them.[7]

Villeroy again went to see Anjou at the beginning of July, in the wake of Catherine who was accompanied by Pinart. His

[1] *C.S.P.F.*, 1577-8, p. 502, 15 February 1578, Poulet to the secretaries; B.N., Mss. it. 1730, f. 235, 15 February 1577/8; Petitot, xlv, Pierre de l'Estoile, *Journal de Henri III*, 164; ibid., xxxvi, *Mémoires de Cheverny*, 75-6.

[2] Gomberville, *Mémoires de Nevers*, i, 148-51.

[3] *C.S.P.F.*, 1583-4, p. 16, 11 July 1583, Cobham to Walsingham.

[4] B.N., Mss. it. 1730, f. 244, 25 February 1577/8.

[5] *Ibid.*, f. 250, 5 March 1578.

[6] *C.S.P.F.*, 1577-8, p. 515, 1 March 1578, Poulet to the secretaries.

[7] Cabié, 393, 25 February 1578, Villeroy to Saint-Sulpice.

object was not only to make one final effort to dissuade him from going to the Netherlands, but also to try to divert him with the prospect of a Spanish marriage, carrying with it part of the Netherlands as his wife's dowry.[1] But Villeroy was no more successful than Catherine had been and, after their meeting, Anjou left for Mons.

On 21 August Villeroy went on another mission, this time to see Catherine who had gone to contact Navarre in Guienne, in an effort to enforce the peace. Villeroy must have overtaken her somewhere between Poitiers and Cognac. He probably went to take Catherine a copy of the treaty that Anjou concluded with the States of the Netherlands on 13 August,[2] and possibly also to discuss the Spanish marriage project. Having rejoined the court at Fontainebleau by 6 September, Villeroy departed again on the 13th to see Anjou in the Netherlands.[3] The purpose of this journey was not generally known, but the Florentine ambassador observed that it was not without great mystery that men of such quality travelled to and fro.[4] Villeroy came back on 29 September, and for once with an agreeable reply, for Anjou found that his fortunes in the Netherlands were less glorious than he had hoped.[5]

Brulart was lucky in having escaped any direct dealings with Anjou during these harassed and restless months of 1578, which he spent at court. But he was fully aware of what was happening, and was critical of Anjou's reactions to some propositions of the States which, he said, were 'bien estranges', indicating that Anjou had not studied them and had no understanding of that country.[6] Fizes was also at court, at least during the months of August and September, and he had been doing his utmost to

---

[1] B.N., Mss. it. 1730, ff. 170, 197, 22 November, 27 December 1577; Baguenault de Puchesse, *Lettres*, vi, 386, 2 July 1578, Henry to Villeroy.

[2] P. L. Muller and A. Diegerick, i, 408, Anjou's treaty with the States, 13 August 1578; *C.S.P.F.*, 1578–9, p. 131, 13 August 1578, p. 104, 31 July 1578, Davison to Burghley, is alone in saying that Villeroy went to the Netherlands to help negotiate this treaty. This appears to be an error for Bellièvre, who went towards the end of July and remained there for some months.

[3] B.N., Mss. fr. 15905, f. 138, 7 September 1578, Fizes to Bellièvre; Mss. it. 1730, f. 291, 15 September 1578.

[4] Desjardins, *Négs. Tosc.*, iv, 200, 6 October 1578.

[5] B.N., Mss. it. 1730, ff. 294–5, 3 October 1578.

[6] B.N., Mss. fr. 15905, f. 184, 10 November 1578, Brulart to Bellièvre.

persuade the king to release the unfortunate Bellièvre, who was stranded in the Netherlands as councillor to the ungrateful duke.[1]

We have seen that Pinart, more than the other secretaries, worked in close co-operation with Catherine. He did not at first accompany her when, on 2 August 1578, she left Ollainville to see Navarre in Guienne, but went instead to Paris with the king.[2] But it was not long before Catherine needed him and he joined her at Bordeaux about 27 September, with a number of documents and memoirs from the king. He shared Catherine's hardships and fatigue, and he complained to Bellièvre at the outset of being overworked and very tired, a fatigue which remained with him for several months and which was reflected in his large, sprawling scribble. In Catherine's service he had to write for many hours a day and the size and illegibility of his writing increased with his fatigue. Pinart did not know that he had embarked on a journey which was to take him from Guienne to Languedoc, Provence and Dauphiné and which would keep him away from the court and from home until November 1579, for Catherine met with problem after problem in her efforts to enforce the edict of Poitiers, and she would not give up. Not only Pinart, but also Villeroy would have been dismayed, had they known that the journey would last for so long. Villeroy deplored Catherine's absence which, he said, 'nous a faict et fera grand faillir en ceste endroit'. In fact they needed her, and Brulart also expressed his great regret that they could not hope to see her back before the end of February.[3]

Catherine kept in close touch with the secretaries, who sent on her letters and provided her with news while she was in the provinces. They must have written to her very frequently, for once, after a silence of only five days, she complained of being greatly troubled by not having heard from them for such a long time.[4] She asked Brulart to write to her as often as he could and to send her news of the king, a constant request with which the

[1] B.N., Mss. fr. 15905, f. 138, 7 September 1578, Fizes to Bellièvre.

[2] B.N., Mss. fr. 3389, f. 74, 1 August 1578, Pinart to Matignon.

[3] B.N., Mss. fr. 15905, f. 151, 9 October 1578, Villeroy to Bellièvre; Mss. fr. 3389, f. 101, 16 December 1578, Brulart to Matignon.

[4] Baguenault de Puchesse, *Lettres*, vii, 513, 31 August 1579, Catherine to Villeroy.

secretaries became familiar.[1] But it was Villeroy who acted
almost as her lieutenant; during Henry's frequent absences, it
was he who opened and studied her immensely long and complex letters to the king. To Villeroy she expressed herself frankly
and sometimes secretly, requesting that no one but he and the
king should see her letter.[2] If the king were away, Villeroy
would send him on such letters privately.[3] During her absence
she relied on Villeroy to guide the king's policy along what she
considered the right lines.[4] But, trusting his judgement, she was
also prepared to accept his advice: 'Voilà mon advis,' she wrote
to him one day, after making a suggestion, 's'il est mauvais,
jettez le au feu; s'il est bon, montrez le au Roy. . . . Mandez moy
toujours de ses nouvelles et de toutes autres choses.'[5] Villeroy
did his best to get replies back to Catherine as quickly as possible,
constantly reminding the king what he ought to do and asking
him to hurry. When the king omitted to write to Catherine in
his own hand, Villeroy rebuked him for being so inconsiderate,
and pressing the point right home, he wrote: 'I beg you to consider how distressed the queen your mother will be, amidst so
many other things in which she is immersed for your service, to
remain for so long without hearing from you.'[6] Catherine's
return was repeatedly postponed, thereby increasing the burden
of the secretaries' work. They missed her constantly: 'Il me
tarde infiniment qu'elle n'est icy', Villeroy wrote to Mauvissière,[7] and Brulart to the comte de Matignon expressed the
same opinion, that her presence at court was greatly desired.[8]
Anxiously as they awaited her return, Villeroy and Brulart, as
well as Pinart, greatly admired Catherine's strenuous efforts in
the south, exerted in the interests of that peace which they also
had so much at heart. Pinart would refer to her affectionately
at this time as 'la pauvre princesse' and 'la reine ma bonne

[1] Baguenault de Puchesse, Lettres, vi, 126, 18 November 1578, Catherine to
Brulart.
[2] B.N., Mss. n.a.f. 5128, f. 61, 28 January 1579, Villeroy to the king.
[3] Id.
[4] Baguenault de Puchesse, Lettres, vi, 59, 7 October 1578, Catherine to Villeroy.
[5] Ibid., 60, 7 October 1578, Catherine to Villeroy.
[6] B.N., Mss. n.a.f. 5128, f. 61, 28 January 1579, Villeroy to the king.
[7] B.N., Mss. Cinq Cents Colbert, 472, f. 93, 9 April 1579, Villeroy to Mauvissière.
[8] B.N., Mss. fr. 3354, f. 24, 1 May 1579, Brulart to Matignon.

maitresse', and remembered to tell his friends how she did not waste 'une seule occasion',[1] of her 'extreme et si grand travail',[2] that there was 'aucune sorte de moyen qu'elle ne l'ayt tente',[3] and of her 'grande patience'.[4] Villeroy justly commented to Mauvissière that 'nul autre qu'elle eust sceu venir a bout'.[5] These opinions, which the secretaries freely expressed in private letters, are of great interest considering the process of vilification to which many historians have subjected Catherine's character and achievements. The Venetian ambassador refers to her prestige at this period, saying that whereas, at one time, the French were unwilling to recognize her qualities, now they had come to regard her as something superhuman: it was obvious to him that it was Catherine who was doing everything.[6]

After Villeroy had returned, in October 1578, from the last of his five visits to Anjou, he was able to enjoy a relative calm for the next four months. He laboured to carry out Catherine's wish[7] that he should maintain as friendly relations as possible between the king and Anjou, and this is well illustrated by the powerfully worded instruction with which he armed his envoy who went to see the duke in December 1578.[8] In it Villeroy exhorted Anjou to co-operation, to restrain his followers from sabotaging his mother's hard-won achievements with the protestants, and warned him of the danger from a secret league in Burgundy and Normandy. In February 1579, when the envoy was sent to Navarre about the *places de sûreté* which he ought to have restored, according to the terms of the treaty of Bergerac, Villeroy, in drafting his instructions, again did all he could to help Catherine. His anger at the protestants' behaviour —their refusal to comply with the terms of the edict he had made, their demands for ever greater security and more articles, and their lack of respect and obedience for the queen—overflowed in clear and stringent language in instructions which

[1] B.N., Mss. fr. 15905, f. 196, 16 November 1578, Pinart to Bellièvre.
[2] B.N., Mss. fr. 3389, f. 72, 30 December 1578, Pinart to Matignon.
[3] B.N., Mss. fr. 15905, f. 238, 6 January 1579, Pinart to Bellièvre.
[4] *Ibid.*, f. 261, 23 January 1579, Pinart to Bellièvre.
[5] B.N., Mss. Cinq Cents Colbert, 472, f. 9, 23 July 1579, Villeroy to Mauvissière.
[6] Tommaseo, ii, 627.
[7] Baguenault de Puchesse, *Lettres*, vi, 59, 7 October 1578, Catherine to Villeroy.
[8] B.N., Mss. Dupuy, 537, f. 119, 13 December 1578.

P

were extremely able, well written and cogently argued, revealing his mastery of public affairs.

Early in 1579, Villeroy was dealing with everything of importance. Henry III had never enjoyed life at court and, from about
this time, he began to absent himself increasingly, regardless of
his duties. In January 1579 the news which came in from the
provinces, particularly from Provence and Poitou, was alarming. The council agreed that the king's presence was necessary
in face of this crisis and Villeroy, who was possibly weary of
sending the king despatches, replies, advice, reminders and
warnings, told him plainly that his negligence would have
serious results: 'il ne fault pas que vous faciez estat que pendant
vostre absence vos affaires se puissent si bien faire et depescher
quil est de besoin'.[1]

During the spring of 1579 Villeroy was still hard-pressed.
Anjou suddenly erupted into court—as usual during the night—
Brulart fell ill, and Fizes nearly died, 'qui on a cuide laisser les
bottes ces jours passes', as Villeroy graphically put it.[2] It is
probable that Fizes never fully recovered, since he died later in
the year. Villeroy was therefore all alone, and he said that his
work fell into such arrears that he hardly had time to breathe,
so it is small wonder that he was longing for Catherine's return,
and with her, Pinart.[3] Again in September he made the same
complaint, and said that his work weighed heavily on him. This
was not without good reason, for Anjou's return from a sudden
visit to England, and his cooling relations with his brother, coincided with such a serious illness of the king that Catherine was
urgently summoned. The king had an abscess in the ear, closely
resembling that which was the immediate cause of the death of
Francis II. It left Henry deaf in that ear for life.

It soon became clear that nothing permanent had been
achieved by Catherine's long journey and struggles in the south.
The situation in France remained critical, not to say dangerous,
and Villeroy gave much thought to the problem of what could
and ought to be done about it. We possess a remarkable docu-

[1] B.N., Mss. n.a.f. 5128, f. 61, 28 January 1579, Villeroy to the king.
[2] B.N., Mss. Cinq Cents Colbert, 472, f. 93, 9 April 1579, Villeroy to Mauvissière.
[3] Id.

ment, nineteen pages of a heavily corrected draft in his own handwriting, entitled: 'Advis au Roy sur le reiglement des affaires de son Royaume', in which he made a penetrating analysis of the principal troubles of his country, and urged a demonstration of strength and authority to rectify them.[1]

Villeroy began with three general recommendations. These were that explicit instructions should be issued to all local officials to enforce the edict of Poitiers, if necessary by force of arms; that *gouverneurs*, lieutenants-general and officers of justice were to be constantly harried to do their duty; and that each *parlement* should be presided over by a trustworthy person of honour and probity. Turning to Guienne, Villeroy said that there would never be peace in that province so long as Navarre, the *gouverneur*, and Biron, the lieutenant-general, continued to quarrel there. If it were impossible to reconcile them, then Biron must be recalled, swiftly but also tactfully and honourably. Order must be restored and royal fortresses preserved, and Villeroy suggested making temporary local adjustments in order to inspire confidence in the just administration of the edict; this would cut the ground from under the feet of Navarre. It was necessary to make a stand against him, and to insist that he restore the towns he held illegally. A further danger spot was La Fère, in Picardy, where Condé's relations within and without the kingdom were suspect. Condé must be made to feel that the king could chastise him if he attempted any act of disloyalty ('chose malapropos'). Garrisons must be well paid and troops sent to certain key towns in Picardy. The financial problems were the greatest and most dangerous of all. For these Villeroy suggested no immediate remedy. He did, however, make a number of recommendations, largely based on drastic economies— though in fact the king's wildest extravagances still lay in the near future—and he made it quite clear that, in his opinion, the fearful lack of money sprang more from maladministration than from any deeper cause.[2] Troops should be regularly paid,

[1] B.N., Mss. fr. 15562, f. 50, 28 January 1580.
[2] The Venetian ambassador, Priuli, reported that the finances were so corruptly administered that the king received only one half of his real revenues. The king himself diverted money from its proper uses and, in four years, he had given more than four million to four favourites. Albèri, *Relazioni*, ser. i, vol. iv, 411, 1582. A little book published in 1581 by N. Froumenteau called *Le Secret des finances de France*

placed under able commanders, and the marshals of France should be ordered to carry out frequent inspections. If and when all these things had been accomplished, then the king could summon the States General with some hope of success and co-operation. Villeroy also considered that it would be a good thing to send out to the provinces 'gens de qualite et de bien', and then for the king to visit them himself, provided that his court behaved with propriety—'se comporte comme il appartient'. This was indeed outspoken criticism.

The king, Villeroy continued, should begin by terminating the English marriage negotiation, which had been dragging on for a long time, make sure of the Swiss ('car avec eux vous pouvez faire tete a tout le monde') and, suitably accompanied, go in person to Guienne. Finally, Villeroy issued a warning against the ever-increasing power of Spain. The best way of gaining the consideration of foreign princes, he concluded, was to demonstrate that France had the power to do them good or ill.

The only apparent oversight in this interesting document was the problem of Anjou, unless Villeroy intended—and this is not clear—that he should marry queen Elizabeth. It is a striking illustration of how intensely practical and sensible Villeroy was, for it contains no verbiage, no rhetoric, no idealistic theories and virtually no generalization. Everything that he proposed was possible, necessary and urgent. The king, if it ever reached his eyes, probably applauded it and subscribed to it, for he was genuinely anxious to do better; but, as was his way, he omitted to act upon it.

The events of 1580 did not conform to Villeroy's pattern, nor was his work of the kind he would have liked. By the spring most of the south of France was in a state of anarchy; all parties were arming for their separate reasons, and there began another series of visits to Anjou.

gives the following figures (p. 142) for the period 1547–80. He says that the total revenue for those years was 1,453,000,000 *livres*, and the total expenditure was 927,206,000 *livres*. The king should, therefore, have had 525,794,000 *livres*, which equalled 175,264,666 2/3 *écus*, instead of which he was desperately in debt. While one may query the accuracy of these astronomical figures, one cannot doubt the magnitude of the disaster. Already at the time of the States at Blois, de Morvillier had written to d'Ormesson about the finances, that no one dared to investigate them thoroughly because they were too much afraid of what they would find. Baguenault de Puchesse, *Jean de Morvillier*, 341–4.

Pinart accompanied Catherine to see Anjou in April and several times wrote to Villeroy on her behalf. Then on 5 May Villeroy himself was sent. This was considered to be a very important mission, and it was believed that he was authorized to offer the duke substantial concessions in return for his mediation with Navarre, who was in arms. Villeroy had to see Anjou a second time, in September,[1] before he agreed to co-operate and, as a result, Villeroy and Bellièvre departed for Guienne at the end of September to negotiate yet another treaty. The Venetian ambassador put the situation in a nutshell: 'Things in this kingdom, are in their usual state: they treat for peace and continue the war.'[2] It was indeed becoming monotonous.

It was the measure of Villeroy's prestige that he was placed in charge of this negotiation, and the treaty of Fleix, which he concluded on 26 November 1580, consolidated his triumph at Bergerac. To the annoyance of the king's favourites, he emerged as second in importance only to the king and Catherine themselves.

The negotiation lasted for the remarkably short period of one month, and the most vexed questions were those of the administration of justice and, as usual, the *places de sûreté*.[3] Although, on this occasion, Anjou did everything he could to help Villeroy and Bellièvre, their problems were still great, partly, as Bellièvre told the king, because the licence of war had opened the way to every kind of corruption and dissolution of morals. The province was in a state of acute danger, there being no security of life or property for gentlemen or peasant, and, said Bellièvre, with restraint, during that month they had to endure as much as any servitor possibly could. Bellièvre's letter shows that the insistence of the protestants on their *places de sûreté* did have some foundation in necessity, the royal administration having virtually collapsed.[4]

At the end of November Villeroy departed to take the articles to the court at Blois and, with them, a word of praise in a letter

---

[1] B.N., Mss. fr. 3407, f. 11, 11 September 1580, Brulart to Nevers.
[2] B.N., Mss. it. 1731, f. 387, 7 September 1580.
[3] B.N., Mss. fr. 15563, ff. 207–8, 14–16 November 1580.
[4] B.N., Mss. fr. 15891, f. 74, 22 November 1580, Bellièvre to the king.

from Bellièvre. He told the queen that Villeroy had been very clear-sighted in that negotiation and had rendered the king great and good service. Villeroy, with equal modesty, disclaimed the credit and praised Bellièvre.[1]

Villeroy was in a hurry, but his journey proved to be both slow and hazardous. The bad roads were so deeply flooded that he actually feared the loss of his coach. On 28 November he only came within nine long and wearisome leagues of Angoulême, where he had hoped to spend the night, before he was obliged to abandon his coach and all his luggage.[2] But he soon had greater worries than those provided by travelling in the winter, for he met a courier with letters which made him fear that he would be very ill-received at court. Bellièvre would see, he wrote dejectedly, what a welcome they would give him where he was going, and how they would receive that which had been done. 'I foresee it all too clearly', he said. He felt crushed by the heavy burden of his responsibilities.[3]

We do not know what alarmed him so much, but Villeroy's fears proved to be unfounded, and the king was very well contented with the peace. Soon he wrote to Bellièvre that he would be sending Villeroy back, 'tirer ceste charrue avecques vous', as Villeroy put it himself.[4] Brulart was full of admiration for this treaty. He called it 'chose emerveillable' that in so short a time they should have reached a conclusion.[5]

During the first half of December, therefore, Villeroy had good reason to feel pleased and relieved. Peace had been concluded and he was ready to return to Guienne, for not only did he make the peace, but he was also expected to execute it. Then suddenly, Anjou precipitated a serious crisis.

He had worked himself into a state of physical sickness over the town of Cambrai, in the Netherlands, which was in danger of starvation and which, he said, he was committed to provision. He therefore despatched two officers to command his forces, which

---

[1] Baguenault de Puchesse, *Lettres*, vii, 452, 22 November 1580, Bellièvre to Catherine; *ibid.*, 309, December 1580, Catherine to Bellièvre.

[2] B.N., Mss. fr. 15905, f. 530, 28 November 1580, Villeroy to Bellièvre.

[3] B.N., Mss. fr. 15906, f. 558, 30 November 1580, Villeroy to Bellièvre.

[4] B.N., Mss. fr. 15905, f. 545, 3 December 1580, the king to Bellièvre; Mss. fr. 15906, f. 563, 4 December 1580, Villeroy to Bellièvre.

[5] B.N., Mss. fr. 15905, f. 606, 4 December 1580, Brulart to Bellièvre.

were being illegally raised in many parts of France, and sent a messenger, La Fin, to court, to press the king for men and money. This news threw the court into a turmoil and, over and above the tremendous task of enforcing the peace, Villeroy was once again burdened with that of trying to restrain Anjou. This was the more immediate of the two, for his troops were due to march in less than three weeks. The situation was indeed very serious. The peace was not established and Anjou was involving France in the risk of war with Spain. France was in difficulties over the renewal of the Swiss alliance because of unpaid debts. There was a rising in the marquisate of Saluces and there was serious news of unrest in Dauphiné, where the peace was not in force. Furthermore, Anjou's troops were arousing the most widespread discontent. 'Believe me,' Villeroy wrote to Bellièvre, 'more harm will come of it than I can describe', if Anjou did not revoke his decision. It was absurd, he insisted, to attempt so difficult an operation in a hurry, and Anjou's troops, who were nothing but a rabble of self-seekers, were ruining the duke's reputation by the grave damage they were doing. In Villeroy's opinion, he was very ill-advised and very ill-served. There were only two possible courses of action, he went on, the one to restrain him by persuasion, and the other 'en usant de l'authorite souveraine'. 'No one knows which saint to invoke nor what decision to take . . . their majesties are in great distress about it', he said, and, for his own part, 'j'ai grande pitie de tout cecy et nen attend que tout mal'.[1]

Bellièvre urged that it was already too late to restrain Anjou, and that to allow him to go and be defeated—the result that everyone expected—would be more dangerous than to help

[1] B.N., Mss. fr. 15905, f. 640, 24 December 1580, Villeroy to Bellièvre. It is difficult to determine the king's precise attitude to Anjou's intended expedition to the Netherlands, although he opposed it angrily from December 1580 to July 1581. It may be assumed that his attitude fluctuated according to how dangerous and threatening Anjou appeared to be, and what other dangers were pressing simultaneously. Certain factors, however, were stable. At no cost did the king want a war with Spain, neither did he wish to give the catholics any just grounds for complaint. Nor did he love his brother, and was probably not over-anxious to help him personally. He firmly believed that his departure would be fatal to the peace in Guienne, and he was convulsively angry about the ravages of Anjou's illegal levies in different parts of France. On the other hand, if it could be done safely, if not secretly, he was not averse from repaying Spain in her own coin in the Netherlands, when she was notoriously helping the protestants to sustain civil war in France.

him.[1] Anjou himself claimed that he had done his best to make peace in France, and that he was in despair because no one was willing to do anything for him. Spain, he said, was only waiting to make war on France in any case, and that if he were to take either Biron or Navarre with him, peace would follow in Guienne. There was undeniably some point in this startling argument. The separation of Navarre and Biron was what Villeroy himself had proposed.

This crisis and its aftermath during the next four months are well documented and will be discussed in some detail because they provide an excellent illustration of Villeroy's position in the state, and also add to our knowledge of him personally.

Everyone looked to Villeroy in the moment of crisis, and in every letter Bellièvre insisted with increasing desperation that it was only by his quick return to Guienne that anything could be achieved. Villeroy wrote no less desperately, 'I implore you that monseigneur ... may do me the honour of waiting for me.'[2] This much Bellièvre achieved, and Villeroy left Blois on 26 December with orders not to quit Anjou,[3] for the king had faith in his powers of persuasion and believed that by his constant presence he would be able to restrain him. He also trusted Villeroy to make Anjou understand that the damage done by his troops had created the imminent danger of a general rebellion.[4] Together Villeroy and Bellièvre succeeded in keeping Anjou in Guienne for almost four months, during which time they laboured to enforce their treaty.

Villeroy himself has left a clear analysis of the chief problems which faced him in Guienne.[5] In spite of the fact that this province was in his *département*, and that he admittedly knew more about it than anyone else, the central government was so far away that it was not until he resided and worked there in person that he came to understand the local situation in any detail. It was not encouraging, for the more he learnt of the diversity of the troubles with which the province was afflicted,

[1] Baguenault de Puchesse, *Lettres*, vii, 453, 11 December 1580, Bellièvre to Catherine.

[2] B.N., Mss. fr. 15905, f. 640, 24 December 1580, Villeroy to Bellièvre.

[3] *Ibid.*, f. 646, 26 December 1580, Henry to Bellièvre.

[4] B.N., Mss. fr. 15565, f. 187, 28 December 1580, Henry to Villeroy.

[5] B.N., Mss. fr. 15564, f. 7, 11 January 1581, Villeroy to the king.

and the partialities, quarrels and ill humour of its people, the less hope he had that the king would enjoy the fruits of the peace. The first of the major problems he reported was one to which he had already drawn the king's attention fully a year before, that of the perpetual quarrels between Navarre—as well as Anjou and his sister the Queen of Navarre—and the lieutenant-general, Biron, to whom they refused even to be civil. In the second place it was essential that the king should reward, as liberally as possible, those of the local nobility who, at great loss and danger to their persons and property, had remained loyal to him. Their services had gone unrecognized and they had received no compensation, whereas if they had joined the enemy they could have prospered in safety. If the king omitted to do this, he ran a grave risk of losing the whole province, which was one of the finest jewels in his crown. 'And do not imagine', Villeroy wrote to him sternly, 'that they can be satisfied with letters and words.' For this purpose he considered that it was necessary to raise a special fund. The town of Bordeaux itself was only kept loyal because of the existence of fortifications, for Navarre had many adherents among the officers, magistrates and the *parlement*, that is to say, in influential circles. It was possible for such people to prevent the payment of taxes to the king. The third outstanding obstacle preventing a return to peace and order was Biron's army, which could not be disbanded until the men were paid. His troops had received nothing for six months and were reduced to such a state of necessity that they were 'almost naked'. Villeroy's fourth problem was the administration of justice, about which, he said, Bellièvre was writing in detail.

While Villeroy was with Bellièvre in Guienne in sole charge of enforcing the peace, Pinart and Brulart were at Chenonceaux with Catherine. The council was at Blois, and the king, who became ill at Christmas, had retired to Saint-Germain where he remained until 10 April 1581. It may therefore justly be said that, with Pinart constantly at her side, and Brulart playing a by no means insignificant part, it was Catherine and Villeroy who were ruling the country. At least it was they who did or who prompted everything that was done, though they were not all-powerful.

Villeroy's despatches to the king went first to Pinart, who studied them himself and read them to Catherine. Pinart then wrote in the margins what action they had taken, or were going to take, and sent them on to the king, particularly drawing his attention to any action which was required of him personally. D'O, one of Henry's favourites, who was with him at Saint-Germain, where the king appears to have had no secretaries, also wrote in the margin any comment he had to make on the king's behalf and sent them back to Pinart.[1] Villeroy's letter of 11 January 1581, quoted above, provides us with an excellent example of how this worked. Villeroy began this letter by saying that he had informed Pinart of everything that he had already done about the publication of the peace, and he knew that Pinart would therefore have informed the king. Here Pinart wrote in the margin that he had sent the letters to Monsieur d'O, to read them to the king. Villeroy requested that the king and Catherine should both write to Navarre—in their own hands for greater authority—about his hostile attitude to Biron. Pinart underlined this request and against it he wrote: 'Il plaira au Roy prendre la peine d'escrire cette lettre et a Monsieur d'O l'envoyer par la premiere.' Pinart also underlined the request that the king should gratify the loyal nobles of Guienne and wrote beside it that if the king were agreeable, Catherine, Cheverny and the finance officers would do all they could to find the money needed, and letters would be prepared for Villeroy to give the nobles. Underneath d'O wrote that the king was agreeable. Point by point, business was dealt with in this way, the king being kept fully informed, but only being asked to do the things that required his personal intervention.

Catherine, for her part, did not fail to inform Villeroy of all that she was doing, or trying to do, to implement his advice and, where necessary, of how she was using her influence with the king. She and Villeroy worked together in an easy partnership because they knew what to expect of each other. While helping in every way she could, Catherine had confidence in Villeroy and Bellièvre and she left them alone to do their best without bothering them with instructions. 'Il n'y a qu'à s'en remetre à

[1] Baguenault de Puchesse, *Lettres*, vii, 334, 27 January 1581, Catherine to Villeroy; original written by Pinart.

vous,' she wrote to them, 'comme verrez que faisons.'[1] Her
letters to Villeroy are frank, friendly and warm with approval:
'You are so wise', she wrote to him about Anjou, by the hand of
Pinart late one night, 'that you do not need any further advice
about that or any other matter.' She also praised his advice
that the king must on no account disarm until peace was firmly
established, not only in Guienne, but also in Languedoc and
Dauphiné, and until all danger of war with Spain, as a result of
Anjou's activities, had passed.[2]

The necessity of this was quickly proved by the treaty which,
in spite of everything, Anjou concluded on 23 January, with
deputies who came from the Netherlands. But Catherine did not
blame Villeroy or Bellièvre. On the contrary, she wrote, 'No
one could do better or more worthily than you have done and
are doing . . . and rest assured . . . that the king also entertains
this same good opinion of you both, with very great and good
reason.'[3] Furthermore, it was to Villeroy that she unburdened her
private feelings—the trouble of a queen who has to face affairs
of state in which she is also emotionally involved. She was at
her wits' end to know what to do with Anjou: 'Quent à moy, je
ne sé plus que lui en mender; car je croy qu'il set moque de
tout. . . .' When his enterprises ended in ignominy, he would
realize the wisdom of her advice but, she added sadly, she
would be nonetheless distressed: 'je ann auré le regret que je
douys pour lui estre mère et l'aymer'.[4]

Brulart and Pinart also kept in constant touch with their colleagues in the west, and Pinart not only encouragingly confirmed the queen's confidence in their work but also assured
them that she had made her good opinion of them perfectly
clear to the king. Pinart was terribly hard worked at this time,
as may be imagined, and he was also involved in preparations
for a coming embassy to England. One night he wrote limply
to Bellièvre, 'I assure you that I am worn out from standing, and
writing on the end of the queen's chest [*coffre*] besides which it is so

[1] Baguenault de Puchesse, *Lettres*, vii, 346, 7 February 1581, Catherine to
Bellièvre.
[2] *Ibid.*, 318, 12 January 1581, Catherine to Villeroy.
[3] *Ibid.*, 334, 27 February 1581, Catherine to Villeroy.
[4] *Ibid.*, 353, 7 and 8 February 1581, Catherine to Villeroy.

late that I can hardly stand up straight from sleep and overwork.'[1]

It was about 18 February 1581 that Villeroy once more left the west to go to court to sort out as many problems as possible with Catherine and the king, and also with a mission from Anjou. Glad as he was to escape, he expected to return without delay, although he swore that were it not for the sake of Bellièvre, whom he held in great esteem, he would sooner endure at least four stabs from a spur than ever to return to Guienne.[2] Poor Bellièvre had already declared that, for his part, he would rather be in Poland than Guienne. From Châtellerault, on 23 February, Villeroy wrote again, deeply disturbed by the presence in Poitou of companies of foot levied for Anjou to take to the Netherlands. They were committing every kind of brigandage and terrorizing the people. 'God knows what they will say to me when I arrive at the court', he wrote, as though it were his fault.[3] Yet this time he had an accurate premonition of trouble ahead.

Villeroy rejoined the court at Blois on 24 February, concealing his despondency and anxiety, for he appeared gay and cheerful as usual.[4] The purpose of his coming was kept secret, but it was not supposed, despite his cheerfulness, that a person of his rank and quality would have made the long journey to Blois if everything were going well in Guienne.[5] His message, in fact, appears to have been no less than an ultimatum from Anjou, to the effect that the huguenots would not proceed with the restitution, under the treaty, of towns which they held, unless the king would help his expedition to the Netherlands.[6] This position was both extremely delicate and profoundly distasteful to Villeroy, particularly when, having done nothing to control the undisciplined marauding of his troops, Anjou wrote to Villeroy asking to see the effects of his 'promise'. 'I do not know what he means by it', Villeroy wrote indignantly. 'The truth is that I promised him I would give their majesties a faithful account of his plans.'[7]

[1] B.N., Mss. fr. 15906, f. 84, 27 January 1581, Pinart to Bellièvre.
[2] Ibid., f. 174, 19 February 1581, Villeroy to Bellièvre.
[3] Ibid., f. 192, 23 February 1581, Villeroy to Bellièvre.
[4] Desjardins, Negs. Tosc., iv, 351, 28 February 1581.
[5] Id.
[6] B.N., Mss. it. 1732, f. 1, 2 March 1581, f. 4, 10 March 1581.
[7] B.N., Mss. fr. 15906, f. 219, 3 March 1581, Villeroy to Bellièvre.

But he dissociated himself from them absolutely, for he never had the least intention of pleading so poor a cause. Besides, he was shortly to learn that these troops of Anjou's were ravaging his father's lands. 'Ce sera trop', he said, for they had already lodged on three of his own estates, including that at Villeroy.[1]

If Villeroy's mission was unpropitious, circumstances at court were equally so. He had been encouraged to expect a warm reception, but it was so chilling and unrewarding that he wrote to Bellièvre in bewildered dejection, 'je confesse ne mestre jamais trouve en telle perplexite que je suis. Car je veoi que lon mesure icy la fidellite des hommes aux evenements des choses et non au debvoir quils font.' The king had taken exception to one of Villeroy's letters, besides which he was so angry about the enormity of the harm done by his brother's troops as to have become quite irrational.[2] Anyone who approached him could therefore expect to be angrily repulsed, and Villeroy was aware of the personal and the political danger so long as this lasted. Besides, the king was in one of his withdrawing moods. He was said to have been suffering from a manifestation of some kind of venereal disease which, at that time, affected his face and one of his legs. There is no doubt that his health was bad, and it is a partial explanation of his conduct. But even when he was no longer ill, he obstinately remained at Saint-Germain and refused to attend to affairs of state.[3] No one was allowed to see him; Villeroy said so twice—'cest chose deffendue sans son conge',[4] and 'il nest loisible'.[5] In spite of the trouble he had taken to reach the distant court as fast as possible, it was 7 March before he was able to leave Blois for Saint-Germain. To make matters worse, Pinart had gone with an embassy to England; Brulart had a brief illness, and Catherine was seriously ill and could not work. She got up and tried—'vous cognoissez son courage', said Villeroy—but she had a severe relapse.[6] For the moment, at least, Villeroy was expected to do everything, yet he was obstructed at every turn. Everyone was quick to lay the blame

[1] B.N., Mss. fr. 15906, f. 245, 9 March 1581, Villeroy to Bellièvre.
[2] Ibid., f. 197, 26 February 1581, Villeroy to Bellièvre.
[3] Desjardins, Negs. Tosc., iv, 342, 25 December 1580.
[4] B.N., Mss. fr. 15906, f. 210, 1 March 1581, Villeroy to Bellièvre.
[5] Ibid., f. 219, 3 March 1581, Villeroy to Bellièvre.
[6] Id.

on others but not to offer constructive help for they were all pre-occupied with their own concerns. 'Il ny a celui qui ne fasse proffession de blasmer le mal et reprendre les actions des autres,' he complained at this time, 'mais je nen veoi point [qui] donnent meilleur conseil et sefforcent de mieulx faire. Chacun a habondonne le timon du vaisseau pour pensser a ses affaires vivant au jour la journee et s'engraissant du travail d'autruy.'[1] He considered the problems with which he was faced to be insuperable, because of the divisions and conflicting desires of the protestants; no one could satisfy them all.[2]

If the queen's illness further delayed his departure for Saint-Germain, it was possibly a blessing in disguise, for, when he finally arrived, the king received him well, and even attended— in a mask—an entertainment which Villeroy gave the next evening.[3]

The result of Villeroy's mission is not clear; it appears to have been that the king offered Anjou some limited help, but only if he agreed to remain in France to carry out the peace. But Anjou was straining to leave for Cambrai and Bellièvre was following him from place to place. If he left before the peace were in force, Navarre and Biron would take up arms. Bellièvre was distraught, and in every letter, whether to Catherine, the king, Brulart or to Villeroy himself, he urged and pleaded the immediate necessity of Villeroy's return. Even Anjou was begging for Villeroy, because no one had confidence in anyone else.[4]

Villeroy had been ready to return, and had told Bellièvre he would not be long, but then he had to wait to hear the demands made by deputies from Dauphiné, where peace had still not been enforced. The king sent him back to Blois to consult Catherine and he found her piteously ill. 'Elle ne faict plus que languir. Elle fait pitie a tout le monde et vous jure que j'en ay le cueur si serre que je ne me puis remetre.'[5] It is no wonder that he was overjoyed to escape for a moment to relax over Easter with his uncle Limoges. Villeroy was probably very tired; certainly he was in great perplexity of mind and felt overwhelmed

[1] B.N., Mss. fr. 15906, f. 197, 26 February 1581, Villeroy to Bellièvre.
[2] *Ibid.*, f. 228, 5 March 1581, Villeroy to Bellièvre.
[3] Desjardins, *Negs. Tosc.*, iv, 358, 13 March 1581.
[4] B.N., Mss. fr. 15891, f. 184, 30 March 1581, Bellièvre to the king.
[5] B.N., Mss. fr. 15906, f. 288, 23 March 1581, Villeroy to Bellièvre.

by so many demands upon him. There was the very dangerous deadlock between the royal brothers. Villeroy wished that they would only meet and fight their own battles and make their own decisions, instead of sending him to receive at either end the brunt of their displeasure.[1] News which came in from all sides was going from bad to worse. The affairs of Dauphiné, which delayed him at Blois, were serious, yet he knew that if only the duc de Maine, commanding a royal army there, had been sent 50,000 *écus* two months before, as he had advised, the situation would have been quite different. The real problem was, as he said, that 'we cannot either make war or peace. That is our trouble for which there is no remedy without the help of God.'[2] Indeed, for the last twenty years, the periods of war and peace in France had been very much the same. Villeroy was also showered with agonized letters from Bellièvre beseeching him to return. He sympathized with his plight and understood his difficulties, for he certainly knew what Anjou was like: 'Je cognois bien quel est sa nature et combien elle se bande contre quiconque lui contredit. Il n'est jour que je ne le dis et naie devant les yeux les mesmes considerations.'[3] But if Villeroy felt drawn to Bellièvre and the unfinished work in Guienne, he also knew that with Pinart in England, Brulart desperately needed him at court. Villeroy was always considerate of his colleagues and Brulart was vigorous in defending his claims. Villeroy's departure, he said, would 'crush me and kill me at one blow', adding—whether sourly, humorously or in resignation we cannot tell—that that would not prevent his going, 'for the loss of their good servitors is always the last of our masters' worries'.[4] Brulart had been writing regularly to Bellièvre in Guienne and when Villeroy and Pinart were both away, it was he who received, read and distributed the despatches, as Pinart had done before. Sometimes he would acknowledge them and say that they had been read to the queen, but that it was Villeroy who would reply. But when Villeroy was there, he took charge of this himself. Brulart was not Villeroy's only problem at court.

---

[1] B.N., Mss. fr. 15906, f. 322, 3 April 1581, Villeroy to Bellièvre.
[2] *Ibid.*, f. 288, 23 March 1581, Villeroy to Bellièvre.
[3] *Ibid.*, f. 322, 3 April 1581, Villeroy to Bellièvre.
[4] *Ibid.*, f. 377, 16 April 1581, Brulart to Bellièvre.

With Catherine too ill to work, he could hardly leave Blois until the king arrived. From week to week, however, Henry delayed both his coming and the most urgent decisions. The king and Catherine were relying entirely on Villeroy, or so he explained to Bellièvre.[1] As if all this were not enough for anyone to bear, Villeroy received the news that his wife was dangerously ill with a continuous fever. 'Je vous laisse a penser,' he groaned to Bellièvre, 'quel plaisir ce me sera de m'en esloigner.'[2] This trouble stirred not only his emotions, but also his strong sense of duty. If he owed obedience to the king, did he not also owe something equally binding to his wife, when she might be going to die? But he remained anxiously at court, constantly expecting to be sent to Guienne.

The king's arrival on 10 April brought Villeroy little relief. Indeed, considering the bad news from Dauphiné and the activities of Anjou's levies, Villeroy knew precisely what frame of mind to expect in the king.[3] Nor was he mistaken. If he had no desire to return to Guienne, it was not for his pleasure that he remained at court.[4] The king was still so very angry about Anjou's levies and the problem of the Netherlands that there was not a soul at court, Villeroy told Bellièvre, whom he did not seem to be attacking when he mentioned the subject. There are some grounds for thinking that Villeroy had come over to Bellièvre's opinion that it would be safer to help than to oppose Anjou, as no one could restrain him, since he said that the king's orders to oppose all his brother's levies would end by placing France in great danger, and would cost her dear. 'When means are lacking,' he said, 'one ought to have recourse to prudence and vigilance. But it is all one to us and we continue to live as usual.'[5] Villeroy dared not do more, in writing, than hint at what it was like to be at court and, even so, he told Bellièvre to burn his letter. But it is clear enough what he thought of the way of life at court and the king's conduct, or misconduct, of affairs. The king would do everything in his power, Villeroy said, to establish the peace. But, if Bellièvre objected that the establishment of the peace depended upon a proper handling of Anjou,

[1] B.N., Mss. fr. 15906, f. 340, 8 April 1581, Villeroy to Bellièvre.
[2] Ibid., f. 344, 10 April 1581, Villeroy to Bellièvre.
[3] Id.   [4] Ibid., f. 371, 16 April 1581, Villeroy to Bellièvre.   [5] Id.

'I will reply', he said, 'that no one believes it.'[1] It was also in an effort to establish the peace at this time that Villeroy was privately conferring with envoys from Navarre. If Navarre could only be induced to come to court, that would greatly reduce the likelihood of further trouble, and would separate him from Anjou.[2] In April the moment came when Bellièvre could restrain Anjou no longer. He crept gradually north, protesting his innocence at every stage, and finally left, not for the Netherlands, but for England.

For Villeroy, relief came only at the end of May, when he went home to the comfort of his house and gardens at Villeroy which, contrary to his expectations, had been left undamaged by Anjou's unpaid rabble. Indeed, he told Bellièvre, that in the Ile-de-France, his property alone had been spared, which was possibly a measure of the respect he commanded, or of his popularity.[3]

For Villeroy personally the treaty of Fleix was probably—within the period of this study—his greatest achievement. His subsequent experience in Guienne serves to reveal to us the extent to which the royal administration in the provinces had broken down. There were no foundations left upon which to build the peace. Nevertheless, neither Catherine nor the secretaries despaired of salvaging some kind of settlement from the ruins. The years 1578–81 show the secretaries working in their different capacities, both at home and abroad, and in the closest co-operation with Catherine and each other, while the king chose to play only a secondary role. These were years of strenuous endeavour, in which they did everything within their power to enforce the peace at home and to restrain Anjou from bringing disaster upon himself and foreign war upon his country.

It was for the sake of Anjou, to try to negotiate a marriage between him and queen Elizabeth, that Pinart took part in an embassy to England in 1581, leaving shortly before Villeroy returned from Guienne. The embassy had first been mooted in August or September 1580, but was only finally decided upon in

---

[1] B.N., Mss. fr. 15906, f. 371, 16 April 1581, Villeroy to Bellièvre.
[2] C.S.P.F., 1581–2, p. 112, 8 April 1581, Cobham to the secretaries.
[3] B.N., Mss. fr. 15906, f. 288, 23 March 1581, Villeroy to Bellièvre.

February 1581. It was confidently expected, at least by Pinart, that the marriage would be concluded without difficulty.[1] Ville-roy never expressed himself very clearly on this subject in any document that has survived, but he appears to have regarded the project with reserve, owing to the seeming impossibility of reconciling Anjou and the king. At the time of this embassy he believed that Anjou had no intention of marrying Elizabeth. He was therefore anxious that the duke should extricate himself from the situation as gracefully as possible, and not allow his hostile relations with the king to appear too obvious.[2] That Elizabeth may have had no intention of marrying Anjou, he did not mention. Brulart did not believe that the embassy would succeed, and therefore disapproved of it. He wished the money —certainly a considerable sum since about seven hundred people went to England—could have been spent on chastising the protestants in Dauphiné. In his opinion, France was merely rendering England a service and raising her prestige abroad.[3] Brulart may possibly have been influenced by his annoyance, and justifiable dismay, at being left alone at court. 'I shall not be without occupation', he wrote to Villeroy on 18 February— Villeroy was actually on his way to Blois at the time—'or rather in a short while I shall be quite prostrated [he had recently been ill] and unable to serve'. 'Et suis marry que pour une facon de peu d'honneur et dutilite pour ce Royaulme quils vont jouer jaccroisse tant de peine et de travail si je suis longuement seul.'[4] Pinart was not unsympathetic, and took care not to leave his work in arrears for Brulart. He felt for him, and told Bellièvre as much, for he was left with too great a burden in the work of their combined offices.[5]

There were thirteen ambassadors, led by the prince Dauphin, son of the duc de Montpensier. Their instructions were written by Pinart himself, and signed by Brulart on 1 February 1581, for no secretary ever countersigned instructions in which he was in-cluded, even though he may have drafted them.[6] Their com-

---

[1] B.N., Mss. fr. 15906, f. 170, 19 February 1581, Pinart to Bellièvre.
[2] Ibid., f. 381, 18 April 1581, Villeroy to Bellièvre.
[3] Ibid., f. 298, 26 March 1581, Brulart to Bellièvre.
[4] Ibid., f. 160, 18 February 1581, Brulart to Villeroy.
[5] Ibid., f. 170, 19 February 1581, Pinart to Bellièvre.
[6] B.N., Mss. fr. 3308, ff. 1-2, 1 February 1581.

mission was solely to negotiate a marriage, on the basis of articles concluded in November 1579. The details of the affair are extraordinarily complex, and need not detain us here except in so far as they shed light on Pinart and his career. Pinart appears, at least at this time, to have favoured the marriage, and did his best to bring it about. Elizabeth, as she was wont to do, blew warm, hot and cold in turn, producing considerable confusion, and playing for time in a masterly demonstration of the art of procrastination. Whatever may have been the advantages or otherwise of the marriage as a possible solution to the problem of Anjou—who was little short of an international embarrassment—it seems reasonably certain that Elizabeth was at least anxious for an alliance.

The ambassadors' departure was constantly and tiresomely delayed.[1] Pinart left Blois for Paris on 20 or 21 February, but the embassy had to wait at Calais until 12 April before everyone was ready. They finally arrived about 18 April, and were most honourably received at Somerset House on the Thames, where the chief of them were lodged.[2] Pinart was by no means an unimportant member of this large and dazzling embassy. In the first place, England being in his *département*, he probably had a more complete knowledge than anyone else on the French side of what had gone before; certainly he was one of the effective negotiators. He was also, in a literal sense, their secretary, and besides writing letters, he wrote a memoir for each day. Some of these are preserved in one of his letter-books. They are well and colourfully written and reveal a lively eye for detail.

From the start Elizabeth, who meant to avoid any decision, spent much time in entertainment and in speeches. She first received the ambassadors in a large and beautiful room at Westminster palace where, sumptuously dressed, she descended from the dais to kiss the prince Dauphin. Letters, brought by Pinart, were handed to her and he was one of seven commissioners personally presented to the queen, who spoke to them

---

[1] B.N., Mss. fr. 15906, f. 170, 19 February 1581, Pinart to Bellièvre.

[2] B.N., Mss. fr. 3308, f. 15v, 22 April 1581. This volume is one of Pinart's letter-books and the documents which it contains on this mission to England have evidently been used but, with one exception, not quoted by La Ferrière, *Les Projets de mariage de la reine Élizabeth*, ch. x.

each in turn.[1] Elizabeth, he reported, was in a festive mood, and gaily threatened the prince Dauphin that she would attach his cap to his head if he insisted upon remaining uncovered. Negotiation did not begin in earnest until after dinner and a ball on 26 April, when Elizabeth raised a number of difficulties, which had all been discussed before, and said that she had to wait for the reply to a letter to Anjou. Her deputies later raised the same points, and mixed affairs of church and state with the separate consideration that a pregnancy would endanger the queen's life.

It was only on May day that Elizabeth made herself perfectly clear. She invited the French to watch bull- and bear-baiting from a window, while Pinart, for one, would sooner have got on with the work. Then she took them to hear lute players in a long gallery hung with maps and pictures and afterwards entertained them by playing the spinet herself. Only then did she come to the point: there were difficulties in the way of concluding the marriage, therefore they must try to make 'une bonne et etroite ligue'—which the French had no commission to do. It was Pinart who replied to her that she had already been fully satisfied on religious grounds, and that a marriage would indeed form an indissoluble link with France, such as she proposed, and which the king and Catherine equally desired.[2]

The ambassadors remained in England until the middle of June, wrangling over a marriage contract which contained a clause allowing Elizabeth to contract out of it. This Pinart rightly thought a waste of time. Finally they returned to France laden with honours and silver plate—said to have been fashioned from treasure captured by Drake—but without having obtained anything else from the astute Queen of England.[3]

Five months later, on 15 November, the king sent Pinart back to England in pursuit of Anjou.[4] Since their departure in June, the negotiations had continued, and Elizabeth had gone so far as to give Anjou a ring, which gave rise to rumours that the

[1] B.N., Mss. fr. 3308, f. 17, 24 April 1581.
[2] Ibid., f. 26v, 1 May 1581.
[3] Desjardins, Negs. Tosc., iv, 372, 27 June 1581.
[4] B.N., Mss. it. 1732, f. 216, 16 November 1581; Mss. fr. 3307, f. 50.

marriage had been concluded. Then she blew cool again, and once more placed everything in doubt. Unfortunately we have only one account of Pinart's second mission, written by Mendoza, the Spanish ambassador in England. He believed that Pinart came with instructions to concede everything demanded of him, provided the marriage took place. We may reasonably assume that he was sent to try to clinch the marriage, but not to concede all Elizabeth's demands, since they included the restitution of Calais. Although Mendoza can hardly have been a sympathetic onlooker, his account of what took place does Pinart credit. Elizabeth emerges as baffling and undecided, Anjou as most despicable, and Pinart as having dealt firmly with them both. He returned to France on 14 February 1582. He had not brought off the English marriage but, if Mendoza is to be believed, he had at least shown spirit and initiative.[1] Later, when he was Spanish ambassador in France, Mendoza alleged that Pinart received £3,000 from the English ambassador, Sir Edward Stafford, some time in 1586, and described him as queen Elizabeth's pensioner. What was behind this we do not know, but the sum mentioned is too large to carry much conviction.[2]

[1] *C.S.P.Sp.*, 1580–6, p. 229, 4 December 1581, p. 269, 24 January, p. 273, 27 January 1582, Mendoza to Philip II; B.N., Mss. fr. 3307, f. 50.
[2] *C.S.P.Sp.*, 1587–1603, p. 63, 9 April 1587, Mendoza to Philip II.

CHAPTER XV

The Absentee King, 1582-4

THE years 1582-4 show the secretaries at their most independent and powerful. This was partly because they
were trusted and esteemed by the king and Catherine, but
also very much because the king spent about two-thirds of his
time withdrawn from the court. Catherine was usually there but
she travelled about a certain amount and suffered from rather
frequent illnesses. But, as far as the secretaries were concerned,
she mostly acted in an advisory capacity: they had constantly to
obtain the king's consent and signature to the many acts that
needed royal sanction. The king and a secretary together formed
the nucleus of the executive and ought, therefore, to have been
working in the closest co-operation. As the secretaries had to do
their best, in spite of the king's shortcomings, and as it was upon
them that any extra burden of work and responsibility fell, the
king's whereabouts and disposition, his absences and his eccen-
tricities very closely affected them and the circumstances in
which they worked, as the history of the next six years will show.
If this was true of all three secretaries, it applied particularly to
Villeroy. His position in the state was unique and he stood in a
special relationship to the king, who cherished him more than
his two colleagues, and above all other ministers.

The king's retiring disposition had been noticed at the outset
of his reign. In 1578 and 1579, his departures at times of crisis
had excited adverse comment and a stern rebuke from Villeroy.
But from the time of his illness and long absence at the beginning of 1581 this, and other unfortunate tendencies, were to become much more pronounced. This illness was an inauspicious
crisis and turning-point in his life, after which he never regained
either a satisfactory state of health or his pristine sanity. That is

not to imply that the king was insane, but that the neurotic tendencies always present in his character began, from then on, to grow and to develop, with effects that were felt first by those closest to him, and then in ever-widening circles. Journeying restlessly from château to spa, and from one spa to another, partly to escape from court, creditors, and the burdens of the crown, and partly in the forlorn hope that he might yet have a son to prevent the dangers of a disputed succession, Henry III began to behave with increasing eccentricity and immoderation. In his actions, reactions and emotions, he gave way more and more to extremes and excesses which were highly dangerous both to his country and to himself. There were five ways in which this was particularly noticeable: in the lengthy absences from court which have already been mentioned, in his treatment of his favourites, Joyeuse and Épernon, in his attitude to finance, in his religious life and in his emotional instability.

Henry had always preferred the counsel and the company of a few intimates. This, if unwise, was legitimate, but his exaltation of his two favourites was not. Upon them he loaded offices, titles, riches and estates, and they quickly became not only the very powerful creatures of a bankrupt king, but also the objects of envy, hatred, fear and the utmost hostility. Many people were alienated from the king on account of Joyeuse and Épernon. Henry exalted them because the old nobility, who were the *gouverneurs* of his provinces, the office holders in his state, the apex of French society and the natural supporters of a monarchy, could no longer be trusted. He also exalted them because he was as prodigal of his affections as of his country's wealth. He craved and needed affection himself, and he gave it freely to those who were close to him.

The king, like most of his family, had always been extravagant. He had no conception of public finance and he spent large sums on festivities, entertainments and the purchase of animals. He was, besides, generous to the point of folly. The wedding of Joyeuse to the queen's sister, which took place in September 1581, and on which the king spent an estimated 1,000,000 *écus*, was widely regarded as an outrage, both because Joyeuse was considered socially unworthy and because disorders in Guienne, Languedoc and Dauphiné were largely due to lack of money.

Money was owed to the Swiss on whose alliance so much depended; money was owed to the Venetians; money was needed
to provide against the threat of war with Spain; lack of money
was, in fact, the continual lament and stumbling-block of everyone who tried to serve the crown.

It was a matter of common knowledge that the king was
deeply religious and his devotions had for long attracted attention. But, from this time onwards, Henry gradually began to
indulge in veritable religious orgies, to the despair of the secretaries, whom he often declined to see, and to the anxiety of
Catherine and Villeroy who feared the possible effects upon his
health.

With all this, when the pressure of affairs of state became
sufficiently great, and when his negligence brought him to the
verge of some fresh disaster, Henry would be shocked into a
state of awareness. But each time he was aroused only when it
was too late for effective action, to find that he was already
wounded in his pride, his vanity and his estate. Then he fell a
prey, first to the anguish of self-recrimination and remorse—
inflicting on himself and on Villeroy, whose warnings went unheeded, a devastating analysis of his failings which, at such times,
were perfectly clear to him—and then to anger; anger which
began to smoulder and to grow in him like a poison. The full
consequences for the secretaries emerged only gradually, but it
was the king's absences which most immediately affected their
work.

Even during the reign of Charles IX, the secretaries had, on
occasions, opened the despatches, but from about 1578 or 1580
they did so constantly,[1] each despatch being delivered to the
secretary whose *département* it concerned. In the king's absence
they would study them and read them to Catherine if she were
there. They would then write the reply, in the king's name, often
on Catherine's advice, and send it to the king for signature.
Sometimes they would send a draft and ask him to copy it in his
own hand for greater authority, and sometimes they simply sent
the incoming despatch, with a request for instructions. In every
case this meant delay and additional work, because they had to
write covering letters of explanation and sometimes impatient

[1] Petitot, xliv, *Mémoires d'Estat de Villeroy*, 100.

reminders before they obtained what they wanted. Not only did
the secretaries open the despatches and draft the replies, which
gave them opportunities to influence or modify the king's
official opinions, but they also maintained a private correspondence upon public matters with the officers and ambassadors
working within their *départements*. They had done this for years,
to some extent, but not on so large a scale. There were various
reasons for this. In the first place the officers and ambassadors
concerned were often personal friends. But, apart from this, a
despatch was at least a semi-public document and there were
many things and much information, advice and explanation
which were more usefully kept private. There was also another
reason. Despatches were not normally answered until the king
had seen them and not—unless exceptionally by Catherine—
until he had signed the reply. When he was away the delay
could be considerable; and when he returned there was frequently an accumulation of business to be dealt with. Again and
again Villeroy apologized to Maisse, ambassador in Venice, for
missing the regular post, the *ordinaire* from Lyons, because of
the king's absence, because he had been unable to show him the
despatch, or because the reply had not been signed in time.[1] In
these circumstances, a private letter from the secretary served
every purpose but that of an official instruction, and provided
much more interesting comment on affairs.

The problem of showing the king the despatches and getting
them answered promptly and in time to catch the posts, was a
perpetual one, for even when he was there the secretaries did not
have free access to him. Several of them have left us evidence of
this. The normal time for reading the despatches to the king
was at his levee—early in the morning—and if this opportunity
were missed, they were liable to have to wait until the following
day.[2] If the king decided upon the reply immediately, it could
be prepared and taken for signature the next morning, and the
secretaries could never be certain of getting the answer ready
more quickly than that. 'There is not much chance of showing

---

[1] Maisse went to Venice in August 1582, and the first of these apologies and a
warning that Villeroy would not always be able to prevent this from happening
was dated 25 December 1582. B.N., Mss. fr. 16092, f. 21.

[2] B.N., Mss. fr. 3337, f. 138, 28 July 1577, Fizes to Nevers.

the despatches to the king except in the morning,' Pinart once wrote to Matignon in explanation, 'which I did yesterday, and this morning which is the following day, his majesty has seen and signed the answer.'[1] Villeroy himself explains in his memoir how necessary it was for the secretaries to open and deal with the despatches, 'because the king did not permit them to take them to him at any time, and the greatest difficulty they had, whether the king were present or absent, was to read him the despatches or to have them shown to him, especially since by failing to do so at the critical moment, they could not, as was necessary, answer the correspondent promptly'.[2] In his erratic attention to business and the inadequate access allowed to the secretaries, Henry placed great difficulties in their way. Ville-roy would have been greatly relieved if the king had attended to his affairs and given the secretaries his instructions every day. 'Quel plus grand contentment peuvent recevoir les secretaires,' he wrote, 'que quand leur maistre void tous les jours ses affaires, et leur ordonne ce quils ont à faire? C'est leur descharge et leur honneur; car il void et considere mieux le devoir qu'ils font en leurs charges, et peuvent mieux satisfaire à ceux qui s'adressent à eux, et leur correspondre.'[3] It was the secretaries, Villeroy said, who received the blame for delays and the king's affairs suffered. Sometimes, therefore, they would make a synopsis of the salient points of a despatch to send to the king if he were away—adding 'comme il advenoit trop souvent'—or else to explain it to him in person, the more easily to extract the answer.[4]

Villeroy justly pointed out that either the secretaries must be trusted with the despatches in this way, or else the king must be ready and willing to attend to them himself at any hour, other-wise he would be very ill served: 'sinon qu'il face estat d'estre très-mal servy, et de ne se prendre qu'à luy-mesme du mal qui en succedera'.[5] The same arguments applied to the habit of writing private letters on public affairs—a practice which was never denied or concealed. This, said Villeroy, who had written

[1] B.N., Mss. fr. 3389, f. 70, 22 July 1578, Pinart to Matignon.
[2] Petitot, xliv, *Mémoires d'Estat de Villeroy*, 101.
[3] *Ibid.*, 101–2.
[4] *Ibid.*, 101.
[5] *Id.*

thousands of letters of the kind, added very greatly to the burden of their work, but was of the utmost service to the king.[1]

The secretaries sent the king not only despatches but also reports of council meetings, drawing his attention to such matters as had been reserved for his own decision. If occasion arose they would receive deputations, interview ambassadors and take discretionary action in the affairs of their *départements*.[2] Sometimes, if he were not too far away, the king would send for the secretaries or for Villeroy alone, 'ne voulant antrer au goufre de la cour', he wrote to Villeroy on one such occasion.[3] 'Villeroy vene me trouver incontinant a quelque heure que seste letre vous trouve,' he wrote another time, 'car je ne vous puis dire la cause . . . venez je le vous dis ancores une foys. Adyeu.'[4]

The year 1582 opened in this way with the king at Ollainville, where he sent for Villeroy, who then returned to Paris burdened with business like a donkey, as he told Bellièvre.[5] A great deal devolved upon the secretaries because in February not only was Catherine very ill, but the king went away on a pilgrimage to Chartres, wading in mud up to the knees, as a result of which he had to go to bed.[6] In March Catherine departed to Chenonceaux to convalesce, and Villeroy wrote to Matignon that Catherine, 'notre bonne maistresse', was not lacking in courage, 'principallement puis quil est question de bien faire'.[7] No doubt because she was resting, she did not take Pinart with her. He had only recently returned from his second mission to England, and he remained in Paris to attend to the affairs of his *département*.

Sometimes when he was absent, the king would reply to the secretaries in his own hand, but more often he would simply do what they asked of him, or else write his comments down the margins of their own letters or of the documents they sent him.

[1] Petitot, xliv, *Mémoires d'Estat de Villeroy*, 102.

[2] B.N., Mss. fr. 6628, f. 113, 26 June 1582, Pinart to the king; *ibid.*, f. 102, 2 June 1582, Villeroy to the king; *ibid.*, f. 70, 26 June 1582, Villeroy to the king.

[3] B.N., Mss. n.a.f. 1245, no. 44, f. 101, undated. This and the volumes 1243, 1244 and 1246 are copies of letters contained in the 'Collection des autographes de la bibliothèque de Saint-Petersbourg', vols. 13–16.

[4] B.N., Mss. n.a.f. 1246, no. 62, f. 63, undated.

[5] B.N., Mss. fr. 15906 (2), f. 272, 9 February 1581/2, Villeroy to Bellièvre.

[6] B.N., Mss. it. 1732, f. 272, 9 February 1581/2.

[7] B.N., Mss. fr. 3354, f. 51, 20 February 1582, Villeroy to Matignon.

However, he frequently wrote to Villeroy, and would give him orders for all three secretaries, as in March 1582, when he wrote: 'Faites et le faites fayre a vos compaygnons des letres partout . . . pour empescher les levees et assamblees de jans.'[1] He was referring to the levies being raised for Anjou which were causing great alarm and which he intended to disperse. The secretaries wrote accordingly to the *gouverneurs* of their provinces and sent the letters to Henry for signature.[2]

In these circumstances it was natural for the secretaries to send the king advice on whatever business arose; indeed the king expected it. 'Mandez m'an vostre advis,' he once wrote to Villeroy, 'car j'an suis importune et presse.'[3] But it is unlikely that they all three expressed themselves as plainly as Villeroy, and even he was careful to excuse himself sometimes, as he did in the case of an ordinance on precedence, which he had firmly opposed. But the king only replied in the margin with the unexpected words to find on a state paper—'je vous aime.'[4] The chief problem at this time on which Villeroy felt the need to advise the king was that of Languedoc, which, together with Guienne, was in a state of intense unrest. Villeroy was afraid, and rightly so, that the protestants would never recover from their lack of confidence or the 'maudite maladie de deffiance', as he called it.[5] It was widely rumoured—and it was true—that Montmorency, *gouverneur* of Languedoc and leader of the protestants there, was in league with Spain.[6] In April 1582, Villeroy sent the king a solemn warning about the conditions in this province—a warning which, like all his others, went unheeded —but which the king was later to remember with bitter regret. The king had recently ordered Montmorency to disband his troops in the towns, and Villeroy pointed out that the king would see from his replies which way the wind was blowing, and advised him to take the necessary precautions. 'Sire cest ung

[1] B.N., Mss. n.a.f. 1244, no. 51, undated, Henry to Villeroy.
[2] B.N., Mss. fr. 6628, f. 84, 12 March 1582, Brulart to the king; *ibid.*, f. 86, 13 March 1582, Pinart to the king.
[3] B.N., Mss. n.a.f. 1243, no. 1, f. 4, undated, Henry to Villeroy.
[4] B.N., Mss. fr. 3385, f. 125, 4 April 1583, Villeroy to the king. Although this letter belongs to the following year, the circumstances were similar.
[5] B.N., Mss. fr. 3354, f. 64, 25 March 1582, Villeroy to Pontcarré.
[6] Desjardins, *Negs. Tosc.*, iv, 397, 7 September 1581.

affaire aussi facheux que nul autre . . . et duquoi vous ne sortirez qu'avecques grande peine.'[1]

During May 1582 the court was united at Fontainebleau but in June it dispersed again. Though they continued to do their work as usual, Villeroy went home to Villeroy, and Brulart went to Paris to see his mother and his wife, who were both ill. All three of the secretaries were gravely inconvenienced and worried by this further dispersal of the court which, said Villeroy, was very inopportune, both because of the pressure of business at that moment, and because he could not achieve the same results by writing letters as he could by reasoning with the king in person—'par lettre comme de bouche'.[2] Nevertheless, he did his best to continue to wield his influence from a distance. In sending the king for signature three letters which he had been commanded to write, but with which he did not agree, Villeroy warned the king to consider very carefully before he signed them.[3] Later in the month he returned a despatch to the pope which the king had written in his own hand, and told him that it must be modified.[4]

Brulart, from his house at Crosnes, also complained of the difficulties of getting anything done when the king and Catherine were in a different place from the council.[5] He and Villeroy were equally preoccupied with an attack by the duke of Savoy —who was in league with Spain—on Geneva, Villeroy because Savoy was in his département and Brulart because he was trying to renew the French alliance with the Swiss. Upon this depended a regular supply of Swiss mercenaries in case of need and, almost more important, the undertaking that they would not fight for anyone else. The trouble as usual was that of raising the money to pay them, though there had been plenty of money to squander on the wedding of Joyeuse the previous summer. To Brulart's entreaties, the council replied unsympathetically that he was lucky to have had so much money already, and so he wrote to ask the king to write to the council himself—a slow and

[1] B.N., Mss. fr. 3385, f. 117, 9 April 1582, Villeroy to the king.
[2] B.N., Mss. fr. 15566, f. 13, 8 June 1582, Villeroy to Hautefort.
[3] B.N., Mss. fr. 6628, f. 102, 2 June 1582, Villeroy to the king.
[4] Ibid., f. 70, 26 June 1582, Villeroy to the king.
[5] B.N., Mss. fr. 15566, f. 17, 21 June 1582, Brulart to Hautefort.

unsatisfactory process.[1] 'La necessite de finances nous talonne de si pres', he complained to Bellièvre.[2]

Pinart, who remained at Fontainebleau, was not less in trouble, for he had a miniature war on his hands in his province of Picardy against Anjou's illegal levies. He took action on his own authority, appointing one Torcy, an officer of the crown, and then writing to ask the king to confirm the appointment.[3] In July the court reassembled, but it was only five weeks before the king again withdrew, suffering from an attack of such severe depression that the court actually feared for his sanity.[4]

While Pinart and Villeroy followed Catherine and the council to Saint-Maur-des-Fossés, Brulart and Bellièvre left, on 31 July, on a mission to the Netherlands. They returned on 28 August and at once went to see the king. Pinart took over Brulart's work until the beginning of September and then he went home, and we have no further trace of him for ten months until July 1583.

The object of the journey by Brulart and Bellièvre was to investigate an incident caused by Salcède who was then a prisoner. He was said to have plotted to murder Anjou, and he accused a number of people in France, including Villeroy, of being in league with Spain. Villeroy was extremely upset. He wrote despairing letters to his friend Bellièvre, beseeching his help, for any hint of a slur upon his integrity was the one thing which destroyed Villeroy's otherwise remarkable tranquillity. 'I would sooner endure exile than to see my honour compromised', he wrote. He said he would consider himself very unfortunate if the king would not allow him to defend himself, for he was afraid that from then on all his actions would be open to misinterpretation. According to the English ambassador, Lord Cobham, the king declared on this occasion that 'whatsoever others meant he was sure that Villeroy would not betray him, for in seeking his harm he would betray himself'.[5] Though Villeroy was not

---

[1] B.N., Mss. fr. 15566, f. 16, 9 June 1582, Brulart to Hautefort. Joyeuse and Épernon were said to have controlled the finances for the last two years. Desjardins, *Negs. Tosc.*, iv, 444, 22 July 1582.

[2] B.N., Mss. fr. 15906, f. 703, 28 June 1582, Brulart to Bellièvre.

[3] B.N., Mss. fr. 6628, f. 113, 26 June 1582, Pinart to the king.

[4] Desjardins, *Negs. Tosc.*, iv, 443, 15 July 1582.

[5] B.N., Mss. fr. 15906 (2), f. 729, 3 August 1582, Villeroy to Bellièvre; *C.S.P.F.*, 1582, p. 433, 4 November 1582, Cobham to Walsingham.

involved, he knew it was true that Spain had secret connections
in France, and he sent the king a despatch to that effect, that he
might see for himself the harm that would come of it.[1] Villeroy
was also worried because Navarre was raising forces in Poitou,
and because he was afraid that duke Casimir of Bavaria might
bring to France troops he had levied for use in Switzerland, because the king owed him money. 'I assure you', he wrote to
Hautefort, 'that this business worries me, for if such a storm
were to break upon us in our present state of want and confusion, it would do us a great deal of harm.'[2] Villeroy was
desperately conscious of this lack of order, foresight and fixed
purpose; the government was muddling dangerously on from
day to day—'au jour la journee', as he often said, and it gave
him a feeling of personal frustration. 'Je vous declare et proteste,'
he had already written to Bellièvre some months before, 'que je
ny puis servir de riens, et toutesfoys que je faicts et ferai tout
pour ce que je pourrai pour le service de nostre maitre.'[3] Meanwhile so many things were simply lying waiting for the king's
return from Lyons.[4] Henry arrived at court on 10 October, still
in poor health.[5] He stayed for a few weeks, went on another pilgrimage in November and was away again at Christmas, delay-
ing business on both occasions.

If 1582 had been hard and frustrating for the secretaries, 1583
was to be even worse. It began in much the same way, with the
king absent from court and Villeroy having to remind him of the
work he had neglected. It also continued in much the same way,
with Villeroy struggling to achieve what he could, for he alone
had an overall grasp of affairs. In January he sent the king one
of his solemn warnings, this time to say how necessary it was for
him to be strong in order to prevent renewed trouble. 'Je vous
ramenterai seullement comme votre tresfidelle et oblige serviteur que le seul remede a tous maulx est de se rendre fort par la
gendarmerie pour nestre plus subget a personne.'[6] It was the dis-
turbing news that Anjou's affairs were going badly in the

[1] B.N., Mss. fr. 6628, f. 123, 31 August 1582, Villeroy to the king.
[2] B.N., Mss. fr. 15565, f. 78, 10 September 1582, Villeroy to Hautefort.
[3] B.N., Mss. fr. 15906 (2), f. 542, 8 November 1581, Villeroy to Bellièvre.
[4] B.N., Mss. fr. 16092, f. 10, 5 October 1582, Villeroy to Maisse.
[5] Desjardins, Negs. Tosc., iv, 447, 8 October 1582.
[6] B.N., Mss. fr. 6629, f. 3, 20 January 1583, Villeroy to the king.

Netherlands which supplied the pretext for this warning. However, Villeroy was probably also thinking of the ever-growing authority of Épernon, for feeling against him and Joyeuse was so strong that there was some danger of rebellion. But Henry ignored the hint. Instead he made Épernon *gouverneur* of Metz, Toul and Verdun, which was certain to annoy the duc de Guise, whose lands were in the east and who was already quarrelling with Épernon over the famous madame de Sauve, widow of Fizes. Villeroy's warnings about Languedoc went equally unheeded. Instead of taking firm precautions, the king did his best to alienate the *gouverneur* Montmorency, by attempting to confiscate his office in favour of Joyeuse's father.

In warning the king how necessary it was to be strong, Villeroy was still sincere in wanting peace with Spain. The Spanish ambassador, however, told him in March that his master could not believe that France sincerely wanted peace. Villeroy dutifully wrote to warn the king of this, pointing out that the frontier towns were open and unfortified and that France, divided as she was, and with trouble all through the south, would be a very easy prey. But Henry was absorbed in founding a new order of flagellants, and so long as Villeroy were at his post, he was lulled by a false sense of security. Instead of attending to business, he went away on a pilgrimage to Chartres, walking as much as eight leagues a day; when he returned he retired to Saint-Germain to diet for forty days, and to work out the articles for his new order of penitents.[1] In June he went to drink the waters of Mézières.

It was therefore with Catherine that the secretaries had once again to turn their attention to the problem of watching and restraining Anjou. Having recently suffered a severe setback at Antwerp, he was once more considered to be a danger to France. It was feared that he was in league with Navarre and the trouble-makers in the south, and that he might use in France the many troops he was still raising.

On 7 July, Catherine, Villeroy and Pinart left Mézières—where according to Villeroy the king was drinking his waters better than the greatest German drunkard his wines—to see her

[1] B.N., Mss. it. 1733, f. 75, 29 April 1583; Desjardins, *Negs. Tosc.*, iv, 462, 28 April 1583.

unrepentant son at Chaune. Brulart was also to have gone with them but he fell ill a few days before with a 'fascheuse febvre tierce',[1] which was to worry him off and on for a long time to come. Together Villeroy and Catherine faced the now familiar task of reasoning with Anjou. Villeroy's first concern was to inform the king of his brother's declining health. However, it was not bad enough to prevent him from making a long speech full of demands. The queen, Villeroy told Henry, had answered him 'en bons termes et par bon ordre'. Their purpose was to persuade him to cancel his new levies, for the formation of such an army on the northern frontier was a grave danger. Villeroy therefore strongly advised the king, 'with the liberty you are pleased to allow me', that he ought to approve the agreement that Anjou planned to make with the Netherlands, thereby to obtain the cancellation of the levies, for there was nothing which Villeroy dreaded so much as the presence of armed forces in France. They were, he said, likely to cause a further outbreak of war, which the king was in no position to risk. That was plain language, and Villeroy sugared the pill by adding more gently that the king had won over many of his subjects by showing his determination to keep his word and to enforce the peace. 'Sire je parle comme votre tresfidelle serviteur,' he wrote, 'et vous diray encores une foys que japprove laccord affin de retirer ce prince de la poursuitte de ses premieres conceptions et sil est possible le regagner a votre majeste.'[2]

In August Villeroy went home. Pinart, and this time Brulart also, accompanied Catherine to La Fère in Picardy, to see Anjou a second time because, although he had promised to cancel the levies, as Villeroy wished, he had again not kept his word. At Verneuil, on the way, Pinart and Brulart received an unpleasant shock when Catherine became ill enough to frighten them. Both of them immediately wrote to the king at length, describing the intimate details of her illness. So did her doctor, Miron, who diagnosed choleric and melancholic humours in the stomach, which were the cause of much pain.[3] From La Fère,

---

[1] B.N., Mss. fr. 15907, f. 144, 4 July 1583, Brulart to Bellièvre.
[2] B.N., Mss. fr. 6629, f. 29, 13 July 1583, Villeroy to the king.
[3] *Ibid.*, f. 47, 12 August 1583, Brulart to the king; *ibid.*, f. 44, 12 August 1583, Pinart to the king.

R

where they extracted from Anjou a repetition of his former promises, the two secretaries went with Catherine to Gaillon, a quiet and beautiful place which they enjoyed, for plague was raging in the cities. From there Brulart wrote angrily to Bellièvre that Anjou, who had received 35,000 *écus* to pay off his troops had not kept his promise. 'Nous ny avons pas beaucoup profficte de quoy,' he added querulously, 'nous serons tous blasmez.'[1]

During Villeroy's absence, Brulart and Pinart shared his *département* between them, Brulart attending to Languedoc and Rome, and Pinart to Spain, Guienne and Venice. Pinart informed Longlée, the ambassador in Spain, that they were alone with the queen, with whom the king had left them to open and read all the despatches, and to send them on to him at Lyons.[2] Brulart was ill all this time. He finally collapsed in September and went home for ten months; even then he had not fully recovered.

Villeroy had gone home to his properties of Villeroy and Hallincourt early in August, 'planter des choux en mon village' he said,[3] and he remained there until the end of September, when he joined the queen at Saint-Maur-des-Fossés. Brulart was by then seriously ill, and Pinart had gone to Cambrai to remonstrate with Anjou yet again, for not keeping his promises.[4] Villeroy at least must have had a proper holiday, for when he returned to work he was quite out of touch with events; nor were his colleagues there to enlighten him.[5]

The secretaries did not return to something like a normal routine until October, when the king attended to business for the first time for five months. Already in April he had shown some signs of wishing to make reforms and amends, but he had only dismissed his musicians and returned to his diets and devotions. In November, he held an assembly of notables at Saint-Germain, 'quil pretend faire pour pourveoir a ses affaires',

[1] B.N., Mss. fr. 15907, f. 207, 29 August 1583, Brulart to Bellièvre.
[2] B.N., Mss. fr. 3321, f. 117v, 26 August 1583, Pinart to Longlée.
[3] Cabié, 135, 10 August 1583, Villeroy to Matignon. Cabié incorrectly dates this letter 1585 when Villeroy was, and remained, at court.
[4] B.N., Mss. fr. 6629, f. 88, 20 September 1583, Pinart to the king; Mss. fr. 16092, f. 141, 20 September 1583, Pinart to Maisse.
[5] B.N., Mss. fr. 16092, f. 147, 30 September 1583, Villeroy to Maisse.

wrote Villeroy sceptically to Hautefort.[1] This was little more than a statement of fact, but Villeroy did sometimes criticize the king in a few telling phrases of this kind, in private letters to his friends, because he so hated inefficiency, confusion and disorder, and because he so sincerely regretted that France, as he wrote to Maisse in July, 'est fort decheu de son ancienne dignite et reputation'. Nor was it only a question of reputation, for Villeroy endured, in his own mind at least, all the burden of responsibility that the king declined; and it was not easy—vigilant and clear-sighted as he was—to watch with equanimity while the country moved helplessly towards inevitable disaster, in which the king only half believed, and never for long at a time.

Public affairs had not improved during the five months in which Henry had done virtually nothing but sign the documents which were sent to him, so that by the autumn of 1583 Villeroy was wishing with an ever-increasing urgency that the king were strong enough in money, forces and organization to be able to face both the external and the internal dangers with confidence, and that he would discharge the obligation, and take the precaution of paying his foreign debts, particularly to Casimir, whose mercenaries were a continual threat to France. Villeroy was seriously alarmed at the king's disastrous impoverishment and the daily loss, which he felt personally, of what little prestige remained to his country.[2] But the magnitude of Villeroy's forbearance was far more remarkable than the mild criticism he sometimes voiced. He had too much sense to blame the king for everything and, indeed, he was too charitable and too humble to be much concerned with blame at all. He did not forget that the king had succeeded to a fearful heritage, that the times they lived in 'n'engendre que des monstres',[3] as he once put it himself, or that, as he also said, it was a 'siecle corrompu et par la posterite remarque dingratitude et perfidie par dessus tout autre'.[4]

Indeed, life in France had ceased to flow in its ancient

---

[1] Institut de France, Mss. Godefroy, 260, f. 154, 1 October 1583, Villeroy to Hautefort.

[2] Id.

[3] Cabié, 393, 25 February 1578, Villeroy to Saint-Sulpice.

[4] B.N., Mss. fr. 16911, f. 126, 4 February 1584, Villeroy to Revol.

channels. The restraints and barriers which curb men's passions had all crumbled away. There was no justice and no order in the land, but only the three scourges of God: war, plague and famine. Twenty years of violence, brutality, and poverty had so coarsened men's minds that neither the opinion of the world, the fear of punishment, the hope of reward, nor religion itself any longer influenced their actions. France was abandoned to envy, hatred and malice, to fear, suspicion and greed. Villeroy, and a few of his associates who shared his sentiments, realized that, in the moral sphere at least, this tide of wickedness was overwhelming, and that there could be no salvation for France until her citizens proved themselves more worthy of it. This was why, particularly when he felt most anxious and depressed, Villeroy frequently reiterated his firm resolve to do his duty as he saw it. If all his efforts failed and all his achievements were soon destroyed, honest motives, a clear conscience and the esteem of his friends were not only the greatest satisfactions he could have, but also the greatest contributions he could make.[1]

It is therefore not surprising that Villeroy should have distinguished clearly between Henry the king, who was a tragic misfit, and Henry the man, who was his friend; who, like himself, was in many ways outstanding, and whose qualities he still admired even when distracted by his negligence; for his incompetence did not blind Villeroy to his humanity. 'Le Roi Monseigneur', he wrote to Nevers in September 1583, 'est homme comme un autre. Je veult dire subjet aux perturbations et passions de ceste malhereuse vie . . . il a le naturel si benin et gratieux que quiconque en voudra cherir par les voyes convenables en obtiendra tousjours plaine satisfaction.'[2]

Satisfaction of this kind Villeroy received in full. The king wrote him a vast number of letters, long and short, formal and informal, nearly all undated and most of them undatable, which leave us in no doubt as to the especial warmth of his feelings for Villeroy, whom he was always glad to gratify when he

[1] Petitot, xliv, *Mémoires d'Estat de Villeroy*, 19.

[2] B.N., Mss. fr. 3350, f. 131, 9 September 1583, Villeroy to Nevers. Villeroy's attitude to Henry III is well summed up by the following incident. When, during the reign of Henry IV, it was said that Villeroy better than anyone else could write a history of the times, he is alleged to have replied, 'Je suis trop obligé à la mémoire de Henry III pour l'entreprendre.' Matthieu, 48.

could—for Villeroy was the reverse of importunate. It was well known that he was not covetous, 'nor a taker of anybody, nor that asketh of his master, of whom he may have what he listeth . . . [but he] careth not for it'.[1] Sometimes, however, he did accept gifts from the king, as in 1586 when he thanked Henry for what he had done 'to relieve my purse of which I beseech you to believe I have every need . . . but I also have a good master without whom I would die of hunger'.[2] This was doubtless an exaggeration, but prices had soared and Villeroy had probably begun to fall into debt. To Villeroy Henry confided things which he kept secret from everyone but Catherine,[3] and often he would express his affection and appreciation of Villeroy's work and services in hurried little notes. 'Vous etes trop honnete pour vostre fait vous scavez comme je vous ayme . . . Adieu', he wrote perhaps as early as 1579.[4] 'Mes yeux ont eu le plaisir d'avoyr veu vostre memoyre tres bien faict', he wrote appreciatively, probably in February 1581. 'Il ne sort ryen de vostre boutique qu'il ne soict bien livre',[5] and about this same time he wrote, dropping into the rarely used second person, 'Je t'ayme car tu me sers selon ma vollantte.'[6] Not only did Henry appreciate Villeroy's competence but also his gentle, persuasive manner, 'doulcement', he once advised, 'comme vous le scavez bien faire'.[7]

If the king did not see Villeroy before his sudden departures, he would send him a little note such as this one: 'Je m'an vais mays non si loing que l'on ne sache ou je seray . . . s'il vous ou vos compagnons avez a m'anvoyer vous me l'adresserez. Adieu adieu . . . aimez moy tousjours.'[8] Henry had a touching faith in Villeroy, whose warnings he so consistently ignored, and whose work he so consistently undermined. When he was away, it gave

[1] B.N., Mss. n.a.f. 1244, no. 21, f. 56, undated; 1245, no. 53, f. 120, undated; 1246, no. 45, f. 43, undated; C.S.P.F., 1583-4, p. 621, 17 July 1584.
[2] B.N., Mss. fr. 6631, f. 76, 19 September 1586, Villeroy to the king.
[3] B.N., Mss. n.a.f. 1243, no. 38, f. 77, undated.
[4] B.N., Mss. n.a.f. 1244, no. 39, f. 79, undated, quoted by Nouaillac, 68.
[5] B.N., Mss. n.a.f. 1243, no. 69, undated, Henry to Villeroy, quoted by Nouaillac, 68.
[6] B.N., Mss. n.a.f. 1246, no. 34, f. 25, undated, Henry to Villeroy.
[7] B.N., Mss. n.a.f. 1245, no. 59, f. 138, undated, Henry to Villeroy, quoted by Nouaillac, 72.
[8] B.N., Mss. n.a.f. 1243, no. 64, undated, Henry to Villeroy.

him a feeling of security to know that Villeroy was there, 'cependant que je n'i sois vous ne laissez d'y estre byen necessaire
estant toujours mes afaires byen quant vous i estes pour la
raison du tamps ou nous somes. Dyeu vous conserve car je suis
byen an repos quant je vous i scay. Je voudroys que tous heussent
le soing que vous y avez.'[1] This appreciation was, very naturally,
a source of encouragement to Villeroy, who felt that a man of
integrity could crucify himself in the service of a master who
showed that he had full confidence in him and who distinguished the quality of his service from those whose work was
inferior—'ceux qui versent mal'.[2]

Henry's affection for Villeroy increased with his adversities,
and most of these letters would appear to belong to the eighties.
Sometimes he would abandon all pretence of formality, ending
brief little notes, 'bon soyr Bydon' and 'je t'ayme Bydon',[3] a
strange little name which had other variations: 'Adieu By-
doust'[4] or 'Adieu Bidon Bidonet'.[5] He might, on occasions,
even refer to Catherine not as 'la reine ma mere' or 'la reine
madame et mere' but quite simply as 'maman'.[6] Sometimes
he would write 'adieu' two, three, four and even five times
in great big letters, not unlike a child who ends with a row of
crosses.[7]

When he was away, Henry would often confide to Villeroy
the ups and downs of his personal well-being, as in 1581, when
he had suffered from his leg: 'Adieu. Tout se porte tres byen et
jambe et corps et tout';[8] when his appetite was good, for normally he ate little, 'je mange comme un loup',[9] or when he was
in pain, 'O quel mal Villeroy.'[10]

It was from the end of 1583 that the secretaries were first

[1] B.N., Mss. n.a.f. 1245, no. 38, f. 89, undated, Henry to Villeroy.
[2] Petitot, xliv, *Mémoires d'Estat de Villeroy*, 99.
[3] B.N., Mss. n.a.f. 1243, no. 50, f. 104, undated; 1246, no. 32, f. 21, undated,
Henry to Villeroy.
[4] B.N., Mss. n.a.f. 1244, no. 25, f. 68, undated, Henry to Villeroy.
[5] *Ibid.*, no. 24, f. 66, undated, Henry to Villeroy, quoted by Nouaillac, 69.
[6] *Id.*
[7] *Ibid.*, nos. 30, 32, 35, ff. 80, 85, 92, all undated, from Henry to Villeroy. The
letter no. 35 is quoted by Nouaillac, 69.
[8] B.N., Mss. n.a.f. 1243, no. 69, f. 145, undated, Henry to Villeroy.
[9] B.N., Mss. n.a.f. 1244, no. 34, f. 90, undated, Henry to Villeroy.
[10] B.N., Mss. n.a.f. 1245, no. 29, f. 71, undated, Henry to Villeroy.

seriously inconvenienced, as well as alarmed, by the king's religious zeal, which had begun to exceed all reasonable limits, and which increased the number and length of his absences. His behaviour was far from normal; in December 1583 he even attended the funeral of the chancellor Birague dressed as a penitent. Not content with his frequent and strenuous pilgrimages, his new order of penitents, and a church he had built near the château of Madrid for twenty-four capucins,[1] early in 1584 he founded a monastery at Vincennes, containing at first twelve, then thirty and later a hundred and twenty cells. The affairs of this foundation occupied an ever-increasing amount of his time and thought.[2] Vincennes was not very far away, but the king might be as effectively absent there as he was at Lyons, for he did not like to be bothered or disturbed. Villeroy would be asked not to send any despatches unless they were very urgent. This, it went without saying, applied equally to his colleagues.[3] Sometimes the king would tell Villeroy that he did not want to see anything or anyone at all: 'while I am with the Capuchins if there are any urgent and important things . . . you should, all of you, show them to the queen without sending them to me. Adieu and tell your colleagues.'[4]

In this way the king sent orders to Pinart and Brulart through Villeroy, referring a great deal to their discretion. Sometimes he caused Villeroy to study and report on packets relating to the *départements* of Pinart and Brulart—a way of doing business which was hardly fair to any of them—perhaps because he would be willing to admit Villeroy when he refused to see anyone else.[5] Because it was to Villeroy that the most urgent business was confided, the king wanted him to join the community at Vincennes and to have a private place there, like a parlour, in which to receive the packets and interview the couriers.[6] This was more than even the patient Villeroy could endure in silence, and he sent the king a strongly worded rebuke for his neglect of affairs of state.

[1] Desjardins, *Negs. Tosc.*, iv, 465, 25 June 1583, 467, 8 August 1583.
[2] *Ibid.*, 485 ff., 23 January 1584.
[3] B.N., Mss. n.a.f. 1243, no. 15, f. 29, undated, Henry to Villeroy.
[4] *Ibid.*, no. 20, f. 13, undated, Henry to Villeroy.
[5] *C.S.P.F.*, 1584–5, pp. 308–9, February 1585.
[6] Matthieu, 39.

'Sire, duties and obligations are considered according to the circumstances and older debts ought to be settled before more recent ones. You were King of France before you became the leader of this company and your conscience requires that you render to royalty that which you owe it, before rendering to the congregation that which you have promised. You can excuse yourself from the one but not from the other. Sack-cloth you wear only when you choose, but the crown is always upon your head; and it is not less heavy in this solitude than it is in the midst of your affairs.'

'C'est parler', was his friend Matthieu's admiring comment.[1]

Villeroy, as he wrote in confidence to Revol, the French agent in Savoy, was very depressed during the early months of 1584. Brulart was ill, and Pinart appears to have been mostly with Catherine, who devoted her time to Anjou, firstly to restrain him and then because he was mortally ill. Villeroy therefore had a great deal to do, and the king's absorption in his monastery at Vincennes ill accorded with his authoritative mood which, once again, made him wish—when it suited him—to control everything himself.[2] The affairs of Languedoc, about which Villeroy had been warning him for at least two years, had reached the proportions of a crisis, and Montmorency, who was still said to be in the pay of Spain, was openly arming against the king. 'Languedoc . . . is already in flames', wrote Villeroy to Maisse, and they were preparing for defence.[3]

Villeroy's *département* was in a state of turmoil, and France gravely menaced. News of the crisis in Languedoc arrived about the same time as a warning from Navarre that Spain, in conjunction with Savoy, was planning to invade France through Burgundy and Picardy, to coincide with a rising led by the ducs de Guise, Maine, Nevers and Nemours.[4] This plot was communicated to only six people, besides the king and Catherine, including of course Villeroy, and also Pinart, but not Brulart.

Faced with this crisis, the king appeared autocratic and

1 Matthieu, 39–40.
2 B.N., Mss. it. 1733, f. 340, 16 March 1584.
3 B.N., Mss. fr. 16092, f. 203, 4 March 1584, Villeroy to Maisse.
4 B.N., Mss. fr. 16911, f. 144, 18 February 1584, Villeroy to Revol.

querulous.[1] This was a false façade, hiding the bitterness of his real feelings: but not from Villeroy. 'Je vous descharge mon cœur', he wrote to Villeroy in a long, tormented letter, which was none the less extravagant for being perfectly sincere, for this was one of the occasions upon which the king was shocked into a state of awareness and some understanding of the real danger of his position. He protested that he had no money and was faced with total ruin and the loss of his realm, his authority and his reputation. He was in despair, for he would sooner die than lose the province of Languedoc. Then it was that Henry recalled Villeroy's warning, and the fact that he had not always approved of his counsels, and he blamed himself so bitterly that he had done so little for this province, as almost to revel in his guilt and remorse. At the same time, he was furiously angry with the traitor Montmorency, who took his towns, his money and his realm, 'et nous le laissons jouir du tout', he wrote, as though in surprise at this discovery. 'Nous avons ce que nous y an meritons et m'estonne ancores que nous n'avons pis.' He wished that he had never been born, if Languedoc were going to be lost, for he had no stomach to endure such things without becoming enraged. 'Je scay qu'on dira que je suis trop violent,' he continued to Villeroy, whose gentleness he loved, 'je le suis et an ma religion catholique et [?contre] ceux qui me font mal c'est chose naturelle et ancores ne le suis je pas assez.' In a post-script he wrote: 'Great distress is at least permitted to complain and I do so to you in whom I have every confidence.'[2]

Thus the king could hardly have humbled himself more com-pletely before Villeroy, from whom he had no secrets, and his near raving should not be dismissed as mere histrionics. When Henry said that he could not endure 'teles choses que je n'an enraige' he was speaking the sober truth. His anger had been kindled and it was not to be extinguished.

Each time that the king was overwhelmed with depression and remorse and the calamities in which he had refused to be-lieve, he turned again to Villeroy. 'Shall I speak my mind freely,' he began another outpouring of distress, 'yes, for it is to a servitor of mine who is very faithful and devoted and then I

[1] B.N., Mss. it. 1733, ff. 339-40, 16 March 1584.
[2] B.N., Mss. fr. 3385, f. 1, undated, Henry to Villeroy.

shall at least feel relieved by having unburdened my heart to
someone who will never do anything but that which is necessary
for the good of my service.' He praised a reply from Villeroy—
quite possibly to his letter quoted above—which, he said, was
indeed full of prudence and worthy of great consideration. He
acknowledged quite simply that these 'considerations' proceeded from his own mis-government, his lack of judgement and
his failure to follow 'la voye salutaire . . . avec le couraige quil
estoit necesayre et requis n'ayant esgard que la ou il se falloyt
avoyr et non user de crinte . . . pour des respects indignes'.
Otherwise, he said, 'nous foussions veu le beau chemin que la
providence divine nous avoyt prepare au termes tous contraires
a ceulx que nous sommes et tomberons desormais de plus en
plus', enlarging upon his strong sense of doom, against which he
felt it was too late to struggle.[1] In other words, Henry admitted
to having strayed from the proper path, and to having been
fearful when he ought to have been resolute. As a result he had
missed the glories which ought to have been his, and was
afflicted by troubles which would grow worse and worse. This
was hardly reassuring for Villeroy.

If Henry III revealed to Villeroy the sometimes abysmal
depths of his shame and remorse, he also shared with him his
moments of rejoicing: 'Villeroy I am so beside myself with joy
and contentment'—unfortunately we cannot tell why—'that I
do not know what I am doing. Come tomorrow morning about
eight o'clock . . . and give this good news to the chancellor,
Bellièvre and Brulart. My friend I am overjoyed . . .'[2]

About the time of this crisis, early in 1584, Villeroy was reported to have said that he wished the King of Spain had taken
two or three of the best towns in the realm, for the king would
never be brought to see anything until necessity constrained him
to look to himself.[3] Whether or not this is true, we may be sure
that it was due to Villeroy's influence that the king now sent for
a levy of Swiss troops and took some defensive measures. Villeroy says in his memoir that the troubles which followed in 1585
could have been forestalled, if proper attention had been given,

[1] B.N., Mss. fr. 3385, f. 8, undated, Henry to Villeroy.
[2] B.N., Mss. n.a.f. 1245, no. 37, f. 87, undated, Henry to Villeroy.
[3] *C.S.P.F.*, 1583-4, p. 476, 2 May 1584, Stafford to Walsingham.

during the period of his illness (August 1584–March 1585), to the payment and organization of the royal forces which were stationed in the provinces at the beginning of 1584, and if the military regulations had been enforced.[1] It therefore appears that he was using his influence to achieve what he had always advised, that the king should be strong enough to defend himself. But Villeroy did not receive the degree of co-operation and direction that the situation demanded, or that one might have supposed, from the king's recent utterances, he would be willing to accord. Instead, some time early in March, Villeroy received the following letter: 'I am going away to Chartres . . . I entrust to you all my affairs with which you are concerned. Tell your colleagues, and see that no one sends me anything unless it is something really necessary. . . . Adieu; show everything to the queen. Keep your eyes open in this city during my absence.'[2] At the beginning of March Catherine was ill, and in the middle of the month she took Pinart with her to see Anjou at Château-Thierry, where he was dying. Brulart was still away ill, and Henry must have known that in fact he was leaving Villeroy to do everything. The worsening of Anjou's illness—since he was heir apparent to the throne—increased the gravity of the crisis Villeroy was left to face.

Villeroy was not only desperately inconvenienced, for Henry was away almost the whole of March and April and part of May, but he now became seriously worried lest the exertions of the king's devotions might injure his already delicate health. In particular, he wished the king would not do so much on foot[3] for in March he walked eighty leagues, dressed as a penitent, and spent many hours together on his knees.[4] With Anjou slowly dying, it would have been very dangerous if the king were to be ill.

During the months of March, April and May—when, in the king's absence, he could do very little—Villeroy's letters show his concern over Anjou, and over the active desire of Philip II

[1] Petitot, xliv, *Mémoires d'Estat de Villeroy*, 33–4. This paragraph (p. 33), labelled 1581, is printed in the wrong place in the text, and should form the beginning of that (p. 36) labelled 1585, the year to which it refers.

[2] B.N., Mss. n.a.f. 1246, no. 42, f. 36 [March 1584], Henry to Villeroy.

[3] B.N., Mss. fr. 3357, f. 94, 17 March 1584, Villeroy to Matignon; Mss. fr. 16092, f. 208, 16 March 1584, Villeroy to Maisse.

[4] B.N., Mss. it. 1733, f. 348, 30 March 1584.

for universal monarchy. These two preoccupations were closely related, because Anjou's death would leave the protestant King of Navarre heir apparent to the throne of France. It was generally suspected that the Guises were in league with Spain, and against the protestant heir they championed the catholic cardinal of Bourbon, a harmless, talkative old man, whom Guise could easily dominate.[1]

The fact that a man who was old enough to be the king's father was seriously proposed as heir presumptive to the throne, shows how strong was the conviction that Henry III had not long to live. This conviction was based, not on the state of his health, but on the predictions of astrologers, and at least in part explains the king's almost obsessive preoccupation with prayer, and probably also the resigned hopelessness of his outlook.

Villeroy had been primarily concerned with making peace in France and restraining Anjou. Now the struggle between Guise and Navarre—which left the king dangerously isolated—was the main problem, for Anjou died on 10 June, and proved as dangerous and disrupting in his death as he had been in his life. In a letter to Revol, Villeroy referred to their 'perte inestimable . . . pour la consequence et suitte d'icelle', which, he said, would cause new 'discours et desseings'.[2] He was too honest to pretend to an emotion that he did not feel, and all his regrets were reserved for Catherine. He was touched and distressed by her grief, which made her ill again.[3]

In the summer of 1584, the secretaries were once more attached to Catherine to receive, open and answer all the despatches.[4] Instead of preparing to face the new situation in France, the dangerous beginnings of which were clear enough, Henry went to Lyons, while Catherine went to Chenonceaux with Pinart and Brulart. Villeroy was to have gone with them— to eat melons, so he said[5]—but, in August, he fell seriously ill and was away for eight months.

---

[1] B.N., Mss. fr. 3282, f. 99, 1 September 1580, 'Discours sur le droict pretendu par ceux de Guise sur la Couronne de France.'

[2] 'Talking and scheming.' B.N., Mss. fr. 16911, f. 301, undated draft, Villeroy to Revol; *ibid.*, f. 284, 5 July 1584, Villeroy to Revol.

[3] B.N., Mss. fr. 15907, f. 481, 11 June 1584, Villeroy to Bellièvre.

[4] B.N., Mss. fr. 16902, f. 263, 4 August 1584, Villeroy to Maisse.

[5] *Letters to Matignon*, 126–7, 30 July 1584.

This breakdown was certainly attributable to overstrain and overwork, for his burden of both had been and still was constantly increasing. Sir Edward Stafford, the English ambassador, reported at this time that the King reposed the whole weight of the state on Villeroy.[1] He was worried during that summer by the situation which Anjou had left in the Netherlands, and also, as he had been for some time, by the disorder in Languedoc. He wrote to tell the king that, in his opinion, he ought to go to Languedoc at the head of an army and hold the provincial States in person, sending the commissions not to the rebel *gouverneur*, Montmorency, but to Bellièvre. But the king did not do so, any more than he had gone in person to Guienne in 1580. Furthermore, Villeroy was anxious about the menacing attitude of the Guise family. They had retired to their *gouvernements*, 'tres mal edifies de la court et en jalousie tres grande' because, on the death of his brother, the king had sent Épernon (with an enormous suite costing 400,000 *écus*) to see Navarre, to urge him, it was said, to become a catholic.[2] The Guises and the duke of Savoy were connected with the Spanish danger and, hoping to achieve something useful, Villeroy took it upon himself to try to arrange a meeting in Lyons between the king and the pro-Spanish duke of Savoy, in the hope that he might yet marry one of Catherine's grand-daughters, and be won back to France.[3] Shortly before he was taken ill, Villeroy wrote to Bellièvre confessing this great anxiety and the grave view he took of the dangers in the kingdom which, he said, was moving towards a precipice; and so it was.[4]

Brulart, who had been ill since September 1583, appears to have returned to work about July 1584, or a little before. He alone accompanied Catherine to Chenonceaux in the middle of August, where, although he was still suffering from a slow fever, he did Villeroy's work, just as Villeroy had for long done his.[5] He was later joined by Pinart, who had remained in Paris for the wedding of his brother-in-law, Claude de Laubespine, (Catherine's secretary and also a cousin of Villeroy's wife),

[1] *C.S.P.F.*, 1583-4, p. 621, 17 July 1584, report from Stafford.
[2] B.N., Mss. fr. 15907, f. 516, 21 July 1584, Villeroy to Bellièvre.
[3] B.N., Mss. fr. 16911, f. 299, 15 July 1584, Villeroy to Revol.
[4] B.N., Mss. fr. 15907, f. 522, 25 July 1584, Villeroy to Bellièvre.
[5] B.N., Mss. fr. 16092, f. 273, 2 September 1584, Brulart to Maisse.

although Villeroy's illness meant the cancellation of his holiday.[1]

There, at Chenonceaux, Pinart and Brulart dealt with affairs of state as they were now accustomed to do during the king's absences. The news which came in from the provinces was far from reassuring, particularly that from Brulart's own province of Champagne, where there were rumours that the gentry were being stirred up to prepare to follow in war 'aucuns seigneurs'— the Guises.[2] The rest of the year 1584 passed in this way, with Pinart and Brulart working as best they could between the king's absences, for even after he returned from Lyons, he went often to Vincennes and other places.

It had become all too clear, by 1584, that peace could not be enforced in France, or not unless the king could be induced to pay proper attention to finance and the army. Furthermore, a situation had materialized which Villeroy must have feared and dreaded ever since he had become aware of Anjou's declining health: the protestant King of Navarre had become heir apparent to the throne. Many catholics could be expected to deny his claim, and to use it as a pretext for renewing the wars. Villeroy himself was placed in a terrible quandary: he firmly believed in the principle of legitimacy, yet he could not—and never did—support Henry of Navarre so long as he remained a protestant. On the other hand, he had no illusions about the nature and intentions of the sinister young duc de Guise. Meanwhile, with their hopes of salvation running out, the secretaries had been left very much to themselves, through three long years, to do the best they could from day to day, and it is hardly surprising that both Brulart and Villeroy should have collapsed under the strain.

[1] B.N., Mss. fr. 6630, f. 61, 23 August 1584, Pinart to the king.
[2] B.N., Mss. Dupuy, 537, f. 213, 19 September 1584, Brulart to d'Inteville.

CHAPTER XVI

The Gathering Storm, 1585–7

SHORTLY before he fell ill, in the summer of 1584, Villeroy had said that France was moving towards a precipice. By March 1585 and before Villeroy had recovered, the significance of this was so clear that not even the king could any longer close his eyes to it. The years 1585–8 witnessed the beginning of that total ruin of the kingdom which the secretaries had for long foreseen, and which even their predecessors in office had feared.

When the crisis came at the end of March 1585, the first thing the king did was to recall Villeroy, without whom he was lost. From then until September 1588 Villeroy was as closely involved in the fate of Henry III as it was possible for a minister to be. He returned on 28 March and although, after eight months, he was still suffering from a quartan fever, he was continually in council with the king.[1] In a letter to Maisse in Venice, Villeroy himself explains the nature of this crisis, the outcome of which was to involve his own downfall and that of Pinart and Brulart. It was no less than a revolt of the Guises, supported by Spain, as well as by their own widespread and powerful organization, the catholic league in France. To Maisse, Villeroy wrote that he found the king without troops, and still half doubting the reality of the conspiracy, although it was known that it was planned for 6 April—which was in one week's time.[2] Guise's intention was to march on Paris, but it is not very clear what he meant to do with the king. Brulart himself informed the king of this: 'I advise

[1] Desjardins, *Negs. Tosc.*, iv, 558, 5 April 1585; B.N., Mss. fr. 16092, f. 353, 30 March 1585, Villeroy to Maisse; Mss. n.a.f. 7260, f. 7, 1 August 1594, letter to Du Vair.

[2] Villeroy and Brulart knew of this date on 30 March although it is said that Villefallier, father-in-law of Guise's secretary Péricart, betrayed the plot on 1 April. De Croze, i, 281, n 2; B.N., Mss. fr. 3420, f. 31, 1 April 1585.

you', he wrote, 'that the day on which those of the league are to mount their horses and take up arms is the 6th of this month.' Longlée, the French ambassador in Spain, also wrote to warn the king that trouble was about to recur in France, and that plans had been prepared.[1] It was the cardinal of Bourbon, Villeroy continued to Maisse, all the princes of the house of Guise and several others[2] who were the leaders of this plot. Their ostensible purpose was: to exterminate the protestants; to oblige the king to adopt a catholic—namely Bourbon—as his heir, to distribute the honours and offices of the country to the princes and nobles who were worthy of them—that is to say to disgrace the favourites Joyeuse and Épernon and distribute the spoils among the Guise family; and, finally, to decrease taxation. This conspiracy, said Villeroy, was supported by the pope and financed by Spain, and the Guises had considerable forces assembled in the region of Châlons and others coming from Germany. The protestants were naturally also taking up arms. Thus, wrote Villeroy, who did not deceive himself as to the gravity of the situation, the king would have to defend himself against them both, 'en quoi consiste notre plus grande malheur'. He was certainly in danger of being overthrown, and many even thought that his life was in danger.[3] Catherine, Villeroy continued, was seriously ill, but she was nevertheless going to Épernay to try to negotiate with the Guises. Though it brought tears to his eyes, Villeroy said, he had to admit that he had very little hope of her being successful. For this reason Villeroy and Catherine advised the king to send for a levy of Swiss, and to raise other forces in France, 'pour soubtenir le choc qui sera le plus rude quait jamais receu Roi de France alors quil cuidoit estre en plaine prosperite'.[4] This was tantamount to saying that not until he had been shaken from his throne, would Henry face the fact that he was not 'en plaine prosperite'.

Although he had been absent from court, Villeroy had long

[1] De L'Epinois, 10, n. 2, 30 March 1585, Brulart to the king; B.N., Mss. fr. 16109, f. 217 (f. 220 decoded), 29 March 1585, Longlée to the king.

[2] The ducs de Nevers and Nemours were also of the league although Nevers was later outwardly reconciled to the king, and the secretaries played a large part in bringing this about.

[3] C.S.P.F., 1584–5, p. 390, 1 April 1585, Stafford to Walsingham.

[4] B.N., Mss. fr. 16092, f. 353, 30 March 1585, Villeroy to Maisse.

foreseen this crisis, and not merely in general terms.[1] It has already been seen how he deplored the king's defencelessness. But, for affairs of state, Villeroy was 'all in all', and during his absence they had been treated with even greater insouciance than usual.[2] The atmosphere at court had certainly not been one of alarm—except for the growing hatred between the king and Guise, and increasing ill-feeling against Joyeuse and Épernon—for the king spent much of the early part of the year 1585 in festivities, entertainments and banquets.[3] Brulart, who had been doing Villeroy's work during his illness, does not appear to have taken the warning signs very seriously. He played them down in a letter of 14 January to Maisse in Venice, and as late as 1 March, he wrote rather casually, also to Maisse, '. . . nevertheless we hope that, with God's help, things will calm down'.[4] Not until the end of March did he appreciate the danger and, finally, wrote in a very different tone.[5]

It was already the eleventh hour when Villeroy was recalled, and everyone had suddenly become very much afraid.[6] Villeroy tried to excuse himself from returning to court on the grounds that he was ill, but Brulart unkindly described his plea of ill-health as 'uncivil'. He was thoughtless enough to send Villeroy the last despatch from Venice, of 12 March, unopened, and without having read it to the king, with the result that Villeroy had to begin on arrears of work and missed the post to Maisse.[7] To add weight to the belief that Brulart had not taken the warnings of the Guise conspiracy very seriously, and to the suspicion that he had not been doing Villeroy's work with a very good grace, we find Villeroy expressing his great astonishment that Maisse had not been 'earlier informed of that which had been foreseen four months ago'.[8]

Pinart and Catherine left Paris for Épernay on 30 March in the afternoon, to try to reason with the Guises. They treated the

---

[1] B.N., Mss. fr. 16092, f. 361, 12 April 1585, Villeroy to Maisse.
[2] C.S.P.F., 1584–5, p. 308, February 1585.
[3] Desjardins, Negs. Tosc., iv, 544 ff.
[4] B.N., Mss. fr. 16092, ff. 320, 342, 14 January, 1 March 1585, Brulart to Maisse.
[5] De L'Epinois, 10, n. 1, 30 March 1585, Brulart to the king.
[6] Desjardins, Negs. Tosc., iv, 553, 29 March 1585.
[7] B.N., Mss. fr. 16092, f. 353, 30 March 1585, Villeroy to Maisse.
[8] Ibid., f. 361, 12 April 1585, Villeroy to Maisse.

S

queen with the grossest disrespect, and dragged out the negotiations for over three months.[1] Meanwhile they continued to
bring up troops, seize towns and appropriate revenues.[2]
Throughout these weary and sometimes dangerous weeks,
Pinart was in constant attendance on Catherine. She was ill and
had to be carried, and for two months she conducted the
negotiations from her bed. Not only was she ill at that particular
moment, but her general health was failing. This greatly increased her dependence on Pinart, who seldom left her. Even
when she was able to get up, she had some painful trouble in her
right arm and hand, which lasted for many months and prevented her from writing. The correspondence covering this
negotiation, which can be traced from day to day through all its
tortuous stages, is remarkably complete and, almost without
exception, it was Pinart who wrote it.[3] Catherine would dictate
to him in her room and often in a great hurry, while he sat at
the foot of her bed. Sometimes she would make him close down
the packets in her room, work which was normally done by a
clerk.[4] At other times she might simply ask him to write the
necessary letters for her. The result was that he had little time
left for personal letters, or at least not many have survived.
Those he did write were mostly to Brulart, who was doing his
work in Paris. There was not much to add to Catherine's letters
but he did send news of her health, which was far from reassuring and, although she was old and gouty and stout, he still
referred to her touchingly as 'la pauvre princesse,'[5] and 'ma
bonne maistresse'.[6] When the behaviour and demands of the
Guises became outrageous, he wrote to Brulart with concern

[1] B.N., Mss. it. 1734, f. 26, 2 April 1585. Guise was said to have 'very exalted
ideas'. Ibid., f. 25, 29 March 1585.
[2] On the attitude of the duc de Guise, see his letter to Nevers, de Croze, i, app.
x, 347, 18 May 1585.
[3] The correspondence covering this negotiation is principally contained in the
volumes, B.N., Mss. fr. 3403, 3368, 3369, 3370, 3371, 10297, 15569, 15908. See
also Édouard de Barthélemy, 'Catherine de Médicis le duc de Guise et le traité de
Nemours', Revue des questions historiques, xxvii (1880). This account leaves much to
be desired considering how complete the material is. The author states that Brulart
also went to Épernay, but he has mistaken him for his cousin, known as le présiden
Brulart.
[4] B.N., Mss. fr. 15569, f. 33, 3 April 1585, Pinart to Bellièvre.
[5] B.N., Mss. fr. 3403, f. 59, 13 May 1585, Pinart to Brulart.
[6] B.N., Mss. fr. 3369, f. 7, 4 May 1585, Pinart to Brulart.

that she was 'more angry and troubled than he had ever known her', although he had seen her in all her troubles for many years past.[1] Pinart refrained from writing personally to the king, partly no doubt because he had nothing to add to his official letters, but also out of consideration for Brulart, who would have had to answer them in the king's name.[2] Equally, to save time and trouble, he mostly confined himself to sending Villeroy friendly messages.[3]

Pinart was by no means simply Catherine's scribe. She travelled with a number of councillors and he was one of the closest of them. He attended all the conferences, was one of the effective negotiators and he drafted and wrote the many memoirs to which the work gave rise.

Perhaps because Villeroy had not yet recovered from his long illness, it was Brulart who received the despatches sent by Pinart, and who acted as his intermediary with the king. This may also have been partly because Catherine and the Guises were then in Brulart's province of Champagne. Brulart wrote to Catherine regularly. His letters have not survived but Catherine frequently thanked him for them. She also thanked him for keeping her informed of what was happening in other parts of France, which was of great help to her—for the league was active in many different provinces—and sometimes for getting her rapid answers from the king.[4]

It seems likely that Villeroy, though he remained at court, did not work normally for some weeks, though he does not mention his health in his letters. In the middle of April Pinart feared that he must still be ill, since he had not written to the queen,[5] and early in May Catherine wrote to say how sorry she was to hear of his illness, especially when he was indispensable.[6] He was suffering at the time from something which caused him pain in his side.[7] It is likely that he kept his correspondence down to the minimum in order to concentrate on his role as

[1] B.N., Mss. fr. 3403, f. 59, 13 May 1585, Pinart to Brulart.
[2] B.N., Mss. fr. 3371, f. 7, 8 April 1585, Pinart to Brulart.
[3] *Ibid.*, f. 16, 15 April 1585, Pinart to Brulart.
[4] Baguenault de Puchesse, *Lettres*, viii, 283, 10 May 1585, Catherine to Brulart.
[5] B.N., Mss. fr. 3371, f. 16, 15 April 1585, Pinart to Brulart.
[6] Baguenault de Puchesse, *Lettres*, viii, 273, 4 May 1585, Catherine to Villeroy.
[7] B.N., Mss. it. 1734, f. 91, 13 May 1585.

councillor. A number of fragments in Villeroy's writing show
that he was very much concerned with the problem of raising
troops and arming the king, and Pinart and Catherine were
continually emphasizing the urgent need for military preparations. One of the fragments, marked 'conseil de guerre', concerns troop movements.[1] Another, a list of places, within a
radius of twelve leagues of Paris, where troops could be lodged,
refers to the problem of holding points on the rivers which were
the strategic keys to Paris.[2] A third fragment is simply a list of
things which Villeroy had to do, all of them concerned with
military preparations.[3] But, as Villeroy was well aware, it was
much too late; it was no fault of his that these preparations were
both ineffective and inadequate, for he had tried to make them
in good time. He wrote in his memoir that if the king had continued to maintain the forces which he agreed to station in certain provinces at the beginning of 1584—and which he did until
August when Villeroy fell ill and could no longer attend to the
matter—then the league would neither have dared nor been
able to develop.[4] Now it had become extremely difficult to
raise forces for the king because the Guises had monopolized the
available manpower, which had been decreasing, and had
bought up most of the horses.[5] Besides, the king as usual had no
money. Late in March, Sir Edward Stafford informed Walsingham that in the council 'great ado was made for money'.
This 'ado' had little effect because, he said, the council was corrupt and treacherous, and only Villeroy and Bellièvre could be
trusted. His condemnation did not include Pinart and Brulart
because Stafford did not consider them to be important in the
council, which was not, at that time, a formal body. Villeroy
stood up and told them all that it was shameful, in so important
a matter, 'to stagger upon getting of money'. Though the king
had never given him as much as he had given to some of them—
meaning of course the so-called *mignons*, and though he had no
money because 'he ever had been a spender', nevertheless, he
willingly offered to engage all his lands for the king's service,

[1] B.N., Mss. fr. 15569, f. 201, 16 May 1585.
[2] *Ibid.*, f. 236, 23 May 1585.
[3] *Ibid.*, f. 158, 7 May 1585.
[4] B.N., Mss. n.a.f. 7260, f. 7, 1 August 1594, letter to Du Vair.
[5] B.N., Mss. it. 1734, f. 29, 2 April 1585.

'which quickly would find means to make money'. But none of the rest would follow.[1]

The misgivings which Villeroy felt as to the probable outcome of Catherine's negotiation increased from week to week and were shared by Pinart, who was on the spot. 'I very much fear', Villeroy wrote to Maisse early in April, 'that the [disturbances] will not be suppressed without firing a shot.'[2] A week later he wrote, 'Jacrois que les cartes soient fort brouillees et que le mauvais fois passe trop avant . . . croiez que voiez une miserable guerre . . . plus miserable que je ne le vous puis escrire.'[3] In May he said that it was time for the French to weep for their sins 'et se resoluent d'espouser pour jamais un corps de cuirasse et une perpetuelle et tres sanglante guerre',[4] and in June he wrote to Longlée in Spain that there was even less hope of peace than ever.[5] These letters bear out Villeroy's statement, in his memoir, that he had never been so stricken with grief and affliction as he was by that rising, which he had not expected to see so long as the king lived. This statement makes it perfectly clear that in his opinion the battle was for the throne and not for religion. To Matignon he confessed that he was so bewildered and perplexed by the affairs of the moment that he did not know what to say, 'sinon que je suis de ceux qui ont résolu de crever plutôt que de faire une lâcheté'.[6]

Villeroy's perplexity arose from his uncertainty as to how to advise the king, for he was always reluctant in the extreme to propose any course which might lead to violence. In the circumstances, he advised the king to unite the catholics to himself by every means in his power, and rather make war on the huguenots than permit the formation of a catholic party separate from the crown. Villeroy gives three reasons for this advice: he was aware of the king's strong catholic convictions and his hatred of heresy; he was moved by his own conscience and religious conviction which, he said, had influenced him more strongly than anything else; and, finally, he was afraid of

---

[1] *C.S.P.F.*, 1584-5, p. 390, 1 April 1585, Stafford to Walsingham.
[2] B.N., Mss. fr. 16092, f. 358, 4 April 1585, Villeroy to Maisse.
[3] *Ibid.*, f. 361, 12 April 1585, Villeroy to Maisse.
[4] *Ibid.*, f. 371, 11 May 1585, Villeroy to Maisse, quoted by Nouaillac, 85.
[5] B.N., Mss. fr. 16109, f. 256, 2 June 1585, draft, Villeroy to Longlée.
[6] *Letters to Matignon*, 130, 3 April 1585, quoted by Nouaillac, 78-9.

the consequences of a break between the king and the catholic leaders. At the time he still hoped this might be avoided.[1]

For these reasons some kind of an agreement with the duc de Guise, however disadvantageous, was considered indispensable, though there was little hope of it. On 11 June Pinart wrote to Brulart saying that all their time was wasted; they had not been able to achieve anything; they were faced with war and in its wake there would be plague and famine: indeed there were signs of this already.[2] The reason for their failure was that Guise would only negotiate on the basis of the revocation of the edict of pacification and an agreement to make war on the huguenots, and his demands became daily more exorbitant.

It was at this moment that the king sent Villeroy to Épernay, but he says that he did not go to make the treaty.[3] He wrote in his memoir that he would not disclose the reason, because those were things which should not be divulged, least of all by himself. He made a point of stating that he went against his will and contrary to his own advice, although he did not oppose the treaty, signed at Nemours on 7 July, because he considered it to be necessary.[4] The king, for his part, did not send Villeroy to Épernay without having carefully considered his decision. He was afraid, if Villeroy went, of the aggravating effect that it might have on the huguenots, and that it would reveal to Guise the extent of his anxiety for peace. He was also afraid that the effort might cause Villeroy to have a relapse. On the other hand, as Henry wrote to him, if he did not go, the negotiations would continue to drag on for too long and end disastrously: 'si vous seul ne vous an meslez car je n'an sache d'autre en qui me puisse fier que jauray pas cette paix le pis quil me scaurait arriver'. Again Henry wrote, if Villeroy did not go, 'mes affaires iron tres mal. . . . Reguarder de vous conserver votre sante car je ne veut pas que vous soyiez malade il m'importe trop a mon service mais de vous acheminer comme vous jugez le mieux. Bref j'ai tout en esperance sur vous et crois fermement que si vous n'y estes mes afaires iront tres mal.' It is evident that Henry

[1] Petitot, xliv, *Mémoires d'Estat de Villeroy*, 37–8.
[2] B.N., Mss. fr. 3368, f. 45, 11 June 1585, Pinart to Brulart.
[3] B.N., Mss. n.a.f. 7260, f. 7, 1 August 1594, letter to Du Vair.
[4] Petitot, xliv, *Mémoires d'Estat de Villeroy*, 37.

placed all his hopes in Villeroy but without any clear idea of
what he expected him to do. Besides wanting him to go, he also
wanted him at court. 'Si vous pouvez faire que la Reine fist aler
et venyr vers moi quelque coup sella serait tres apropos. Vous
y ferez comme vous le jugerez le mieux car sil sela etayt je vous
parleroyt plus franchement qu'a un autre et vous me represen-
teriez myeulx les faits quil serait besoing que je seusse.' Forgetting at first about Villeroy's health, Henry hoped the queen
could be induced to send him back to court again, so that he
could talk to him frankly and learn the truth from him. 'Je prie
Dieu,' he concluded, unable to reconcile his conflicting desires,
'que vous me raportiez la paix mais conservez aussy votre
sante.' This was the king's real hope, which Villeroy later refused to divulge. Henry made the point quite clear: 'Si vous
pouriez tant guaigner . . . que le faict de la religyon ne se fist si
rigoureux et trouver moyen de ne nous metre a la guerre, mais
je le tiens impossible.'[1] Perhaps Villeroy, by some miracle, might
yet manage to avert another war.

Villeroy arrived at Épernay on 13 June and Catherine was
very glad to see him, for she too had confidence in him.[2] After
four days of waiting for Guise at Épernay, Villeroy became
annoyed, or so Pinart wrote to Brulart. He was also worried
because Brulart was alone with the king and could not be left
for very long to struggle single-handed with so much work.[3]

Villeroy had to wait until 19 June. The next afternoon a
meeting was held at which only Catherine, Villeroy and Pinart
represented the king. They agreed upon the essentials of a
treaty, as Pinart wrote joyfully to tell Brulart in Paris.[4] To what
extent this conclusion was due to Villeroy it is impossible to say,
except that success, which had eluded Catherine for so many
weeks, coincided with his arrival. But the approach of a royal
levy of Swiss troops also had something to do with it.

Villeroy left for Paris on 22 June taking with him the articles to
show the king. Pinart and Catherine must have returned to

---

[1] B.N., Mss. n.a.f. 1244, no. 60, f. 157, undated but evidently of June 1585,
Henry to Villeroy.
[2] Baguenault de Puchesse, *Lettres*, viii, 318, 14 June 1585, Catherine to Brulart.
[3] B.N., Mss. fr. 3368, f. 62, 17 June 1585, Pinart to Brulart.
[4] *Ibid.*, f. 73, 'le jour de feste dieu' [20 June] 1585, Pinart to Brulart.

court soon after the publication of the peace on 7 July. Then we have no further knowledge of Pinart for almost a year, from 15 August 1585 to 24 June 1586, and very little knowledge of Brulart either for roughly the same period.

Villeroy feared and expected the worst from the peace he had regretfully helped to conclude. They would send up fireworks for joy, he wrote to Maisse in Venice, if peace were what it really meant. But it did not. It meant filling France with fire and blood and desolation,[1] and he likened his country to a man who, emerging from a sharp fever, feels even more debilitated than during the crisis of his illness.[2] 'I cannot hope to see her risen and restored, as she should be, during our life time', he told Maisse in September. 'I tell you rather that everyone has conspired to ruin her . . . these are judgements of God that man can neither comprehend nor evade. . . . This century produces only miscreants and extraordinary ingratitude, infidelity, avarice and other similar vices.'[3] Villeroy saw this 'total ruin', which he had so often predicted, as something inexorable to be worked through—'Il me semble y avoir en cela de la fatalite'[4]—and it was his reward that he did live, not only to see France rise again but to play a leading part in her recovery.

Knowing, as we do, little or nothing of the work and movements of Pinart and Brulart at this time, Villeroy appears to us even more isolated than can really have been the case. Nevertheless he was alone in a very real sense, as the Venetian ambassador realized in November 1585 when he described him as 'principal secretary of state through whose hands everything of importance now passes, and which, moreover, is for the most part initiated and concluded on his advice and authority'.[5] Besides the isolation of his personal position, Villeroy was also left to work alone because the king became ever more completely abandoned to his life of seclusion and strenuous devotions.

The king was at Vincennes for much of August, September,

---

[1] B.N., Mss. fr. 16092, f. 411, 29 August 1585, Villeroy to Maisse.
[2] Ibid., f. 402, 4 August 1585, Villeroy to Maisse.
[3] Ibid., f. 416, 13 September 1585, Villeroy to Maisse.
[4] B.N., Mss. n.a.f. 7260, f. 7, 1 August 1594, letter to Du Vair.
[5] B.N., Mss. it. 1734, f. 323, 25 November 1585.

November and December 1585. Twice during this summer we hear of Villeroy going out there to do a day's work with the king.[1] In December, after walking to Chartres in bad weather, the king refused to see anyone, even Villeroy. Catherine herself, to whom the secretaries could usually turn, was away a good deal, perhaps to avoid the plague in the cities, perhaps because she was growing old, or because of the beginning of an estrangement between herself and the king. Nothing was being done, and preparations for the war were making little progress because, if Villeroy had acquired an unusual degree of initiative, he still could not do everything alone. It was Catherine who came to his rescue, by going to Vincennes to remonstrate with the king. She urged that he was endangering his health, jeopardizing his affairs and creating an impossible task for his ministers.[2] She succeeded in making him work for a week, but he returned to Vincennes over Christmas, and in January 1586 not only Villeroy and Joyeuse, but even Catherine herself received orders not to disturb him. He was fasting strictly and spending twenty hours a day at his devotions.[3] Villeroy and Catherine were grievously worried because the cold was intense and the king was ill.

Villeroy's burden was very great. He was aware that a German protestant levy was expected in the summer and that no defensive measures had been taken. The king was away for most of January and February and was still ill when Guise arrived in March for a council of war. This illness, like that of 1581 which kept him away from court for three months, marked another stage in the steady deterioration of his physical and mental health. Also like the other, it was followed by an aggravation of his unbalance, and a period in which he behaved with the most exaggerated eccentricity, doing even less work than usual. In March the king agreed with Guise to raise seven armies. Presumably he was not serious, since this was quite impossible. Then in April he spoke to Guise of making peace and negotiating with Navarre. He appeared to oscillate between a fierce determination to fight to the death and an overwhelming desire

[1] B.N., Mss. it. 1734, f. 217, 19 August 1585, f. 253, 30 September 1585.
[2] *Ibid.*, ff. 349-50, 20 December 1585.
[3] *Ibid.*, f. 355, 3 January 1586.

for peace. He squandered more money on Joyeuse and Éper-non,[1] went on an exceptionally strenuous pilgrimage to Char-tres and, leaving the situation still unresolved, returned to his prayers.[2] But one should not assume that this was entirely due to incompetence or eccentricity: Henry was probably playing for time. He was well aware, as Mendoza, the Spanish ambassador, informed Philip II, that Guise and the league were in touch with Spain. He felt that things had gone so far that it was too late to stop them, and seeing how great the danger was, he had begun to hope that Navarre might be induced to declare him-self a catholic.[3] There was nothing but his religion which stood between them.

It was natural that Villeroy's perplexity and apprehension should have increased with every month that passed. 'When we see forty or fifty thousand foreigners in this kingdom, then we will realize our errors', he wrote to Maisse in the cold, frustrating month of January.[4] In March, while Guise was at court, he wrote that the impotence of the 'men of good will surpassed even their distress although that was extreme', and in April, that they were blinded by passion and he himself despaired of there being any cure for it.[5]

To understand more fully the extent of this burden, the strain which it placed on Villeroy and the real significance of these restrained comments, it is necessary to know something more of the sinister and poisoned atmosphere in which he and his asso-ciates were living and working, and of the desolation of the country, which resulted in a kind of slow paralysis. We learn of these things from the brilliant, penetrating reports of Cavriana, a Florentine political agent, which are heavily charged with suspense and an atmosphere of impending doom. They make eerie reading, for it is difficult to imagine and to bear in mind the corrosive distrust and suspicion in the court, which was secretly divided between Guise and the king, the growing im-possibility of fully trusting anyone, and the ever-present fear and danger of sudden death. The king had already hated Guise with

---

[1] B.N., Mss. it. 1735, f. 20, 28 March 1586.
[2] *Ibid.*, ff. 25–6, 11 April 1586.
[3] *C.S.P.Sp.*, 1580–6, p. 575, 11 May 1586, Mendoza to Philip II.
[4] B.N., Mss. fr. 16093, f. 5, 4 January 1586, Villeroy to Maisse.
[5] *Ibid.*, ff. 35, 45, 14 March, 12 April 1586, Villeroy to Maisse.

a hatred which Cavriana described as *immortale*, before the recent crisis. After it he said: 'The king is offended, and the anger of kings is ever to be feared in all ages.'[1] This was extremely pertinent, for the anger which periodically flared up in the king was increasing and could become dangerous. It was also increased by his own inability to take action, which rendered him so vulnerable. Even in peace, Cavriana said, Guise and the king would never disarm because there was no confidence between them.[2] Confidence had in fact been totally and for ever destroyed, and already the tension showed signs of becoming so great that some kind of explosion was to be feared.[3] Reporting was not part of Villeroy's business, therefore he did not write these things. But he knew and understood them as well as Cavriana; they were behind the few agonized comments he allowed himself to make to his friends, while he watched the king and the duke playing cat and mouse with each other, and waited helplessly for the invasion which, whether sooner or later, was bound to come. When it came it would be to a country which Cavriana described as poor, exhausted, divided, sick, fraudulent and in decline.[4] Not only was there plague and other epidemic sickness in all but the coldest months, but by April 1587 a measure of corn which had cost 25 *écus* in 1585 was selling at 95–100 *écus*, and the cost of wine had increased four times.

In the second half of 1586, Villeroy and Brulart continued to have to work alone. It was therefore Villeroy who received and conferred with the deputies who arrived from the King of Navarre, late in May or early in June, possibly in response to a direct appeal from the king. Mendoza at least was fully convinced that the king and Villeroy were plotting with Navarre.[5] The deputies requested an audience, but Villeroy's vitally important task was complicated because, at this crucial moment, when life and death themselves were in the balance, he found the King of France not even at prayer, but touring about outside Paris, hunting at night by torchlight in the forest of Vin-

---

[1] Desjardins, *Negs. Tosc.*, iv, 613, 11 June 1585.

[2] *Ibid.*, 612, 27 May 1585.

[3] 'qualche sinistro accidente,' *ibid.*, 621, 4 August 1585.

[4] *Ibid.*, 661, 30 September 1586.

[5] *C.S.P. Sp.*, 1580-6, p. 574, 11 May 1586, Mendoza to Philip II.

cennes and absorbed in the collection from all over France, and
the purchase at any price of an infinite number of different kinds
of dogs.[1] It is of course possible that the king deliberately elected
to hide behind his reputation, in order to evade responsibility
for negotiations with the protestants. Whatever his shortcomings
as a monarch may have been, he at least succeeded in keeping
his enemies guessing.

It was almost certainly as a result of Villeroy's labours with
these envoys that, on 24 July, Catherine, accompanied by Pinart,
set out on yet another long journey, this time to see Navarre in
the south-west. The king, wrote Villeroy to Maisse in July,
desired peace, 'plus que je ne le vous puis escrire', and the only
hope for this lay in Catherine.[2] In accordance with the harsh
terms of the treaty of Nemours, which obliged the king to make
war on the protestants, the army was, at least to some extent,
being mobilized. However, we may be reasonably certain that the
king's military slothfulness proceeded more from a determination that he himself would not make war upon the King of
Navarre, if he could possibly avoid it, than from an inability to
make up his mind. On the other hand, he meant to allow some
kind of war to take place between his rival subjects because his
greatest hope, and increasingly his only hope, was that the duc
de Guise might be overthrown in the field by protestant mercenary troops invading from the east. It was unfortunate that
the duc de Guise happened to be a competent soldier.

We know that Catherine tried to persuade Navarre to change
his religion, but it is not very clear what else she hoped to obtain. Villeroy was never really hopeful about the outcome of the
negotiation. He did not trust Navarre, and was soon to blame
him bitterly for not declaring himself a catholic. If this seems a
curious attitude from someone of Villeroy's integrity, it was
because he knew that Navarre had been a catholic before,
believed that his religion was a matter of policy, and was convinced that he could never hope to succeed to the throne in
peace until he were a catholic. Villeroy came to believe that by
declaring himself a catholic, Navarre could have prevented the

[1] B.N., Mss. it. 1735, f. 70, 9 June 1586.
[2] B.N., Mss. fr. 16093, f. 76, 5 July 1586, Villeroy to Maisse; Desjardins, *Negs.
Tosc.*, iv, 621, 4 August 1585, 625, 17 September 1585, 614, 9 July 1585.

troubles then about to break. This is a debatable point, but coming from Villeroy, it cannot lightly be dismissed.[1]

Only a small number of Brulart's letters of this period have survived and they nearly all deal with the routine matters of his and Pinart's *départements*. In the absence of Catherine as well as the king, Villeroy and Brulart read the despatches to the council, then drafted the replies and sent both together to the king.[2] 'I have found all the replies to the despatches to be good', the king wrote to Villeroy some time in August.[3] Commenting in another letter to Villeroy on the despatches that he and Brulart had sent, Henry wrote, 'Je vous parle comme a celui que je scai qui m'estes tres asure et fidelle', and continued unceremoniously about the Queen of England: 'Je creve de pancer que ceste fame d'Angleterre face de tels secours [she was helping Navarre] et ancores responds a mon ambassadeur en la sorte qu'elle faict.' As for a despatch from Spain, and for the help which Spain was giving the league, without which Guise would be too poor to be dangerous, Henry wrote in the same letter, 'telles choses me donnent tant d'annuy que je voudroys quelque foys estre a la fin de ma vye et quant et quant estrangler tels jans qui me font tant de mal sans occasyon'. Thus, again revealing to Villeroy his growing anger, he admitted to a desire to strangle those who did him so much wrong.[4]

Villeroy's principal task in the summer of 1586 was to try to persuade the council to produce enough money to prevent the duc de Maine's army in Guienne from disbanding, for, if it did, Navarre could dictate his own terms and Catherine's effort to negotiate peace would be predestined to failure. Villeroy was distraught by the impossibility of raising this money and told the king that they were in great perplexity.[5] It was possibly in reply to this letter of Villeroy's that Henry wrote to him insisting that Maine's army must indeed be paid, because it would be terrible

[1] B.N., Mss. fr. 16092, f. 449, 6 December 1585, Villeroy to Maisse; Mss. fr. 16093, ff. 5, 82, 4 January, 2 August 1586, Villeroy to Maisse; *C.S.P.F.*, 1585-6, p. 442, 14 March 1586, Stafford to Walsingham.

[2] B.N., Mss. fr. 16093, f. 82, 2 August 1586, Villeroy to Maisse.

[3] B.N., Mss. n.a.f. 1243, no. 3, f. 8, undated but clearly of summer 1586, Henry to Villeroy.

[4] B.N., Mss. n.a.f. 1244, no. 63, f. 165, undated but of August 1586, Henry to Villeroy.

[5] B.N., Mss. fr. 6631, f. 48, 13 August 1586, Villeroy to the king.

if it disbanded. 'Villeroy,' he wrote, 'seeing that so many expenses are overwhelming us, and with so little or no means at all of raising money, I am in despair.'[1] Though the sentiment was perfectly sincere at the time, Villeroy might still be forgiven if he reflected that the king's despair was considerably less than his own, for Henry soon spent another 100,000 *écus* on the purchase of little dogs.[2] 'Villeroy, my friend,' the king wrote in another letter, 'we must . . . make the effort to raise money. . . . Send this to the members of my council.'[3] Yet again he explained to Villeroy his anguish over money: 'C'est chose quil me tourmante fort que tant est si grandes [tant de choses sont si grandes] et si peu de deniers que nous avons pour fournyr. Je ne say sur cella que respondre tant j'an suis annuie et contrie.' He needed money for so many important things and could raise so little. The problem seems also to have aroused in him some sense of guilt.[4] The king's affection for Villeroy and his confidence in him were unchanged at this time: 'You have seen my letter,' he wrote, 'and the satisfaction which it conveys . . . furthermore you have a good master who cares for you and places great trust in you.'[5] When Villeroy went to his house at Villeroy in the middle of August, either because he was ill or for some other personal reason, the king wrote to him sympathetically. 'Je suis byen aise car je desire vostre conservatyon pour l'amitie que je vous porte que vous n'aies poinct heu de mal. Demeures ches vous jusques au lendemyn de la Nostre Dame de septembre cest asez car vous estes necessayre avec les autres de mon conseyl. Se sont peu de jours pour vous reposer,' he said, almost apologetically, but in his own absence, Villeroy's presence was necessary for his peace of mind. 'Quant vous i estes se m'est un partyculier contantemant car j'an suis au grant repos estant absant comme je suys.' He wanted Villeroy to go home, but at the same time he wished him to remain at his post.[6]

Villeroy—like everyone else—was still unable to see the king

---

[1] B.N., Mss. n.a.f. 1245, no. 8, f. 18, undated, but of August 1586, Henry to Villeroy.
[2] Robiquet, ii, 241.
[3] B.N., Mss. n.a.f. 1245, no. 61, f. 143, undated, Henry to Villeroy.
[4] *Ibid.*, no. 10, f. 26, undated, Henry to Villeroy.
[5] *Ibid.*, no. 1, f. 2, undated, Henry to Villeroy.
[6] *Ibid.*, no. 10, f. 26, undated, Henry to Villeroy.

for several weeks after he returned to Vincennes from the waters of Bourbon-Lancy. Henry now did a certain amount of work all alone and himself made the major decisions. But he was like a phantom king. Although he was only thirty-six, his hair and beard were already entirely white. The Florentine ambassador said at this time that he was secretive and patient, quick to reply and somewhat given to subterfuge.[1] Not only was he angry and dangerously provoked but, as had happened at other times of stress, an undiscriminating suspicion had begun to possess him.

It was from about this autumn of 1586 that Henry very gradually began—if at first almost imperceptibly—to withdraw the hitherto unbounded confidence and affection which Villeroy had enjoyed, even as he was beginning to lose faith in his still devoted mother. This withdrawal of confidence was not the result of any direct cause, nor was it personal to Villeroy. It was simply the way in which Henry reacted to the troubles which were closing in on him, making it impossible for him to ignore them as he would have preferred.

Besides his work at court and for the king, Villeroy remained in constant touch with Catherine and Pinart during their long absence in the west from July 1586 to March 1587. Villeroy's letters have not survived, but this is clear from Catherine's. They were nearly all written for her by Pinart because she was still suffering from pain in her right arm and hand, and was frequently ill in bed. It was Villeroy who kept Catherine in touch with what was happening, and informed her of the movements of the armies in the west. Indeed, Catherine said that it was from Villeroy that she received almost her only news of the king.[2] It was also Villeroy who drafted and sent off her commission to negotiate with Navarre.[3] Brulart, for his part, kept them informed about the affairs of his own and Pinart's *départements*, but his letters have also been lost.[4]

We do not know what personal contribution Pinart may have made to the negotiations with Navarre. After much correspondence, waiting and travelling about, they took place at Saint-

---

[1] Desjardins, *Negs. Tosc.*, iv, 659, 30 September 1586.

[2] Baguenault de Puchesse, *Lettres*, ix, 28, 10 August 1586, Catherine to Villeroy original written by Pinart.

[3] *Ibid.*, 35, 24 August 1586, Catherine to Villeroy, original written by Pinart.

[4] *Ibid.*, 28, 10 August 1586, Catherine to Villeroy.

Brice near Cognac in December.[1] We only know that he never left Catherine during these months. He was, in a very literal sense, her right hand, her close counsellor and doubtless as close a friend. He worked for her at all hours of the day and night and he did not have an easy time. 'Ce mardi de trop grant matin et trop tard pour lundi', he ended one letter to Villeroy, which he was writing 'en dormant quasi' at one o'clock in the morning, while the queen was at prayer. He had to wait up to read out her letter to Villeroy before she retired.[2] He sent Villeroy news of Navarre's movements, of those of his troops and, as usual, of Catherine's health. In November Villeroy sent Pinart a cipher through which they could communicate more freely.[3]

Catherine was making little progress and, according to Sir Edward Stafford, there was talk of sending Villeroy to help her. We may imagine that the king dared not part with him, though in Stafford's opinion, only Villeroy could have brought the negotiation to a successful conclusion. 'I do not think,' he wrote to the English secretaries, 'that till he go, the bottom of the King's will shall ever be delivered, for Villeroy is his viceroy in all matters of weight, and I have not seen any treaty of peace or matter of that weight concluded (whosoever may have begun them) till Villeroy has been sent.'[4] The observation was just.

At the same time as he was negotiating with Navarre, Henry was trying to draw closer to Navarre's old ally, the Queen of England. But everything was uncertain. Mendoza told Philip II that 'such is the confusion of the court, the vacillation of the King and the jealousy, hatred and suspicion of the courtiers, that . . . even Villeroy, who holds the helm, says that such is the state of the King that it is impossible to predict whether it will be peace or war'.[5] The Florentine agent, Cavriana, confirmed this sinister impression of affairs at court. Guise, he said, was of a haughty and ambitious disposition. What else, therefore, could

---

[1] On this conference see G. de Brémond d'Ars, *Les Conférences de Saint-Brice entre Henri de Navarre et Catherine de Médicis, 1586–7*; A. de la Fontenelle, *Journal de Guillaume et de Michel Le Riche*.

[2] B.N., Mss. fr. 15573, f. 225, 3 November 1586, Pinart to Villeroy.

[3] Baguenault de Puchesse, *Lettres*, ix, 89, November 1586, Catherine to Villeroy.

[4] *C.S.P.F.*, 1585–6, p. 153, 25 November 1586, Stafford to the secretaries.

[5] *C.S.P.Sp.*, 1580–6, p. 689, 24 December 1586, Mendoza to Philip II.

he desire but alarms and excursions?[1] Everyone thought only of personal advancement, despising the public interest and careless of justice and royal authority. At court the talk was all of quarrels and duels, and a day rarely passed in which there was no hand-to-hand fighting. 'If it does not come to homicide and the assassination of certain of the great,' wrote Cavriana, 'it will be a miracle.'[2] Villeroy became increasingly alarmed. Out of discretion, he only referred in his letters to the disunity among the catholics, but what he meant was the mortal enmity between the king and the Guises. He knew that they could never act together in sincerity—whether in war or peace—and probably not even in safety because, as he wrote to Maisse, 'ils ne tendent a meme but'.[3] He, too, confirmed the terrible state of affairs in Paris. 'This city', he wrote in the same letter to Maisse, 'has been full of alarm and still is full of suspicion, distrust and enmity which proceed from the plotting and scheming . . . of those who desire to fish in troubled waters. In a word,' he concluded, 'things are as bad as they could possibly be.'[4]

During the first three months of 1587 the king, ostrich-like, mostly hid himself away. He had recalled his armies—such as they were—from the field, and begun to disarm in the hope of winning over Navarre. Guise, on the other hand, not only remained in arms but became increasingly menacing. It was little wonder, therefore, that Villeroy should have been alarmed. The strain was possibly becoming too great for, in March, he obtained the *survivance* of his office for his cousin by marriage, Claude de Laubespine.[5] He wanted to take him into immediate partnership in order to reduce the burden of his *département* and probably to give himself more time for his work as minister in a broader sense.

Some time after 14 March, Villeroy went to meet Catherine at Estampes. There had been definite news of her failure and imminent return. She was hurrying back although she was

---

[1] 'rumori e novità.' Desjardins, *Negs. Tosc.*, iv, 675–6, 16 February 1587.
[2] *Ibid.*, 670, 675–6, 5 January, 16 February 1587.
[3] B.N., Mss. fr. 16093, f. 142, 28 February 1587, Villeroy to Maisse.
[4] *Id.*, quoted by Nouaillac, 97.
[5] B.N., Mss. it. 1736, f. 29, 30 March 1587. Claude de Laubespine was one of Catherine's personal secretaries.

T

ill again. It may be assumed that Villeroy went to inform her of a revelation made to him by Poulain, a member of the league's council of sixteen in Paris. He had given warning of a conspiracy against the king's person, also involving Épernon and the city of Paris.[1] Villeroy and the king had actually been discussing whether or not he ought to arrest Guise. Villeroy advised against it because the king was too ill-prepared 'pour commencer le jeu', in the queen's absence, and with the duke armed to the teeth. 'It is not enough to undertake things,' Villeroy commented, 'one must also be resolute and properly equipped . . . otherwise it is more temerarious and imprudent than courageous and wise.'[2] In other words, the king was too weak, in all senses, to arrest the duke. Villeroy's real opinion was that Guise ought to be arrested. If his advice had been followed earlier the king would have been in a position to arrest him with safety. As it was Henry could not be trusted to take effective action: 'Ce prince etait si bon et facille a desmouvoir que rarement il executait ce qu'il avoit resolu du facon que les conseils que l'on lui donnait et les resolutions pour bonnes qu'elles fussent souvent luy apportaient plus de mal que de bien.'[3] In deciding what advice he ought to give the king, Villeroy took his weaknesses into consideration. Clearly, in this case, an unsuccessful attempt to arrest the duke was too dangerous to be contemplated.

It was to this plot against the king that Villeroy referred when he wrote to Maisse upon his return from Estampes: 'Our wretchedness increases every day as everyone is trying to feather his own nest without a care for the public good. . . . Everyone wants to control the government and few are willing to obey the pilot, so that if the tempest lasts much longer I have no doubt that the vessel will be wrecked.' The duc d'Aumale,[4] he said, was troubling Picardy; Guise remained in arms, and all the towns were divided. The protestants took advantage of this and the English and Spanish poured oil on the flames. 'Everything', he groaned, 'is upside down.' 'C'est un theatre de confusion de

---

[1] Desjardins, *Negs. Tosc.*, iv, 677, 681, 3, 31 March 1587; Petitot, xlv, Pierre de L'Estoile, *Journal de Henri III*, 427.

[2] B.N., Mss. n.a.f. 7260, f. 7, 1 August 1594, letter to Du Vair. This statement indicates the influence which, by her mere presence, Catherine was able to wield.

[3] *Id.*

[4] Aumale was a first cousin of the duc de Guise.

desordre et de pauvrete d'impiete et de toute autre espece de calamite.'[1]

From January to April 1587 only one letter of Brulart's has survived. Those for April to June are exclusively addressed to Nevers, whom the king sent to Picardy where Aumale was taking control of the towns for the league, and rallying the nobility against the hated favourite, Épernon. Picardy was of course strategically important for the introduction of Spanish forces into France.

It is possible that Pinart now went on holiday after his long absence with Catherine. However that may be, we know nothing of his movements until, on 12 May, he left with Catherine on another mission to the Guises. They went to complain of the revolution in Picardy, and to try to bring the catholics to some measure of agreement, because the outstanding problem to be faced was the protestant force of Germans and Swiss who were preparing to invade the country. Pinart well knew what temper to expect. He wrote to Nevers from Reims on 8 June that nothing had yet been decided and that he did not see any great hope.[2] If Pinart could not see much cause for hope, neither could Villeroy. He at last declared quite openly to Matignon that the Guises cared about nothing but their own desires. 'Le masque de la Religion est levé. C'est l'ambition qui nous régente, l'imprudence qui nous maîtrise et l'irrésolution qui nous ruine.' Characteristically he went on, 'Dieu est tout puissant, j'ai mon recours à lui et ne me départirai de mon devoir. Je veux encore moins perdre courage.' Nevertheless he calmly wrote of making one more effort before they died, for he knew it was possible that the end was near.[3] To Maisse he said that it was therefore time to fit their armour and resolve to endure all the disasters which attend upon such a war. It caused them such anguish and occupied so much of their attention that they had neither the time nor the money to attend to anything else.[4]

Villeroy's attitude to the catholics in the summer of 1587 was very different from what it had been two years earlier, at the

[1] B.N., Mss. fr. 16093, f. 150, 28 March 1587, Villeroy to Maisse.
[2] B.N., Mss. fr. 3398, f. 105, 8 June 1587, Pinart to Nevers.
[3] Letters to Matignon, 180, 24 May 1587, partially quoted by Nouaillac, 101.
[4] B.N., Mss. fr. 16093, f. 171, 18 June 1587, Villeroy to Maisse.

time of the treaty of Nemours. So useless was it any longer to
pretend that the king and the catholics could be united that
Villeroy actually declared to Matignon, 'il me semble que le
Roi et tous ses serviteurs endurent toutes les hazardes et
opprobres du monde sans s'en revancher'. He did not think
that this could go on, and said that he would rather die that day
than the next, if such usage was to continue. 'Je suis bon
catholique,' he went on, 'et affectioné à ma religion autant
qu'homme de ma sorte; mais non pour supporter qu'on gour-
mande le Roi et que l'on le prive d'autorité sous prétexte de
piété. . . . Si l'on en abuse on le déséspéra.'[1] Villeroy was
gradually being forced to choose between two principles. But
apart from that, he knew that the king could not stand much
more strain and provocation.

In July Villeroy and Brulart accompanied the king to Meaux
to meet Guise and to hold a council of war. Villeroy was so overworked that he hardly had time to breathe, for, if the king had
less confidence in him than previously, nevertheless he would
not listen to anyone else, except Bellièvre. The outcome of the
conference was vital. 'Ce coup emportera la piece', Villeroy
said to Matignon,[2] 'la piece' being nothing less than the crown
of France. Villeroy was not reassured by the decision to oppose
the invading force, not only because the catholics were so
divided that he did not know whom to trust, but also because
the conference had been anything but successful.[3] Villeroy had
had occasion to observe that someone had contrived to make the
king resent the advice that he should see Guise and reconcile him
to the crown. Henry had come to entertain so great a jealousy of
the duke, that he almost forgot his fear of the army which was
about to invade France.[4] Thus the king's anger, hatred and
fear—which were already great—were still being fomented by
those same people who elected to fish in troubled waters. This,
Villeroy pointed out, produced a vicious circle, for Guise,
having grievously offended the king, had very good reason to be

[1] *Letters to Matignon*, 191, 14 June 1587, quoted by Nouaillac, 85.
[2] *Ibid.*, 197, 5 July 1587.
[3] B.N., Mss. it. 1736, f. 103, 16 July 1587; Mss. fr. 16093, f. 176, 18 July 1587,
Villeroy to Maisse.
[4] Petitot, xliv, *Mémoires d'Estat de Villeroy*, 41; see also on this conference, Desjardins, *Negs. Tosc.*, iv, 693 ff., 24 June 1587.

afraid.[1] Villeroy thought the king had made a fundamental mistake. He considered that the last thing a sovereign prince ought
to do is to show himself displeased and offended with one of his
subjects and then, instead of chastising him, to allow him even
greater powers and opportunity to do him wrong.[2]

Catherine wanted Villeroy to dissuade the king from taking
the field in person. But Villeroy did not share her opinion which,
on this occasion, was based on maternal solicitude. The
secretaries therefore spent the summer preparing for the war
which was expected after the harvest, and for all the calamities
and miseries it was possible to conceive of.[3]

Definitely anxious as to the outcome of the campaign, Villeroy and Brulart accompanied the king when he left Paris to join
his army at Gien on the Loire. He departed at two o'clock in the
afternoon of 12 September, amidst the tears of the queens and
their ladies.[4] Villeroy had not been in the field for eighteen
years, since the time when the king had won himself a military
reputation in his brother Charles' reign. Pinart remained in
Paris with Catherine, who was in control of the government, but
virtually none of his correspondence for the rest of the year has
survived.

Villeroy and Brulart attended the king from beginning to end
of the campaign, which lasted just over three months. Their
work was very much the same as usual, but they shared the
privations and discomforts of the army for, once shaken from
his lethargy, the king himself lived and worked as a simple cap-
tain. But not even the activity of going to war distracted Villeroy
from the sad, reproachful thoughts with which his letters had
for long been filled. He deplored the fact that so few of his
countrymen obeyed the command to love one another and, in
his peculiar loyalty to the king's person, he distressed himself
with the thought that it was on him that all their present trouble
would fall, 'which', he said, 'is what afflicts and torments me most
for the obligation which we owe him'. His intentions were good,
but he was ill-served, everyone thinking first of himself and not

[1] Petitot, xliv, *Mémoires d'Estat de Villeroy*, 41.
[2] *Ibid.*, 42.
[3] B.N., Mss. fr. 16093, f. 180, 1 August 1587, Villeroy to Maisse.
[4] B.N., Mss. it. 1736, f. 186, 14 September 1587.

of the king's service, an attitude which was doubly apparent in the camp.[1] Villeroy in fact thought very little of 'cette compagnie'—meaning those who were in the field with the king,[2] and Brulart shared his evil opinion of their loyalty and reliability. He wrote to Bellièvre, after the defeat of Joyeuse at Coutras, 'I am very much afraid that worse is yet to come since matters are so ill directed and evilly disposed.'[3] During this curious campaign, Henry and Navarre did their utmost to avoid engaging the other's forces. The battle of Coutras—at which Villeroy's son was captured—was forced on Navarre by the king's treacherous favourite Joyeuse, who was in league with Guise. Instead of following up his victory, Navarre retreated into the south-west and remained there. He may have feared a Spanish invasion in his rear, or he may have had some secret agreement with the king.

The king turned west, away from the invading force and, at Saint-Aignan, on the way to Blois, there occurred an incident which upset Villeroy profoundly. It influenced his future actions, and others believed that it did more than anything else to bring about the disgrace which he shared with his colleagues the following year. While this is incorrect, the incident, nevertheless, had other sad and far-reaching consequences.

Épernon made a savage attack on Villeroy, on 30 September, when, in the presence of de Retz, Biron, La Guiche and Brulart, Villeroy read the king a report from the council, sent by Pinart. It dealt with a financial matter, and Épernon first accused Villeroy of diverting to other uses money promised to his brother, and then of acting as he pleased, on his own authority, instead of upon the king's orders. Villeroy, who was standing behind the king's chair, denied this accusation, but the king rose and silenced him. Épernon then reaffirmed his charges, abusing Villeroy and calling him 'un petit gallant a qui il fallait apprendre a parler'. Villeroy remained silent and the king went over to speak to Biron, and Nevers who entered the room at that moment. La Guiche tried to calm Épernon, who declared that were it not for the king's presence he would have assaulted Ville-

---

[1] B.N., Mss. fr. 15908, f. 461, 20 September 1587, Villeroy to ?Bellièvre.
[2] *Ibid.*, f. 464, 22 September 1587, Villeroy to Bellièvre.
[3] *Ibid.*, f. 493, 27 October 1587, Brulart to Bellièvre.

roy and shortly after told him so directly, 'que je remertiasse hardiment la presence du Roi que sans icelle il m'eust bien traite en une autre facon'.[1]

Villeroy was so severely shaken and upset that he remained in his room for two days before he could summon the courage to return to his papers. To relieve his feelings he wrote at great length to his friend Bellièvre, whom he esteemed above every-one else. 'Je vous escript,' he began, 'outre de douleur autant que peult estre un homme de bien. Ung malheur ou pour mieulx dire ung coup de tonnere . . . m'est tombe sur la teste.' He explained the whole incident and concluded, 'Voila mon-sieur l'histoire de ceste tragedie pour moi qui ma afflige grande-ment.'[2]

The next day, or the one after that, the king sent for Villeroy and said he was annoyed at what had happened, but that it was no time for his councillors to quarrel; he actually bade Villeroy forget the matter. Villeroy defended himself, complained that the situation was intolerable, that there was no certainty that Épernon would not renew his onslaughts and, finally, asked leave to go home.[3] The king refused his request, and com-manded him to obey—a summons to which Villeroy was always responsive, even in extremity, for he did not want to be re-proached with having deserted his master at such a time, at the desire of another, and for a personal reason.[4] Their conversation was interrupted by the entry of Épernon himself.

Villeroy need not have feared for the spotless reputation which was so dear to him. Neither then nor later did anyone take seriously accusations levelled against him by those who wished him ill. He received many condolences from those about him—who also tried to placate Épernon—so much so that only then did Villeroy realize the full extent to which Épernon was hated. Not the least gratifying and consoling was an autograph letter from Catherine, who was deeply shocked by this news. She

---

[1] B.N., Mss. fr. 15908, ff. 477, 483, 2, 4 October 1587, Villeroy to Bellièvre, partially quoted by Léo Mouton, 177. In his account of this incident (pp. 174-7), Mouton says that Épernon also accused Villeroy of selling council secrets to Spain. Had he really said this, Villeroy would certainly have told Bellièvre.

[2] Ibid., f. 477, 2 October 1587, Villeroy to Bellièvre.

[3] Id.

[4] Id.

had not, she said, been so upset by anything that had happened
for a long time, both for the sake of Villeroy, and for love of the
king, that he should be so far reduced that anyone dared, in his
presence, to abuse his good and experienced servitors.[1]

Unfortunately this incident had more serious effects than the
anguish of mind it caused Villeroy. In the first place it altered,
or rather undermined, his still close if already changing relations
with the king. Probably from helplessness, dislike of trouble and
fear of the possible consequences, Henry brushed the matter
aside with wounding indifference and a notable lack of understanding. In his memoir Villeroy confessed that he could never
have believed that the king would allow Épernon—or even a
person of higher rank—to treat a favoured councillor and official
in this way, and before his very eyes.[2]

It was from the time of the conference with the Guises at
Meaux, and no doubt more particularly after the scene with
Épernon, that Villeroy began to feel a change in the king's
attitude to him.[3] Catherine wrote Villeroy a sympathetic letter
at this time, mingling condolence with her apprehensions. The
letter clearly shows how anxious she was that Villeroy's discomfiture should not result in his estrangement from the king.
This was because she, better than anyone, knew that Villeroy's
importance was paramount. No one else could be relied upon to
tell the truth, and, if he refused to listen to Villeroy, then he
would not listen to anyone. But it had not then occurred to her
that the king might be as much to blame as Épernon, if such an
estrangement occurred. She wrote, she said, not so much to
comfort Villeroy—for she did not doubt that the king himself
had already done this, as became him—but rather to beg that
the incident might not prevent him from serving the king with
his accustomed frankness. 'Vous conesé vostre mestre, qui vous
douyt donner une tele aseuranse que les préventions des aultres
ne vous deust empècher la lyberté requise pour son servyse. Je
vous dys sesi, car le je voys [le roi] en tel aystat que il ne faut

[1] Baguenault de Puchesse, *Lettres*, vii, 405, 5 October 1587, Catherine to
Villeroy. The editor, who was unable to trace the incident to which Catherine's
letter refers, has made the error of printing it under the year 1581, instead of 1587.

[2] Petitot, xliv, *Mémoires d'Estat de Villeroy*, 51.

[3] B.N., Mss. fr. 15909, f. 188, 5 October 1587, Villeroy to Bellièvre.

ryen creyndre à luy dyre, affin que, pour ne savoyr la véryté, il souyt encore pys . . . Je prye à Dieu qu'i delyvre le Roy de tant de yndygnytés.'[1]

Villeroy had his own explanation of Épernon's hostility. Épernon had opposed and thwarted a good marriage arranged for Villeroy's son. He therefore imagined that Villeroy must be ill-disposed towards him, and that he used his influence and authority to damage him in the eyes of the king. Doubtless Épernon also resented the friendly relations which existed between Villeroy and his own hated rival, Joyeuse. Besides these personal reasons, of which there were several, Villeroy, in his memoir, implies a further explanation. The previous July, when the king had gone to Meaux to confer with the duc de Guise, Villeroy had advised him to master his distrust and dissemble his annoyance. Épernon, on the contrary, had been one of those who poured oil on the flames, because he and the duc de Guise were mortal enemies.[2]

Villeroy and Bellièvre later did all they could to soften Épernon's attitude to Guise because they realized that the effects of this hostility—the 'contre-coup'—would be visited upon the king, which was precisely what happened. But the only result was to increase Épernon's evil opinion of themselves, and in turn he fed the king with suspicions. Thus Épernon's outburst in the council gave publicity, as well as form and shape, to a difference of opinion between himself and Villeroy which, on Villeroy's side, was not personal to the duke. In addition, it had the effect of removing Villeroy from the impartial position of a disinterested councillor, of dragging him, in spite of himself, into a quarrel with the king's favourite, and of involving him on a personal level in intrigues and enmities which were extremely dangerous. This destroyed his peace of mind and interfered with his work. Thereafter he was haunted by a sense of insecurity, and a by no means baseless fear that his life was in danger; for Épernon's attitude was menacing. Épernon was jealous of Villeroy's influence, and feared his advice to the king. Henry, for his part, was becoming afraid of Épernon, and Villeroy, through no fault of his own, also had cause to fear him. In

[1] Baguenault de Puchesse, *Lettres*, vii, 405, 5 October 1587, Catherine to Villeroy.
[2] Petitot, xliv, *Mémoires b'Estat de Villeroy*, 49.

this way, normal human relationships, and that degree of confidence which is the essential basis of co-operation, were being subtly destroyed.

Villeroy made a great effort to carry on as usual, for they were, after all, at war. To Bellièvre he said that he had been struggling since last he wrote to raise sufficient confidence to enable him to remain there at his post, in order not to abandon the king or his work, although their danger was so great and so imminent that it made his hair stand on end to think of it. Their forces, he said, were weak in all respects.[1]

As usual, in such circumstances, Villeroy and Brulart kept in constant touch with Catherine—and no doubt with Pinart who must have been shouldering a triple burden—but their letters to her have not survived. We learn from her own that they sent her day-to-day accounts of what was happening, and she sent them any papers which had to be shown to the king. One of the chief services which she required of them was, as always, that they should continually reassure her as to the king's personal well-being. On this occasion the normally calm and courageous Catherine confessed in a poignant letter to Brulart that she was almost sick with fear and anxiety over the king, knowing that he was exposed to the danger of battle as well as to the danger of treachery. The smallest scraps of news were precious to her. It would give her life, she said, only to hear every day where he was, where the enemy was, and that he was well, even if there was no other news.[2] Whether touched or merely dutiful, Brulart complied with this pathetic request, and the queen did not omit to thank him.[3] But it was to Villeroy that Catherine confided any delicate matter, trusting in him to make the king understand whatever she felt unable to write to him directly.[4]

---

[1] B.N., Mss. fr. 15908, f. 486, 7 October 1587, Villeroy to Bellièvre.

[2] 'Je vous prye fayre tent pour moy que je aye tous les jours des nouvelles du Roy enquore que ne se presante aultre afayre ne novelles; mès seulement: yl èt en tel lyeu, et les ennemys en tel, et se porte byen. Croyés que s'èt me donner la vye; car il fault que je confese mon ynfirmyté aveques la grende craynte que j'ann é. Je an suys an une ayxtreme pouyne de panser que il fault qu'i souyt à l'asard d'un combast ou d'une mechanceté, nous voyant si byguarés come nous soumes tous.' Baguenault de Puchesse, *Lettres*, ix, 250, 15 October 1587, Catherine to Brulart.

[3] *Ibid.*, 302, 309, 24 November, 3 December 1587, Catherine to Brulart.

[4] *Ibid.*, 279, 12 November 1587, Catherine to Villeroy.

Though we know that Villeroy and Brulart wrote to Catherine and to others during these months in the field, the few letters which have survived provide us with little information either about themselves or the strange events which they witnessed— for this was surely the most extraordinary and most confused campaign that had ever been fought in France.[1] When they returned to Paris, just in time for Christmas, Villeroy and Brulart were rather more cheerful than they had been for some time, doubtless from sheer relief. The foreign invader had been quickly despatched, even though the method was unorthodox, and, if Guise had not been defeated in battle, it was at least something to be thankful for that the king and his army had survived intact.[2]

Because he knew what Guise was doing, and how the king was likely to react, Villeroy foresaw a final catastrophe, the ruin of the monarchy and the collapse of France. At least from 1585, if not before, he entertained no further hope that this could be averted. What he expected was that a war of succession together with a Spanish invasion would be added to the plague and famine which were already causing widespread misery in France. He felt that this catastrophe was going to be so overwhelming, that France would not rise again within his lifetime. Only in this did he prove to be wrong. The events of 1585-7 offer a picture of almost complete disintegration, while the succeeding years fulfilled Villeroy's worst forebodings.

---

[1] On this campaign see the despatches of the Venetian ambassador, B.N., Mss. it. 1736, 186 ff.; Archives de France, Fonds Simancas, K. 1565, 1566, correspondence of the duc de Guise. See also Baguenault de Puchesse, *La Campagne du duc de Guise dans l'Orléanais—octobre et novembre, 1587*. This account is very slight.

[2] B.N., Mss. fr. 3975, f. 194, 27 December 1587, Brulart to Nevers; Mss. fr. 16093, f. 219, 16 December 1587, Villeroy to Maisse.

CHAPTER XVII

The Dismissal of the Secretaries, 1587–8

WHEN the king returned to Paris at Christmas 1587, it was not for very long that Villeroy and Brulart continued to feel hopeful either that he would again take the field, this time in Poitou, according to his declared intention, or that there would be any effective co-operation between the king and Guise against the heretics. A situation quickly developed which was very similar to that of 1585, only this time it was even more dangerous. Guise remained in arms in the east while Aumale sustained a revolution in Picardy which effectively kept the king near Paris. This was very much in the interests of Spain, which was about to launch the great Armada and, it was thought, simultaneously to invade the north of France, or at the least to attack Cambrai.[1]

It was neither Villeroy, nor Catherine and Pinart (about whom we have no information before the month of May) but Bellièvre who was sent to reason, argue and plead with the Guises. His instructions were prepared, written and signed by Brulart[2] who remained in touch with him during his critical negotiation at Soissons in March and April 1588. But, when he received an urgent and important despatch from Bellièvre, Brulart experienced great difficulty in obtaining the king's answer. In spite of his anger and his menacing words against Guise, Henry still inconvenienced the secretaries and impeded their work by his repeated absences, as he had done for the past ten years. On 25 March, Brulart sent Bellièvre's letters on to the king—we do not know where— and they missed him. The king spent the whole of the next morning in council with Catherine

---

[1] Desjardins, *Negs. Tosc.* iv, 742, 31 January 1588.
[2] B.N., Mss. fr. 15892, f. 151, 27 February 1588.

and Villeroy and by the time Brulart had a chance to remind him of Bellièvre's letters, it was late, and he went away to mass and to dinner. The next day, 27 March, Brulart found that the king had departed for Vincennes at five o'clock in the morning. It was therefore not until 28 March that he was finally able to see the king, although Bellièvre had particularly requested an immediate reply.[1]

Bellièvre—an eminently suitable envoy—was doubtless chosen on this occasion because the king needed Villeroy in Paris. It was to Villeroy that Poulain—a member of the league's council of sixteen—gave his warnings and information as to the duke's real intentions.[2]

Villeroy, whose attitude to the catholic league and their supporters had been steadily hardening, was coming to think that the king ought to take the field in Picardy against the Guises, who were threatening his state and his person alike, and who were clearly far more to be feared than the protestant King of Navarre. The papal nuncio, Morosini—a man of considerable stature, whose vision penetrated far beyond the political aspirations of the Holy See—reported Villeroy to have said that there were two ways of pacifying the troubles, either by reason or by force. The king had tried the former but Bellièvre had obtained no results. Therefore only force remained to the king, if he were to preserve his honour and his kingdom.[3] He knew that if the king fought the Guises in Picardy, or anywhere else, he might lose a certain amount of catholic support, but, on the other hand, he could not stand by with his hands in his pockets and watch the kingdom being seized.[4] In any case, the king himself was actually threatening to lead an army into Picardy. But, although Villeroy thought this politically desirable and even necessary, when it came to the point he advised against it.[5] The reason is not far to seek: he knew that Guise was in

[1] B.N., Mss. fr. 15909, f. 58, 27 March 1588, Brulart to Bellièvre, f. 64, 28 March 1588, Brulart to Bellièvre, f. 62, 28 March 1588, the king to Bellièvre.

[2] Cimber et Danjou, xi, 'Le Procès verbal d'un nommé Nicolas Poulain', 289 ff. This is also printed by Petitot, xlv, Pierre de L'Estoile, *Journal de Henri III*, 411 ff.

[3] De L'Epinois, 120, quoting the despatches of the nuncio in the Vatican library.

[4] *Ibid.*, 121.

[5] *Ibid.*, 120, 129.

league with the pope and could quite possibly obtain the king's excommunication as easily as he had Navarre's. This would have been far the most terrible of all possible disasters. Villeroy was therefore in the grim position of being unable to offer any advice which he himself considered valid. In this predicament, and aware no doubt of the paradox, he did his utmost through Morosini to invoke some papal sanction against the subversive political activities of the league, which was playing into the hands of the protestants, and to induce Guise to desist from making war on the king. Morosini himself was by no means hostile to the king, but his instructions were not conciliatory.[1]

Villeroy was well aware, as hope in the success of Bellièvre's mission declined, that the king was becoming desperate, for though he was increasingly withdrawing into himself, he still trusted Villeroy more than anyone else, and occasionally favoured him with something of his former frankness, if not affection. Thus he wrote to Villeroy that he must call up troops into the region of Paris and 'parler an Roy', for he was resolved no longer to endure such a situation. On the other hand, he confessed that he still cherished hopes in Bellièvre's ability to keep Guise away from Paris—hopes which Villeroy knew to be entirely vain. 'La passyon a la fin blessee se tourne en fureur,' Henry added menacingly after his signature, 'qu'ils ne m'y metent poynct.'[2] Besides this, Villeroy himself wrote to Bellièvre, in the king's name, and presumably to his dictation, expressing a new resolution to stand firm against the menace of the league. '[Je] suis resolu de faire tout ce qui est en moy jusques a y metre tout . . . pour y remedier . . . J'ai deslibere de . . . me rendre la plus fort quil me sera possible et apres faire tout ce que je cognoistrai estre necessaire pour me deslivrer du danger et de la peine en laquelle je veis.'[3] 'The king has declared that he can no longer live as he has lived up till now', Villeroy wrote to Matignon at this time. 'He wants to be obeyed or else to die. These are his words, which I wish to God he had uttered

---

[1] On Henry's relations with the pope, see de L'Epinois, 'La Politique de Sixte-Quint en France', *Revue des questions historiques*, xxvii (1880).

[2] B.N., Mss. n.a.f. 1246, no. 35, f. 27, undated but of March or April 1588, Henry to Villeroy, quoted by Nouaillac, 69–70.

[3] B.N., Mss. fr. 15909, f. 70, 24 April 1588, Henry to Bellièvre.

sooner. . . . But they are better late than never.'[1] Villeroy knew from Poulain of Guise's intention to create a revolution in Paris and that—as Mendoza, the Spanish ambassador, said with graphic inelegance—the abscess was about to burst.[2]

There is little reliable information about the secretaries during the stormy days in May 1588 when Guise came to Paris with sinister designs upon the king. We know for certain that they were all three there, Villeroy and Brulart in attendance upon the king, and Pinart, as usual, with Catherine. According to Robiquet—who is not always reliable—Villeroy was at dinner when he heard of the arrival of Guise in Paris on 9 May, and he was the first to inform the king; but we do not know whether he was present at the king's interview with Guise in the Louvre that day.[3] On 12 May in the evening, the famous day of the barricades, Pinart wrote quite calmly to Nevers to tell him what had happened.[4] Robiquet also says that on 13 May, Catherine sent Pinart to the king to warn him of Guise's menacing attitude.[5] Pinart found the king at the Tuileries upon the point of departure. This is borne out by Cheverny, who says that Pinart was with them, but that the king sent him back to Catherine. Villeroy and Brulart—as well as Bellièvre and Cheverny—left with the king on his precipitate departure for Chartres. Many of

---

[1] *Letters to Matignon*, 218, 28 April 1588.

[2] De Croze, ii, 62, app. xxxiii, 333, 7 May 1588, Mendoza to Philip II.

[3] Robiquet, ii, 314, n. 1.

[4] *Ibid.*, 351.

[5] Petitot, xxxvi, *Mémoires de Cheverny*, 110. Secondary accounts of the *journée des barricades* vary in detail and should all be used with caution. The best first-hand accounts are to be found in the despatch of the Venetian ambassador, B.N., Mss. it. 1737, f. 71, 20 May 1588, and in a letter from the king to Nevers, B.N., Mss. fr. 3976, f. 84, 17 May 1588. See also B.N., Mss. fr. 5315, ff. 139v seq., Nicolas Brulart, *Histoire de notre temps depuis le 8 mai 1588*. The king has been criticized for running away, whereas his departure was an astute move which assured the failure of Guise's *coup d'état*. It was originally intended to coincide with the appearance of the Spanish Armada and a simultaneous invasion of France and England. But the Armada was delayed, and consequently Guise's arrival in Paris, and the whole plan miscarried. De Croze, ii, app. xxxv, 337, 15 May 1588, Mendoza to Philip II. 'Puisque l'abcès n'a point crevé comme on s'y attendait, les choses demeurent dans un si mauvais état qu'il sera difficile d'y apporter remède.' Nevertheless, he went on, 'le roi est dans une impossibilité absolue de venir en aide à la reine d'Angleterre'. On the movements of the Spanish Armada see the despatches of Longlée, the French ambassador in Spain, B.N., Mss. fr. 16110, *passim* and Mattingly, *The Defeat of the Spanish Armada*.

the company were not even booted and spurred and they took whatever horses they could find.

In the midst of this crisis Villeroy did a remarkable thing: he wrote a long, personal letter to the King of Navarre. He asked him to receive his letter in good part, but considering the danger and the imminent desolation of the state, it would belie his whole life if he did not bear witness, at least to Navarre, that he was not afraid to voice his opinion, even though he were power-less to avert disaster. Villeroy considered that, after God, the well-being of the state depended upon the existence of good relations between the king and Navarre, although this had been rendered difficult by the bitterness of war and the problem of religion. But, indicating the path of duty, Villeroy said that it was now for Navarre to make up his mind to sever at the root the troubles and disasters which threatened them. Villeroy urged that any action which tended to perpetuate civil war would arouse hatred against Navarre, and increase the catholic depen-dence on Spain, who coveted the inheritance of France at the expense of the legitimate heirs. The hindrance caused by the difference in religion must be removed, otherwise it was only with the utmost difficulty that Navarre could ever hope to pre-vail against Spain and succeed to the throne of France. Villeroy therefore begged him to declare himself catholic and come to their help before forces were assembled and another war broke out. He wrote as from himself alone, but his action was entirely in line with the king's policy and wishes. It is a striking illustra-tion of the eminence of his position and the way in which he strove to defend the real interests of France. He and Navarre had known each other for many years and doubtless already felt that mutual esteem, even in disagreement, which later bore fruit in close co-operation.

Navarre did not respond to this appeal, and a profound de-pression descended upon Villeroy while he was at Chartres with the king. 'C'est dieu qui nous a voulu *punir*,' he wrote to Nevers, 'et vous confesse quant a moi que je me y trouve *si confus et failli de cueur* que je ne scai plus que faire sinon me *resoudre a mourir en bien faisant*.'[1] Villeroy—and everyone else—had been

---

[1] B.N., Mss. fr. 3976, f. 80, 16 May 1588, Villeroy to Nevers, quoted by de L'Epinois, 149. Italics represent Villeroy's underlining in the original.

expecting something like the events in Paris, or even worse, for he wrote in his memoir that everyone had foreseen that some kind of violence would come of the suspicions and hatreds, that this would place the king in very great distress and likewise his affairs in great confusion.[1]

It was Villeroy's last great task in this first part of his public career, to try to reduce this confusion to some semblance of order and agreement. At first he tried to excuse himself from going to Paris to join in Catherine's negotiations with Guise. This was because he knew that Épernon was urging the king not to make peace, and blamed those who advised him to seek an agreement. Villeroy was aware that Guise would never agree to a peace which excluded the disgrace of this hated royal favourite. He already had cause to fear the effects of Épernon's implacable hostility, and did not wish to attract to himself the anger and hatred that Épernon's disgrace would inevitably arouse. The king accepted Villeroy's excuses and sent his doctor Miron, while Villeroy did what he could to help Catherine from Chartres. She thanked him for sending her news of the king, for which she still craved.[2]

It seems likely that Pinart, who remained in Paris with Catherine, may have attempted to retire at this time for, on 15 May, Villeroy drafted a letter from the king instructing him to remain in Catherine's service throughout her stay in Paris, to receive her commands and to keep the king informed of her news and other important matters.[3]

After Miron had made several unsuccessful journeys to Paris, the king prevailed upon Villeroy to undertake the negotiation. He departed on Whit Sunday—17 May—from Vernon, where the king was on his way to Rouen. 'I offered to go and willingly resolved to do this,' wrote Villeroy, 'moved by a great zeal for the service of God, the king and the public welfare and by a great desire to release the king from the uncertainty in which he lived.'[4] In his absence Brulart took over his work.

---

[1] Petitot, xliv, *Mémoires d'Estat de Villeroy*, 53.

[2] Baguenault de Puchesse, *Lettres*, ix, 344, 22 May 1588, Catherine to Villeroy, original written by Pinart.

[3] B.N., Mss. Cinq Cents Colbert, 9, f. 159v, 15 May 1588, Henry to Pinart, draft by Villeroy.

[4] Petitot, xliv, *Mémoires d'Estat de Villeroy*, 55-6.

U

We know very little about this important negotiation. It afterwards became a subject of controversy because Villeroy was accused in some quarters of having played into the hands of Guise. This was the most obvious stick with which to beat a minister, and virtually no one believed the accusation. But it is the reason why our only brief and incomplete account of the negotiation, in Villeroy's memoir, is couched in the form of an apology. Aware that any agreement which he and Catherine might conclude, would be a source of grave dissatisfaction, Villeroy proceeded with great caution, taking care to do everything in the presence of witnesses. He wrote his first instruction himself, to the king's dictation and upon Miron's advice. It included the important offer to make Guise lieutenant-general, and Villeroy made sure that it was signed by the king.[1] When he reached Paris, Villeroy avoided displaying his goods in the shop window. He confided his instruction to Catherine alone, and allowed it to be thought that he had none, but rather came to obtain a clearer idea of what the Guises were really claiming. As he expected, they wanted many things which he did not believe the king would grant. In this negotiation Villeroy was up against circumstances entirely beyond his control. Peace might have followed from his first mission to Paris, if the negotiation had not been disrupted by the Spanish ambassador, whose reason for doing this was to keep everything in France in a state of dangerous uncertainty, while awaiting definite news of the Spanish Armada.[2] Guise, in his bid for the throne of France, was entirely guided by Mendoza and entirely dependent on Spanish gold. In fact there were disruptive forces at work on both sides, as Villeroy wrote to Nevers on 13 June: 'Il y a des gens de part et dautre qui nourissent les troubles et en veullent vivre.'[3]

The following day, 14 June, Villeroy left Paris to report to the king at Rouen.[4] He gave a full account before the council of everything that he had negotiated in Catherine's presence in Paris. Brulart wrote the king's comments and replies in the

[1] Petitot, xliv, *Mémoires d'Estat de Villeroy*, 56.
[2] B.N., Mss. it. 1737, f. 125, 17 June 1588.
[3] B.N., Mss. fr. 3976, f. 147, 13 June 1588, Villeroy to Nevers.
[4] *Id.*

margin against each item, and this served as Villeroy's second instruction. The only point which he discussed with the king in private was the question of the authority which Guise demanded over the army, and the relative authority contained in the commissions of a constable and a lieutenant-general. But Villeroy had not got his registers with him, which listed in detail the functions and powers of these officers. He was authorized to offer the duke the authority over the army of a *grand maitre*, and to work out the details later.[1]

On Catherine's advice, Villeroy continued to keep secret the king's offer to allow Guise some authority over the army. On the eve of his second departure for Rouen, the Florentine agent Cavriana reported that Guise had been advised by someone at the court not to cede an inch in his demands, because the king was afraid and wanted peace at all costs. He also reported Guise to have been annoyed with Villeroy, who proceeded with such circumspection, and to have said to him: 'Mortdieu, je scay bien ce que vous avez eu en charge d'accorder; parquoy, si vous ne le faites, vous vous repentirez.'[2] If Villeroy's instructions had been betrayed to Guise—and this is clearly the inference— then the very gravest suspicion must fall upon Miron. Villeroy was still profoundly depressed and discouraged at this time, for he knew that this treaty, when concluded, would solve nothing. 'You see the wretched state to which the king is reduced', he wrote to Nevers, adding that it afflicted and tormented him so much that sometimes he felt in despair and wanted rather to die than to live.[3]

On 2 July Villeroy arrived in Rouen, where he was again careful to make his report before the entire council, and Brulart, as before, wrote the answers in the margin against each item.[4] Villeroy took with him the necessary registers and showed the king a commission of lieutenant-general and one of constable. The commission which was drafted for Guise was partially drawn from them both. The king corrected it three times and signed the final version. But it was not handed to Guise until

[1] Petitot, xliv, *Mémoires d'Estat de Villeroy*, 69.
[2] Desjardins, *Negs. Tosc.*, iv, 793, June 1588.
[3] B.N., Mss. fr. 3976, f. 167, 22 June 1588, Villeroy to Nevers.
[4] Petitot, xliv, *Mémoires d'Estat de Villeroy*, 70.

later, at Chartres. Villeroy afterwards said that the king did this with regret, and determined to disgrace those who had advised it.[1]

Villeroy went back to Paris a third time—we do not know which day—and an agreement was reached on 12th and signed on 15 July. The following day Villeroy took the articles to the king, who was still at Rouen.[2]

At the end of July the two secretaries accompanied the king back to Chartres, where they were joined by Catherine, Pinart and Guise himself. The atmosphere there was one of the most extreme tension, and both the king and Guise received warnings of personal danger.[3] Villeroy continued to suffer from his profound depression: 'If we are lulled by this reconciliation, you may be certain that it will do us more harm than good', he wrote to Maisse. He had done his utmost in making the agreement, and had served the king faithfully but, he said, 'si mes raisons et mes arguments eussent este fortifies de quelque prosperite et bons effets en nos affaires de la guerre peut estre quils eussent este mieulx recus'.[4]

Just as he had feared and foreseen, Villeroy was further troubled at this time by another disquieting manifestation of Épernon's hostility, from which the king had so far done nothing to protect him. Épernon had been disgraced and ordered to remain in his *gouvernement*. He went to Angoulême and the king, who was afraid of him, wanted to have him arrested. For whatever reason, the attempt on the part of the mayor of the town to arrest the duke, turned into an assault upon his person. The mayor was killed, but the duke survived to visit his anger upon Villeroy, whom he accused of having planned to murder him.[5] The chief significance of this event lies outside the period of this study, but it served to increase Villeroy's depression and discouragement in the summer of 1588, as well as his fears for his safety and that of his family. The whole story is no longer available to us, but Villeroy's fears were certainly not imaginary.

[1] Petitot, xliv, *Mémoires d'Estat de Villeroy*, 74.
[2] B.N., Mss. it. 1737, f. 171, 18 July 1588; Mss. fr. 3976, f. 187, 18 July 1588, *articles de l'Union*.
[3] B.N., Mss. it. 1737, ff. 188-9, 29 July 1588.
[4] B.N., Mss. fr. 16093, f. 226, 29 July 1588, Villeroy to Maisse.
[5] On this incident, see Léo Mouton, ch. ix.

Twice in the month of August, Stafford wrote to Walsingham that Épernon had sworn Villeroy's death, 'whatsoever it cost him and in what kind so ever he can have it'.[1] Besides, the mere fact that Épernon was his enemy, would tend to link his name with that of Guise in the mind of anyone inclined to suspect his politics. No one, in fact, was immune from suspicion at that time when the personal confidence, which is the basis of all co-operation in public affairs, had been destroyed.[2]

For some time past Villeroy had wanted to be at least partially relieved from the burdens of his office. His health had never fully recovered from his long illness in 1584-5, and he was too overworked to be able to attend to everything properly. His desire to retire had greatly increased since the episode in which the king had permitted Épernon to level outrageous accusations against him, thereby implying either that he believed them to be true, or else that he cared very little for his minister's honour and reputation, not to mention his safety. Villeroy says that he spoke to his friends and relations of this desire to retire, but that they tried to dissuade him from it. Catherine was the first to approach the king on his behalf, at Mantes, where she met him in July after the conclusion of the treaty with Guise. The king refused, but subsequently consented at Chartres in August. By the same evening, however, he had changed his mind, and said that he needed Villeroy for the meeting of the States to be held at Blois in September.

Since he could not retire, Villeroy asked to be allowed to delegate a large part of his work to Claude de Laubespine, who already held the *survivance* of his office. To this the king agreed, and on 23 August Villeroy went home on holiday, prepared to return in time for the States. 'And I must say', he wrote in his memoir, 'that I had never quit the king and the court with greater assurance of favour.'[3] To Matignon he wrote on this occasion: 'I am leaving for my house to see if I can find more peace there than here. If so, I assure you that I shall have as little as possible to do with public affairs.'[4]

[1] *C.S.P.F.*, July–December 1588, p. 145, 20 August 1588, p. 154, 23 August 1588, Stafford to Walsingham.

[2] For Villeroy's account of this affair, see Petitot, xliv, *Mémoires d'Estat de Villeroy* 76–81.   [3] *Ibid.*, 85–92.

[4] *Letters to Matignon*, 222, 21 August 1588.

From his house at Villeroy, he wrote to assure Bellièvre that it was not on account of Épernon that he had left the court, because he had obtained permission to go on holiday some time before. 'If M. d'Épernon was unable to banish me when he was all-powerful and puffed up with favour at the king's side, I would be wrong and greatly lacking in devotion to the service of my master if, being where he is [Angoulême], I departed on his account. When M. d'Épernon satisfies the king, I will be his good servitor. This is the nature and extent of my malevolence and wickedness.'[1] Villeroy's departure from court at that particular moment was clearly subject to misintepretation and it aroused considerable interest and speculation among the foreign ambassadors. They did not know the explanation, but they attached importance to the event. Some thought that the king had entered into 'some jealousy' of Villeroy, and others that he was destined for a higher office. 'Some', wrote Stafford to Walsingham, 'think he knoweth so much of the King's mind that he knoweth some particular thing to make him retire himself.'[2] Whatever the truth may be, Villeroy, contrary to his original intention, never returned during the reign of Henry III.

For Pinart and Brulart we have nothing but a few routine letters during this sinister period. They both accompanied the king when he left Chartres on 29 August 1588 and went to Blois to prepare for the States General. On 7 September, Brulart wrote to Nevers and said that he was going home on holiday.[3] Evidently no suspicion of what was about to befall him and his colleagues had ever crossed his mind. The next day, 8 September, the three secretaries, Bellièvre, the chancellor Cheverny, and Combault, master of the king's household, were summarily dismissed by the king, without warning, explanation or compensation.

Pinart, Brulart and Bellièvre were all at court when they each received a note in the king's own hand informing them of their disgrace. Villeroy's was brought to his house by Benoise, one of the king's personal secretaries. He was deeply mortified at receiving his dismissal in this way, at the hands of an inferior,

---

[1] B.N., Mss. fr. 15909, f. 132, 27 August 1588, Villeroy to Bellièvre.
[2] C.S.P.F., July–December 1588, p. 120, 9 August 1588, Stafford to Walsingham.
[3] B.N., Mss. fr. 3407, f. 9, 7 September 1588, Brulart to Nevers.

together with a request to return such state papers as he might have in his possession. Besides, it was particularly galling to be dismissed when he had repeatedly been refused permission to retire. He replied respectfully, but adding the verbal message, 'que s'il eust pleu à Sa Majesté me laisser sortir de la cour par la porte à laquelle j'avois tant heurté devant que d'en partir, sans me faire sauter par les fenestres, qu'elle eust mis mon esprit en grand repos'.[1]

It chanced that Villeroy's son was at court about the time of the dismissals. He was graciously received by the king who told him that he was 'the son of a father who had served him so well that he had only to emulate his example and follow the path which he had indicated to acquire honour in his profession and the king's favour and protection in all things'.[2] Villeroy was greatly comforted when he heard this from his son. He also received from Catherine an assurance of the king's goodwill, and his associate, de Laubespine, told him that he and Bellièvre still stood high in credit at the court.[3]

In his misfortune, Villeroy derived much comfort and consolation from his old friend Bellièvre. 'Your letters and your example', Villeroy wrote to him on 28 September, 'serve to guide and console us in our misfortune. I have found healing in them for much of the distress which afflicts me. As you so justly say, why should we be vexed by our absence from the court, save that we cannot serve the king . . . now when his need is greatest. . . . Monsieur, I certainly believe that God has done much for us in withdrawing us from the throng at this time when those who betray the king are more esteemed than those who crucify themselves in his service. . . . Let us therefore praise God . . . and rejoice in our release in tranquillity of mind . . . that we may avoid the fury of our mutual enemies who reproach us and blame our conduct in vain. . . . Monsieur, we must wish that the officials of the king and the kingdom may prosper, that God may be glorified . . . that justice may reign and this poor people be succoured. If those whom the king has retained in his service can procure him this happiness, I will gladly honour them all my

[1] Petitot, xliv, *Mémoires d'Estat de Villeroy*, 92–3.
[2] *Ibid.*, 93–4.
[3] B.N., Mss. fr. 15909, f. 188, 5 October 1588, Villeroy to Bellièvre.

life. This, Monsieur, is my resolution derived from your own, and from the fine precepts of our late good master and friend, M. de Morvillier.'[1]

What distressed Villeroy most of all was the fear that his actions might be judged by their results: 'plustot par le succez de leurs fortunes que par la verité et justice d'icelles'.[2] Bellièvre, for his part, was upset because his dismissal had coincided with that of a number of thieving finance officers. On the one hand, they were glad to have escaped from the strain and stress of the court, where they were liable to make enemies; on the other they had lost the power to serve the king as they thought he should be served. Villeroy, for his part, had to go away into the country, in order to reconcile his feelings with his better judgement. He was particularly upset by the effect of his dismissal on other people. 'Il fault que je vous confesse comme a mon meilleur ami,' he wrote to Bellièvre, 'que rien ne me agitte et donne tant de peine en ma fortune que de veoir mes parens et amys sen afliger plus que moy . . . pour . . . trouver dautres remedes que ceulx que nous debvons recouvrer en la boutiqcue de nostre ame si elle est bien rangee et composee.'[3] These troubles, he wrote a week later, on 5 October, had brought a quartan fever on his father, and so distracted his little family that this distressed and tormented him more than anything else.[4]

We know rather less about the reactions of Pinart and Brulart. Cavriana reported that Pinart sighed over his misfortune and said that if he had served God as well as he had served the king, he would be the most devout man in the world.[5] To Nevers he wrote with dignity: 'Thanks be to God, I consider myself most fortunate, since their majesties are pleased to continue their good will towards me . . . to be relieved at this calamitous time of so heavy a burden . . . and to have a little peace in which to serve God, to whom I pray every day that he may grant the king all good prosperity and the success that he himself desires in his affairs, with long life and presently a fine son.'[6]

---

[1] B.N., Mss. fr. 15909, f. 178, 28 September 1588, Villeroy to Bellièvre.
[2] Petitot, xliv, Mémoires d'Estat de Villeroy, 94.
[3] B.N., Mss. fr. 15909, f. 178, 28 September 1588, Villeroy to Bellièvre.
[4] Ibid., f. 188, 5 October 1588, Villeroy to Bellièvre.
[5] Desjardins, Negs. Tosc., iv, 822, 13 September 1588.
[6] B.N., Mss. fr. 3407, f. 45, 22 November 1588, Pinart to Nevers.

We cannot be sure that Brulart accepted his disgrace with equal dignity. In a letter to Bellièvre of 18 September, he confined himself to regretting that the king had blackened their reputations as well as dismissing them. He said he had heard from the court that he was accused of belonging to the league; also that the king had claimed to feel as though he had been set at liberty, for his ministers had held him in subjection.[1] He did not, like Pinart, reflect that henceforth he would have more time in which to serve God or, like both Pinart and Villeroy, that he had been relieved of a crushing burden. Neither did he, like his colleagues, expressly wish the king success and prosperity in his affairs.

This sensational dismissal of the secretaries aroused universal astonishment and disapproval. 'The whole of France', wrote Cheverny in his memoir, 'was greatly astounded by this very sudden alteration in the king's will, without any apparent cause, and directed against persons of our station, towards whom, until then, he had always displayed so much friendship and trust.'[2] The nuncio, Morosini, said that the king's decision had thrown the whole court into a state of suspicion and uncertainty. Again, on another occasion, he said that the whole court marvelled exceedingly, especially in the case of Villeroy, because of his great favour, his authority over the king, his gentle ways and his dexterity in handling the king's affairs.[3] Cavriana's reactions were identical: he said that this very sudden change had caused everyone to marvel greatly.[4]

Bellièvre received a number of letters of condolence, all of them expressing extreme astonishment.[5] One of these, from his friend Épinac, is particularly interesting, and typical of the climate of opinion at that moment. Épinac said that he heard the news of the dismissals as he was going to wait upon the king. He could hardly believe his ears, and could not refrain from speaking his mind to the queen-mother. He said that as the king had removed all the oldest members of his council, his affairs would certainly suffer. There was no one left in office who had

[1] B.N., Mss. fr. 15909, f. 152, 18 September 1588, Brulart to Bellièvre.
[2] Petitot, xxxvi, *Mémoires de Cheverny*, 116.
[3] De L'Epinois, 212, n. 1, quoted from the Vatican archives.
[4] Desjardins, *Negs. Tosc.*, iv, 822, 823, 13 September 1588.
[5] B.N., Mss. fr. 15909, ff. 142, 144, 146, 166, 172.

any comprehensive grasp of them, and the king and Catherine could not hope to attend to everything themselves. Therefore things were bound to fall into arrears, or be less carefully done. The queen replied that she had been no less astounded than Épinac. 'In short, sir,' he concluded, 'I foresee that these dismissals will do more harm to the public service than to the individuals concerned, and am well aware that those who are furthest from the court will not be the most unhappy. . . .'[1]

Morosini, who had an audience with the king on the day of the dismissals, expressed the same thoughts. He said that in effect his majesty had deprived himself of all the persons who had a grasp of his affairs, to introduce new men into the government. 'Were they the best in the world, they would still have to learn the ways of good service and would need time in which to reach that degree of perfection which their predecessors, by their good qualities. . . and long experience, had already achieved.'[2]

Catherine, said the Venetian ambassador, was beside herself.[3] Neither she, Guise, nor anyone else had been consulted about this decision. Everyone was asking themselves and each other the same question: what was the significance of the dismissals? 'I see many important people here . . .' wrote Jacques Faye to Bellièvre, on 18 September, 'but I do not know of anyone who is not astounded about M. de Villeroy and yourself, or who can offer a single explanation.'[4] Cavriana said that no one knew, but many people believed that it was because the ministers had divulged information; some said that they had been of the league, and others that it was because the king wanted to be his own councillor and secretary.[5] Morosini, like Cheverny, suggested that the king wanted to be free of his ministers before he held the States, because it was believed that they would be attacked for the imposition of heavy taxes, and also that perhaps the king wanted to be rid of ministers who were too closely linked with Catherine, for she had appointed all three of the secretaries. But they were only improvising.[6] The Venetian

[1] B.N., Mss. fr. 15909, f. 140, 8 September 1588, Épinac to Bellièvre.
[2] De L'Epinois, 213, quoted from the Vatican archives.
[3] B.N., Mss. it. 1737, f. 238, 23 September 1588.
[4] B.N., Mss. fr. 15909, f. 154, 18 September 1588, Faye to Bellièvre.
[5] Desjardins, Negs. Tosc., iv, 822, 13 September 1588.
[6] Petitot, xxxvi, Mémoires de Cheverny, 116–17; de L'Epinois, 213.

ambassador, normally well informed, gave no other reason than that Guise had been receiving state secrets.[1]

Villeroy himself examined a number of reasons that were in the air, but without conviction: that he had had too much authority; that the secretaries had opened the despatches; that he was accused of not having obtained the best possible terms for the king during the recent negotiation; that the secretaries were too closely linked with Catherine from whom the king was supposedly estranged, and so on. Everyone gave some different explanation, 'chacun diversement selon son sens et sa passion', said Cheverny, but 'la raison certaine' was never found.[2]

Historians have been no less mystified than contemporaries, and not one of them has offered a plausible explanation. De Luçay in his book on the secretaries and Nouaillac in his book on Villeroy, both say that Henry dismissed his ministers because he was contemplating violence against the duc de Guise. This is neither relevant nor an explanation, for the king did not require permission or approval for his actions. De Luçay also says that the king may have become appalled by the great authority of the secretaries, and Nouaillac that Villeroy's political conduct had become suspect. But this does not explain the simultaneous dismissal of the other ministers. De Croze says that it was to escape from what he calls 'l'inquiète surveillance de sa mère', and to put an end to the treachery of the council.[3] The former reason is not very convincing since Catherine was showing marked signs of old age and for some time past had done extremely little, and the latter would rather explain an alteration in the composition of the council than the dismissal of those members whom the king had most cause to trust.

There is no explanation of this event susceptible to documentary proof but an examination of the various elements of the situation against the background of Henry's reign sheds light upon it. Mendoza came near to what is almost certainly the truth when he wrote to Philip II: 'The actions of this prince all contradict each other to such an extent that these dismissals

---

[1] B.N., Mss. it. 1737, f. 237, 23 September 1588.
[2] Petitot, xxxvi, *Mémoires de Cheverny*, 116–18.
[3] De Luçay, 23–4; de Croze, ii, 108–9; Baguenault de Puchesse, in his introduction to the ninth volume of Catherine's letters, gives no explanation at all.

. . . do not appear to be the result of a plan drawn up in advance.'[1] No one was consulted because Henry acted on impulse; and one would be as mistaken in assuming that he was clear in his own mind why he deprived himself of the only dependable and expert help he had, as one would be in expecting to find a complete and rational explanation of what was a profoundly irrational thing to do. But that Henry should have done this at such a moment was in keeping with what we know of his character. He was wandering on the borders of insanity, and for three years he had been ever more closely hounded by the resolute, efficient duc de Guise until, by September 1588, he was king only in name. Demented and afraid, he was more than ever before possessed by that undiscriminating suspicion which, it has been seen, was his characteristic reaction to adversity. While he did not really believe that his ministers could not be trusted, part of him still feared this might be so. Everyone was suspect, and had not all his secrets been betrayed? When this mood possessed him, Henry always became secretive and autocratic and tried, as far as possible, to do everything himself, swinging from extreme indolence to extreme application, for immoderation characterized almost everything he did. This tortured state of mind found expression in a dramatic demonstration of authority which served, for a moment, to bolster his exhausted morale and perhaps, in hurting those to whom he owed the most, it was also an expression of his own suffering.

Apart from the reasons implicit in his character, there were other, contributory reasons for the king's action. Besides dismissing the secretaries, he replaced their entire staff, as well as his council, and appointed two new secretaries who barely had the powers of a clerk. By making a clean sweep, the king certainly hoped to be rid of the traitor who kept betraying him to his enemies. He also thereby made it theoretically possible to do everything himself. Cheverny, in a letter to Bellièvre, said how hard the king was working at that time.[2] It was also said, and it was Villeroy's opinion, that the king harboured a resentment against those who had advised him to give Guise a com-

---

[1] Baguenault de Puchesse, *La Politique de Philippe II*, 41; de Croze, ii, app. liii, 373, 24 October 1588, Mendoza to Philip II.
[2] B.N., Mss. fr. 15909, f. 160, 25 September 1588, Cheverny to Bellièvre.

mission of lieutenant-general at Chartres, although he himself had previously approved and signed it.

The manner in which the dismissals were made has aroused no comment among historians, but it was nevertheless extremely curious and does much to explain what were probably the king's real intentions. All three secretaries are alleged to have received an identical message, and the Florentine agent Cavriana is alone in saying anything about it. It was the dismissal of Villeroy which attracted most attention and so Cavriana's report referred to him. If it is correct—and there is no reason to doubt this—the king's letter of dismissal was a very strange document indeed. This is how it began: 'Villeroy, I remain very well contented with your service; do not fail however to go away to your house where you will stay until I send for you; do not seek the reason for this my letter, but obey me.'[1] In his memoir Villeroy tells us that the king also promised, 'de me faire plaisir en autre chose'.[2]

What then were the secretaries meant to understand by such a message? The first effect was undoubtedly one of shock, for clearly no one had anticipated such a move. To judge from the possible explanations which he considered, Villeroy for one was entirely mystified. He never seems to have doubted the rectitude of Henry's motives, for it was six years later when he wrote to Du Vair: 'Ce prince etait trop bon et equitable pour a mon avis traiter ainsi qu'il feist sans croire en avoir occasion apres l'avoir servy si longuement et confidemment.'[3] He still sounded mystified; but we must not assume that Villeroy never suspected the truth because he never said what he thought it was. He knew the king as well as, if not better than anyone else, and he was far too accomplished a diplomat to suppose that a document necessarily said what it meant, or meant what it said. When, shortly after his dismissal, Villeroy received a heart-warming message from his son, followed by other assurances from the court—and we know that Pinart also received similar assurances—he cannot

[1] 'Villeroy, io resto molto ben contento del vostro servizio; non lasciate però di andarvene a casa vostra, dove voi starete sino che vi mandi a dimandare; non cercate la cagione di questo mio scrivere, ma ubbiditemi.' Desjardins, *Negs. Tosc.*, iv, 822, 13 September 1588.

[2] Petitot, xliv, *Mémoires d'Estat de Villeroy*, 92.

[3] B.N. Mss. n.a.f. 7260, f. 7, 1 August 1594, letter to Du Vair.

have failed to consider the king's letter carefully, or to search between the lines.

If Cavriana's extract is correctly rendered, it is clear that the letter was mysterious and ambiguous; this could hardly have been an accident. In the first place, after opening with the friendly, familiar 'Villeroy', the king began his letter of dismissal with a categorical statement of complete satisfaction. What interpretation should be placed on '. . . where you will stay until I send for you', and how could the king expect his ministers not to seek the reason for this apparent outrage? This was not the letter of a king who believed his ministers to be guilty of treason, or who bore them any malice. It was friendly in tone, and there was nothing final or conclusive about it. With its implicit promise of a future explanation, it sounded more like a temporary expedient. Why, then, did the king dismiss his ministers? Why did he firmly refuse to see any of them personally although Pinart, Brulart, Bellièvre and Cheverny were all at court? Why did he refuse to hear them, or to grant them any compensation for their loss, which was considerable, although he was known to be generous to the point of folly?

This mysterious incident was evidently linked with the king's fear of the States General, which he had been forced to summon. In so far as he may be supposed to have thought clearly about the dismissals at all, he was probably guided by this fear. It was widely believed that when the States assembled, the ministers would be fiercely attacked. To dismiss them beforehand would therefore serve the curious, multiple purpose of making them scapegoats for his own faults and failures—which he well knew to be great—of saving them from the hopeless task of trying to defend him, and also of protecting them from personal attack; Henry III was by no means lacking in penetration, neither was ingratitude one of his faults. This opinion is borne out by what took place when the States assembled. Referring to the king's harangue to the deputies, Villeroy wrote to Bellièvre: 'Ce n'a este sans draper sur les absens quil a charge de negligence et dautres defaults.'[1] It was also the opinion expressed by Stafford

---

[1] B.N., Mss. fr. 15909, f. 205, 26 October 1588, Villeroy to Bellièvre, quoted by Nouaillac, 149, n. 5, who gives 'frapper' for 'draper'; Petitot, xxxvi, *Mémoires de Cheverny*, 117.

in reporting the dismissals to Walsingham. 'This', he said, 'is a thing that I have heard to be in the King's mind . . . and which carrieth likelihood.'[1]

The only credible explanation of the dismissal of the ministers, which accounts for every known aspect of the situation, is that the king's original intention was first to appear to have disgraced them, and then to recall them after the States had been dissolved. Had he not said that they must stay at home *until he sent for them*? Everything was so disposed that, provided they were willing, it would have been easy to recall them.

If this were indeed what Henry intended, events did not conform to his plan. Guise had effectively packed the States and everything went against the king. He never had a chance to recall the secretaries because, in the meanwhile, he reached the limit of endurance and the point of breakdown. He may possibly have sunk into the abyss of insanity; certainly he gave up in despair, murdered the duc de Guise, and precipitated a further revolution. He was finally defeated and no longer capable of making a constructive effort.

[1] *C.S.P.F.*, July–December 1588, p. 178, 1 September 1588, Stafford to Walsingham.

CONCLUSION

THE dismissal of the secretaries in 1588 was a minor revolution which completed a chapter in their history. The long period from the tenth century, or before, up till 1547, produced the *secrétaires des finances*, the office on to which that of *secrétaire d'État* was grafted. We do not know whose idea this was, how it came to be developed or who drafted the letters patent of 1 April 1546/7, though it is probable that the constable Montmorency was responsible for them. Neither do we know what their author hoped to achieve, for at that date no one could have anticipated the growth of an institution whose members might eclipse the landed classes and the great officers of state. The development of the office, therefore, cannot be attributed to a recognition of its potentialities.

Whatever its original purpose may have been, the founding of this institution was a stroke of administrative genius. Its extreme simplicity afforded a high degree of flexibility which enabled it to grow and develop as need arose. Thus in the councils and the government—if not in the provinces or the field— the secretaries were at least partially able to fill the gap created by the defection of the old nobility. Under Henry II, they were subordinate but not insignificant officials. Catherine, as regent and queen-mother, chose them and trusted them, and Henry III largely abandoned the government into their hands. This, how- ever, did not mean that the institution which they represented was necessarily bound to evolve from strength to strength. In fact it did survive until the Revolution, but in the 1580s the importance of the secretaries related more to the individuals, Villeroy, Pinart and Brulart, than to the office which they held. Their friends Bellièvre and Cheverny were also important and, although not secretaries, they shared the same disgrace.

The dismissal of the secretaries broke their tradition, which was personal, and interrupted that deliberate transmission of

x

the coveted office from one carefully chosen individual to another, which largely explained the consistently high standard of their services. These services could no longer be dispensed with altogether, if only because of the need for a secretary's signature, but, because they had never been defined or clearly specified, the functions of the secretaries could, to a large extent, be superseded. This is what Henry III tried to do.

On 18 September 1588, he appointed two secretaries, Martin Ruzé, seigneur de Beaulieu, who had been in his service since before his accession, and had accompanied him to Poland, and Louis Revol, formerly the French agent in Piedmont. Two others cautiously declined the offer.[1] Thus Ruzé and Revol divided everything between them, Ruzé taking all the provinces of France and all military matters (*la guerre*), and Revol foreign affairs.[2] On 1 January 1589, the number of secretaries was restored to four; Ruzé's *département* then became the households of the king and queen, war, and Paris with the Ile-de-France. Revol's remained unchanged, thirteen foreign countries being listed under his name. The two new secretaries, Louis Potier, seigneur de Gevre, and Pierre Forget, seigneur de Fresne, divided the provinces of France between them, except for Paris and the Ile-de-France.[3] This *département* was included in a lengthy ordinance which regulated the position and functions and the public and private conduct of the secretaries in considerable detail, a thing which had never been done before. The ordinance reflected both the king's extreme fear of delegating work, and his inability to govern without secretaries. He therefore compromised by an attempt to control them rigidly. He decreed that they were all to be good catholics over the age of thirty-five, and obliged them to swear a revised and unequivocal oath, not, as formerly, before the chancellor, but to himself.[4] They were no longer allowed to open or answer the despatches; indeed they were not even allowed to receive them. Neither was anyone else, and the king reserved these functions to himself. As a

[1] B.N., Mss. fr. 16216, f. 487, September 1588. This is an original draft of a new *département* intended for four secretaries.
[2] B.N., Mss. fr. 21432, f. 125v; Mss. n.a.f. 7226, f. 187. There are three different versions of this *département* but this appears to be the correct one.
[3] B.N., Mss. fr. 18243, f. 55, 1 January 1589.
[4] *Ibid.*, f. 68, the revised oath.

phrase of the text made clear, the explanation of this extreme measure lay in the king's desire to control his own affairs: 'Sa Majeste veut plus que jamais embrasser l'intelligence et conduitte de ses affaires. . . .' We know that he began to work hard about the time of the dismissals but, in the confusion which followed the death of the duc de Guise, it seems unlikely that he succeeded in enforcing his ordinance to any significant extent. More probably the new secretaries carried on as best they might, according to custom and the circumstances.

Pinart and Brulart never recovered their former offices, possibly only because there was no vacancy before they died. After suffering various losses and vicissitudes during the civil wars which followed the death of the duc de Guise, they lived to serve Henry IV as councillors only, until 1605 and 1608 respectively. Villeroy, however, was immediately reinstated by Henry IV, upon the death of Revol in 1594. Principally in the conduct of foreign affairs, he continued to render outstanding services— indeed he became far more important than ever before—and remained in office until his death in 1617. Without making a further detailed study, it is impossible to pronounce upon the importance or insignificance of the role of the other secretaries early in the seventeenth century, except that Pierre Forget undoubtedly achieved a certain distinction, and is said to have been responsible for the famous edict of Nantes.[1]

There is much more that we shall never know about the twelve secretaries of this study, some of whom may have been less virtuous than now appears. They were human and presumably had faults and failings. But no well-founded criticism has survived against them, and we cannot but admire their fortitude in the face of calamity, their rejection of the vice, corruption and self-interest surrounding them, and their refusal to take sides or to despair. Indeed—without underestimating the importance of their political and administrative work—when the state failed to maintain order and justice, and the church to provide inspiration and moral leadership, the most valuable contribution that the secretaries made was in the moral, rather than in the political sphere. The best of them—the two de

[1] Du-Toc, 189.

Laubespines, du Thier, Bourdin, Alluye, Pinart and Villeroy—share, with several of their relations and friends, the notable distinction of having upheld in public life those moral qualities without which they themselves believed that France would never be restored to her ancient splendour and prosperity.

APPENDICES

I. The Secretaries

1547	Guillaume Bochetel	Cosme Clausse
	d. 1558	d. 1558
1558	Jacques Bourdin	Florimond Robertet
	d. 6 July 1567	seigneur de Fresne
		d. Oct. 1567
1560		
1567	Claude de Laubespine II	Simon Fizes
	d. Sept. 1570	baron de Sauve
		d. 27 Nov. 1579
		no successor
1569		
1570	Claude Pinart	
	dismissed 8 Sept. 1588	
	d. 14 Sept. 1605	

Family interconnexions

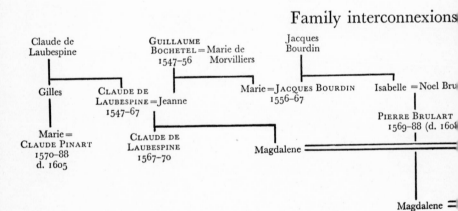

f State 1547–88

Jean du Thier   Claude de Laubespine I
d. 17 March 1560   d. 11 Nov. 1567

Florimond Robertet
seigneur d'Alluye
d. 6 June 1569

Nicolas de Neufville
seigneur de Villeroy
dismissed 8 Sept. 1588
reinstated 1594
d. 12 Nov. 1617

Pierre Brulart
dismissed 8 Sept. 1588
d. 12 Apr. 1608

f the Secretaries

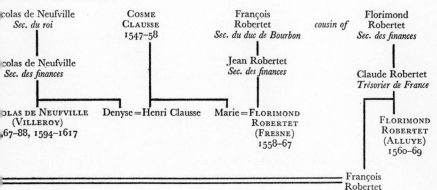

Nicolas de Neufville	COSME CLAUSSE	François Robertet		Florimond Robertet
Sec. du roi	1547–58	*Sec. du duc de Bourbon*	*cousin of*	*Sec. des finances*
Nicolas de Neufville		Jean Robertet		
Sec. des finances		*Sec. des finances*		Claude Robertet
				Trésorier de France
NICOLAS DE NEUFVILLE (VILLEROY) 1567–88, 1594–1617	Denyse = Henri Clausse	Marie = FLORIMOND ROBERTET (FRESNE) 1558–67		FLORIMOND ROBERTET (ALLUYE) 1560–69

François
Robertet

II

Chronological List of Events

1547	Mar.	Death of Francis I.
1552		Metz campaign.
1556	Feb.	Truce of Vaucelles.
1557	Aug.	Battle of Saint-Quentin.
1558	Jan.	Siege of Calais.
1559	Apr.	Treaty of Cateau-Cambrésis.
	June	Death of Henry II.
1560	Mar.	Tumult of Amboise.
	Oct.	Arrest of Condé.
	Dec.	Death of Francis II.
1561	Jan.	States General of Orléans.
	Mar.	Formation of the *triumvirat*.
	Aug.	States General of Pontoise.
	Sept.	Colloque of Poissy.
1562	Jan.	Edict of January, granting limited toleration.
	Mar.	Massacre of Vassy.
	Apr.	Condé takes Orléans.
		Outbreak of civil war.
	Oct.	Siege of Rouen, death of Navarre.
	Dec.	Battle of Dreux, death of Saint-André.
1563	Feb.	Assassination of the duc de Guise.
	Mar.	Peace of Amboise.
	July	Recapture of Le Havre from the English.
1564	Apr.	Treaty of Troyes with England.
1564–6		Journey of Catherine de Medici and the king round France.
1565	June	Meeting at Bayonne between Catherine, the king and the Queen of Spain.
1566		Trouble in the Netherlands.
1567	Sept.	*Entreprise de Meaux*, outbreak of the second civil war.
	Nov.	Battle of Saint-Denis, death of Montmorency.

1568   Mar.   Treaty of Longjumeau.

        Aug.   Flight of Condé and Coligny from Burgundy to La
                   Rochelle.
                Outbreak of the third civil war.

1569   Mar.   Battle of Jarnac, death of Condé.
        Oct.   Battle of Montcontour.

1570   Aug.   Peace of Saint-Germain.

1572   Aug.   Marriage of Navarre and Marguerite de Valois.
                Massacre of Saint Bartholomew.
                Outbreak of the fourth civil war.

1573   Jan.–
        June   Siege of La Rochelle.
        May   Election of Anjou to the throne of Poland.
        June   Peace of La Rochelle.

1574   Fifth civil war.
        May   Death of Charles IX.
        Sept.   Return of Henry III from Poland.
        Dec.   Death of the cardinal of Lorraine.

1575   Sept.   Escape from court and revolt of Alençon.

1576   Feb.   Escape from court of Navarre.
        May   Peace of Monsieur.
        June   Beginning of the catholic league of Picardy.
        Nov.   States General of Blois.

1577   Mar.   Outbreak of the sixth civil war.
        Sept.   Peace of Bergerac.

1578   Feb.   Second flight of Alençon from court.

1578–80   Catherine's voyage of pacification.

1580   Outbreak of the seventh civil war.
        Nov.   Peace of Fleix.

1582–4   Anarchy in Languedoc and other parts of southern
                   France.

1583   Anjou in the Netherlands.

1584   June   Death of Anjou.
        Dec.   Formation of the catholic league of Paris.

1585   Jan.   Treaty of Joinville between the Guises and Spain.
        Mar.   The Guise revolt and Catherine's negotiation at
                   Épernay.
        July   Peace of Nemours.

1586–	July–	Catherine's negotiation with Navarre in the south-
1587	Mar.	west.
		Outbreak of the eighth civil war.
	Oct.	Battle of Coutras.
1588	May	Guise revolt and the day of barricades in Paris; flight of the king to Chartres.
	July	Articles of Union, Henry capitulates to the league.
	Sept.	Dismissal of the secretaries.
		States General of Blois.
	Dec.	Murder of the duc de Guise.
1589	Jan.	Death of Catherine.

Biographical Notes

D'ANDELOT, François de Coligny, seigneur, 1521–69; brother of Gaspard de Coligny and of Odet, cardinal of Châtillon; colonel-général de l'infanterie 1555.

ANNEBAUT, Claude d', baron de Retz, seigneur de Saint-Pierre; marshal of France 1538; lieutenant-general in Turin and Piedmont 1541; admiral of France 1543; ambassador to Venice; chief minister to Francis I; d. 1552.

BELLIÈVRE, Pomponne de, 1529–1607; b. Lyons; son of Claude de Bellièvre; several times ambassador to Switzerland and went on many extraordinary embassies; surintendant des finances 1575, disgraced 1588; chancellor of France 1599–1604; trusted councillor of Catherine de Medici and life-long friend of Villeroy.

BIRAGUE, René de, c. 1509–83; conseiller privé to Francis I; lieutenant-general in Piedmont; gouverneur of Lyonnais, Forez and Beaujolais; chancellor of France 1573, discharged 1578 and made a cardinal.

BIRON, Armand de Gontaut, baron de, c. 1524–92; chevalier des Ordres du roi; lieutenant-general in Guienne; marshal of France 1577.

BOUILLON, Henri de la Tour d'Auvergne, duc de, vicomte de Turenne, 1556–1623; marshal of France 1592; memoirist.

BOURDILLON, Imbert de la Platière, seigneur de; gouverneur and lieutenant-general in Piedmont; marshal of France 1562; d. 1567.

BRISSAC, Charles de Cossé, comte de, 1507–63; chevalier des Ordres du roi; lieutenant-general of the army in Piedmont; marshal of France 1550; gouverneur of Picardy and the Ile-de-France 1559.

BRISSAC, René de Cossé, seigneur de; father of the more famous marshal Brissac.

CASIMIR, duke Jean, prince of Bavaria; son of duke Frederick III; m. Elizabeth of Saxony.

CAVRIANA, Filippe; a Mantuan doctor, resident in France; served the duc de Nevers and later Catherine de Medici. His letters are an important source for the later years of the reign of Henry III. Between 1580 and 1589 there was no accredited Florentine ambassador in France, but Cavriana was the secret correspondent of the grand duke Francis I of Tuscany.

CHÂTILLON, Odet de Coligny, cardinal of, 1515–71; brother of the admiral Coligny and of d'Andelot; became a protestant and married; d. in England, buried in Canterbury cathedral.

CHEVERNY, Philippe Hurault, comte de, 1528–99; chancelier de l'Ordre du Saint-Esprit; conseiller au parlement; maître des requêtes; conseiller d'État; chancelier du duc d'Anjou (later Henry III); garde des sceaux 1578; chancellor of France 1581; disgraced 1588; recalled by Henry IV and made gouverneur of Chartres.

COLIGNY, Gaspard de, seigneur de Châtillon-sur-Loing, 1517–72; admiral of France; gouverneur of Picardy 1552; leader of the protestant party after the death of the prince de Condé in 1569; murdered on the night of the massacre of St. Bartholomew, 24 August 1572.

CONDÈ, Louis Ier de Bourbon, prince de, marquis de Conti, comte de Soissons, 1530–69; brother of Antoine, King of Navarre; gouverneur of Picardy; leader of the protestants with Gaspard de Coligny; killed after the battle of Jarnac.

DAMVILLE, Henri de Montmorency, comte de, duc de Montmorency 1579, 1534–1613; younger son of the constable Montmorency; gouverneur of Languedoc 1563; marshal of France 1567; leader of the politiques in Languedoc; took up arms with Henry of Navarre in 1585; constable of France 1593.

DU FAY, Michel Hurault de l'Hôpital, seigneur; grandson of the chancellor de l'Hôpital; conseiller au parlement 1581; maître des requêtes 1585; conseiller d'État; chancellor of the kingdom of Navarre; ambassador for Henry of Navarre to Holland and Germany; d. 1592.

DU MORTIER, André Guillart, seigneur and seigneur de L'Isle; premier président au parlement de Bretagne; ambassador to Rome and the council of Trent.

ÉPERNON, Jean-Louis de Nogaret, duc d', 1554–1642; favourite of Henry III; gouverneur of Metz, Toul and Verdun, Boulonnais, l'Angoumois, Saintonge, l'Aunis, Touraine, Anjou, Normandy; colonel-général de l'infanterie 1581; admiral of France 1581 (ceded to his brother); disgraced 1588; later submitted to Henry IV; present when this king was murdered; powerful under Marie de Medici.

ÉPINAC, Pierre d', archbishop of Lyons; became a servitor of the duc de Guise; member of the league, though still in the king's council; quarrelled with the duc d'Épernon.

ESTAMPES, Anne de Pisseleu, duchesse d', 1508–c.1576; m. Jean de Brosse, created duc d'Estampes; maid-in-waiting to Louise of Savoy; mistress of Francis I.

FOIX, Paul de, 1528–84; diplomat; conseiller au parlement 1547; arrested with Anne du Bourg for favouring protestantism; ambassador to Mary Stuart, and to England 1564; ambassador to Venice; archbishop of Toulouse 1577; ambassador to Rome 1579, where he died.

GASSOT, Jules; secrétaire du roi; served under the secretaries Alluye and Villeroy; went on many missions; was honest, cultured and a strong catholic; wrote a memoir which is a valuable source for the period.

GONNOR, Artus de Cossé, comte de Segondigny, seigneur de, c. 1512–82; brother of marshal Brissac; chevalier des Ordres du roi; surintendant des finances 1563; grand pannetier of France 1564; marshal of France 1567; gouverneur of Anjou, Touraine and Orléans 1570; imprisoned in the Bastille for conspiracy 1574; nicknamed 'le maréchal des bouteilles' because he drank a great deal.

GUISE, François de Lorraine, comte, then duc d'Aumale 1548, duc de Guise 1550, 1519–63; son of Claude, duc de Guise and Antoinette de Bourbon; m. Anne d'Este; grand maître, grand chambellan, grand veneur of France; gouverneur of Dauphiné and Savoy; lieutenant-general of France; wounded by an assassin at Orléans on 18 February, d. 24 February 1563.

GUISE, Henri de Lorraine, duc de, prince de Joinville, 1550–88; grand maître of France; gouverneur of Champagne and Brie; leader of the catholic league 1581–8; lieutenant-general of France; assassinated at Blois by order of Henry III.

HUMIÈRES, Jean d', seigneur de Mouchy; chevalier des Ordres du roi; gouverneur of Péronne, Montdidier and Roye 1519; ambassador to England 1527; governor of the dauphin 1535; lieutenant-general of Dauphiné, Savoy and Piedmont 1537; chambellan du dauphin 1542.

JOYEUSE, Anne, duc de, 1561–87; created duke and peer of France; m. Marguerite of Lorraine, sister of the Queen of France; admiral of France; gouverneur of Normandy; favourite of Henry III; d. at the battle of Coutras.

JOYEUSE, Guillaume, vicomte de, c. 1520–92; father of the duc de

Joyeuse; gentilhomme ordinaire de la chambre du roi; lieutenant-general in Languedoc in the absence of Montmorency; marshal of France 1579.

LA MOTHE-FÉNELON, Bertrand de Salignac, marquis de; diplomat; ambassador to England 1572–4; d. 1589.

L'HÔPITAL, Michel de, c. 1507–73; conseiller au parlement de Paris 1537; maître des requêtes 1553; conseiller d'État; premier président en la chambre des comptes 1554; chancellor of France 1560, disgraced 1568; considered one of the most distinguished men of his time for his virtue, judgement and moderation.

LONGLÉE, Pierre de Ségusson, seigneur de; ambassador to Spain.

LONGUEVILLE, Henri Ier d'Orléans, duc de, 1568–95; peer of France; m. Catherine Gonzagues, daughter of the duc de Nevers; chevalier des Ordres du roi; grand chambellan of France; gouverneur of Picardy 1588.

L'ORME (LORME), Philibert de, abbé de Saint-Serge-lès-Angers, and Saint-Eloi de Lyon; royal architect; aumônier to Henry II.

LORRAINE, Charles de, archbishop of Reims, cardinal of Guise 1547, and of Lorraine 1560, 1524–74; younger brother of François, duc de Guise; chief minister to Henry II and Francis II.

MAISSE, André Hurault, seigneur de; ambassador to Venice; ambassador extraordinary to England.

MATIGNON, Jacques de Goyon, comte de, comte de Thorigny 1565, baron de Saint-Lô, 1525–97; captured at Saint-Quentin 1557; gouverneur of lower Normandy; marshal of France and chevalier de l'Ordre du Saint-Esprit 1579; lieutenant-general in Guienne 1580; loyal to Henry III and served Henry IV.

MAUVISSIÈRE, Michel de Castelnau, seigneur de, baron de Join-ville, c. 1520–92; m. Marie Bochetel, daughter of Jacques La Forest Bochetel; chevalier des Ordres du roi; capitaine des cinquante hommes d'armes; gouverneur of Saint-Dizier; several times ambassador to England; close friend of Villeroy.

MAINE, Charles de Lorraine, marquis, then duc de, 1554–1611; younger brother of Henri, duc de Guise; leader of the catholic league after the death of his brother in 1588.

MONTLUC, Jean de, c. 1503–79; elder brother of Blaise de Montluc, marshal of France; bishop of Valence 1553; ambassador to Poland 1572.

MONTMORENCY, Anne, baron, then duc de, 1493–1567; marshal of France 1522; grand maître 1526; gouverneur of Languedoc 1526;

constable of France 1538; duke and peer of France 1551; captured at Saint-Laurent 1557 and Dreux 1562; died of wounds after the battle of Saint-Denis.

MONTMORENCY, François de, duc de, 1567, 1530–79; eldest son of the constable Montmorency; m. Diane de France, daughter of Henry II, 1557; marshal of France 1559; gouverneur of the Ile-de-France; imprisoned in the Bastille for conspiracy 1574.

MONTPENSIER, François de Bourbon, dauphin d'Auvergne, duc de, 1582, c. 1542–92; known as the prince Dauphin; gouverneur of Normandy.

MONTPENSIER, Louis de Bourbon, prince de la Roche-sur-Yon, dauphin d'Auvergne, duc de, 1513–82; gouverneur of Anjou, Maine, Touraine 1561.

MORVILLIER, Jean de, 1506–77; ambassador to Venice 1547; bishop of Orléans 1552; garde des sceaux 1568–70.

NAVARRE, Antoine de Bourbon, King of, 1518–62; m. Jeanne d'Albret; father of Henry IV of France; lieutenant-general of France 1560; gouverneur of Guienne; died from wounds after the siege of Rouen.

NEMOURS, Jacques de Savoie, duc de, 1531–85; m. the widow of François, duc de Guise; the most elegant and polished courtier of his day.

NEVERS (NIVERNOIS), Louis de Gonzague, duc de, and duc de Rethelois, prince of Mantua, 1539–95; m. Henriette de Cleves 1565; came to France 1549, naturalized 1550; peer of France 1566; chevalier des Ordres du roi; gouverneur of Champagne and Brie 1589; ambassador to Rome 1593; surintendant des finances 1594.

POITIERS, Diane de, duchesse de Valentinois 1548, 1499–1566; daughter of Jean de Poitiers, seigneur de Saint-Vallier; m. Louis de Brezé, grand sénéchal of Normandy; mistress of Henry II; retired to her château, Anet 1559.

RETZ, Albert de Gondi, comte, later duc de, 1522–1602; Florentine; marshal of France 1573; gouverneur of Provence 1573; chevalier de l'Ordre du Saint-Esprit; said by some to have been one of the instigators of the massacre of Saint Bartholomew.

REVOL, Louis; native of Dauphiné; royal agent in Savoy by 1584; served under Épernon as intendant of the army of Provence; secrétaire d'État 1588 when Villeroy, Pinart and Brulart were dismissed; d. 1594.

SAINT-ANDRÉ, Jacques d'Albon, seigneur de, marquis de Fronsac, *c.* 1505–62; m. Marguerite de Lustrac 1544; premier gentilhomme de la chambre du roi; marshal of France 1547; gouverneur of Lyonnais, Beaujolais, Forez and Bourbonnais; died at the battle of Dreux.

SAINT-GELAIS, Louis de Lezignan de, seigneur de Lansac, baron de La Mothe-Saint-Héraye; chevalier des Ordres du roi; ambassador to Rome and the council of Trent 1554; envoy to Spain 1564; capitaine des cent gentilshommes de la maison du roi; conseiller privé; chevalier d'honneur to Catherine de Medici 1573, chef de son conseil, de sa maison; d. 1589.

SAINT-SULPICE, Jean d'Ebrard de; gentilhomme ordinaire de la chambre du roi; ambassador to Spain 1562; governor of the duc d'Alençon.

TAVANNES, Gaspard de Saulx, seigneur de, 1509–73; chevalier des Ordres du roi; lieutenant-general of Burgundy, Dauphiné and Lyonnais 1560; marshal of France 1569; admiral of the Levant 1572; gouverneur of Provence 1572.

DU VILLARS, François Boyvin, seigneur; maître d'hôtel to Elizabeth of France (later Queen of Spain); secretary to marshal Brissac; memoirist.

VILLARS, Honorat or Honoré de Savoie, comte, then marquis de, comte de Sommerive and Tende after 1572; m. Jeanne-Françoise de Foix; chevalier de l'Ordre du Saint-Esprit; lieutenant-general in Languedoc 1560, Guienne 1570; marshal of France 1572; admiral of France 1572; d. 1580.

VILLEQUIER, René de, baron de Clairvaux; favourite of Henry III; gouverneur of Paris and Ile-de-France; chevalier de l'Ordre du Saint-Esprit 1578.

IV

'Provisions de Secrétaire des Finances pour Cosme Clausse Sieur de Marchaumont'[1]

HENRY, par la grace de Dieu, Roy de France: A tous ceux qui ces presentes Lettres verront, Salut. Comme de nos premiers ans, et du vivant de feu nostre Frere aisné Dauphin, nostre amé et feal Conseiller Maistre Cosme Clausse Sieur de Marchaumont, eust par le feu Roy nostre tres-cher Sieur et Pere, qui Dieu absolve, esté fait Secretaire de nos Finances, auquel Estat il a servy seul nostredit Frere tant qu'il a vescu, et nous jusqu'icy en telle diligence, loyauté et fidelité, que nous avons bonne et juste occasion, maintenant qu'il a plû à Dieu nostre Createur nous faire Successeur à la Couronne, non seulement de le continuer en cet Estat, mais aussi de l'avancer et augmenter en honneurs et bienfaits, estant asseurez si par le passé il a fait bon et entier devoir ès choses dependans dudit Estat, et concernans l'administration des Affaires que nous avons eu mesme en nostre Duché de Bretagne et ailleurs durant que Nous avons esté en Exploict de Guerre, il sera pour de bien en mieux nous servir ès Affaires de plus grande importance qui de present s'offrent. Pour ces Causes, et autres bonnes justes et raisonnables considerations à ce nous mouvans, confians à plien de ses sens, vertu et longue experience; Iceluy en continuant, avons fait institué, ordonné et étably, faisons, instituons, ordonnons et etablissons nostre Conseiller et Secretaire de nos Finances, et ledit Estat et Office luy avons par ces Presentes donné et octroyé, donnons et octroyons, pour l'avoir, tenir et exercer aux honneurs, authoritez, prérogatives, prééminences, franchises, libertes, droicts, profits et émolumens qui y appartiennent, et aux gages, pensions et entretenements de *seize cens vingt-trois livres dix sols six deniers tournois*,[2] que ont accoustumé d'avoir et prendre les autres Secretaires ordinaires de nos Finances. À commencer du jour et datte de ces Presentes, nonobstant que d'ancienneté lesdits Secretaires de nos Finances eussent esté reduits à nombre

[1] B.N., Mss. fr. 18236, f. 53, 1 April 1546/7; Du-Toc, 33–6.
[2] Du-Toc's italics.

certain, qui depuis par feu nostre tres-cher Sieur et Pere le Roy
dernier decedé, que Dieu absolve, a esté creu et augmenté, comme de
present encore nous faisons en creant et erigeant de nouvel en tant
que besoin seroit, cetuy present Office de nostre Conseiller et
Secretaire de nos Finances, en chef et titre d'Office, formé comme
ceux de nos autres Secretaires en semblable estat et qualité. Si
donnons en mandement par ces Presentes, à notre amé et feal
Chancelier, que pris et receu dudit Clausse de Serment en tel cas
requis et accoustumé, iceluy mette et institue . . . en possession . . .
dudit Estat et Office. . . .

V

Notes on the Catholic League and the Guise Connection with Spain

THE catholic league was originally organized in 1576, and was revived and reorganized upon the death of Anjou in 1584.[1] Paris was divided into five areas under a council of sixteen (*le comité des seize*) with a budget and an army—in fact a shadow government. Spain had been intriguing in France probably since 1559 but, more recently, had been active at least since 1581.[2] The connection of Guise with Spain was already suspected in July 1582, and in November of that year Navarre sent to warn the king of his complicity.[3] In 1583, he warned the king a second, and in 1584 a third time.[4] In fact Guise was actively in touch with Spanish agents in 1578.[5] He appeared in the Spanish correspondence as 'Hercules' from 1581, and as 'Mucius' from 1584.[6] So far as we know, he received his first payment of 10,000 écus from Spain in September 1582, and in the last six years of his life received 500,000.[7] At Joinville, on 31 December 1584, the Guises concluded a formal, secret treaty with Mendoza, the Spanish ambassador in France. This was an inviolable, defensive, offensive alliance, binding their respective heirs, by which Philip II was to pay the Guises 50,000 écus a month so long as they made war in France to exterminate the protestant religion and place the cardinal of Bourbon on the throne.[8] Longlée, the French ambassador in Spain, made it quite clear to the king that the Guises were fighting not for religion, but for the throne.[9]

[1] Robiquet, ii, 192; de Croze, i, 273 ff.
[2] B.N., Mss. it. 1732, f. 100, 13 July 1581.
[3] Desjardins, *Negs. Tosc.*, iv, 443, 449, 15 July, 16 November 1582.
[4] Duplessis-Mornay, *Mémoires et correspondance*, i, 145–7; H. Omont, *Registre journal de Pierre de L'Estoile*, 14–15. This is a series of additions not previously published with the *Registre journal*, taken from the B.N., Mss. n.a.f. 6888.
[5] De Croze, i, 247.
[6] De L'Epinois, 32, n. 2.
[7] *Id.*
[8] B.N., Mss. fr. 3363, f. 9, 31 December 1584.
[9] B.N., Mss. fr. 16109, ff. 228, 236, 14 and 23 April 1585.

BIBLIOGRAPHY

The abbreviations and short titles which follow in brackets are those
used in the footnotes.

I. MANUSCRIPT SOURCES

Paris

Bibliothèque nationale
Fonds Français [*cited as* Mss. fr.]
Nouvelles Acquisitions Françaises [*cited as* Mss. n.a.f.]
Fonds Clairambault
Cinq Cents Colbert
Fonds Dupuy
Fonds Moreau
Pièces Originales
Dossiers Bleus
Cabinet d'Hozier
Fonds Italien [*cited as* Mss. it.]

Archives nationales
Fonds Simancas

Institut de France
Fonds Godefroy

London

British Museum
Additional Mss. [*cited as* Add. Mss.]

II. PRINTED SOURCES

A. *Collections of Documents*

Albèri, E. *Relazioni degli ambasciatori Veneti al Senato*, ser. i, 1856–62.

Baguenault de Puchesse. *Lettres de Catherine de Médicis*, vols. vi–ix,
1897–1905 [cited as Baguenault de Puchesse, *Lettres*]. Valuable
introductions.

Cabié, Edmond. *Guerres de religion dans le Sud-Ouest de la France,
1561–90*, 1906. Principally the correspondence of Saint-Sulpice.

Calendar of State Papers Domestic and Foreign [cited as *C.S.P.D./F.*].

Calendar of State Papers Foreign [cited as *C.S.P.F.*].

Calendar of State Papers Spanish [cited as *C.S.P.Sp.*].

Catalogue des Actes de François Ier. Académie des Sciences Morales et Politiques, 8 vols., 1887–1905 [cited as *Catalogue*].

Charrière, E. *Négociations de la France dans le Levant*, 4 vols., 1848–60.

Cimber et Danjou. *Archives curieuses de l'histoire de France depuis Louis XI jusqu'à Louis XVIII*, 20 vols., 1834–8.

De La Ferrière, H. *Lettres de Catherine de Médicis*, vols. i–v, 1880–95 [cited as La Ferrière, *Lettres*]. Valuable introductions.

Desjardins, Abel. *Négociations diplomatiques de la France avec la Toscane*, 5 vols., 1859–75 [cited as Desjardins, *Negs. Tosc.*]. French translation of the despatches of the Florentine ambassadors.

Douais, C. *Dépêches de M. de Fourquevaux*, 1896–1904.

François, Michel. *Lettres de Henri III, roi de France*, i, 1959.

Isambert, F. A. *Recueil général des anciennes lois françaises*, 29 vols., 1821–33.

La Ferrière, see De La Ferrière.

Lettres . . . de Villeroy ecrites à Matignon, 1749 [cited as *Letters to Matignon*]. This is a printed collection of letters from Villeroy to Matignon, the originals of which have disappeared. It should be used with caution since the editor, who is anonymous, confesses in his preface to having found Villeroy's writing difficult to read. He has misdated a number of the letters and there also appear to be other copyist's errors.

Muller, P. L. and Diegerick, A. *Documents concernant les relations entre le duc d'Anjou et les Pays-Bas, 1576–83*, 5 vols., 1889–99.

Paris, L. *Négociations, lettres et pièces diverses relatives au règne de François II*, 1841. Principally taken from the papers of Sébastien de Laubespine, bishop of Limoges.

Ribier, G. *Lettres et Memoires d'Estat*, 2 vols., 1666. Miscellaneous documents.

Rott, E. *Histoire de la représentation diplomatique de la France auprès des cantons Suisses*, 10 vols., 1900–35.

Rymer, T. *Foedera*, 17 vols., 1704–17.

Tommaseo, N. *Relations des ambassadeurs Vénetiens sur les affaires de France au XVIe siècle*, 2 vols., 1836. French translation of the reports of the Venetian ambassadors; incomplete.

Valois, Noel. *Inventaire des arrêts du conseil d'État, règne de Henri IV*, 1886. Valuable introduction.

Weiss, C. *Papiers d'état du Cardinal de Granvelle*, 9 vols., 1841–52.

B. *Contemporary Works*

Brantôme, Pierre de Bourdeille, seigneur de. *Œuvres complètes*. Ed. Lalanne, 11 vols., 1864–82.

De La Noue, François. *Discours politiques et militaires*, 1587.

De La Planche, Régnier. *Histoire de l'estat de France sous le regne de François II*, 1576.

Du Tillet, J. *Recueil des roys de France . . .*, 1580.

Froumenteau, N. *Le Secret des finances de France*, 1581.

Matthieu, Pierre. *Histoire des derniers troubles de France sous les regnes des roys Henry III et Henry IV*, 1600.

——. *Remarques d'estat et d'histoires sur la vie et les services de Monsieur de Villeroy*, ed. 1620 [cited as Matthieu].

Memoires de l'Estat de France sous Charles IX, 3 vols., 1578.

Paradin, Guillaume. *Continuation de l'histoire de notre temps depuis l'an 1550 jusqu'à l'an 1556*, 1575.

Paschal, Pierre de. *Journal de ce qui s'est passé en France durant l'année 1562 principalement dans Paris et à la cour*. Ed. Michel François, 1950.

Pasquier, Estienne. *Des Recherches de la France*.

——. *Lettres*, 2 vols., 1619.

Ronsard, P. *Œuvres complètes*. Ed. Laumonier, 8 vols., 1914–19.

Serres, J. de. *Mémoires de la troisième guerre civile, et des derniers troubles de France*, 1570.

C. *Memoirs*

All the memoirs should be treated with caution and carefully compared with other sources.

Chandon, Jean. *Vie et testament*, 1857.

Mémoires de Condé, 6 vols., ed. 1743. This is not a memoir but an extensive collection of documents.

Du Plessis-Mornay, see Mornay.

Gassot, Jules. *Sommaire mémorial*. Ed. Pierre Champion, 1934. Extremely valuable; reliable on fact but not on dates.

Le Riche, Guillaume et Michel. *Journal*. Ed. A. de La Fontenelle, 1846.

Mémoires de M. le duc de Nevers. Ed. Gomberville, 2 vols., 1665.

Michaud et Poujoulat. *Nouvelle collection des mémoires pour servir à l'histoire de France,* ser. i.

    vol. vi, *Mémoires-journaux du duc de Guise.*

Mornay, Philippe de, seigneur du Plessis-Marly (called Du Plessis-Mornay). *Mémoires et Correspondance,* 12 vols., 1824–5.

Omont, H. *Registre-journal de Pierre de L'Estoile,* additions, 1900.

Petitot, M. *Collection complète des mémoires relatifs à l'histoire de France,* ser. i, 1819–26.

    vol. xxx, *Mémoires de du Villars.*

    vol. xxxv, *Mémoires du duc de Bouillon.*

    vol. xxxvi, *Mémoires de Cheverny.*

    vol. xxxvii, *Mémoires de Marguerite de Valois.*

    vol. xliv, *Mémoires d'Estat de Villeroy.* This valuable work is not a memoir but two long, selective apologies. There are strong grounds for thinking that, in its present form, it was not entirely written by Villeroy himself. Parts of it are in obscure and complex French, unlike his invariably lucid style. It may have been compiled or completed by his son, Charles, from his father's notes and papers. However, there is no reason to suspect that it is not a true representation of Villeroy's actions and opinions.

    vol. xlv, Pierre de L'Estoile, *Journal de Henri III.* Very misleading.

Syrueilh, François de. *Journal, 1568–85.* Ed. G. Clément-Simon, 1873.

III. SECONDARY WORKS

Aucoc, Léon. *Le Conseil d'État avant et depuis 1789,* 1876.

Baguenault de Puchesse. *Les Ducs François et Henri de Guise,* 1867.

—. 'Négociations de Henri II avec le duc de Ferrare, 1555–7', *Revue des questions historiques,* v, 1868.

—. *Jean de Morvillier évêque d'Orléans, garde des sceaux de France,* ed. 1870.

—. 'La Politique de Philippe II dans les affaires de France, 1559–1598', *Revue des questions historiques,* xxv, 1879. A good summary of Franco-Spanish relations.

—. *La Campagne du duc de Guise dans l'Orléanais en octobre et novembre, 1587,* 1885. Very slight.

—. 'Les Négociations de Catherine de Médicis à Paris après la journée des barricades', *Séances et travaux de l'Académie des Sciences Morales et Politiques,* nouv. ser. lix, 1903.

—. *Les Opérations de l'armée royale dans le Limousin en juin 1569 d'après les lettres inédites de François de Laubespine*, 1909.

Barthélemy, Édouard de. 'Catherine de Médicis le duc de Guise et le traité de Nemours', *Revue des questions historiques*, xxvii, 1880. Makes poor use of unusually complete material.

Bèze, Théodore de. *Histoire ecclésiastique des églises réformées de France*, 3 vols., 1580.

Boislisle, A. de. *Les Conseils du roi sous Louis XIV*, 1884. Confusing, but still contains the best short account of the councils in the sixteenth century.

Bondois, P. M. 'Les Secrétaires d'état sous François II, 1559–60', *Revue Henri IV*, iii, 1909.

Bonnerot, J. 'Esquisse de la vie des routes au XVIe siècle', *Revue des questions historiques*, cxv, 1931.

Bouard, A. de. *Manuel de diplomatique*, 2 vols., 1929.

Bourciez, Édouard. *Les Mœurs polies et la littérature de cour sous Henri II*, 1886.

Brémond d'Ars, G. de. *Les Conférences de Saint-Brice entre Henri de Navarre et Catherine de Médicis, 1586–7*, 1884.

Briquet. *De l'Origine et du progrès des charges de secrétaires d'État*, 1747.

Butterfield, H. *Man on his Past*, 1955. Contains a bibliography of the massacre of Saint Bartholomew.

Caillet, J. *De l'Administration en France sous le ministère du cardinal de Richelieu*, 1857.

Capefigue, J.-B.-H.-R. *Histoire de la Réforme, de la Ligue et du règne de Henri IV*, 8 vols., 1834–5.

—. *Catherine de Médicis, mère des rois François II, Charles IX et Henri III*, 1856.

Castan, A. *La Mort de François Ier et l'avènement de Henri II d'après les dépêches secrètes de l'ambassadeur impérial, Jean de Saint-Mauris*, 1879.

Champion, Pierre. *Ronsard et son temps*, 1925.

—. *Ronsard et Villeroy*, 1925.

—. *Catherine de Médicis présente à Charles IX son royaume, 1564–6*, 1937.

—. *Charles IX. La France et le contrôle de l'Espagne*, 1939.

Chénon, Émile. *Histoire générale du droit français public et privé des origines à 1815*, 1929.

Church, W. F. *Constitutional Thought in Sixteenth-Century France*, 1941.

Corlieu, A. *La Mort des rois de France depuis François Ier, études médicales et historiques*, 1892.

De Coste, H. *Les Eloges et vies des reynes, princesses, dames et damoiselles illustres* . . ., 2 vols., 1647.

De Croze, J. *Les Guises, les Valois et Philippe II*, 2 vols., 1866. De Croze is one of the few historians to have used the Spanish archives.

Decrue de Stoutz, F. *La Cour de France et la société au XVIe siècle*, 1888.

—. *Anne duc de Montmorency connétable et pair de France sous les rois Henri II François II et Charles IX*, 1889 [cited as Decrue].

Delaborde, J. *Les Protestants à la cour de Saint-Germain lors du colloque de Poissy*, 1874.

—. *Gaspard de Coligny amiral de France*, 3 vols., 1879–82 [cited as Delaborde].

De La Ferrière, H. *Le XVIe siècle et les Valois*, 1879.

—. *Les Projets de mariage de la reine Élizabeth*, 1882.

—. *L'Entrevue de Bayonne de 1565*, 1883.

—. 'La Paix de Troyes avec l'Angleterre', *Revue des questions historiques*, xxxiii, 1883.

—. 'La Seconde guerre civile. La Paix de Longjumeau', *Revue des questions historiques*, xxxvii, 1885.

—. 'La Troisième guerre civile et la paix de Saint-Germain, 1568–70', *Revue des questions historiques*, xlii, 1887.

—. 'Les Dernières conspirations du règne de Charles IX', *Revue des questions historiques*, xlviii, 1890.

De La Saussaye, L. *Blois et ses environs*, ed. 1862.

De L'Epinois, H. 'La Politique de Sixte-Quint en France', *Revue des questions historiques*, xxvii, 1880.

—. *La Ligue et les papes*, 1886 [cited as De L'Epinois].

De Luçay, H. *Des origines du pouvoir ministériel en France. Les Secrétaires d'État* . . ., 1881.

De Ruble, A. *Antoine de Bourbon et Jeanne d'Albret*, 4 vols., 1881–6.

—. *Le Duc de Nemours et Mademoiselle de Rohan, 1531–92*, 1883.

—. *Le Traité de Cateau-Cambrésis, 2 et 3 avril 1559*, 1889.

'Le Colloque de Poissy (septembre–octobre 1561)', *Mémoires de la Société de l'histoire de Paris et de l'Ile de France*, xvi, 1889.

De Thou, J.-A. *Histoire universelle*, 16 vols., ed. 1734. Incomparably the best of the old histories and generally reliable.

Desjardins, Abel. *Charles IX, deux années de règne, 1570-2*, 1873.

Desjardins, Albert. *Les Sentiments moraux au XVIe siècle*, 1887.

Devic, C. et Vaisseté, J. *Histoire générale de Languedoc*, 18 vols., 1872–1904.

Dickinson, G. Ed. *The 'Instructions sur le Faict de la Guerre' of . . . Fourquevaux*, 1954.

Dodu, Gaston. *Les Valois*, 1934.

Doucet, R. *Les Institutions de la France au XVIe siècle*, 2 vols., 1948. Useful bibliography.

—. 'La Mort de François Ier', *Revue historique*, cxiii, 1913.

Du Cerceau, Androuet. *Les plus excellents Bastiments de France*, 2 vols., ed. 1868–70. Contains many engravings, some of buildings long since demolished.

Dumas, A. 'L'Action des secrétaires d'état', *Annales de la Faculté de Droit d'Aix-en-Provence*, 1954.

Duruy, G. *Le Cardinal Carlo Carafa, 1519–61*, 1882.

Du-Toc, see Fauvelet Du-Toc.

England, S. *The Massacre of Saint Bartholomew*, 1938.

Evennett, H. O. *The Cardinal of Lorraine and the Council of Trent*, 1930.

Fauvelet Du-Toc. *Histoire des Secrétaires d'Estat*, 1668 [cited as Du-Toc].

Flassan, see Raxis de Flassan, G. de.

François, Michel. *Le Rôle du Cardinal François de Tournon dans la politique française en Italie, janvier-juillet, 1556*, 1933.

—. *Le Cardinal François de Tournon, 1489–1562*, 1951.

Furgeot, Henri. 'L'Attitude de Henri II au lendemain de la journée de Saint-Quentin', *Revue des questions historiques*, xxxii, 1882.

Gigon, S.-C. *La Troisième guerre de religion. Jarnac, Montcontour, 1568–9*, 1911.

Girard, Etienne. *Trois livres des offices de France*, 1645.

Guillard, R. *Histoire du Conseil du roy depuis le commencement de la monarchie jusqu'à la fin du règne de Louis le Grand*, 1718.

Guillemin, J. *Le Cardinal de Lorraine, son influence politique et religieuse au XVIe siècle*, 1847.

Hauser, H. *François de La Noue*, 1892.

—. *Les Sources de l'histoire de France au XVIe siècle*, 4 vols., 1906–15.

—. *La Prépondérance espagnole, 1559–1660*, 1933.

—. 'Les Caractères généraux de l'histoire économique de la France, du milieu du XVIe siècle á la fin du XVIIIe', *Revue historique*, clxxiii, 1934.

Héritier, Jean. *Catherine de Médicis*, ed. 1959.

Jouan, A. *Voyage de Charles IX en France*, 1759.

Lacombe, B. de. *Catherine de Médicis entre Guise et Condé*, 1889.

La Ferrière, see De La Ferrière.

Lambert, Gustave. *Histoire des guerres de religion en Provence, 1530–98*, 2 vols., 1870.

Marchand, C. *Charles Ier de Cossé, comte de Brissac et maréchal de France, 1507–63*, 1889.

—. 'Documents pour l'histoire du règne de Henri II', *Extrait du Bulletin historique et philologique*, 1901 [cited as Marchand].

—. 'Le Traité des Huguenots avec les Anglais en 1562', *Revue des questions historiques*, lxxvii, 1905.

Marlet, Léon. 'Florimond Robertet, son rôle à la cour et ses missions diplomatiques', *Revue des questions historiques*, xlvii, 1890.

Mattingly, Garrett. *The Defeat of the Spanish Armada*, 1959.

Maulde de La Clavière, *Les Origines de la Révolution française au XVIe siècle*, 1889.

Miraulmont, P. de. *Traicté de la chancelerie*, 1610.

Moreri, L. *Le Grand dictionnaire historique*, ed. 1759.

Mousnier, R. *La Vénalité des offices sous Henri IV et Louis XIII*, 1946.

Mouton, Léo. *Un Demi-roi, le duc d'Épernon*, 1922.

Noell, H. *Henri II et la naissance de la société moderne*, 1944.

Nouaillac, J. *Villeroy, secrétaire d'État et ministre de Charles IX, Henri III et Henri IV, 1543–1610*, 1909. This life of Villeroy is not reliable. Nouaillac made only a superficial study of the first half of Villeroy's career, and his transposition of evidence results in much confusion. The narrative is based on Villeroy's *Mémoires d'Estat*, which are not memoirs properly speaking, but two long apologies. As such they are selective in content and particular in treatment. Although Nouaillac gives the date 1610 in his title, Villeroy actually died in 1617.

Pagès, Georges. 'La Vénalité des offices dans l'ancienne France', *Revue historique*, clxix, 1932.

Paillard, C. 'La Mort de François Ier et les premiers temps du règne de Henri II d'après les dépêches de Jean de Saint-Mauris (avril–juin 1547)', *Revue historique*, v, 1877.

Picot, Émile. *Les Italiens en France au XVIe siècle*, 1901–18.

Raxis de Flassan, G. de. *Histoire générale et raisonnée de la diplomatie française . . .*, 6 vols., 1809 [cited as Flassan].

Robertet, G. *Les Robertet au XVIe siècle*, 1888. The register of Florimond Robertet, *secrétaire des finances* to Francis I. Contains no biographical material.

Robin, Pierre. *La Compagnie des secrétaires du roi, 1351–1791*, 1933.

Robiquet, P. *Paris et la Ligue sous le règne de Henri III, étude d'histoire municipale et politique*, 2 vols., ed. 1886.

Romier, L. *La Carrière d'un favori: Jacques d'Albon de Saint-André, maréchal de France, 1512–62*, 1909.

—. 'Le Sommaire des choses accordées pour la Conspiration du Triumvirat', *Revue Henri IV*, iii, 1909.

—. *Les Origines politiques des guerres de religion*, 2 vols., 1913–14. Mostly about Italy. Vol. i contains an excellent chapter on the court of Henry II.

—. *Le Royaume de Catherine de Médicis*, 2 vols., 1922.

Roy, M. 'Discours', *Annuaire-bulletin de la Société de l'Histoire de France*, lxvi, 1929. The subject of this paper was the secretary Jean du Thier.

Schweinitz, Margaret de. *Les Épitaphes de Ronsard*, 1925.

Société Académique de Saint-Quentin. *La Guerre de 1557 en Picardie*, 1896.

Tessereau, A. *Histoire chronologique de la Grande Chancelerie de France*, 2 vols., 1710.

Van Dyke, P. *Catherine de Médicis*, 2 vols., 1923.

Varillas, Antoine. *Histoire de Henry second*, 3 vols., 1692.

Vindry, F. *Les Ambassadeurs français permanents au XVIe siècle*, 1903.

Viollet, Paul. *Histoire des institutions politiques et administratives de la France*, 4 vols., 1890–1912.

Weaver, F. J. 'Anglo-French Diplomatic Relations, 1558–1630', *Bulletin of the Institute of Historical Research*, iv–vii.

Wedgwood, C. V. *William the Silent*, 1944.

Whitehead, A. W. *Gaspard de Coligny, Admiral of France*, 1904.

Yates, F. A. *The French Academies of the Sixteenth Century*, 1947.

—. *The Valois Tapestries*, 1959.

Zeller, Gaston. *La Réunion de Metz à la France*, 1552–1648, 2 vols., 1926.

—. 'Les Gouverneurs de provinces au XVIe siècle', *Revue historique*, clxxxv, 1939.

—. 'L'Administration monarchique avant les intendants', *Revue historique*, cxcvii, 1947.

—. *Les Institutions de la France au XVIe siècle*, 1948.

INDEX

Z